FRIEDRICH A. HAYEK

FRIEDRICH A. HAYEK

Critical Assessments of Leading Economists

Second Series

Edited by
John C. Wood and Robert D. Wood

Volume III

Routledge
Taylor & Francis Group

LONDON AND NEW YORK

First published 2004
by Routledge
11 New Fetter Lane, London EC4P 4EE

Simultaneously published in the USA and Canada
by Routledge
29 West 35th Street, New York, NY 10001

Routledge is an imprint of the Taylor & Francis Group

Typeset in Times by Wearset Ltd, Boldon, Tyne and Wear
Printed and bound in Great Britain by
TJ International Ltd, Padstow, Cornwall

British Library Cataloguing in Publication Data
A catalogue record for this book is available from the British Library

Library of Congress Cataloging in Publication Data
A catalog record for this book has been requested

ISBN 0–415–31055–5 (Set)
ISBN 0–415–31058–X (Volume III)

Publisher's Note
References within each chapter are as they appear in the original
complete work.

CONTENTS

ACKNOWLEDGEMENTS

The publishers would like to thank the following for permission to reprint their material:

Critical Review for permission to reprint Ryszard Legutko, 'Was Hayek an Instrumentalist?', *Critical Review* 11(1) (Winter 1997): 145–164.

The American Economic Association for permission to reprint Bruce Caldwell, 'Hayek and Socialism', *Journal of Economic Literature* 35 (December 1997): 1856–1890.

Blackwell Publishing for permission to reprint Chris Guest, 'Hayek on Government: Two Views or One?', *History of Economics Review* 0(26) (Winter–Summer 1997): 51–67.

Blackwell Publishing for permission to reprint Jeremy Shearmur, 'Hayek, Keynes and the State', *History of Economics Review* 0(26) (Winter–Summer 1997): 68–82.

Duke University Press for permission to reprint William N. Butos and Roger G. Koppl, 'The Varieties of Subjectivism: Keynes and Hayek on Expectations', *History of Political Economy* 29(2) (1997): 327–359. Copyright 1997, Duke University Press. All rights reserved. Used by permission of the publisher.

Elsevier Science Ltd. for permission to reprint P. Boettke, 'Economic Calculation: The Austrian Contribution to Political Economy', *Advances in Austrian Economics*, 5, 1998, pp. 131–158. Copyright 1998, with permission of the publisher.

Kluwer Academic for permission to reprint Douglas Glen Whitman, 'Hayek contra Pangloss on Evolutionary Systems', *Constitutional Political Economy* 9 (1998): 45–66.

Critical Review for permission to reprint Edward Feser, 'Hayek, Social Justice, and the Market: Reply to Johnston', *Critical Review* 12(3) (Summer 1998): 269–281.

Blackwell Publishing for permission to reprint John F. Henry, 'Keynes, Hayek, and "Religion" as a Necessary Social Institution', *History of Economics Review* 0(28) (Summer 1998): 126–128.

Blackwell Publishing for permission to reprint Riccardo Bellofiore, 'Between Wicksell and Hayek: Mises' theory of money and credit revisited', *American Journal of Economics and Sociology* 57(4) (October 1998): 531–578.

Indian Journal of Applied Economics for permission to reprint Harald Hagemann, 'Monetary Causes of the Business Cycles and Technological Change: Hicks vs. Hayek', *Indian Journal of Applied Economics* 7(4) (1998): 61–77.

Duke University Press for permission to reprint Bruce Caldwell, 'Why Didn't Hayek Review Keynes's *General Theory?*', *History of Political Economy* 30(4) (1998): 545–569. Copyright 1998, Duke University Press. All rights reserved. Used by permission of the publisher.

St Martin's Press for permission to reprint James Angresano, 'Toward Developing a Twenty-First Century Economic Paradigm: Lessons from Myrdal, Schumpeter, and Hayek', W. E. Halah and K. B. Taylor (eds), *Twenty First Century Economics: Perspective of Socioeconomics for a Changing World*, London: St Martin's Press, 1999, pp. 227–250.

History of Economic Ideas for permission to reprint Thierry Aimar, 'Time, Coordination and Ignorance: A Comparison between Hayek and Lachmann', *History of Economic Ideas* 7(1–2) (1999): 139–165.

History of Economic Ideas for permission to reprint Jack Birner, 'The Surprising Place of Cognitive Psychology in the Work of F.A. Hayek', *History of Economic Ideas* 7(1–2) (1999): 43–84.

History of Economic Ideas for permission to reprint Richard Arena, 'The Hayek/Keynes Controversy in the Light of Modern Business Cycle Theory', *History of Economic Ideas* 7(1–2) (1999): 227–253.

The publishers have made every effort to contact authors/copyright holders of works reprinted in *Friedrich A. Hayek: Critical Assessments of Leading Economists*. This has not been possible in every case, however, and we would welcome correspondence from those individuals/companies who we have been unable to trace.

45

WAS HAYEK AN INSTRUMENTALIST?

Ryszard Legutko

Source: *Critical Review* 11(1) (Winter 1997): 145–164.

In a certain respect Roland Kley's *Hayek's Social and Political Thought* (Oxford: Clarendon Press, 1994) is tediously predictable. Page after page, section after section tells us that Hayek's theses are "hardly comprehensible," "implausible" and "fatally flawed," that his theory "founders," "crumbles," and "aborts," that his conclusions are "foregone," that each argument he raises is "untenable," "weak," "self-defeating." When in the concluding parts of his book Kley argues that Hayek's theory is essentially instrumentalist, one cannot help feeling that this last charge is superfluous to the overall critique; instrumentalist or not, this theory must be regarded as indefensible since all its constitutive parts have been previously demolished. The picture of Hayek's philosophy as it emerges from Kley's book is that of a gigantic intellectual failure that hardly justifies the effort to refute it.

The structure of the book, in which each chapter and subchapter, each comment on each part of Hayek's theory, is followed by a critique, is a methodological trap, constraining the author to produce rebuttals almost automatically, even when there is no obvious need for them. This compulsion to score as many points as possible is probably the major reason that many of the book's arguments are unpolished; that some are methodologically inconsistent (intrinsic ones are mixed with extrinsic, empirical with analytical, etc.); and that several are unnecessary or simply false. Those arguments that are valuable and interesting become lost in a chaotic and indiscriminate series of critical punches. Kley's study certainly has not reached the standard set by other books on Hayek written during the last fifteen years (Barry 1979; Gray 1984; Kukathas 1989).

Hayek's epistemological economics

Let us illustrate Kley's method by considering his refutation of what is considered to be Hayek's major insight into social theory: the epistemic role of the market. According to Hayek, the indispensability of the market is primarily epistemological: it helps to discover, utilize, and develop knowledge. To support this claim Hayek offers several arguments, of which three seem to me the most interesting. The first of these derives from economic calculation: only the market generates the conditions in which a system of prices, being a reflection of countless individual transactions, gives us reliable information about the costs and benefits involved in any economic undertaking. The second argument stems from plurality: market society is sufficiently diversified in opportunities to create a demand for individuals' knowledge and abilities, which would be ignored in a less pluralist system and which, when utilized, enrich the general pool of knowledge and open up possibilities for other individuals. The third argument is from evolutionary adaptability. In the process of history, individuals have developed abilities and gained skills—often passed from one generation to another within families and other small communities—that enabled their adaptation to the social and natural environment and constituted practical knowledge of how to handle those unique problems that are characteristic of a given social group or a given set of historical circumstances; the market, by dispersing authority, increases this social potential, making for greater responsiveness to reality.

The epistemic role of the market is, if I am not mistaken, the only aspect of Hayek's philosophy for which Kley has some—albeit, few—positive words to say (though ultimately these words further *reculer pour mieux sauter* tactics). The epistemological argument, he notes, "seems extremely powerful" (57); "it is ... an original contribution of Hayek's to have demonstrated that only in markets and in a market price-system do the relative scarcities of resources and goods find expression accurately and promptly enough to make efficient production and allocation possible, thereby advancing general welfare" (199). Kley's apparent admiration for Hayek's epistemological argument extends only to the thesis that economic calculation is possible exclusively in the market. This thesis is not original to Hayek; Ludwig von Mises is usually credited with its formulation. What Hayek did was to complement Mises's argument by recognizing that economic calculation is a "discovery process, developing and spreading otherwise unavailable, latent information that is part of price formation by a multitude of economic agents" (de Jasay 1990, 11; also Lavoie 1985, 158–73). Kley finds little value in the other two arguments: that the market affords more opportunities for the use of individuals' knowledge, and that it induces people to acquire and to transmit adaptive skills.

2

The main objection Kley raises against Hayek's epistemic argument is that it "in no way goes sufficiently far to justify *liberal* institutions" (199, italics his). One cannot help noting—before any concrete assessment of the objection is made—that it seems somewhat mistargeted. It is not at all clear that Hayek intended his argument to answer these notoriously difficult questions, and one may wonder whether any one argument could possibly answer them. Moreover, there is nothing in the epistemic function of the market that would suggest direct and specific institutional conclusions rather than general guidelines; no epistemology can have such obvious practical application.

One gets the impression that the major reason for Kley's early praise of the epistemological argument as "powerful" was to allow him to launch a critique along the following lines. If the argument is "powerful," then it should solve difficult problems. It turns out that the argument does not solve those problems, e.g., it does not tell us who should build opera houses and whether to curb pornography (60–61); so we have to conclude that it is not so powerful after all.

On the other hand, Kley is no more satisfied when Hayek's theory permits a more specific implication. The epistemic function of the market clearly favors a great number of economic agents, which in turn strongly implies a system of private property. In that sense one can say—contrary to Kley's initial objection—that Hayek's argument "goes sufficiently far to justify" at least one liberal institution, that of private property. Yet Kley asserts that "at least in theory" markets may be grounded on other property arrangements (59). Whatever the merits of this claim, it amounts to saying that Hayek's thesis is in fact too specific in its institutional implications. At this point Kley's critique ceases to be an intrinsic assessment of Hayek's theory and becomes extrinsic: there are better theories than Hayek's, judged according to non-Hayekian criteria, such as the need for a large public sphere. This may be true, but Kley does not substantiate it with a single argument. Moreover, having conceded to Hayek that "only in markets and in a market price-system do the relative scarcities of resources and goods find expression accurately and promptly enough to make efficient production and allocation possible, thereby advancing general welfare," the *onus probandi* rests on Kley to show that a property system other than the one favored by Hayek would perform the epistemic function—Hayek's criterion—at least equally well as some theoretical alternative.

With respect to the liberal state—the other liberal institution about which Hayek's thesis allegedly fails to be sufficiently unequivocal—Kley's case fares no better. At first he mentions two specific problems about which Hayek has little to say: the limits of the consumer's freedom (the consumer may desire products, such as pornography, which are socially damaging or morally dubious), and the question of public goods. The

3

Hayek Kley gives us could hardly have any solutions to such problems, since his epistemic argument is reduced "essentially [to] the contention that only market competition can discover the relative scarcities of resources, establish a price-system mirroring them, and thus provide the information needed for an economy efficient and sensitive to people's wants" (63). Obviously, the knowledge provided by prices cannot say anything about the importance of spending tax money on an opera house or about the damaging effects of pornography. Such judgments cannot come from the price system—and Hayek never said they could. They must stem from the rules that constitute the legal and moral order of a society.

Summing up his critique of Hayek's epistemic argument, Kley makes a more general point: "Hayek's epistemological considerations are by themselves inconclusive and do not furnish a general argument against any interventionism" (62–63). While Kley concedes that "government intervention may indeed distort the price-system," he goes on to claim that "nothing Hayek says excludes the possibility of endogenous market disturbances and informational uncertainties which only government action can abate" (62). Previously he argued that there are certain specific problems which Hayek's epistemological thesis, although "powerful," cannot solve. Now he contends that the thesis does not give us any *general* grounds against *any* interventionism. This contention not only does not follow from the claim that disturbances and uncertainties may call forth government intervention as an exceptional measure, but it is false as an interpretation of Hayek.

Hayek's epistemological argument clearly excludes the possibility that the state would *systematically* act as a corrective to the kinds of market failure Kley briefly mentions. The government cannot intervene for the sake of social welfare if this would mean tampering with the general rules of cooperation; its role is to defend those rules rather than to manipulate them in order to achieve particular ends. Here Hayek's position is in line with that of several prominent twentieth-century German liberals, particularly of the so-called Freiburg School (Vanberg 1994, 454–57). Looked at differently, Hayek's position may be compared to a certain version of the subsidiarity principle. The primary agents are individuals, communities, and voluntary associations; if they fail, there is a possibility for a government action; but if the government intervenes, it is preferable that action be taken by "local authorities," which would generally offer "the next-best solution where private initiative cannot be relied upon to provide certain services and where some sort of collective action is therefore needed" (1960, 263; also 1979, 41–51). Kley is perfectly entitled to reject this notion of the state, but he cannot claim that Hayek has little to say about government intervention.

Famine and the epistemic argument

Strictly speaking, Kley has only one argument that may serve to undermine the epistemic role of the market. There are situations, he says, when "people get the price signals wrong," which in turn might result in a drastic market failure. "Hayek never considers the possibility," Kley writes,

> that massive market changes may leave large parts of a population suddenly without access to the most basic goods. But, as Amartya Sen has argued, this is precisely what happened in various famines. People died not because the aggregate availability of food had fallen but because huge price shifts had put it above their reach. Martin Ravallion has analyzed one such case, the 1974 famine in Bangladesh, and concludes that the rice prices were high and unstable largely as a result of speculation.... Now, to be sure, market situations of this sort may be exceptional in various ways. Still, the example drastically demonstrates that there is more to individual adjustment than the informational side Hayek stresses. Moreover, it points to limits of adjustment, showing that sometimes no amount of individual flexibility will suffice to enable people to link up again with the existing web of exchange relations. Finally, it also warns against making the claim about the market's informational capacities an article of faith.
>
> (66)

Upon inspection, there is less here than meets the eye. If the epistemological argument is indeed powerful, then one would expect an effort to relate the market's informational capacity to the famine in Bangladesh; in other words, one would expect an explanation of how this particular empirical fact should make us reevaluate the analytical assertion about the market's epistemological function. To say that "there is more to it," and that this function should not be "an article of faith," is far from satisfactory.

In saying that "massive market changes may leave large parts of a population suddenly without access to the most basic goods," moreover, Kley implies that the market may be the cause of the famine. But while there is no doubt that the state was the sole agent responsible for the gigantic famines in the Ukraine following the Russian Revolution and in China during the Great Leap Forward, it cannot be argued that the market bears responsibility for the famine in Bangladesh. Sen and Ravallion contend that the market was unable to *cope with* the famine, and sometimes aggravated it, but they do not say that the market produced it. If, as they maintain (Sen 1981, 131–66; Drèze and Sen 1989, 27–30; Ravallion 1987, 1–23, 57–83), the high price of rice in Bangladesh was the result of mistaken anticipations of future prices, it does not in any way contradict the epistemic role of the market. Nothing in Hayek's theory would suggest that people cannot "get the price signals wrong," especially in the face of floods, political crisis, and social upheaval. If, in a certain situation, people get the price signals wrong, it does not mean that there is a more reliable and universally applicable instrument to get them right.

Hayek's instrumentalism

To review a book like Kley's, where there is no clear organizing principle, is a thankless, if not impossible, task: a thorough analysis would require that all its arguments be enumerated and given a separate assessment. Since I cannot do that, I will take up the only idea in Kley's book which, hypothetically at least, might give it a unifying structure: an instrumentalist interpretation of Hayek's thought. That such an interpretation was the intention of Kley's project we learn in the Introduction. Unfortunately, in the subsequent portions of the text the concept of instrumentalism virtually disappears and does not reappear until the concluding part. There, to our surprise, we find the author saying that he had been arguing for the instrumentalist interpretation of Hayek all along (183), a claim unwarranted by the actual content of the book.

As to why Hayek's thought is instrumental, Kley explains that Hayek

> thinks liberalism is the right political doctrine because, unlike socialism and other collectivist creeds, it is committed to institutions that do take account of the social world as it is. He even deems the liberal market society the only feasible alternative because it alone admits of those self-co-ordinating mechanisms, such as the market, on which modern society vitally depends. Similarly, he portrays the institutions of the liberal market society as the work of a singular evolutionary development in the course of which they have proved their value and wisdom. So it is concerns of viability that are decisive when, in his political philosophy, Hayek endeavors to justify the institutions of the liberal market society. Feasibility considerations are characteristic of instrumental reasoning.
>
> (184)

Let us summarize Kley's argument: (a) Hayek believes that liberalism, unlike socialism, "takes into account the social world as it is"; (b) from this it follows that his main concern is the "viability" and "feasibility" of institutions; (c) such concerns are typical of instrumentalist thinking; ergo, Hayek is an instrumentalist.

I have serious doubts about this argument. First, it should be noted that

(a) is very vague while (b) contains an ambiguity. Feasibility and viability are not identical; communism, to give an example, was feasible but it was certainly not viable. Consequently, (a) and (b)—if the latter is limited to feasibility—generate an extremely weak notion of instrumentalism which could be applied indiscriminately almost to any position. All social and political theories "take into account the social world as it is," in the sense that none is created in a blatant indifference to what the world tells us. The whole point of controversy between Hayek and the socialists was not about taking or not taking into account the world as it is, but about what constitutes the "as it is" of the world. Even the most bizarre conceptions of the ideal human order—for instance, Plato's ideal *polis* or Fourier's pha-lansteries—were thought to have been derived from an accurate diagnosis of reality. All of them were considered to be feasible. At the same time one can claim with equal persuasiveness that all theories—even the most conservative ones—"take into account the world as it should be," since they reject some aspect of the status quo in the name of an optimal stan-dard. Hayek's *Road to Serfdom*, which contained a call for a thorough reform of capitalism, is a case in point.

To improve the argument we may dispense with "feasibility" and take (b) to mean "viability," if this signifies the ability to foster "self-co-ordination." We would then say that an institution is viable if it is able to generate and sustain itself without the interference of an external factor, such as, for instance, a government. Socialism, according to Hayek, was not viable, that is, it did not develop the mechanisms of self-generation and self-sustenance that would have given its institutions a sufficient stability; for that reason it was bound, sooner or later, to fall apart. On this interpreta-tion we begin to understand what Kley means by "the world as it is." Hayek—the argument would run—accepted and promoted only those institutions that, through a long process of adjustment and improvement, have become more in tune with the complexities of the world; those that have not gone through this process—and are thus the product of a "con-structivist" spirit, as Hayek would say—carry too little social experience and too little practical knowledge to withstand the pressure of reality. Via-bility is thus not only a technical notion—institutions that are viable are more responsive and have a longer life—but also has a metaphysical or quasi-metaphysical side to it: viable institutions give us a better insight into the nature of the social order.

This interpretation of Hayek is congruent with a lot of what he wrote, but it has one drawback from the point of view of Kley's argument: there is little in it in terms of instrumentalism. A similar notion of viability is found in many conservative writers (such as Russell Kirk and Roger Scruton) who, while having nothing to do with instrumentalism, also favor self-generating and self-sustaining institutions that have emerged through an evolutionary process of adjustment.

There is another way to interpret the quoted passage, one that modifies the previous version. The view ignores (a) as referring to an obscure problem of social ontology; as to "feasibility" and "viability," we can use these terms interchangeably to convey loosely the simple idea that, for Hayek, a social order is "a mechanism" that, by definition, should be judged by whether it functions properly, where the word "properly" denotes efficient coordination. Thus, when asked why he prefers some social and economic arrangements to others—capitalism to socialism, for example—Hayek would answer that capitalism provides a better system for coordinating political and economic agents. I believe this explanation is closest to Kley's intention, though, as noted, it does not seem to be entirely consistent with the text. In the quoted passage we are told that Hayek believed in an evolutionary process that gives a mechanism "value and wisdom." If so, one might say that he was not a strict instrumentalist, because he also relied on non-instrumental notions. Referring to "value" and "wisdom" presupposes that Hayek's order is not only operationally efficient, but that this efficiency is subservient to the good it produces (leaving aside the question what this good, i.e., this value and wisdom, might be). As other passages in the book show, Kley will argue that in Hayek we can separate the notion of the market as a coordinating mechanism from the notion of cultural evolution which creates "value and wisdom" (an argument I will comment on in the last part of the paper).

Hayek and the fall of communism

In order to find more in Kley's use of the category of instrumentalism one should turn to other, less ambiguous, formulations. Of the few that are available in the text, the most telling is the following one from the Introduction. "What is, in Hayek's perspective, distinctive about liberalism is less a particular set of moral and political concerns deriving from a powerful ideal of individual liberty than its unqualified espousal of the market and its system of rules. To be a liberal is, for Hayek a question not primarily of having the right political morality, but of possessing the correct social and economic theory and, therefore, endorsing the only effective coordination mechanism. Liberalism is an instrumental doctrine" (8).

Here, as in the last of the above interpretations, Hayek is said to be an instrumentalist because, for him, the superiority of the liberal order consists in its efficient mechanism of coordination. To this two more points may be added which are stated explicitly in this as well as other passages. First, in Hayek there are no "moral and political concerns" derived from some independent ethical standpoint, irreducible to the criterion of efficiency; especially it would be a mistake to attribute to Hayek the view—typical of liberals—that the independent ethical standard for political and economic institutions is some notion of individual freedom. Second, the preoccupation with efficiency at the expense of the moral principles that underlie the value of individual freedom makes Hayek liable to an even more serious charge. He was not only an instrumentalist, but also a holist (68): what mattered to him was the evaluation of whole social systems (such as capitalism and socialism), whose efficiency could be measured by the degree to which they secure peace and prosperity.

Let me start with the last two points. They amount to a rather one-sided view of Hayek and one that would be difficult to defend consistently. A holist attitude is there, to be sure, but Kley makes too much of it. We should not forget that until relatively recently, much free-market philosophy was formulated within the context of the East-West communism-capitalism conflict, which inevitably gave them a partly holist character. Even in Ludwig von Mises's aprioristic theory of the market, which was definitely more individualistic than Hayek's, one could find a holist tinge. Kley is of course not unaware of this historical circumstance, but he tends to see it as spawning simplified dichotomies that, characteristically, he dismisses with the epithet "Manichean" (4).

But a dualistic perspective need not be identical with political-economic Manicheanism, and in so far as they both overlap, it need not support the charge of instrumentalism. What the menace of the communist system induced was, indeed, a shift from conceptual nominalism in the interpretation of the market (to which capitalism based on self-interest and individualism has always been prone) to conceptual realism. The latter position, however, by no means obliges us to embrace an image of capitalism as an efficient mechanism of coordination securing peace and prosperity, irrespective of individual freedom. Although, having taken this perspective, we are undoubtedly inclined to view capitalism as a distinct whole—and because of this holistic tendency we might be suspected of betraying its individualistic spirit—this whole is a cultural entity, the civilization of freedom, whose essence could be best grasped in contrast with totalitarianism. Should one look for Manicheanism here, one would find it in a contrast between freedom and serfdom, rather than that between efficient and inefficient mechanisms of coordination. But once we take this position, we are less—or not only—concerned with black-and-white morality (no matter how justified it might be), and more with the theoretical project of identifying and depicting the forces that have generated and sustained a free society. If that approach is holistic, so be it, but it is certainly not instrumentalist in the above-defined sense. My quarrel with Kley's view is that it makes Hayek, at best, an un-self-conscious or, at worst, a dishonest thinker who, while writing about the road to serfdom, the constitution of liberty, and an order of a free people meant in fact something different, namely, the road to poverty, the constitution of prosperity, and an order of efficiently cooperating economic agents.

9

It may very well be that with the fall of communism, the idea of the civilization of freedom has lost the conceptual and cultural distinctness it once was believed to have, so that the search for its foundations would now be carried out in a less "Manichean" way. Such a project, however, has no appeal for Kley, nor, apparently, did it ever. In a short paragraph referring to the collapse of communism, he contends that Hayek's theory has limited "explanatory relevance": the revolution in the Soviet bloc—Kley maintains—was primarily political, focused on the ideas of "citizenship, public discourse, individual rights and procedural fairness," and triggered by "the notorious discrepancies between official rhetoric and actual achievement" that was characteristic of Eastern European socialism (17).

Without minimizing the impact of the factors he mentions, Hayek's theory was equally relevant. He was unquestionably one of the political theorists who substantially influenced the way the Eastern European intellectuals began to view their situation and their objectives during the last decade of communism. What he made them realize was that the error of the ruling system was not a poor implementation of noble ideals. Hence "the notorious discrepancies between official rhetoric and actual achievement" came to matter less than the perception that the whole rationale of the social, political, and economic order under which they lived was essentially flawed. In other words, communism was now thought to be "unnatural" in the sense of being an ill-conceived, artificially constructed system that, since its inception, had been aimed against the form of social existence that generated the institutions of freedom. The categories of "spontaneous development" and "constructivism" not only helped articulate social experience, but led to a reassessment of the place that capitalism and socialism occupied in the Western tradition. From that moment on, freedom was no longer primarily a political postulate expressed in the rhetoric of liberation, but began to be viewed in terms of a larger legal and economic order based on a moral and intellectual tradition different from the one that animated the ideologies of socialism.

It should be also pointed out that the whole debate between the supporters of capitalism and the supporters of socialism had not been, for some time, focused on the efficiency/inefficiency dichotomy for the simple reason that few socialists seriously doubted which system is superior in that respect. The standard charge that Marxist and *Marxisant* circles (represented among others by the Frankfurt School and, in a much less refined form, by communist propaganda) raised against the free market was therefore not that it did not produce wealth but that, firstly, it had become anachronistic in the light of social and cultural processes, and secondly, that it was essentially inhumane (that is, unfair, alienating, spiritually impoverishing, etc.) precisely due to its impersonal, machine-like efficiency. The latter accusation had a further consequence. Whatever claims capitalism might have had to freedom, it was ultimately declared a failure: a man living in a society that is unfair, alienating, and spiritually impoverishing did not have real freedom. He was believed to be eager to trade what freedom he had for more meaningful values that a more humane system could provide.

What Hayek did was to challenge both of the above assertions. He dismissed the alleged anachronism of capitalism by positing a model of evolution that did not make socialism a more advanced, let alone an inevitable stage of social development. And he rebuilt capitalism's ethical foundation by reasserting what its adversaries persistently denied or minimized: that this system lives on and produces freedom, and that this freedom—merely negative and largely illusory, according to Marxists—should not be traded for supposedly more meaningful values, because it is a constitutive element of the whole order. By making those two assertions Hayek put the ideologues of socialism on the defensive: he made them appear, within the framework of his theory, out of tune with the times, unable to cope with the complexities of the modern world. Although this defect expressed itself in socialism's inherent inefficiency, it was in itself a by-product of something more basic—a misinterpretation of reality (here Kley's "the world as it is" formula might have some relevance). Similarly, on the ethical side one could argue that socialism's inefficiency stemmed from its suppression of freedom, which is the fundamental source of human creativity and the condition of meaningful existence. *Toutes proportions gardées*, one could make an analogous argument against slavery: it is inefficient not only, and not primarily because of an organizational failure— this might be at least partly redressed—but because it misinterprets the nature of social order, being therefore unable to withstand the pressure of change: and because it is ethically wrong in depriving people of freedom.

Evolutionism and instrumentalism

To reinforce the view that what Hayek was after was in fact the efficiency of the *mechanism* and nothing more, with freedom playing a subservient role. Kley suggests the following interpretation. Hayek, he says, proposes two separate arguments: traditionalist and proceduralist. According to the first one, "the institutions of the liberal market society—being long-standing traditions of evolutionary origin—are indispensable for the survival of mankind even though a rational justification explaining what precisely their contribution consists in cannot be given"; according to the second one, "the institutional framework of the liberal market society and self-coordination in the market" are indispensable because "they alone are capable of dealing with certain circumstances of modern social life in a way that secures general prosperity and social peace" (185).

In Kley's view both arguments are essentially instrumentalist, which again is somewhat puzzling. Whereas one can easily attribute instrumentalism to the second argument—the market may indeed be conceived as a set of procedures of economic cooperation whose efficiency is measured by the degree to which it secures prosperity (although, as the previous section showed, it is doubtful if this view applies to Hayek)—one should hesitate to characterize the first one this way. Traditionalism requires that people feel attached to their historically rooted institutions and practices regardless of whether these serve any rationally identifiable purpose, and certainly regardless of whether they secure prosperity, peace, or even personal happiness.

Kley explains why Hayek's traditionalism is instrumentalist in the course of a long and complicated argument that I have been unable to put into a coherent whole. Here are some of the points he makes:

(i) "The contours" of Hayek's instrumentalist traditionalism are according to Kley, the following. Hayek's "strategy is to identify an end shared also by the adversaries of the market and to show that only market traditions, but no alternative institutional arrangements, are capable of achieving it." This common end is "the preservation of mankind and the elimination of famine and poverty.... Since everybody endorses the end, everybody must also endorse the only effective means to that end: the rules and institutions of the market" (186).

To this one might reply that what Hayek proposes here is not the justification of the market institutions but an *ad hominem* argument against socialists. Since those socialists who envisaged capitalism as a self-destructive and economically polarizing mechanism would agree that the preservation of mankind and the abolition of poverty are essential criteria of evaluating institutional arrangements, it is natural that Hayek would press them on this point. The actual performance of the socialist economies, in contrast with the achievements of the capitalist economies, provides an argument too tempting not to be raised by market advocates; in fact it is used by most—if not all—free marketeers, regardless of their possible instrumentalist tendencies. The criteria involved are minimalist and largely negative. One cannot hope to *justify* capitalism solely on the grounds that people living under it do not die of hunger and do not destroy one another. This may, however, turn out to be a powerful argument against those who, like some socialists, promised to achieve much more but were unable to attain even this.

(ii) Kley maintains that Hayek's defense of the market is irrational, and can be made rational only on instrumentalist grounds. Here is his line of reasoning. He recapitulates Hayek's notion of his conceptual antagonist, "constructivism," which he characterizes by three tenets: (a) "all social institutions are, and ought to be, the product of deliberate design"; (b) "reason is sufficiently powerful to know, and simultaneously to take into account, all the details of the human conditions necessary to shape the institutions of society according to the preferences of its members"; (c) "all institutions not visibly serving approved ends . . . should be discarded," a tenet Kley calls "explanatory explicitness" (187–88). Kley makes two points about this last tenet: first, that Hayek, in rejecting the possibility of an explicit argument in favor of the market, in fact rejects any possibility of justification, rendering his defense of the market "a truly irrational undertaking and a pointless endeavor" that can only issue in "quietism and blind submission" (189); second, that "to maintain, against the constructivist maxim of accepting only what one *understands*, that we have never been able to comprehend moral rules *in the sense in which we understand how the things that we manufacture function* is to share with constructivism the idea that in principle, if one had the knowledge, moral rules could be understood analogously to how manufactured things work" (190).

The first two tenets of constructivism Kley leaves without comment, which might indicate that he, too, finds them objectionable. This is not a far-fetched conclusion, since they are extremely bold and easily challenged: there are institutions which are not the products of deliberate design, and reason cannot be sufficiently powerful to master all factors that make a good institution. Once we agree on that, we may find the notion of explanatory explicitness suspect and sympathize with Hayek's idea of the social process as the accumulation of practical wisdom, irreducible to explicit formulae. To have confidence in this accumulated knowledge and, consequently, in the institutions that are credited with carrying it need not be irrational; in fact, what would be irrational would be to search for explicit justifications after having rejected (a) and (b). Similarly, since explicit justification may not be possible, it would be unreasonable to claim that whenever it is impossible we are faced with "blind submission." This charge itself may arise only from the constructivist position, for which there is a sharp dichotomy between rational explicit argument and thoughtless quietism. Hayek's point is precisely that such a dichotomy is untenable.

This also undermines the last part of Kley's argument, which seems somewhat bizarre. The fact that one attacks the constructivists on the ground that contrary to their claim, "we have never been able to comprehend moral rules *in the sense in which we understand how the things that we manufacture function*" does not imply that by launching that attack we unwittingly share the constructivist principle that "if one had the knowledge, moral rules could be understood analogously to how manufactured things work." Considering that constructivism for Hayek is equated with a Cartesian epistemology based on deducing from absolute, self-evident first principles a chain of logical consequences, one could make a similar argument proving that Hayek is a crypto-Cartesian: whatever we know about our moral rules and social institutions is not knowledge that accords with Cartesian epistemology, but if we had the knowledge about those rules and institutions it would certainly be of the Cartesian type.

(iii) Kley argues that Hayek's evolutionism cannot give permanent sanction to liberalism and liberal institutions, as evolution is by definition an open-ended process. "Whatever direction institutional change takes, that theory can only note it and explain its occurrence as an increase in societal adaptiveness. It must trace liberal values and institutions back to a certain momentary environmental constellation which, if it changes, gives way to new values and institutions. From an evolutionist viewpoint, there is nothing special about liberalism" (192).

This is, I think, the strongest part of Kley's counterargument. The only reply one can make in Hayek's defense is that the criticism illustrates not really a weakness of the concept of adaptiveness (and indirectly of instrumentalism), but of evolutionism. If we resort to the category of evolution and want to avoid—as Hayek does—falling into historical determinism, with its belief in the inevitability and inexorability of historical laws, we have to admit that no social or economic order deserves a permanent privileged position. And although Hayek might have argued that the transition from capitalism to socialism is not really a spontaneous one, but results from the violation of the rules of cooperation, thus deviating from the evolutionary process, this argument does not have sufficient force. While it may apply to several historical circumstances, especially in twentieth-century history, it cannot be turned into a general rule. From the strictly evolutionist perspective, the market must be seen as something transitory; at least there is no way one can rationally prevent social expectations of new and alternative institutional arrangements. Another possible defense may also be put aside. Although Hayek tried hard to avoid the trap Kley notices by conceiving of evolution as a pattern of change or a framework within which all possible developments may spontaneously occur, rather than a set of specifications of what these developments will be, he could not succeed. The pattern of change is as likely to evolve as the vision of future history.

That said, a more general comment about the interpretation of instrumentalism Kley attributes to Hayek is warranted. Apart from the fact that neither the proceduralist nor the traditionalist arguments are as instrumentalist as Kley wants them to be, his view suffers from a more serious inadequacy, which is, interestingly, indicated *en passant* by the author himself. "Hayek," Kley writes, "does not himself distinguish the two arguments. Perhaps, he would even have insisted that they form a coherent though complex whole" (185). This is exactly right. I would say more: the whole point of Hayek's theory, by which it stands or falls, is precisely the unity of those two arguments.

A lot of what Hayek wrote was determined by the classical problem, going back as far as antiquity, of how to reconcile two apparently irreconcilable aspects of human behavior: freedom and order. His proceduralist argument, as I understand it, was responsible for the freedom part of his message: by concentrating on procedures, Hayek avoided any commitment to rigid hierarchies of ends, leaving their choice to tree agents acting within a framework of rules that constitute the Great Society. The traditionalist argument, on the other hand, is not—contrary to Kley's claim—latently instrumentalist; it is conservative. Hayek's project developed in the context of reflection on the great derailments in the modern societies—a context he shared with many of his contemporaries, haunted by the specters of Nazism and Communism, as well as by their historical antecedents—which led him to believe that the only solution is a combination of individual freedom and accumulated social wisdom. As did many others before him, he turned to the British tradition, which seemed—especially in contrast to the totalitarian regimes that were then at the peak of their power—a perfect illustration of freedom being reconciled with an institutional tradition. The fact that Hayek talks of freedom in the conservative idiom of inherited social practices does not, then, mean that he did not have a strong independent ethical standard, that he diluted this standard in the impersonal forces of the market or historical processes, or that he identified it with the social status quo. For him such freedom was the only real type, that is, the only type that did not turn into despotism or an ideological ploy.

To separate the traditionalist perspective from the proceduralist one, as Kley does, is not only to deprive Hayek of the ethical force that his conception was meant to carry, but is to disregard the tension that characterized it. We cannot rely, Hayek said, on what we have received from the past because by pursuing our individual goals we are necessarily future-oriented; on the other hand, we are not free to think about the future solely in terms of the most effective means to realize our goals, because we ourselves are the products of the past, and this past, in the form of our cultural heritage, is the most reliable source of knowledge that we have.

Hayek clearly belongs to an important, though hard-to-classify, group of thinkers who tried to combine liberal and conservative ideas and are, therefore, often referred to as representing a "liberal-conservative" orientation. They did not form a school or a consistent doctrinal body; some of them were more conservative (like Burke), some more liberal (like Constant and Acton). Among Hayek's contemporaries this idea was popular among some German *ordo*-liberals, Wilhelm Röpke being the best-known of them. If there is anything that all these thinkers had in common, and anything that justifies the use of the otherwise clumsy and oxymoronic "liberal-conservative" label, it is their philosophical anthropology. All of them shared a certain conception of man, without which a good deal of what they said could be dismissed as intrinsically contradictory. The liberal-conservative world they depicted was possible because it was inhabited by liberal-conservative people. Most of these thinkers pointed to the British tradition (or, to be precise, to a certain interpretation of it), with its peculiar mixture of freedom and conservatism, in order to exemplify this anthropology and the forms of social existence it entailed.

Liberal-conservative anthropology describes people in antithetical terms because it is meant to account for the antithetical concept and the antithetical phenomenon of "a discipline of freedom" (Hayek 1979, 163–65). Hayek's human being is individualistically understood because individual innovation is, ultimately, the sole source of creativity and progress; yet he is also understood as a socially embedded being who never indulges in an adversarial attitude toward the rules that underlie the fabric of the social order. He does not believe in absolute ethics of the Platonic type that would petrify norms and institutions, yet he would consider as a major threat to the civilization of freedom prophets of emancipation, such as Marx and Freud, who teach that norms and institutions are the primary vehicles of oppression. Being a member of the Great Society, he no longer cherishes any allegiance to premodern communities, which he regards as the relics of the tribal instincts; but at the same time he relies on mores, social conventions, and inherited practices—tacit norms that are largely the cultural legacy of the premodern tradition, untouched by the constructivist spirit of modern rationalism.

Viewed from this perspective the proceduralist-traditionalist dichotomy presents itself not as an inconsistency—"irremediable" and "palpable," as Kley calls it (11–12)—but rather as an attempt to close within one social order and one anthropological vision the two elements without which, Hayek believed, liberal society could not exist. This anthropology may not be inconsistent, but one may well suspect it of cultural anachronism. Just as one might no longer share Hayek's vision of the clear boundaries and identifiable nature of the civilization of freedom, one might also doubt whether the liberal-conservative human beings who supposedly created it still exist in modern society. The concept of man that goes back to the venerable tradition of British moderate conservatism does not accord easily with today's cultural idiom, which concentrates more on "marginality" (Gray 1993, 263) and "modularity" (Gellner 1994, 97–102); and any theory that is implicitly built on such a man is bound to look anachronistic. At the same time one must be aware of the limited nature of this complaint: we cannot know for certain if what looks anachronistic today may not look appealingly modern after some unpredictable tide of future history.

Acknowledgment

Thanks to the Social Philosophy and Policy Center for providing conditions that made work on this chapter possible, and Jeffrey Friedman for insightful comments on the first draft.

16

References

Barry, Norman P. 1979. *Hayek's Social and Economic Philosophy*. London: Macmillan.

De Jasay, Anthony. 1990. *Market Socialism: A Scrutiny*. London: Institute of Economic Affairs.

Drèze, Jean, and Amartya Sen. 1989. *Hunger and Public Action*. Oxford: Clarendon Press.

Gellner, Ernest. 1994. *Conditions of Liberty: Civil Society and Its Rivals*. Harmondsworth: Allan Lane, Penguin Press.

Gray, John. 1984. *Hayek on Liberty*. Oxford: Blackwell.

Gray, John. 1993. *Post-Liberalism*. New York: Routledge.

Hayek, Friedrich A. 1948. *Individualism and Economic Order*. Chicago: University of Chicago Press.

Hayek, Friedrich A. 1960. *The Constitution of Liberty*. Chicago: University of Chicago Press.

Hayek, Friedrich A. 1979. *Law, Legislation and Liberty*, vol. 3: *The Political Order of a Free People*. Chicago: University of Chicago Press.

Kley, Roland. 1994. *Hayek's Social and Political Thought*. Oxford: Clarendon Press.

Kukathas, Chandran. 1989. *Hayek and Modern Liberalism*. Oxford: Clarendon Press.

Lavoie, Don. 1985. *Rivalry and Central Planning*. Cambridge: Cambridge University Press.

Ravallion, Martin. 1987. *Markets and Famines*. Oxford: Clarendon Press.

Sen, Amartya. 1981. *Poverty and Famines*. Oxford: Clarendon Press.

Vanberg, Viktor. 1994. "Hayek's Legacy and the Future of Liberal Thought: Rational Liberalism vs. Evolutionary Agnosticism." *Journal des Economistes et des Etudes Humaines* 5: 451–81.

46

HAYEK AND SOCIALISM

Bruce Caldwell

Source: *Journal of Economic Literature* 35 (December 1997): 1856–1890.

I. Introduction

Most economists know that Friedrich A. Hayek was a life-long opponent of socialism. But who were his opponents, what were his arguments, and how did he come to develop them?

In the 1930s Hayek attacked the economic feasibility of socialism, drawing on arguments from an earlier German-language debate and taking to task a number of separate proposals for a socialist society. This drew a response from Oskar Lange, who advocated market socialism. The ensuing battle with Lange and others led Hayek to develop a distinctive "knowledge-based" critique of socialism.

Just before the onset of World War II Hayek began work on a series of articles whose ultimate result was the publication in 1944 of *The Road to Serfdom*, his most famous (and in some quarters, notorious) book. *The Road to Serfdom* contains Hayek's political critique of socialism, but also the seeds of more positive work. The fruit was his description and defense of an alternative liberal utopia in such works as *The Constitution of Liberty* (1960) and *Law, Legislation and Liberty* (1973–79).

During the war years Hayek also became fascinated with questions of methodology. This led him, apparently incongruously, to publish a book on the foundations of psychology. *The Sensory Order* (1952a) is, particularly among economists, Hayek's least appreciated book, yet in a letter to an economist prior to its publication he described it as "the most important thing I have yet done ..." (letter to John Nef, Nov. 6, 1948). The book provides a theoretical basis for the "limitations of knowledge" theme that has been recurrent in Hayek's work. This claim in turn implies limits on the ambitions of socialist planners and other "rationalist constructivists," and as such constitutes another set of arguments against socialism. It also implies limits on the ambitions of economists, and from an Austrian viewpoint, may help to explain why the models of economists have so often misled them about the prospects for socialism.

The paper attempts to answer the questions provided at the outset, to survey Hayek's various arguments against socialism and to provide some historical background on why he developed them when he did.

Recent interpretive literature provides the impetus for the emphasis on historical context. Since the events of 1989, the Soviet central planning model has largely been abandoned by academic advocates of socialism, and a renewed interest in market socialism has taken its place. Recent discussions of market socialism by economic theorists, both proponents and opponents, typically draw on insights derived from the "economics of information." This new perspective views general equilibrium approaches as inadequate, if not misleading, for understanding economic phenomena. Because many of the earlier debates on market socialism utilized a general equilibrium framework, they are from the perspective of the economics of information otiose.

A new interpretation of the debates over socialism, one that highlights the contributions of the economics of information, has begun to emerge (Pranab Bardhan and John Roemer, eds. 1993, pp. 3–9; Joseph Stiglitz 1994). These interpretations are designed to provide context for recent work, but they typically run into difficulties when they try to characterize Hayek's contribution. Though it is evident that Hayek (like the information theorists) was critical of using static general equilibrium models for assessing the merits and limitations of socialism, it seems clear (and this despite his frequent invocation of the concept of "knowledge") that Hayek did not directly participate in the development of the economics of information.

How, then, to characterize Hayek's contribution? From a modern perspective, his work seems "fuzzy" (Louis Makowski and Joseph Ostroy, in Bardhan and Roemer, eds. 1993, p. 82). Many may well be tempted to conclude with Jànos Kornai (in Bardhan and Roemer 1993, p. 63) that "the warnings of a Mises or a Hayek about market socialism" should be viewed as "brilliant guesses" rather than as anything resembling "scientific propositions," or with Robert Heilbroner (1990, p. 1098) that "the successes of the farsighted seem accounted for more by their prescient 'visions' than by their superior analyses."

In the final section an alternative, more positive interpretation of Hayek's contribution is offered. As he became ever more deeply entangled in the debates over socialism, Hayek decided that a more integrative approach to the study of complex social phenomena was necessary, that standard economic analysis taken alone might itself be inadequate, if not misleading, for understanding the problems of socialism. To be sure, his decision to branch out was based in part on his recognition of the limitations of the static "equilibrium theory" of his day. But his emphases on the market as a discovery process, his concern with the limits of human cognition, and above all his fascination with questions of knowledge, what John

Gray (1986, p. 134) has aptly called his "epistemological turn," led Hayek to insights that may well be different in kind from those advanced by proponents of the economics of information.

If this alternative account is correct, it means at a minimum that those who would try to read history backwards, who would assess Hayek's contribution solely in terms of whether and how he anticipated the later literature on the economics of information, will perforce misunderstand his arguments against socialism. So one point of the final section is to plea for a less ahistorical history. But it may also be the case that Hayek actually provided an independent set of claims against market socialism, one that has been missed by modern information theorists. If so, then Hayek's apparently "fuzzy" arguments may well prove to be of more than "merely historical" interest today.

II. Hayek and the market socialists[1]

Friedrich August von Hayek was born in Vienna on May 8, 1899. Following war service he entered the University of Vienna, where he completed degrees in 1921 and 1923. After 14 months of study in the U.S., Hayek returned to Austria in 1925. He spent the rest of the decade studying monetary history and developing a theory of the trade cycle. Hayek's life and the academic milieu of Vienna in the 1920s is documented in Hayek (1984, Introduction; 1992, Prologue; 1994, pp. 47–72) and Earlene Craver (1986).

In the spring of 1931 Hayek was invited by Lionel Robbins to deliver a series of lectures on the trade cycle at the London School of Economics (LSE). The next year he was appointed to the Tooke Chair of Economic Science and Statistics at the LSE, a position he would hold until he moved to the United States in 1950, where he ultimately accepted a position on the Committee on Social Thought at the University of Chicago. During the early 1930s Hayek had exchanges with John Maynard Keynes and Piero Sraffa on monetary and trade cycle theory and with Frank Knight on capital theory (Hayek 1994, pp. 75–98; 1995). His debates with the socialists began in 1935 with the publication of *Collectivist Economic Planning: Critical Studies on the Possibilities of Socialism*. The book contained translations of four articles with introductory and concluding essays provided by Hayek as editor.

A. Prelude—Mises and the German language debates

The most important of the translated contributions was an article by Ludwig von Mises that had originally appeared in 1920. The collapse of the German and Austro-Hungarian Empires at the end of the First World War opened the door for a variety of socialist proposals for reorganizing society. Prior to the war Mises was known as a monetary theorist and for his unyielding devotion to liberalism. He was as good a person as any to challenge the socialists; in so doing he initiated the German-language socialist calculation debate. David Steele (1992, ch. 4) identifies some of Mises' predecessors, and a number of writers (Trygve Hoff 1949; Judith Merkle 1980, ch. 6; Don Lavoie 1985; Günther Chaloupek 1990) examine the debates as well as the specifics of various proposals.

The proposal that most provoked Mises was made by the sociologist and philosopher Otto Neurath. Neurath is remembered today as a member of the Vienna Circle of logical positivists and as the inventor of ISOTYPE, the International System of Typographical Picture Education. Before World War I he began to make a reputation as a proponent of a new academic subfield, "war economy." He also participated, along with Mises, in Eugen von Böhm-Bawerk's famous economics seminar. Among the other seminar participants were Joseph Schumpeter, Otto Bauer, who would lead the Austrian Socialist Democratic Party in the 1920s, and Rudolf Hilferding, one of the leading Marxian theoreticians of the 20th century.

According to Neurath, during peace-time, production in market economies is driven by the search for profits, but this leads to recurrent periods of over-production and unemployment. In wartime, by contrast, production is no longer driven by profit-seeking, and the war effort ensures that productive capacity is always fully utilized. Another characteristic of the war economy is the suppression of the price system, which is replaced by extensive planning of materials management from the center. This is all to the good, because for Neurath the monetary system, the search for profits, and the disorderliness of capitalist production all go hand in hand.

Neurath argued that the central planning that emerges within war economies should continue in peacetime. He proposed that a "natural accounting center" be set up to run the economy as if it were one giant enterprise. Most controversially, he insisted that money would be unnecessary in the new planned order: because production would be driven by objectively determined needs rather than by the search for profits, all calculation regarding the appropriate levels of inputs and output could be handled in "natural" physical terms. In Neurath's opinion, attempts to employ monetary calculations within a planned society would render impossible scientific economic management, which had to be conducted in terms of "real" physical quantities.[2]

Mises (1978, pp. 39–41, 133) plainly had a strong negative reaction to Neurath personally, and as a monetary theorist he found his economic claims fantastic. (As Chaloupek 1990, pp. 668–70, has shown, most socialists also soon rejected Neurath's proposals for a moneyless economy.) But he wanted to make a more general case against socialism, one that could be used against other proposals as well, including those that retained a role for some form of money. Mises took as a starting premise that under most forms of socialism "production-goods" (factors of production) are owned by the state, and that as such there is no market for them. But this basic feature of socialism has substantial consequences:

> because no production-good will ever become the object of exchange, it will be impossible to determine its monetary value. Money could never fill in a socialist state the role it fills in a competitive society in determining the value of production-goods. Calculation in terms of money will here be impossible.
> (Mises, in Hayek, ed. 1935, p. 92)

Even if money is retained, in the socialist state no prices for factors of production exist. As such, socialist managers have no way to tell when choosing among a huge array of technologically feasible input combinations which are economically feasible. Without some knowledge of relative scarcities, they are left "groping in the dark." As Mises put it: "Where there is no free market, there is no pricing mechanism; without a pricing mechanism, there is no economic calculation" (in Hayek, ed. 1935, p. 111).

B. Hayek's initial arguments

In his introductory chapter Hayek recounted the debates that had taken place in the German language literature a decade before. In his conclusion he turned to the current scene.

English socialism in the 1930s was a mixed bag. The Fabians, whose leaders included Sidney and Beatrice Webb and George Bernard Shaw, had been arguing for an evolutionary style of socialism since the late 1880s. The British Labour Party, formed in 1906, officially endorsed socialism in its platform. Labour had prevailed in the general election of 1929, but had faltered with Britain's abandoning of gold in 1931 and spent the remainder of the decade regrouping. Though interest in Guild Socialism, a form of syndicalism, had declined following World War I, academic advocates like R. H. Tawney and G. D. C. Cole were still active. Barbara Wootton was the Director of Tutorial Studies at the University of London, and under her influence a "tutorial version of history," one which emphasized the deterioration of the position of the working class under capitalism, was taught in adult education courses throughout Britain. Maurice Dobb was the leading spokesman among economists for Marxism, and a number of prominent natural scientists favored communism. Finally, there existed a nascent interest in market socialism, dubbed "pseudo-competition" by Hayek.[3] With no idea which of his many opponents might respond, Hayek offered a diversity of criticisms of socialism.

22

He began with a review of "the Russian experiment," basing his criticisms on the writings of a Russian émigré Boris Brutzkus. This would serve as a counterweight to a more appreciative assessment of the experiment offered by the Webbs, whose massive study (it filled two volumes) was titled *Soviet Communism: A New Civilization?* when it was published in 1935. With incredibly bad timing, they chose to drop the question mark in the 1937 edition.

Next Hayek took up the argument of Henry D. Dickinson (1933), who claimed that Mises was wrong, that rational calculation under socialism was at least theoretically possible. Because any economy could be formally represented by a Walrasian system of equations, Dickinson claimed that on a theoretical level there is no difference between capitalism and socialism: In a capitalist system the equations are "solved" by the market, whereas in a socialist system they could be solved by the planning authorities.

In his rebuttal, Hayek enumerated many difficulties associated with "the mathematical solution," or any regime that relied on formulating and solving a giant system of equations for the relevant prices and quantities. He mentioned the staggering amount of information that would need to be gathered; the immense difficulty of formulating the correct system of equations; the hundreds of thousands of equations that would then need to be solved, not just once but repeatedly; and the inability of such a system to adapt to change.

Should socialist authorities decide to "solve" the system using a trial and error method, an approach also mentioned by Dickinson, other problems would arise. The most important of these is the inability of any price-changing mechanism to replicate the automatic adjustments that occur in a competitive free market system in response to underlying changes in supply and demand:

> Almost every change of any single price would make changes of hundreds of other prices necessary and most of these other changes would by no means be proportional but would be affected by the different degrees of elasticity of demand, by the possibilities of substitution and other changes in the method of production.
>
> (Hayek, ed. 1935, p. 214)

Next Hayek took up the arguments of the Marxist Dobb (1933), who noted that if consumption decisions were also subjected to central control, most of the problems associated with central planning would be alleviated. Hayek pointed out that the abrogation of consumer sovereignty implied in such an approach would presumably be repellant to most Britons, and that even under such a regime, prices to help guide production would still be necessary.

23

In the last half of his chapter Hayek explicitly engaged market social-ism. Because no concrete proposals were yet on the table, he had to imagine the forms of market organization that his opponents might propose. One possible arrangement is for managers of monopolized indus-tries to be directed to produce so that prices covered marginal costs, thereby duplicating the results of competitive equilibrium. Hayek's most original argument here is that in the real world (as opposed to the static world of perfect competition models) it is typically difficult to know exactly what "true" marginal costs are (Hayek, ed. 1935, pp. 226–31). In a market socialist regime in which firms within an industry do compete, a different problem arises: in decisions concerning capital allocation, central planners would have to take over the role played by thousands of entre-preneurs in a market system (Hayek, ed. 1935, pp. 233–37). Hayek clearly considered this to be a disadvantage, but did not specify the nature of the problem. Finally, he noted that the absence of private ownership in the means of production creates incentive problems for managers, who will put off making difficult decisions and who will tend toward risk-aversion in making investment decisions (Hayek, ed. 1935, pp. 235, 237).

Though Hayek's two early pieces contain fleeting glimpses of his mature position, the modern reader must work to find them. As Israel Kirzner has convincingly argued, the socialist calculation debate served as a

> catalyst in the development and articulation of the modern Aus-trian view of the market as a competitive-entrepreneurial process of discovery.... it was through the give-and-take of this debate that the Austrians gradually refined their understanding of their own position.
>
> (Kirzner 1988, p. 1; cf. Lavoie 1985)

C. Lange's rebuttal

Market socialists are critics of capitalism, but they also acknowledge that under certain conditions perfectly competitive markets have desirable efficiency characteristics. An essential premise of market socialism is the denial that market structures under late capitalism resemble, in any meaningful way, perfect competition. According to this view few competitive industries exist anymore, having been replaced by corporate giants, cartels, and monopolies. Contemporary capitalism thus lacks the beneficial efficiency characteristics of competition, while retaining all of its defects. With careful planning market socialism can replicate the bene-fits of truly competitive markets, correct for remaining problems regard-ing efficiency, and all the while avoid capitalism's pernicious distributional effects. The chief spokesman for this view in the later 1930s was a Polish émigré to America, Oskar Lange, whose two-part paper appeared in the *Review of Economic Studies* in 1936–37, and was soon reprinted in a book of the same title, *On the Economic Theory of Socialism* (1938).

Lange's first argument was directed against Mises. Lange agreed with Mises that prices are necessary for rational calculation. Mises' mistake was to think that prices must be formed in markets. If one instead understands that the correct definition of prices is "terms on which alternatives are offered," and that their determination in markets is not essential but rather a peculiarity of a particular institutional arrangement (capitalism), then Mises' argument collapses. Accounting prices could be supplied by the Central Planning Board, and these could be taken by socialist managers as parameters in their decision making. Rational calculation under socialism is not "impossible" after all (Lange 1938, pp. 60–62).

Lange's next step was to demonstrate how a socialist commonwealth could be made to yield the same results as a true competitive market system. In his model there exists a free market for both consumer goods and labor, but (because of public ownership of the means of production) no market for non-labor productive resources like capital. Because labor incomes would still be market-determined, income inequality would not be eliminated. But because capital ownership is a principal source of income disparities, its elimination would serve to reduce inequality. Individual incomes would also be supplemented by receipt of some share of the "social dividend," the income that had previously gone to owners of capital.

The sticking point for this variant of market socialism is the absence of profit maximizing firms and of a market (and hence of prices that reflect relative scarcities) for non-labor productive resources. Lange proposed that the Central Planning Board provide provisional "prices" for all goods and factors of production. Managers of socialist firms would be instructed to choose, on the basis of these "given" prices, the combination of inputs that minimized their costs and the level of output that maximized profits. Planners in charge of industries would likewise expand or contract them as necessary, thereby replicating the beneficial effects of free entry and exit under competition.

Lange's proposal begged a key question: What if the Central Planning Board fails to choose prices that accurately reflect underlying relative scarcities? Here Lange suggested that planners follow a "trial and error" procedure, one similar to that used in actual markets, adjusting prices up or down in any factor or product markets in which gluts or shortages existed. Through the trial and error method the "right" set of accounting prices will ultimately be found (Lange 1938, pp. 86–89).

Lange responded to Hayek's concerns about replacing entrepreneurs with central planners as follows:

the trial and error procedure would, or at least could, work *much better* in a socialist economy than it does in a competitive market. For the Central Planning Board has a much wider knowledge of what is going on in the whole economic system than any private entrepreneur can ever have, and, consequently, may be able to reach the right equilibrium prices by a *much shorter* series of successive trials than a competitive market actually does.

(Lange 1938, p. 89, emphasis in the original)

What about the skewing of incentives under socialism? Acknowledging the importance of the problem, Lange offered two responses. First, he denied that such agency questions are a proper topic for economists to study: "The discussion of this argument belongs to the field of sociology rather than of economic theory and must therefore be dispensed with here" (Lange 1935, p. 109). Second, he insisted that the real problem was one of *bureaucracy*. But bureaucratization, he continued, is a generic problem that afflicts both capitalism and socialism. Because of the absence of competition, the managers of a bureaucratic modern capitalistic corporation are as likely to be inefficient as are their counterparts under socialism. The separation of ownership from control exacerbates this: the modern capitalist corporation is increasingly run by a professional managerial class whose members care more about their own welfare than about running an efficient firm. Bureaucracy is a problem of modern life, not one that is unique to socialism (Lange 1938, pp. 109–10, 120). To support his case Lange cited Adolf Berle and Gardiner Means (1933), the classic study of the separation of ownership from control in the modern corporation and a forerunner of the modern principal-agent literature. Lange's argument underlines again the crucial importance for socialists of the claim that old-style atomistic competition is rare under late capitalism.

D. Answering Lange—Mises on appraisement and the entrepreneur

Mises never directly replied to Lange. But it is clear from his later writings that he rejected Lange's claim that prices are nothing more than "terms on which alternatives are offered." For Mises, prices are social phenomena "brought about by the interplay of the valuations of all individuals participating in the operation of the market" (Mises 1966, p. 331). They reflect the plans and appraisements of millions of acting individuals at a particular moment in time.

Given its origin in the appraisements of millions of people, the price structure is constantly changing. Even so, it is an essential tool used by entrepreneurs to make calculations about the highest-valued use of scarce resources. Crucially, such calculations are always future-oriented.

In drafting their plans the entrepreneurs look first at the prices of the immediate past which are mistakenly called *present* prices. Of course, the entrepreneurs never make these prices enter into their calculations without paying regard to anticipated changes. The prices of the immediate past are for them only the starting point of deliberations leading to forecasts of future prices. . . . The prices of the past are for the entrepreneur, the shaper of future production, merely a mental tool.

(Mises 1966, pp. 336–37, emphasis in the original)

Entrepreneurs must make decisions about resource use in a world in which production takes time and in which the constant evolution of human plans creates a constantly changing structure of prices. In such an environment errors clearly are unavoidable. But they do not persist, because every mistake made by one entrepreneur is simultaneously a profit opportunity for another: "it is the competition of profit-seeking entrepreneurs that does not tolerate the preservation of *false* prices of the factors of production" (Mises 1966, pp. 337–38, emphasis in the original). Thus the ever-changing structure of prices that exists within a market system, the messy groping that appears so anarchic, ends up being a passably efficient system for revealing relative scarcities. And paradoxically, though the price system operates through the self-interested actions of thousands of individuals, its end result is social cooperation: Paris gets fed.

For Mises, the entrepreneur is the essential actor of the piece, but equally important is that his actions take place within a specific institutional framework. Absent a market system with well-defined and enforced property rights, the entrepreneur would have neither the necessary information nor the proper incentives to perform his essential function.[4] Mises acknowledged that Lange's attempt to introduce prices and competition into a socialist framework showed some recognition of all this (Mises 1966, p. 706). But without the rest of the requisite institutional setting, such efforts must ultimately fail.

E. Answering Lange—Hayek on computation and on knowledge

Hayek initially responded to Lange in a book review (Hayek [1940] 1948), then elaborated on and extended his argument in a series of articles (Hayek [1945, 1946] 1948; [1968a] 1978).

1. The Computation Problem and "Trial and Error"—Recall that Hayek had in 1935 already provided arguments against such approaches as "the mathematical solution" and, more importantly given Lange's arguments, against the feasibility of trial and error methods. In his review he wondered why Lange had failed to address his objections about the latter,

27

and why his opponent had even neglected to answer the obviously important question of how often prices were to be adjusted under his proposed system. Hayek ([1940] 1948, p. 188) added that,

> it is difficult to suppress the suspicion that this particular proposal has been born out of an excessive preoccupation with problems of the pure theory of stationary equilibrium.

Hayek's point was a simple one: static equilibrium theory concentrates on end-points, on a system that has achieved a state of rest. But the notion of a system moving toward some "final" end-point as determined by "given" data is radically at odds with the situation in the real world, "where constant change is the rule" (Hayek [1940] 1948, p. 188). Hayek was suggesting that Lange's use of an equilibrium model had misled him into thinking that the movement toward some final equilibrium set of accounting prices would be a one time adjustment, whereas in reality it would be a never-ending process.

Hayek's arguments about the difficulties of coming up with the necessary data have been challenged by each new generation of socialists, as first input-output analysis, then planometrics, then computable general equilibrium models, then the advent of supercomputers all promised finally to provide an instrument that could replace the market's price adjustment mechanism. As a mature Lange (1967, p. 158) provocatively put it:

> Were I to rewrite my essay today my task would be much simpler. My answer to Hayek and Robbins would be: so what's the trouble? Let us put the simultaneous equations on an electronic computer and we shall obtain the solution in less than a second.

More recently, Allin Cottrell and W. Paul Cockshott (1993) and Steven Horwitz (1996) have offered contrasting assessments of the feasibility of socialist computational proposals.

As a practical matter, though, few convincing examples of the successful replacement of markets exist. Ironically, the practical effects of the computer revolution so far seem to have been to undermine the ability of totalitarian states to restrict access to information, and to enable entrepreneurs to engage in the sort of "atomistic competition" that socialists of the 1930s had assumed had died out. It is also noteworthy that within the artificial intelligence literature the relationship between markets and computers is becoming very nearly the opposite of that imagined by Lange: rather than regarding markets as primitive forms of computers, efforts are aimed at making computers replicate the allocational and adaptative characteristics of markets (Lavoie 1990, p. 76).

2. Hayek's "Knowledge" Arguments—Hayek provided an example of the consequences of taking static theories too seriously in a discussion of Lange's cost minimization rule. Hayek asked: how will planners come to know what the minimum costs are ([1940] 1948, p. 196)? His basic contention was that only through the workings of a rivalrous market process are ever lower cost methods of production discovered or created (cf. Hayek, [1946] 1948, pp. 96–97). Standard equilibrium theory misleads by assuming that an end-state is already reached, so that cost minimizing input combinations are already known. This obscures the process by which they come to be known, and may lead to the erroneous belief that one can dispense with the very process (rivalrous market competition) that generates the knowledge. More generally, the static theory of perfect competition "starts from the assumption of a 'given' supply of scarce goods. But which goods are scarce goods, or which things are goods, and how scarce or valuable they are—these are precisely the things which competition has to discover" (Hayek [1968a] 1978, p. 181). In a phrase: Market competition constitutes a discovery procedure.

Lange had also argued that, because entrepreneurs have knowledge about only a limited set of markets and prices, a Central Planning Board (which would have access to more knowledge than would individual entrepreneurs) could make better capital allocation decisions.

In his 1937 article "Economics and Knowledge" Hayek noted that though standard equilibrium theory assumes that all agents have access to the same, objectively correct information, in reality there is a "division of knowledge." Actually-existing knowledge is dispersed; different individuals have access to different bits of it. Their actions are based on their varying subjective beliefs, beliefs that include assumptions about future states of the world and about other people's beliefs and actions. The "central question of all social science" ([1937] 1948, p. 54) is how such dispersed knowledge might be put to use, how society might coordinate the knowledge that exists in many different minds and places. Equilibrium theory with its emphasis on end-states assumes that the process of coordination has already taken place. By doing so, it assumes away the most important question.

A number of authors (Caldwell 1988a; Kirzner 1988; Meghnad Desai 1994) have argued that "Economics and Knowledge" was a seminal piece both in the development of Hayek's ideas and for its implications for the calculation debate. In his review, Hayek cited the article to show that Lange had again been misled by "equilibrium theory."

> As I have tried to show on another occasion, it is the main merit of real competition that through it use is made of knowledge divided among many persons which, if it were to be used in a centrally directed economy, would have all to enter the single plan.

To assume that all this knowledge would be automatically in the possession of the planning authority seems to me to miss the main point.

(Hayek [1940] 1948, p. 134)

Tracing out the implications of the "dispersion of knowledge" would become another major theme in Hayek's work. In the present context, three related strands may be identified. First, freely adjusting market prices that reflect relative scarcities are profoundly important when errors in perception exist, because they help market participants to bring their subjectively formed expectations in line with the actual state of the world. Next, much knowledge (particularly of business conditions) is localized, what Hayek came to call "knowledge of the particular circumstances of time and place" ([1945] 1948, p. 80). Finally, certain knowledge is tacit; it is "knowledge how" rather than "knowledge that" ([1968b] 1978, p. 38). Localized and tacit knowledge is difficult (and may be impossible) to pass on to others, even if one wanted to.

Modern theorists were quick to pick up on Hayek's insight that, in a world of dispersed knowledge, prices convey information. The same cannot be said about his writings on localized and tacit knowledge, the importance of which is well captured in the following example provided by Leland Yeager:

Often an entrepreneur makes business decisions partly on his intuition or feel for technology, the attitudes and tastes of consumers and workers, sources of financing, and conditions in markets for inputs and for consumer goods and services—all in the future as well as the present. The entrepreneur receives information for judgments about such matters by reading specialized and popular publications, watching television and movies, experiencing various services and products personally, chatting with innumerable people, and strolling through town or the shopping mall. Much of what he thereby observes—or senses—he could not express in explicit words or numbers. A socialist system would let much such entrepreneurial knowledge go to waste even if it emerged in the first place.

(Yeager 1996, p. 138)

The idea that "the pure theory of stationary equilibrium" is inadequate as a tool for understanding the workings of a market economy, and that it should be replaced by a view of the market as a competitive-entrepreneurial process for the discovery and coordination of knowledge, has become a central tenet of Austrian thought.[5] Hayek's arguments are probably most effective if one considers centrally controlled soviet-style economies, where price fixing is extensive and, as a result, the coordination of plans is hindered. But they also apply to many market socialist regimes. In Lange's proposal, for example, prices were still set by central authorities; this is why Hayek insisted that Lange must reveal how often prices would be adjusted under his "trial and error" regime. And Hayek's arguments about discovery, error correction, and the coordination and communication of localized and tacit knowledge apply whenever entrepreneurs acting within an institutional context of market competition make decisions that differ from those of their socialist manager counterparts.

Because of its connection to recent debates on the economics of information, we will delay until the last section our discussion of Hayek's response to Lange on the incentives question. Instead, we will next examine Hayek's political arguments against socialism. He began developing the argument in articles written in the late 1930s, but more famous is the analysis contained in *The Road to Serfdom* ([1944] 1976).

III. The road to serfdom

A. *Origins of the book*

The Road to Serfdom carries the dedication, "To the Socialists of All Parties." This was not just a rhetorical swipe; in the 1930s most British intellectuals (Hayek's presumed audience) *were* sympathetic to socialism (Arthur Marwick 1964). The many differences that might ordinarily separate a Liberal-Labour centrist from a member of the Communist Party of Great Britain were intentionally downplayed once the Popular Front, a union of leftist groups against fascism, emerged in the middle 1930s. In their own way even the Conservatives joined in. In 1938 future Prime Minister (then the Conservative MP from Stockton-on-Tees) Harold Macmillan published *The Middle Way* (1938), in which extensive government control of the economy was extolled. Hayek had little sympathy for such views, dubbing them "the muddle of the middle."

Hayek later reminisced that the original impetus for the book was comments made by Lord Beveridge (Hayek 1994, p. 102). But he was also fighting against the widely accepted view that National Socialism and other fascisms were a natural outgrowth of capitalism, and that only by adopting socialism could the remaining western democracies avoid a similar fate. Karl Mannheim, an academic who had fled Frankfurt in 1933 and who soon gained an appointment in the Department of Sociology at the LSE, was one of the more sophisticated proponents of this position.

Mannheim outlined the causal mechanisms at work in a lecture before his British colleagues first published in 1937. His starting premise was that monopoly capitalism was the root cause of widespread and sustained unemployment. In an age of mass democracy, orators skilled in the use of the latest propaganda techniques can manipulate public opinion. Demagogues

31

emerge who play on the collective insecurity of the masses, providing scapegoats and offering escape into symbols of past glories. There is a gradual breakdown of societal responsibility, and totalitarian forms of government step in to fill the vacuum. The breakdown is aided by capitalists, whose allegiances are few and fleeting, and who see new profit opportunities in every change of regime (Mannheim 1940, ch. 3).

Reflecting on the recent experience of Germany, Mannheim concluded that the nascent democracies of Middle Europe were lost. He held out some hope for England, but only if it would give up liberal democracy and embrace a comprehensive system of planning. In the latter half of the book a variety of modern methods of social control are outlined, all of which could be used to make the transition from a liberal to a planned society. What implications did Mannheim think such planning had for freedom?

> At the highest stage freedom can only exist when it is secured by planning. It cannot consist in restricting the powers of the planner, but in a conception of planning which guarantees the existence of essential forms of freedom through the plan itself. For every restriction imposed by limited authorities would destroy the unity of the plan, so that society would regress to the former stage of competition and mutual control.
>
> (Mannheim 1940, p. 378)

Mannheim's book was received well. The reviewer in *Economica* described it as "epoch-making," adding that "it is devoutly to be wished that the teaching of the book may, through various channels, filter down from the specialist readers and seep into the popular mind, especially into the political mind" (F. Clarke 1940, pp. 330–31).

Hayek's political works of the late 1930s and early 1940s may be read as an attempt to turn arguments like Mannheim's on their head.[6]

Rather than the only means of *counteracting* totalitarianism, Hayek argued that planning itself constituted a significant step along the road toward the totalitarian state.

> The main point is very simple. It is that comprehensive economic planning, which is regarded as necessary to organize economic activity on more rational and efficient lines, presupposes a much more complete agreement on the relative importance of the different social ends than actually exists, and that in consequence, in order to be able to plan, the planning authority must impose upon the people the detailed code of values that is lacking.
>
> (Hayek [1939] 1997, p. 193, cf. [1944] 1976, p. 57)

* * * * * *

32

> In the end agreement that planning is necessary, together with the inability of the democratic assembly to agree on a particular plan, must strengthen the demand that the government or some single individual, should be given powers to act on their own responsibility. It becomes more and more the accepted belief that, if one wants to get things done, the responsible director of affairs must be freed from the fetters of democratic procedure.
>
> (Hayek [1939] 1997, p. 205; cf. [1944] 1976, pp. 62–63)

Because of the absence of a shared code of values, authoritarian government tends inevitably to expand beyond the economic and into the political domain, even under those forms of socialism that may have started out as democratic. Mannheim was wrong to think that only under planning would freedom persist. It was just the opposite: Only if democracy is allied with a free market system will freedom of choice be permitted to exist.

> Democratic government has worked successfully where, and so long as, the functions of government were, by a widely accepted creed, restricted to fields where agreement among a majority could be achieved by free discussion; and it is the great merit of the liberal creed that it reduced the range of subjects on which agreement was necessary to one on which it was likely to exist in a society of free men. It is now often said that democracy will not tolerate "capitalism." If "capitalism" means here a competitive system based on free disposal over private property, it is far more important to realize that only within this system is democracy possible. When it becomes dominated by a collectivist creed democracy will inevitably destroy itself.
>
> ([1944] 1976, pp. 69–70; cf. [1939] 1997, pp. 205–06)

B. Prediction or warning?

Hayek's book found a large popular audience (in America after *The Reader's Digest* came out with a condensed version in April 1945, and among later generations in Eastern Europe when samizdat copies circulated), but its reception within much of the Anglo-American academic community was negative. A common criticism focused on Hayek's apparent prediction that planning must necessarily and inevitably lead to authoritarianism; the last sentence in the quotation above is the sort of passage that gave rise to the criticism.

This criticism was repeatedly raised, for example, by Wootton in *Freedom Under Planning* (1945, e.g., pp. 28, 36–37, 50).[7] Wootton's courteous book was explicitly written as a response to *The Road to Serfdom*. It is also representative of its genre regarding questions of "human nature." In the first nine chapters Wootton assumes that "planners are public-spirited people who seek only to discover the common good, and to do their best for it" (1945, p. 19). Only in the last chapter is this assumption dropped; but even there she invokes such devices as a better informed electorate, more forthright political parties, and oversight by bodies of concerned citizens to accomplish the manifold goals of planning.

Hayek objected to the criticism, arguing that *The Road to Serfdom* was meant to be a warning, not an historical prediction. He noted that the book's introduction contains such caveats as "no development is inevitable" (p. 1); "the danger is not immediate" (p. 2); and, most significantly, "Nor am I arguing that these developments are inevitable. If they were, there would be no point in writing this. They can be prevented if people realize in time where their efforts may lead" (p. 4).

Certain of Hayek's other writings, and in particular his methodological critique of "historicism," may also be mentioned in his defense. Historicism includes the claim that human history consists of "a necessary succession of definite 'stages' or 'phases,' 'systems' or 'styles,' following each other in historical development." But Hayek rejected this historicist endeavor "to find laws where in the nature of the case they cannot be found ..." ([1941–44] 1952b, p. 128). Given his clear statements that there exist no immutable laws dictating inevitable historical trends, he was surprised to find others claiming that he had sought to demonstrate the existence of such a trend.

One can see why the "prediction or warning" issue is an important one. If one takes Hayek's words as predictions of inevitable trends, the events foretold obviously did not come to pass in England, the country Hayek had in mind when writing the book. If one takes them as warnings, however, his later remarks about the negative "psychological effects" of postwar Labour rule in Britain become more comprehensible, perhaps even apposite (Hayek [1944] 1976, pp. x–xvi).

A final point may help put the dispute into perspective: Neither Mannheim's nor Hayek's books were unique in their times. The western world was turned upside down, and all manner of intellectuals, from journalists like Walter Lippmann (1937), to economists like Schumpeter ([1942] 1950) and Karl Polanyi (1944), to philosophers like James Burnham (1941), to historians like Edward H. Carr (1945), felt compelled to ruminate on its past development, present dilemmas, and future prospects.

None of the other authors, though, quite shared Hayek's fate. He had a hard time finding a publisher for the book, when it finally appeared some of his critics' reactions bordered on the libelous (e.g., Herman Finer 1945), and Hayek later was to claim that the book "went so far as to completely discredit me professionally" (1994, p. 103). This is one reason why the book should be read today. Readers who know it only by its reputation will be surprised to find that it contains a number of recommendations for state intervention in the economy, as is evident in the following (admittedly qualified) passages:

> There is no reason why in a society which has reached the general level of wealth which ours has attained the first kind of security [he had earlier mentioned "security against severe physical privation, the certainty of a given minimum of sustenance for all"] should not be guaranteed to all without endangering general freedom. There are difficult questions about the precise standard which should thus be assured; there is particularly the important question whether those who thus rely on the community should indefinitely enjoy all the same liberties as the rest. An incautious handling of these problems might well cause serious and perhaps dangerous political problems; but there can be no doubt that some minimum of food, shelter, and clothing, sufficient to preserve health and the capacity for work, can be assured to everybody.

> * * * * * *

> Nor is there any reason why the state should not assist the individuals in providing for those common hazards of life against which, because of their uncertainty, few individuals can make adequate provision. Where, as in the case of sickness and accident, neither the desire to avoid such calamities nor the efforts to overcome their consequences are as a rule weakened by the provision of assistance—where, in short, we deal with genuinely insurable risks—the case for the state's helping to organize a comprehensive system of social insurance is very strong.
>
> (Hayek [1944] 1976, pp. 120–21)

Hayek's remarks *are* qualified, but it seems clear that, at least in 1944, he was willing to countenance some level of "safety net" policy. In a new preface for the book prepared in 1976, however, Hayek wrote that "I had not wholly freed myself from all the current interventionist superstitions, and in consequence still made various concessions which I now think unwarranted" ([1944] 1976, p. xxi).

C. Liberty and knowledge—Hayek's alternative liberal utopia

Hayek's initial arguments prompted one socialist critic (Dickinson 1940) to challenge him to describe his ideal liberal society in more detail. After

35

reading *The Road to Serfdom*, Keynes also challenged Hayek to state clearly the criteria he would use to distinguish acceptable from pernicious government intervention (Jeremy Shearmur 1997). Though these tasks were begun in his 1944 book, Hayek's most refined response to his critics may be found in *The Constitution of Liberty* (1960).[8] And indeed, Hayek's prolonged effort to explore the origins, nature, and sustainability of a liberal market order is probably the most important legacy of *The Road to Serfdom*.

Hayek (1960, p. 11) began by defining "liberty" as a condition "in which coercion of some by others is reduced as much as possible in society." This produces a dilemma, because the best way to avoid coercion is to set up a coercive power that is strong enough to prevent it. Free society has met the problem by defining a private sphere of individual activity, granting the state a monopoly on coercion, then constitutionally limiting the power of the state to those instances where it is required to prevent coercion. The state's coercive actions are constrained by the rule of law: the laws it makes in protection of the private sphere must be prospective, known, certain, and equally enforced (pp. 205–10). Hayek contrasts these with laws that seek specific outcomes within the private sphere, such as certain redistributive patterns (p. 232). What especially rankled him was the attempt to turn what Hayek viewed as legitimate "safety net" insurance schemes into explicit instruments of redistribution aimed at securing "social justice" (e.g., p. 289). In his discussions of old age and health insurance policy, some of his dark warnings about intergenerational political strife make for timely, if uncomfortable, reading today (e.g., pp. 295–98).

In his political writings Hayek frequently stated that he was no fan of laissez-faire. By this he meant that a market system must be embedded in a set of other institutions—a democratic polity, with strong constitutional protection of a private sphere of individual activity, with enforced and exchangeable property rights—if it is to work. The problems of the Eastern European transition have made these ideas seem almost obvious, and they *are* ancient ideas. But Hayek was stressing them before they (re)gained popularity.

Hayek also linked liberty to his recurring theme, the problem of how to make use of dispersed knowledge. As society progresses the division of knowledge increases, as does our dependence on the knowledge possessed by others: "When we reflect how much knowledge possessed by other people is an essential condition for the successful pursuit of our individual aims, the magnitude of our ignorance of the circumstances on which the results of our action depend appears simply staggering" (p. 24). The most successful societies are those in which each individual is able to put his own local knowledge to its best uses. From this perspective, *The Constitution of Liberty* describes the complex of institutions and beliefs that promote the discovery, transmission, and use of knowledge so that individuals might have the best chance to have success in pursuing their own goals. Chief among the enabling conditions is liberty itself:

> The rationale of securing to each individual a known range within which he can decide on his actions is to enable him to make the fullest use of his knowledge, especially of his concrete and often unique knowledge of the particular circumstances of time and place. The law tells him what facts be may count on and thereby extends the range within which he can predict the consequences of his actions.
>
> (pp. 156–57)

Hayek's political philosophy is not uncontroversial. Critics have pointed out that he mixes a number of different ethical and political philosophies together, positions that may not cohere and all of which have been independently criticized; that in particular it is difficult to square his Kantian ethical ideas about universalizability with his Humean epistemological pessimism; and that the characteristics he requires that laws possess are not adequate to guarantee liberty (Arthur Diamond 1980; Chandran Kukathas 1989; Gray 1986, ch. 6). If one is judging his work against the standard of whether he provided a finished political philosophy, Hayek did not succeed though Shearmur (1996) contains a diagnosis of what would need to be done to build a coherent liberal political philosophy starting from Hayek's foundations, and an admittedly preliminary attempt to begin that enterprise. It nonetheless remains an impressive attempt to construct an integrated system of social philosophy, one that blends insights from such diverse fields as economics, political philosophy, ethics, jurisprudence, and intellectual history. And it is hard to deny Hayek's foundational contention that a liberal order allows individual knowledge to be better used than does socialism.

IV. Hayek and spontaneous orders

A. The critique of rationalist constructivism

Hayek's final set of arguments against socialist planning begin from the premise that the market system and certain other social institutions are examples of spontaneously organized complex phenomena, spontaneous orders which generate unintended beneficial consequences for those lucky enough to live under them. Now especially in mid-century, most of Hayek's readers would have thought it quaint to consider the market system as a paradigmatic example of a self-organizing system. For them it was more like a machine that had broken down, something that required radical repair, if not outright replacement. Hayek labeled this opposing viewpoint "rationalist constructivism," located its origins in the French rationalist variant of Enlightenment thought, and used it as a kind of foil in many later writings. Thus, according to Hayek, rationalist constructivists believed:

> that human institutions will serve human purposes only if they have been deliberately designed for these purposes, often also that the fact that an institution exists is evidence of its having been created for a purpose, and always that we should so redesign society and its institutions that all our actions will be wholly guided by known purposes. To most people these propositions seem almost self-evident and to constitute an attitude alone worthy of a thinking being.
>
> (1973, pp. 8–9; also see his [1964a] 1967; [1970] 1978)

Hayek's earliest critique was aimed at "the engineering mentality" (1952b, ch. 10) of the "men of science" ([1941] 1997; cf. Editor's Introduction), but his target was later broadened to include proponents of rationalism, empiricism, positivism and utilitarianism (1988, pp. 60–62). Hayek's apparently creative historiography has been challenged by both Diamond (1980) and Gray (1988).

Following Carl Menger ([1883] 1985, Book 3), Hayek argued that spontaneous social orders are products of human action but not intentionally designed. Such institutions evolved gradually, and only after they emerged were their advantages recognized, first by certain of the Scholastics, then by various members of the Scottish Enlightenment, and then again by Menger. Hayek's fascination with such orders began back in the 1930s ([1933] 1991, pp. 17–34; Caldwell, 1988b, discusses the importance of the piece), and indeed is evident in the question he broached in "Economics and Knowledge" about how human action gets coordinated even in the absence of a central controlling authority. In his early writings the coordinating role of freely adjusting market prices was highlighted. But soon Hayek began including all sorts of practices, norms, rules and other forms of institutions as aiding social coordination. Thus he would argue that such institutions as language, the law, and money emerged because they contributed to the ability of individuals to pursue their own goals; that our morals went through a similar sort of cultural evolution; and that (as we shall soon see) even the ordering of neural networks within the human brain develops analogously.

Hayek employed his account of cultural and institutional evolution to criticize the view that society can reconstruct institutions or moral codes to be more rational. As always, knowledge questions played a prominent role in the argument. Hayek believed that spontaneously emerging practices, norms and institutions not only allow humans to use knowledge better, they also permit knowledge gained in the past to be preserved, because they are artifacts reflecting the experimentation of many people over long periods of time:

> Far from assuming that those who created the institutions were wiser than we are, the evolutionary view is based on the insight that the result of the experimentation of many generations may embody more experience than any one man possesses.
>
> (1960, p. 62)

As a result, attempts to radically alter or reconstruct these institutions are fraught with dangers; we simply do not have enough knowledge about what they do and how they do it. Given our ignorance, only "the hubris of reason" would lead one to believe that we can rebuild society from the ground up (1973, p. 33). "Reason properly used" understands the limits of what reason can do; like David Hume before him, Hayek sought to "whittle down the claims of reason by the use of rational analysis" (1960, p. 69). The implication for economic analysis was for Hayek straightforward: "what we can know in the field of economics is so much less than people aspire to" (1983, p. 258).

Hayek's evolutionary arguments have been extensively criticized (particularly his reliance in later work on the idea of "group selection"), perhaps most effectively by those like Viktor Vanberg (1994, chs. 5–7 and 12) who believe that the design of constitutions is an essential element in the improvement of liberal orders. And Hayek, after all, was not averse to making proposals about constitutional design himself (1979, ch. 17), in apparent violation of his own strictures concerning constructivism. But he was also concerned with how specific instances of liberal market orders ever came to be created in the first place, particularly because they sit so uneasily with, as he put it (1988, ch. 1), both our "instinct and reason." This is a question that his critics have thus far left unanswered.

In any event, one particular exemplar of Hayek's treatment of spontaneous orders, his book on the foundations of theoretical psychology, *The Sensory Order* (1952a), has not been much studied by economists (exceptions include William Butos and Roger Koppl 1993; Horowitz 1994; and Steve Fleetwood 1995). The book does not deal even peripherally with socialism. But properly understood it provides a key for comprehending the nature and extent of Hayek's divergence from mainstream economics in the postwar period, and so may help to explain why modern information theorists writing about market socialism have had such a hard time understanding him. As such, a short digression follows.

B. A digression—the sensory order

During the war Hayek began a major project, one with both historical and methodological dimensions, on "the abuse of reason." As he later explained (1952b, pp. 10–11), the larger project was never completed, but he did finish an extended piece on methodology entitled "Scientism and the Study of Society" (reprinted in Hayek, 1952b). The essay contains a critique of the idea that the methods that had been so successful in the natural sciences should also be applied in the social sciences; "scientism" refers to what Hayek called the "slavish imitation" (1952b, p. 24) by social scientists of (what often turned out to be a caricature of) such methods. He also offered a positive methodological alternative to scientism. His starting point was to describe what he took to be the central subject matter of the social sciences: the acting individual. Hayek outlined some fundamental premises about the mind of such an individual, and about the relationship between beliefs and action. Among the premises were: the structure of the human mind is everywhere the same; our actions are based on our "opinions" (presumably these include both perceptions and beliefs); these opinions are subjectively held (and as such, some are wrong); finally, perceptions and beliefs differ among individuals.

Turning from a description of the subject matter of the social sciences to a discussion of how best to study it (that is, from ontology to methodology), Hayek proposed a "compositive" methodology in which the social scientist's task is to show how the actions of many such individuals come to constitute broader, more complex social phenomena. In his examination of the issues, Hayek reached a crucial conclusion: when studying complex phenomena, typically one cannot predict individual actions. Pattern predictions, or explanations of the principle underlying the composition of social phenomena, are usually the best one can do (Hayek 1952b, chs. 3 and 4; cf. Caldwell 1989).

Hayek's next step was to try to provide a firmer basis for his statements about the nature of mind. In the summer of 1945 he dug out a manuscript on psychology that he had written during his student days in Vienna nearly a quarter of a century earlier. The essay formed the basis for his next major contribution, *The Sensory Order* (1952a).

It appears that Hayek viewed *The Sensory Order* as providing the physiological underpinning for the various theses he had advanced concerning the relationship between mind, knowledge, and human action in the "Scientism" essay.[9] Hayek began by distinguishing between the physical order existing in the external world and our phenomenal experience of it. Our sensations, our perception of the qualities of objects, our whole mental image of the world, start from stimuli received through our central nervous system. This central nervous system constitutes the common "structure of the mind" shared by all individuals that had been posited in "Scientism."

The system provides a relational ordering of stimuli: the sensory order. The qualitative differences in perceptions and sensations that we experience depend on the specific pattern of neuron firings that a given stimulus produces within various neural networks. The experiences and beliefs of individuals will differ according to the pattern of neural firings that each develops. Thus though the structures of our minds are the same, there is a physiological basis for the notion of a dispersion of perceptions and experiences and, ultimately, of knowledge. The sensory system that results as the individual interacts with and receives feedback from the environment is both self-organized and adaptive, one that is constantly adjusting (strengthening certain pathways and connections, while diminishing the strength of others) as new stimuli come in. The adaptations represent "learning" by the individual.

C. The significance of The Sensory Order

The Sensory Order clearly heralds the full emergence of complex "spontaneous orders" as a theme in Hayek's work. But for our purposes, its import lies in viewing it as Hayek's decisive step away not just from the study of economics, but from standard economic reasoning, as well.

To see this note that, first, *The Sensory Order* provides a naturalistic ontological grounding for a number of methodological prescriptions. Both the recourse to ontology and the specific methodological prescriptions Hayek derived were diametrically opposed to the philosophical world view not just of most mainstream economists of his day, but of psychologists as well.

In mid-century, positivism and instrumentalism were the philosophical doctrines that most influenced the methodological self-consciousness of psychologists and economists. Positivists eschewed talk of ontology or metaphysics, and measured the veracity of theories not by their ontological grounding but by their ability to allow scientists to control or predict phenomena. This was the reasoning that allowed behaviorist psychologists to deny scientific status to any and all attempts to "get beneath" observable behavior to discover its origins in human consciousness. Likewise, both Paul Samuelson's recourse to "revealed preference" and Milton Friedman's "as if" methodology (that is, the claim that the realism of a theory's assumptions is unimportant compared to its ability to predict) share the positivist emphasis on observable phenomena and prediction. (The methodological positions of both Samuelson and Friedman are examined in detail in Caldwell [1982] 1994.)

This aversion to ontology was exactly the sort of view that Hayek attacked in both the "Scientism" essay and in *The Sensory Order*. Furthermore, by providing a grounding for his methodological claims in physiological psychology, Hayek believed that he was the one who was truly being "scientific." Hayek's psychological work is now recognized as an early challenge to behaviorism (e.g., Gerald Edelman 1987, ch. 1; Donald Hebb 1949 was another early dissenter), and his ontological boldness explains his attractiveness to scientific realists of today like Tony Lawson (1994) and Fleetwood (1995).

The specific methodological conclusions that Hayek drew also contradicted the positivistic dogma of the time. As noted above, when considering complex phenomena, Hayek claimed that typically the best that we can do is to explain the principles by which they work. To the extent that prediction is possible at all, only broad "pattern predictions" may emerge (1952b, ch. 8; cf. [1955] 1967, [1964b] 1967). Such pessimistic claims about the ability of economists to predict may sound a bit less controversial today. But when he was writing and for a number of decades to come it would separate him from nearly all mainstream economists, even those, like his colleagues at the University of Chicago, whose views on policy were often very similar to his.

Finally, *The Sensory Order* marked Hayek's further movement away from the constructs used by economists to understand the market order. For mainstream economists, the concepts of "equilibrium" and "rationality" are virtually coextensive with economic analysis. By the middle of the century Hayek believed that neither one shed much light on the most important questions.

Recall that in "Economics and Knowledge" Hayek had asked: How does human action get coordinated when knowledge is limited and dispersed? In light of this question, he felt that the "equilibrium theory" of his day was of little use: in equilibrium, full coordination has already occurred. Standard theory also assumed the presence of rational agents who all share the same, objectively correct information. The individual described by Hayek in *The Sensory Order* had little in common with this "rational (and fully informed) economic man" construct.

Hayek never explicitly tried to change economics, he never argued that his own description should replace "rational economic man" within economic models. And certainly a central question is what difference Hayek's various departures all might make. One way to see is briefly to examine the latest installment of the market socialism debates.

V. Market socialism and the economics of information

A. A new chapter in the history of the debate over socialism

There is renewed interest in market socialism, and emerging with it has been a new stylized history of the debates, one that highlights the contributions of the economics of information (Bardhan and Roemer, eds. 1993, pp. 3–9; Stiglitz 1994).

The first part of this history incorporates the conventional story that had been told about the socialist calculation debate through about the 1970s, with Abram Bergson (1948) being the classic early statement (see Lavoie 1985, however, for a modern revisionist reply). In that account, the debate was opened by von Mises, who declared the "impossibility" of rational calculation under socialism. The "mathematical solution" of Dickinson, which utilized the Paretian or Walrasian general equilibrium model to show the formal similarities between a socialist and capitalist regime, undermined Mises' claim of impossibility. Hayek's contribution via his "complexity argument" was to question the practical feasibility of solving a general equilbrium system. Lange's proposed "trial and error method" undercut Hayek's claim, and the actual feasibility of socialism then became viewed as an empirical matter. Later the emergence of supercomputers and of computable general equilibrium models suggested that the complexity problem might well be soluable, so that the actual establishment of a viable socialist state might only be a matter of time.

But this was not to be. The poor performance of communist regimes suggested that the chief problem was not one of computation, but of "incentive compatibility." In the new account the Walrasian general equilibrium model (or its more recent counterpart, the Arrow-Debreu model) became the villain of the piece, and particularly its implication that a purely competitive system will yield efficient market outcomes, albeit once a stringent set of marginal conditions is met. If information is asymmetric, however, deviations from a Pareto-efficient outcome can occur. While economists in earlier periods may occasionally have hit upon specific instances of information problems (e.g., Berle and Means 1933), the Arrow-Debreu framework posed an obstacle, directing attention away from questions of information.

In contrast, the economics of information provides a systematic means of identifying and classifying the wide array of problems that informational asymmetries can produce. For example, within a planned economy various monitoring problems may arise: production managers might decide to feather their own nests, to seek patronage, to practice favoritism, or in other ways to deviate from the plan; product quality, being multidimensional, is difficult to monitor; and so on. Nor is it an easy matter for the government to design and enforce a system of constraints to prevent managers from behaving opportunistically. A government that is in any way responsive to an electorate will find it difficult to commit itself credibly to stringent actions, such as raising prices for consumer goods, shutting down production lines when product demand declines, firing well-liked but incompetent (or worse, unlucky) managers, or informing redundant workers that they must be retrained or transferred. But plant managers confronted with such "soft budget constraints" (so dubbed by Kornai 1986) are less likely to take their production goals seriously.

Investment decisions also pose problems, because it is difficult to avoid either too much or too little risk-taking behavior, and without competing projects, it becomes problematical even to assess whether an investment once undertaken is in fact economic (Roemer 1993, pp. 91–92).

As these brief examples suggest, the economics of information provides a powerful set of tools for identifying and analyzing the problems of a socialist economy. According to the new history, current models greatly improve on those of the past because they contain a sophisticated understanding of agency problems. Indeed, if one accepts this account, the evolution of the various positions in the socialist calculation debate becomes a paradigmatic example of how theoretical progress can occur, and has occurred, in economics.

Perhaps inevitably, historical accounts that emphasize progress tend toward Whiggism: the work of economists in the past is but a prelude to developments in the present. Stiglitz, for example, invokes the debates of the 1930s, but mostly as window dressing. His book *Whither Socialism?* (1994) is best read as a celebration of the economics of information, one that uses the question of the viability of socialism as its chief application.[10]

Other accounts treat the arguments of the 1930s more carefully (e.g., Bardhan and Roemer 1993, pp. 3–9). Because of their reliance on a full information general equilibrium framework, Lange and other market socialists fare poorly because they (inevitably) ignored the question of incentives. Hayek makes for a harder interpretive case. To be sure, he did understand that the price system is a mechanism for conveying information, and modern theorists are quick to acknowledge this. Thus in his collection *The Informational Role of Prices* (1989), Sanford Grossman quotes in three different articles the same passage from Hayek's "The Use of Knowledge in Society" (1945) about the price system as a communication mechanism. In a popular textbook, Hayek is credited with having provided the initial insight later formalized by Leonid Hurwicz about the low informational requirements of a decentralized price system (Paul Milgrom and John Roberts 1992, p. 85).

But this only raises a new set of questions. Given the limited nature of his tools, how was it that Hayek stumbled onto the insights that he did? And given that Hayek's critique of Lange focused on how changing relative prices convey *knowledge*, why did he make so little headway toward developing an economics of *information*? This last question is pointedly raised by Makowski and Ostroy who, noting that the field of "mechanism design" differentiates between (i) the information/communication requirements of mechanisms, and (ii) the incentive properties of mechanisms, are led to the following assessment of Hayek's contribution:

> Failing to emphasize incentives as he did and concentrating on the problem of communication, Hayek should have arrived at a con-

clusion much closer to market socialism than he did. Of course it could be noted that whereas the division between (i) and (ii) may be analytically useful, it is clearly artificial—any mechanism is a composite of (i) and (ii), If, as it seems to us, Hayek did not recognize the need to separate the two functions (equivalently, to separate communication of information from elicitation of information), his critique of market socialism is "fuzzy."

(in Bardhan and Roemer, eds. 1993, p. 82)

From this perspective, Hayek's major contribution was to point out that in an environment of scarcity in which information is disaggregated or dispersed, the price system is a low-cost mechanism for its aggregation and transmittal. Later theorists formalized this insight, in the course of which it became clear that Hayek (and his opponents) failed to grasp a second problem, that of opportunistic behavior in situations of informational asymmetries. Because Hayek (and the Austrians in general) failed to see the importance of incentives, and of the necessity of developing mechanisms to overcome problems associated with asymmetric information, they could not move the field forward. They missed the salient fact that information problems plague *both* market and socialist regimes, and as a result their analyses were at best incomplete, and at times deficient. These informational issues are the very problems that a new generation of more sophisticated models are able to address.

I will argue that though there is some truth in this account, it also constitutes a paradigmatic example of Whig history, where earlier contributions that do not fit well with contemporary theory perforce are diminished or misunderstood. I will then try to show how such present-centered interpretations of the historical record may have significant consequences for a proper understanding of the issues.

B. The incentives question

First, is it true that Austrians had had no appreciation of the question of incentives? The evidence here is mixed.

Hayek frequently mentioned incentive issues in the final chapter of *Collectivist Economic Planning* (1935). He pointed out that the "Russian experiment" provided a concrete example of the "obvious difficulty of making people follow out the plan loyally" (p. 206). He raised the question of whether private ownership of property is necessary for managers to be properly motivated, and asked what criteria should be used to assess managerial decision making (pp. 219–20, 231–32). Hayek was particularly concerned with the investment decision, and the "tendency to prefer the safe to the risky enterprise" that he believed would prevail among socialist managers (p. 234).

Mises, too, recognized the problem. His 1920 paper contains a section entitled "Responsibility and Initiative in Communal Concerns," where he wrote: "It is now universally agreed that the exclusion of free initiative and individual responsibility, on which the successes of private enterprise depend, constitutes the most serious menace to socialist economic organization" (Mises in Hayek, ed. 1935, p. 116). Other early work that mentioned the incentive problems facing socialism (John Rae 1891, ch. 11, section 4; William H. Mallock 1907) provides evidence for Mises' claim that this limitation of socialist systems had long been recognized.

A concern for incentives is also implicit in some of the later Austrian writings. For example, Boettke (1995) argues that certain sections of *The Road to Serfdom* anticipated some of the public choice literature on government failure. Furthermore, the notion that certain institutional arrangements (i.e., free markets operating under a regime of enforced and exchangeable private property rights) spur and reward entrepreneurial alertness is a direct recognition of how institutions affect the incentives agents face. And as Hayek himself wrote in a late piece,

> We have come to understand that the market and the price mechanism provide in this sense a sort of discovery procedure which both makes the utilization of more facts possible than any other known system, and which provides the incentive for constant discovery of new facts which improve adaptation to the ever changing circumstances of the world in which we live.
>
> ([1976] 1978, p. 236)

The conclusion, no matter how convenient, that the Austrians ignored incentives questions must be rejected.

On the other hand, it is also clear that the Austrians made no sustained systematic contribution to the now enormous literature on the economics of information. More interesting, it is also evident that Hayek sometimes dropped the argument even when he could have used it. Thus in his rebuttal to Lange he was willing to grant, "for the purpose of this argument," that socialist managers "will be as capable and as anxious to produce cheaply as the average capitalist entrepreneur" ([1940] 1948, p. 196). The real question for the historian is: Given Hayek's unrelenting opposition to socialism, given his readiness to develop political and even evolutionary arguments against it, and given his evident knowledge of this line of attack, why was it not pursued more vigorously?

A number of plausible explanations exist. Recall that Lange had offered two responses to Hayek's claim that a socialist regime would be plagued by incentive problems, namely: 1) the only real agency problem is one of bureaucracy, but this is a generic problem that exists whenever corporations are large and competition is absent, and 2) such "sociological" issues are not properly included within the domain of economics.

Hayek never bought the first argument, denying Lange's premise that the emergence of large corporations necessarily implied the end of competition. In "The Meaning of Competition" (1946) Hayek argued that market rivalry is the key to true competition, and that such rivalry can exist even when the conditions for perfect competition do not hold. The assumptions of the theory of perfect competition misled people like Lange to conclude that because so few markets in the real world satisfy the assumptions, they must be monopolistic. Once again static equilibrium theory obscured the nature of reality.[11]

It may be, however, that Hayek at least in part accepted Lange's second argument. Questions of "bureaucracy" had indeed traditionally been the domain of sociologists (e.g., Max Weber 1978, pp. 956–1005). Though the line between economics and fields like sociology was less clearly drawn when Weber was writing before the First World War, by the 1930s under the dual influence of positivism and the professionalization movement the disciplinary divisions were hardening.

It was also an article of faith among intellectuals living in the 1930s that human behavior was supremely malleable. Time and motion studies, techniques of mass propaganda, and other methods of behavior modification were being studied and perfected everywhere; even Lenin had come grudgingly to admire the Taylor System of Scientific Management (Merkle 1980, ch. 4). Who was to say that an appropriately "educated" or "conditioned" manager might not someday be "socially engineered," one whose actions would be indistinguishable from one who was responding to the carrot and stick of pecuniary profits and losses? And what special insight could an economist bring to this question of "psychology"? Indeed, Hayek himself occasionally used the adjective "psychological" when discussing issues of incentives (e.g., 1935, pp. 206, 232).

Had Hayek pressed his argument, he would at a minimum have opened himself up to the charge that he was speaking outside of his area of expertise. That very claim was made at one point. Hayek's occasional reference to "human nature" in *The Road to Serfdom* elicited the following admonition from Evan Durbin (1945, p. 359): "It is a pity that Professor Hayek makes no use of the light that has been thrown upon these matters by scientific inquiry in recent years; and remains content with old-fashioned and unsupported, yet dogmatic, generalizations about human nature and emotional behaviour." It is no small irony, given Durbin's remarks, that Hayek would within a decade complete his book on the foundations of theoretical psychology (Hayek 1952a).

Hayek would also have to contend with the old socialist belief that the opportunistic behavior that gives rise to agency problems is *itself* a product of capitalist society. Marx had long ago argued that one's consciousness was determined by one's social condition, rather than the reverse. While capitalism promoted greed, under socialism a new socialist man, one willing to sacrifice his own comfort for the greater good, was supposed to emerge.[12] Though this utopian vision has long been challenged by opponents,[13] there is no way to falsify it, because it refers to an unspecified point in time in a supposedly radically altered future.

Hayek knew that socialism faced incentive problems, but he didn't want to be drawn into what promised to be an unproductive debate, so he did not pursue the question. The reasons behind his action were complex and subtle, and current historical treatments have not shed much light on them.

Modern theorists might concede the historical point. But they would still insist that the significance of the incentives question has less to do with its history than with the adequacy of Austrian analysis. Because of their failure to provide a systematic analysis of the problems arising from asymmetric information, Austrians have missed certain limitations of markets. As a result, their confidence is misplaced; their defense of the market system is naive.

It is true that, except for the occasional aside (e.g., Hayek [1982b], in Chiaki Nishiyama and Kurt Leube, eds. 1984, p. 61), Mises and Hayek never engaged the economics of information literature. A number of younger Austrians *have* begun that task, however, among them Stephen Boehm (1989), Thomsen (1992), and several of the authors in Boettke and David Prychitko, eds. (1996). And surely it is uncontroversial that the Austrians have much to gain from a continuation of their interaction with this literature.

But the coin may be flipped: mainstream analysts have seldom engaged (and when they have, have not always understood, as is evident in the exchange between Hurwicz 1984 and Kirzner 1984; compare Boehm 1989; Kirzner 1997) the Austrian position, and thus may also have something to gain from a better understanding of the Austrian insights. For those who might doubt that this advice about the advantages of better mutual comprehension is anything more than a bromide, let us get down to cases by examining how Hayek might have responded to the latest iteration of the market socialism debate.

C. An Austrian view of the new debate on market socialism

Information theorists differ over whether some form of market socialism, one that is cognizant of incentive compatibility problems and takes steps to resolve them, can survive or even prosper. We may take the works of Stiglitz and Roemer as representative of the opposing views.

Stiglitz, representing the mainstream, admits that market economies are themselves plagued with agency problems, particularly when it comes to the classic problem of the separation of management from ownership in large corporations. The economics of information provides both the glasses to see what the problems are and, as progress occurs, the tools with which to fix them. The prospects for market socialism, however, are less bright. Because they lack both the market discipline provided by competition and the innovation that a decentralized market economy promotes, socialist regimes invariably will be less successful than their market counterparts (Stiglitz 1994, chs. 7–9).

Roemer demurs, believing that the economics of information can be used to fix socialist regimes, too. Roemer is daring in the sorts of innovations he is willing to countenance. For example, because of the commitment credibility problems that governments face, he does not believe that state ownership of the means of production is necessary (or even desirable) under socialism: "Socialists should be eclectic in their attitude toward property relations: there may be many forms of ownership more amenable to socialism's goals than traditional state ownership of the means of production" (Roemer 1994, pp. 6–7). In the place of the competition that is provided naturally within market economies, he envisions foreign competition, or even separate free market sectors coexisting within socialist economies, as doing the job.

Not all of the proposals put forward by market socialists are as "radical" as Roemer's in terms of the leeway they would permit to markets; indeed, some might question whether Roemer's proposals even qualify as socialism. But all do seek to face the problem of incentives squarely. The middle section of his book with Bardhan (1993), entitled "Microincentives," is devoted to the solution of a variety of incentive compatibility problems that afflict market socialist regimes. For economists who might dismiss these proposals as utopian, Roemer and Bardhan (1994, p. 179) rightly point out that cynicism about reform flies in the face of "much of modern economic theory, which is devoted to designing institutions that will lead self-interested players to arrive at efficient outcomes . . ."

The specifics of the new proposals have been criticized: N. Scott Arnold (1996) claims that monitoring problems would persist even were Roemer's reforms enacted. But surely, from a theoretical standpoint Roemer and Bardhan are right to insist that if the economics of information can help make mixed market economies work better, there is nothing in principle to prevent it from being employed to modify and reform market socialist economies. Unfortunately, because he takes the Arrow-Debreu model as his foil rather than the more recent work of sophisticated market socialists, Stiglitz does not even address this issue. In a review, Roemer (1995) pointedly notes that Stiglitz's *Whither Socialism?* should really be read as an attack on the conventional general equilibrium model rather than on recent models of market socialism.[14]

49

It certainly seems plausible that if the chief difficulty facing market socialism is the presence of the sorts of incentive problems that the economics of information identifies, then it should be possible to construct a model of an efficient market socialist system. In this sense, there is a *similarity* between the economics of information and its theoretical predecessor. (This is ironic, given the frequent emphasis by Stiglitz and other proponents of the economics of information approach on how it differs from general equilibrium theory.) Within the general equilibrium model there was no way on theoretical grounds to distinguish a competitive free market system from a market socialist one. In a like manner, there is no way *within the model* provided by the economics of information to distinguish between a free market system and a market socialist one in which all agency problems have been identified, and to the extent possible, corrected.

It is here that the contributions of the Austrians may make a difference. This has been recognized by advocates of the Austrian view like Boettke (forthcoming), who considers the Austrian analysis of socialism to be *the* most important Austrian contribution to economics, as well as by detractors like Fikret Adaman and Pat Devine (1996), who nonetheless view the Austrian challenge as more fundamental than those provided by neoclassical economics. Precisely because they were at times willing to grant, for the sake of argument, Lange's claim that questions of incentives were not the concern of economists, the Austrian arguments concentrate on areas that are different from those emphasized by information theorists.[15] They focus instead on concerns that lie, as it were, *outside of the model*. The sorts of issues that they would raise are as follows:

1. Knowledge is different from information

Hayek's writings about the ability of the price system to convey information in a world in which knowledge is dispersed may well have inspired others to investigate the design of mechanisms for resource allocation within such environments. But it should also be clear that when he used the term "knowledge," he was referring to something that is different in kind from the concept of "information" as it is used by current theorists.

For Hayek, knowledge is dispersed, as mechanism design theorists picked up on. But some knowledge, especially that generated as a result of day to day contact within specific local markets, is also tacit. Tacit knowledge is not directly communicable. Theories that treat "information" as if it was contained in little packets that can be "elicited" once the appropriate mechanism is "designed" misunderstand the fundamental fact that no mechanism can elicit tacit knowledge. Furthermore, tacit knowledge is important: it affects and informs the decisions of entrepreneurs and ultimately gets reflected in the prices that emerge in a competitive price system. In proposed systems in which entrepreneurial decision making is eliminated, or replaced by managerial processes, this knowledge gets lost. One still has "prices" in such systems, but they contain less "information."

The mainstream often focuses on how markets "convey information." Though Hayek considered this role important, he was concerned additionally with the creation, discovery, and conservation of knowledge. Furthermore, the Austrian notion of "discovery" is quite different from the neoclassical idea of "search." A neoclassical economist like Stiglitz (1994, p. 8) can ask: Are "the expenditures on information acquisition too little, too much, or just right?" To answer this question one must be able to compare the expected costs of additional search against expected benefits. Contrast this with Kirzner's (1997, p. 62) characterization of entrepreneurial discovery:

> For the Austrian approach imperfect information is seen as involving an element which cannot be fitted at all into neoclassical models, that of "sheer" (i.e., unknown) ignorance ... the discovery which reduces sheer ignorance is necessarily accompanied by the element of *surprise* ... one had not hitherto realized one's ignorance. Entrepreneurial discovery is seen as gradually but systematically pushing back the boundaries of sheer ignorance ... (emphasis in the original)

2. The market process is not well captured by mainstream theories of competition

Hayek, like modern information theorists, believed that the theoretical tools of his day were inadequate for understanding the limitations of socialism, and he identified the unrealistic treatment of knowledge as a prime defect. But his response was not to add a more sophisticated account of information to the neoclassical model. Rather, he rejected the ideas of "given" data and of perfect competition, putting in their place the notion of a dynamic market process in which rivalry among participants ensures that knowledge is continually generated and discovered. In doing so, Hayek was actually harking back to an earlier tradition, one whose eclipse in the twentieth century is demonstrated, and lamented, by Frank Machovee (1995).[16]

The Austrian analysis of the market process is not utopian; there is no guarantee of coordination. But it does insist that a system in which prices determined in competitive markets are free to adjust to reflect relative scarcities is one in which the coordination of agents' plans is least likely to be hindered. Soviet-style central planning ignored this insight completely, but the "trial and error" solutions proposed by Lange and others also misunderstand the point. All such proposals understimate the difficulty of playing "catch-up" with a system in which the acts of millions of individual decision makers produce a continuous process of adjustment.

Competition is a key institutional feature within a market system. It is needed to provide incentives, as the economics of information emphasizes. But the "discipline of the marketplace" also assists the process of discovery: of errors, of new processes and products, of knowledge itself.

Competition never has been "perfect," nor need it be. The dual claim of the early market socialists (that atomistic competition was necessary for a market system to work, and that it had disappeared) was not true when they made it, and subsequent history has done little to support a revised judgment. In particular, perfect competition is an inappropriate benchmark for policy, one that is bound to mislead us into thinking that we can accomplish much more with interventions than we really can. To the extent that Austrians accept an efficiency welfare norm, their emphasis is on the dynamic adaptive efficiency of a system (that is, how fast it adapts to the introduction of emerging or new information) rather than on static allocational efficiency, which focuses on the use of existing, known information.

In the real world errors occur all the time. Mainstream theorists typically treat errors as disequilibrium phenomena, so their models seldom directly incorporate this ubiquitous aspect of reality. But as Thomsen (1992) and Kirzner (1997) emphasize, the actions of entrepreneurs in disequilibrium situations constitute a fundamental aspect of the Austrian characterization of the market process. Like their real world counterparts, the entrepreneurial decision makers in the Austrian account also make errors all the time. These errors result in profit opportunities, and the search for profits works to reveal and eliminate divergent expectations. The mainstream emphasis on equilibrium states obscures the fact that one of the chief advantages of a market system is that it contains a built-in mechanism, imperfect to be sure, but constantly operating, for the correction of errors. From an Austrian perspective, mainstream economists tend to overestimate the informational content of equilibrium prices, and to underestimate the informational content of disequilibrium prices (Boettke 1996, pp. 189–90).

3. The rejection of homo economicus

Though homo economicus is a crucial assumption of neoclassical analysis, Hayek had doubts about its usefulness, and even ridiculed it on occasion (1960, pp. 60–61). Rather than continuing to employ the construct, he sought to provide in his psychological work a physiological foundation for perception and, ultimately, for knowledge formation. The mind of the individual described in *The Sensory Order* is a complex adaptive self-organizing neural order, and this is what leads to differences in perceptions and beliefs among people, to our ability to adapt to new environments, and to the possibility of the growth of our knowledge. This is a different creature altogether from homo economicus.

One way to put the contrast is as follows. In standard neoclassical analysis, one starts out with rational agents who by assumption optimize over all the relevant margins, including those that have to do with acquiring more information. In cases in which information is asymmetric, the chief goal is to design mechanisms that will either elicit information or provide an incentive structure to prevent inefficient social outcomes. If the world were really populated by agents resembling homo economicus, such approaches might make some sense.

For Hayek, though, the world does not look like this. Humans are purposeful but imperfect beings, they have limited knowledge, they make mistakes, and whatever knowledge that exists is dispersed, fragmented, and often difficult to communicate. Many of the things that neoclassical economics assumes (at the most fundamental level, the ability of individuals to engage in rational behavior, and to perform marginal analysis) are, from the Austrian perspective, properly viewed as the *results* of certain institutional arrangements rather than as assumptions of the analysis (Hayek 1979, pp. 74–77; Boettke, forthcoming). Austrians ask: what combination of institutions can best assist imperfect individuals to make better decisions and better use of their knowledge? By starting with rational agents, standard analysis gets things exactly backwards.

4. The role of institutions

Instead of studying the design of alternative *allocation* mechanisms (a project that would anyway smack of rationalist constructivism to him), Hayek proposed that we examine the role of various institutions in assisting the creation, discovery, use, conveyance, and conservation of *knowledge*. This led him to make some proposals of his own. It was his focus on knowledge that led Hayek to endorse a system of free markets, operating within a liberal democratic polity, a system with established, enforced and exchangeable property rights, all protected by a strong constitution.

Though he made proposals, Hayek also recognized that the conscious construction or imposition of social institutions is a tricky business. Many such institutions are the product of a long process of evolutionary development; they are themselves examples of complex self-organized adaptive orders. They have histories, and they perform functions that are not well-understood by outside observers. Their emergence was certainly not inevitable, nor is their continuance: this led Hayek to explore why certain institutional forms persist, even though they might not accord well with either our instincts or our reason. But he also saw that those societies in which the right combination of liberal institutions happened to emerge have both prospered and permitted a considerable amount of individual liberty to be exercised.

Attempts to alter such institutions, be it by piece-meal or by full-scale social engineering, will often generate unintended, unanticipated, and unwelcome consequences. "Mechanism design" may be feasible within firms that then face the test of market competition. It is much less likely that one can successfully mimic markets as a whole, or redesign entire societies. As a general rule, those who hope to redesign institutions are over-optimistic about the amount of knowledge that is available to them. It is precisely because knowledge is not readily available that evolutionary processes typically do better than our reason in the area of institutional design. This argument, if true, should make one pessimistic about the prospects for socialism. But it should also give pause to market reformers who hope overnight to install new institutions in countries formerly under communist rule. If such reforms are to have any hope of working, a sensitivity to the previously existing institutional framework is critical. Bardhan and Roemer (1993, p. 16), Boettke (1994), and Peter Murrell (1995, pp. 175–77) offer pertinent observations.

In the end Hayek concluded that many institutions, from our moral codes to the market system, are themselves examples of complex adaptive phenomena. In this regard, though he may have shared the complaints of the information theorists about static equilibrium models, Hayek's basic observations are more in line with recent developments in complexity theory and evolutionary biology than they are with the later development of neoclassical theory. The similarity between Hayek's work and these other areas of research has so far only just begun to be explored (Lavoie 1989; Birner, forthcoming; Mirowski, forthcoming; Ransom 1992, 1996).

VI. Conclusion

Though the Austrians knew about incentives problem, they did not systematically pursue them. For modern day information theorists, this means that, no matter how prescient their conclusions may have been, Austrian analysis is of limited value. If the Austrians were right, they were right for the wrong reasons, because their models ignored the insights revealed by the economics of information.

This final section suggests at a minimum that modern information theorists have not fully understood why the Austrians chose not to pursue the incentives problem. As a doctrinal historian, I cannot help adding that such misunderstanding is virtually inevitable in a profession that, at least in the United States, has nearly systematically eliminated the study of history of economic thought from graduate curricula.

But a different point was also made. Getting the history right matters. It matters not only for historical accuracy, but because one can draw the wrong conclusions if one only has recourse to Whig history. If one reads one's history backwards from the present, where today's theoretical analysis provides the sole possible benchmark against which to assess a program, then only one conclusion is possible about Austrian "analysis": it is deficient. But if one goes back and looks at the record, what is immediately apparent is *that the Austrians went another way*. Their path really was different. Furthermore, the mainstream might have something to learn from that alternative path.

The virtue of the economics of information is to permit economists to discuss questions of agency with analytical precision and rigor. Like all theories, its analytic rigor is purchased at the price of an oversimplified picture of reality. This poses a danger if it leads one to think that the only problems facing socialism are agency problems, problems that can be overcome once the requisite incentive compatibility mechanisms are put into place.

Hayek was no opponent of theory; indeed, he frequently defended it from its historicist detractors. But he also understood the limitations of theory. A half century ago well-intentioned socialists demonstrated with simplistic mathematical models that market socialism could duplicate the workings of a competitive market system, plus remove its deficiencies. More elegant models are available today for correcting a system with informational problems. Over 60 years ago Hayek warned about the dangers of an "excessive preoccupation with the conditions of a hypothetical state of stationary equilibrium" (1935, p. 226). It is not altogether outrageous to suggest that today he might warn against an excessive preoccupation with questions of information.

Acknowledgment

I have received many helpful comments on this chapter from participants at the History of Economics Society meetings at the University of British Columbia, at seminars given at the University of Georgia, at the Austrian Colloquium at New York University, at the York University-University of Toronto Workshop on the History of Economics, and at the Duke University History of Political Economy Workshop. Extensive comments were also received from Peter Boettke, William Butos, Neil De Marchi, Greg Ransom, and George Selgin. All remaining errors are the responsibility of the author.

Notes

1 Parts of this section are adapted from the introduction I wrote as editor for Hayek (1997).
2 For more on his views, see Neurath (1973, ch. 5), Nancy Cartwright et al. (1996, ch. 1), and Agnes Miklos-Illès (1996). The resurgence of interest in Neurath among philosophers is chiefly due to his pluralistic and anti-foundationalist

approach to unified science. Austrian economists focused on his physicalism, his insistence that, to be meaningful, scientific terms must refer to observable phenomena. The Austrian economists' opposition to positivism and scientism in the social sciences derives in part from their arguments with such opponents.

3 See Elizabeth Durbin (1985) on British socialism in the interwar years, Gary Werskey (1978) on socialism among the natural scientists, and the essays in Philip Bean and David Whynes, eds. (1986) on Wootton. Hayek, ed. (1954) may be read as a response to the tutorial version of history.

4 Joseph Salerno (1990) recently sparked a lively debate with the provocative claim that the Misesian emphasis on appraisement and entrepreneurship differs from, and is more fundamental than, Hayek's arguments about knowledge. Leland Yeager (1994) and Kirzner (1997) contend that the two positions are better considered complementary, while Boettke (forthcoming) argues that any differences of emphasis that may exist between Mises and Hayek are due to their responding to different audiences.

5 For more on "market process theory" see Kirzner (1973, ch. 1; 1997); Ludwig Lachmann (1976); and Esteban Thomsen (1992). Hayek's was not a blanket rejection of general equilbrium theory. He thought that even the static Walrasian model contained important insights about market interdependence, and he spent much of the later 1930s in an unsuccessful attempt to develop a dynamic intertemporal general equilibrium model of a capital-using monetary economy, as Jack Birner (1994, pp. 2–5) discusses.

6 Hayek explicitly identifies Mannheim as an opponent in the second chapter of *The Road to Serfdom* ([1944] 1976, p. 21); and also mentions him in his ([1941–44] 1952b, pp. 156, 166n) and ([1970] 1978, p. 6).

7 Wootton was not unique; such diverse figures as George Stigler (1988, pp. 140, 147) and Paul Samuelson came away with similar readings. At one point Hayek sent Samuelson a strongly worded letter objecting to the latter's repetition of the inevitability thesis in the 11th edition of his *Principles* text. In a letter dated January 2, 1981, Samuelson graciously apologized and promised to try to represent Hayek's views more accurately in any future work. See the Samuelson file, Box 48, number 5, in the Hayek Archives, Hoover Institution, Stanford, CA.

8 Hayek's other major contribution was the trilogy *Law, Legislation and Liberty* (1973–79), which contained his diagnosis of why liberal democracies were being taken over by special interests, and a proposed legislative reform aimed at strengthening liberal constitutionalism.

9 Hayek links the two essays in a retrospective piece (1982a, p. 289), and in his letter to John Nef (cited earlier). Further, the "Scientism" essay is the only work by Hayek cited in *The Sensory Order*.

10 To be fair to Stiglitz, the book was adapted from his Wicksell lectures and was originally to be on the economics of information, which affected its format. But even so, there is reason for historians to be uneasy when in the bibliography of a book on the economics of socialism, Mises and Robbins, Dickinson and Dobb go uncited and Hayek, Lange, Abba Lerner, and Fred M. Taylor get only one entry each (Hayek's citation is to *The Fatal Conceit*). By way of contrast, there are 122 articles or books written or co-authored by Stiglitz listed in his bibliography.

11 Economists continue to disagree, of course, about the consequences of the fact that few real world markets meet the assumptions of perfect competition. Discussions of "workable competition" in the 1940s and of "countervailing powers" in the 1950s, and the development of "contestable market" theories in

the 1970s and of the "imperfect competition" and "strategic trade" theories in the 1980s, all appear to share this common origin.

12 Even the usually hard-headed modern socialists Bardhan and Roemer (1993, p. 8) exhibit occasional nostalgia for these earlier arguments, leaving the door open a crack for the emergence of the long-hoped-for socialist economic man(ager): "it may be the case that the culture of management in a market-socialist economy, with its Weltanschauung of egalitarianism, would be different, at least to some extent, from the culture of capitalist management."

13 Mises (1935, p. 119) made the point with characteristic flair: "All socialist systems ... proceed from the assumption that in a socialist society a conflict between the interests of the particular and the general could not possibly arise. . . . The obvious objection that the individual is very little concerned whether he himself is diligent and enthusiastic, and that it is of greater moment that everybody else should be, is either completely ignored or is insufficiently dealt with by them. They believe they can construct a socialist commonwealth on the basis of the Categorical Imperative alone."

14 It is strange, however, that Roemer (1995) should characterize Stiglitz's book "An Anti-Hayek Manifesto" rather than, say, "An Anti-Walras Manifesto." Roemer bases his characterization on a few remarks made by Stiglitz in one of his last chapters, in which Hayek's *The Fatal Conceit* is briefly critically discussed. It does not seem to this reader that either Roemer or Stiglitz has fully comprehended Hayek's evolutionary arguments.

15 To be sure, some of the points mentioned below have been made by information theorists, including Stiglitz, whose remarks (1994, p. 134) on the importance of the institutional framework in which competition is embedded could have been written by Hayek. What is less clear is *how such insights follow analytically from the models found in the economics of information literature.*

One referee commented that many of the Austrian insights have been incorporated within other areas in economics, such as in the "bounded rationality" literature. It may be noted, however, that Thomsen (1992, ch. 4) argues that Austrian market process theory differs significantly from Herbert Simon's early work on bounded rationality, and Esther-Mirjam Sent (1997) suggests that the more recent literature on bounded rationality may face historiographical problems of its own.

16 Makowski and Ostroy (1993, p. 74) refer to competition as market rivalry, but it is less clear from their brief paper how what they call an "old and seminal idea" links up to the analytics of their Perfectly Competitive Equilibrium model.

References

ADAMAN, FIKRET AND DEVINE, PAT. "The Economic Calculation Debate: Lessons for Socialists." *Cambridge J. Econ.*, Sept. 1996, *20*(5), pp. 523–37.

ARNOLD, N. SCOTT. "The Monitoring Problem for Market Socialist Firms," in PETER J. BOETTKE AND DAVID L. PRYCHITKO, eds., 1996, pp. 41–58.

BARDHAN, PRANAB AND ROEMER, JOHN E., eds. *Market socialism.* New York and Oxford: Oxford U. Press. 1993.

——. "On the Workability of Market Socialism," *J. Econ. Perspectives*, Spring 1994, *8*(2), pp. 177–81.

BEAN, PHILIP AND WHYNES, DAVID, eds. *Barbara Wootton—Social science and public policy: Essays in her honour.* London: Tavistock, 1986.

BERGSON, ABRAM. "Socialist Economics," in a *Survey of contemporary economics.* Ed.: HOWARD ELLIS. Homewood, IL: Irwin, 1948, pp. 412–48.

BERLE, ADOLF A. AND MEANS, GARDINER C. *The modern corporation and private property.* New York: Macmillan, 1933.

BIRNER, JACK. "Introduction: Hayek's Grand Research Programme," in JACK BIRNER AND RUDY VAN ZIJP, eds. London: Routledge, 1994, pp. 1–21.

——. "The Surprising Place of Cognitive Psychology in the Work of F. A. Hayek." *Hist. Econ. Ideas,* forthcoming.

BIRNER, JACK AND VAN ZIJP, RUDY, ed. *Hayek, co-ordination and evolution: His legacy in philosophy, politics, economics and the history of ideas.* London and New York: Routledge, 1994.

BOEHM, STEPHEN. "Hayek on Knowledge, Equilibrium and Prices," *Wirtschafts Politische Blätter,* 1989, *36*(2), pp. 201–13.

BOETTKE, PETER J. "The Reform Trap in Economics and Politics in the Former Communist Countries," *Journal des Economistes et des Etudes Humaines.* June/Sept. 1994, *5*(2/3), pp. 267–93.

——. "Hayek's *The Road to Serfdom* Revisited: Government Failure in the Argument Against Socialism," *Eastern Econ. J.,* Winter 1995, *21*(1), pp. 7–26.

——. "Book Review: Joseph Stiglitz's *Whither Socialism?*" *J. Econ. Lit.,* Mar. 1996, *34*(1), pp. 189–91.

——. "Economic Calculation: The Austrian Contribution to Political Economy," in *Advances in Austrian economics.* Vol. 5. Greenwich, CT: JAI Press, forthcoming.

BOETTKE, PETER J. AND PRYCHITKO, DAVID L., eds. *Advances in Austrian economics.* Vol. 3. Greenwich, CT: JAI Press, 1996.

BURNHAM, JAMES. *The managerial revolution: What is happening in the world right now.* New York: John Day, 1941.

BUTOS, WILLIAM N. AND KOPPL, ROGER G. "Hayekian Expectations: Theory and Empirical Applications," *Constitutional Polit. Econ.,* Fall 1993, *4*(3), pp. 303–29.

CALDWELL, BRUCE J. *Beyond positivism: Economic methodology in the twentieth century.* London: Routledge, [1982] 1994.

——. "Hayek's Transformation," *Hist. Polit. Econ.,* Winter 1988a, *20*(4), pp. 513–41.

——. "Hayek's 'The Trend of Economic Thinking'," in *The review of Austrian economics.* Vol. 2. Eds.: MURRAY N. ROTHBARD AND WALTER BLOCK. Washington, DC: Ludwig von Mises Institute. 1998b, pp. 175–78.

——. "La Méthodologie De Hayek: Description, Evaluation, et Interrogations." in *Friedrich Hayek: Philosophie, economie et politique.* Eds.: GILLES DOSTALER ET DIANE ETHIER. Paris: Economica, 1989, pp. 71–85.

CARR, EDWARD H. *Nationalism and after.* London: Macmillan, 1945.

CARTWRIGHT, NANCY ET AL. *Otta Neurath: Philosophy between science and politics.* Cambridge: Cambridge U. Press, 1996.

CHALOUPEK, GÜNTHER K. "The Austrian Debate on Economic Calculation in a Socialist Society," *Hist. Polit. Econ.,* Winter 1990, *22*(4), pp. 659–75.

CLARKE, F. "Book Review: Mannheim's *Man and Society in an Age of Reconstruction,*" *Economica,* N.S., Aug. 1940, *7*(27), pp. 329–32.

COTTRELL, ALLIN AND COCKSHOTT, W. PAUL. "Calculation, Complexity and Planning: the Socialist Calculation Debate Once Again," *Rev. Polit. Econ.,* 1993, *5*(1), pp. 73–112.

CRAVER, EARLENE. "The Emigration of the Austrian Economists," *Hist. Polit. Econ.*, Spring 1986, *18*(1), pp. 1–32.

DESAI, MEGHNAD. "Equilbrium, Expectations and Knowledge," in JACK BIRNER AND RUDY VAN ZIJP, eds. 1994, pp. 25–50.

DIAMOND, ARTHUR. "F. A. Hayek on Constructivism and Ethics," *J. Libertarian Stud.*, Fall 1980, *4*(4), pp. 353–65.

DICKINSON, HENRY D. "Price Formation in a Socialist Economy," *Econ. J.*, June 1933, *43*(170), pp. 237–50.

——. "Review: Hayek's *Freedom and the Economic System*," *Economica, N.S.*, Nov. 1940, *7*(28), pp. 435–37.

DOBB, MAURICE. "Economic Theory and the Problems of a Socialist Economy," *Econ. J.*, Dec. 1933, *43*(172), pp. 588–98.

DURBIN, ELIZABETH F. *New Jerusalems: The Labour Party and the economics of democratic socialism.* London: Routledge, 1985.

DURBIN, EVAN. "Professor Hayek on Economic Planning and Political Liberty," *Econ. J.*, Dec. 1945, *55*(220), pp. 357–70.

EDELMAN, GERALD M. *Neural Darwinism: The theory of neuronal group selection.* NewYork: Basic Books, 1987.

FINER, HERMAN. *The road to reaction.* Chicago: Quadrangle Books, 1945.

FLEETWOOD, STEVE. *Hayek's political economy: The socio-economics of order.* London: Routledge, 1995.

GRAY, JOHN. *Hayek on liberty.* 2nd ed. Oxford: Blackwell, 1986.

——. "Hayek the Scottish School, and Contemporary Economics," in *The boundaries of economics*. Eds.: GORDON C. WINSTON AND RICHARD F. TEICHGRAEBER. Cambridge: Cambridge U. Press, 1988, pp. 53–70.

GROSSMAN, SANFORD J. *The informational role of prices.* Cambridge, MA: MIT Press, 1989.

HAYEK, FRIEDRICH A. VON. "The Trend of Economic Thinking," [1933]: reprinted in FRIEDRICH VON HAYEK 1991.

——, ed. *Collectivist economic planning: Critical studies on the possibilities of socialism.* London: G. Routledge, 1935.

——. "Economics and Knowledge," [1937]; reprinted in FRIEDRICH VON HAYEK, ed. 1948, pp. 33–56.

——. "Freedom and the Economic System," [1939]; reprinted in FRIEDRICH VON HAYEK 1997, pp. 189–211.

——. "Socialist Calculation: the Competitive 'Solution'," [1940]; reprinted in FRIEDRICH VON HAYEK, ed. 1948, pp. 181–208.

——. "Planning, Science, and Freedom," [1941]; reprinted FRIEDRICH VON HAYEK 1997, pp. 213–20.

——. *The counter-revolution of science: Studies on the abuse of reason.* Glencoe: IL: Free Press, [1941–44] 1952b.

——. *The road to serfdom.* Chicago: U. of Chicago Press, [1944] 1976.

——. "The Use of Knowledge in Society," [1945]; reprinted in FRIEDRICH VON HAYEK, ed. 1948, pp. 77–91.

——. "The Meaning of Competition," [1946]; reprinted in FRIEDRICH VON HAYEK, ed. 1948, pp. 92–106.

——, ed. *Individualism and economic order.* Chicago: U. of Chicago Press, 1948.

——. Letter to John Nef. Dated November 6, 1948, Located in Box 55, Number 1, in the Hayek Archives, Hoover Institution, Stanford, CA.

——. *The sensory order: An inquiry into the foundations of theoretical psychology.* Chicago: U. of Chicago Press, 1952a.

——, ed. *Capitalism and the historians.* Chicago: U. of Chicago Press, 1954.

——. "Degrees of Explanation," [1955]; reprinted in FRIEDRICH VON HAYEK, ed. 1967, pp. 3–21.

——. *The constitution of liberty.* Chicago: U. of Chicago Press, 1960.

——. "Rules, Perception and Intelligibility," [1962]; reprinted in FRIEDRICH VON HAYEK, ed. 1967, pp. 43–65.

——. "Kinds of Rationalism," [1964a]; reprinted in FRIEDRICH VON HAYEK, ed. 1967, pp. 82–95.

——. "The Theory of Complex Phenomena," [1964b]; reprinted in FRIEDRICH VON HAYEK, ed. 1967, pp. 22–42.

——, ed. *Studies in philosophy, politics and economics.* Chicago: U. of Chicago Press, 1967.

——. "Competition as a Discovery Procedure," [1968a], in FRIEDRICH VON HAYEK, ed. 1978, pp. 179–90.

——. "The Primary of the Abstract," [1968b], in FRIEDRICH VON HAYEK, ed. 1978, pp. 35–49.

——. "The Errors of Constructivism," [1970], in FRIEDRICH VON HAYEK, ed. 1978, pp. 3–22.

——. Law, legislation and liberty: A new statement of the liberal principles of justice and political economy. Vols 1–3. Chicago: U. of Chicago Press, 1973–1979.

——. "The New Confusion about 'Planning'," [1976], in FRIEDRICH VON HAYEK. ed. 1978, pp. 232–46.

——, ed. *New studies in philosophy, politics, economics and the history of ideas.* Chicago: U. of Chicago Press, 1978.

——. "The Sensory Order after 25 Years," in *Cognition and the symbolic processes.* Vol. 2. Eds.: WALTER WEIMER AND DAVID PALERMO. Hillsdale, NJ: Lawrence Erlbaum Associates, 1982a, pp. 287–93.

——. "Two Pages of Fiction: the Impossibility of Socialist Calculation," in *The essence of Hayek.* Eds.: CHIAKI NISHIYAMA AND KURT R. LEUBE. Stanford: Hoover Institution Press, [1982b] 1984a, pp. 53–61.

——. "Nobel Prize-winning Economist." Transcript of an Oral History Interview Conducted in 1978 under the Auspices of the Oral History Program, University Library, UCLA, Regents of the U. of California, copyright 1983.

——. *Money, capital, and fluctuations: Early essays.* Ed.: ROY MCCLOUGHRY. Chicago: U. of Chicago Press, 1984b.

——. *The collected works of F. A. Hayek.* Vol. 1. *The fatal conceit: The errors of socialism.* Ed.: W. W. BARTLEY. London: Routledge, 1988.

——. *The collected works of F. A. Hayek.* Vol. 3. *The trend of economic thinking: Essays on political economists and economic history.* Eds.: W. W. BARTLEY III AND STEPHEN KRESGE. Chicago: U. of Chicago Press, and London: Routlege, 1991.

——. *The collected works of F. A. Hayek.* Vol. 4. *The fortunes of liberalism: Essays on Austrian economics and the ideal of freedom.* Ed.: PETER G. KLEIN. Chicago: U. of Chicago Press, 1992.

——. *Hayek on Hayek.* Eds.: STEPHEN KRESGE AND LEIF WENAR. Chicago: U. of Chicago Press and London: Routledge, 1994.

——. *The collected works of F. A. Hayek.* Vol. 9. *Contra Keynes and Cambridge: Essays, correspondence.* Ed.: BRUCE CALDWELL. London: Routledge, 1995.

——. *The collected works of F. A. Hayek.* Vol. 10. *Socialism and war: Essays, documents, reviews.* Ed.: BRUCE CALDWELL. London: Routledge, 1997.

HEBB, DONALD O. *The organization of behavior: A neuropsychological theory.* N.Y.: Wiley, 1949.

HEILBRONER, ROBERT. "Analysis and Vision in the History of Modern Economic Thought," *J. Econ. Lit.,* Sept. 1990, *28*(3), pp. 1097–1114.

HOFF, TRYGVE J. B. *Economic calculation in the socialist society.* London: W. Hodge, 1949.

HORWITZ, STEVEN. "From *The Sensory Order* to the Liberal Order: Mind, Economy and the State in the Thought of F. A. Hayek." A paper presented at the Mount Pélèrin meetings, Cannes, France, 1994.

——. Money, Money Prices, and the Socialist Calculation Debate," in PETER J. BOETTKE AND DAVID L. PRYCHITKO, eds., 1996, pp. 59–77.

HURWICZ, LEONID. "Economic Planning and the Knowledge Problem: A Comment," *Cato J.,* Fall 1984, *4*(2), pp. 419–25.

KIRZNER, ISRAEL M. *Competition and entrepreneurship.* Chicago: U. Chicago Press, 1973.

——. "Economic Planning and the Knowledge Problem," *Cato J.,* Fall 1984, *4*(2), pp. 407–18.

——. "The Economic Calculation Debate: Lessons for Austrians," *The review of Austrian economics.* Vol. 2. Eds.: MURRAY N. ROTHBARD AND WALTER BLOCK. Washington, DC: Ludwig von Mises Institute, 1988, pp. 1–18.

——. "Entrepreneurial Discovery and the Competitive Market Process: an Austrian Approach," *J. Econ. Lit.,* Mar. 1997, *35*(1), pp. 60–85.

KORNAL JAÑOS. "The Soft Budget Constraint," *Kyklos,* 1986, *39*(1), pp. 3–30.

——. "Market Socialism Revisited," in PRANHAB K. BARDHAN AND JOHN E. ROEMER, eds. 1993, pp. 42–68.

KUKATHAS, CHANDRAN. *Hayek and modern liberalism.* Oxford: Clarendon, 1989.

LACHMANN, LUDWIG M. "On the Central Concept of Austrian Economics: Market Process," in *The foundations of modern Austrian economics.* Ed.: EDWIN G. DOLAN. Kansas City: Sheed and Ward, 1976, pp. 126–32.

LANGE, OSKAR. *On the economic theory of socialism.* Ed.: BENJAMIN E. LIPPINCOTT. Minneapolis: U. of Minnesota Press, 1938, pp. 57–143.

——. "The Computer and the Market," in *Socialism, capitalism and economic growth: Essays presented to Maurice Dobb.* Ed.: C. H. FEINSTEIN. Cambridge: Cambridge U. Press, 1967, pp. 158–161.

LAVOIE, DON. *Rivalry and central planning.* Cambridge: Cambridge U. Press, 1985.

——. "Economic Chaos or Spontaneous Order? Implications for Political Economy of the New View of Science," *Cato J.,* Winter 1989, *8*(3), pp. 613–35.

——. "Computation, Incentives, and Discovery: the Cognitive Function of Markets in Market Socialism," *Ann. Amer. Acad. Polit. Soc. Sci.,* Jan. 1990, *507*, pp. 72–79.

LAWSON, TONY. "Realism and Hayek: A Case of Continuing Transformation," in *The economics of F. A. Hayek. Vol. 2. Capitalism, socialism, and knowledge.* Eds.: MARINA COLONNA, HARALD HAGEMANN, AND OMAR F. HAMOUDA. Aldershot: Elgar, 1994, pp. 131–59.

LIPPMAN, WALTER. *An inquiry into the principles of the good society.* Boston: Little, Brown & Co., 1937.

MACHOVEC, FRANK M. *Perfect competition and the transformation of economics.* London: Routledge, 1995.

MCMILLAN, HAROLD. *The middle way: A study of the problem of economic and social progress in a free and democratic society.* London: Macmillan, 1938.

MAKOWSKI, LOUIS AND OSTROY, JOSEPH. "General Equilibrium and Market Socialism: Clarifying the Logic of Competitive Markets," in PRANHAB K. BARDHAN AND JOHN E. ROEMER, eds. 1993, pp. 69–88.

MALLOCK, WILLIAM H. *A critical examination of socialism.* NY: Harper, 1907.

MANNHEIM, KARL. *Man and society in an age of reconstruction: Studies in modern social structure.* London: Kegan Paul, 1940.

MARWICK, ARTHUR. "Middle Opinion in the Thirties: Planning, Progress and Political 'Agreement'," *English Hist. Rev.,* Apr. 1964. *79*(311), pp. 285–98.

MENGER, CARL. *Investigations into the method of the social sciences with special reference to economics.* Translated by FRANCIS J. NOCK. New York: New York U. Press, [1883] 1985.

MERKLE, JUDITH A. *Management and ideology: The legacy of the international scientific management movement.* Berkeley: U. of California Press, 1980.

MIKLÒS-ILLÈS, AGNES. "Otto Neurath's War Economics." Manuscript, 1996.

MILGROM, PAUL AND ROBERTS, JOHN. *Economics, organization and management.* Englewood Cliffs, NJ: Prentice Hall, 1992.

MIROWSKI, PHILIP. "Machine Dreams: Economic Agents as Cyborgs," in *The new economics and its history.* Ed.: JOHN DAVIS. Durham, NC: Duke U. Press, forthcoming.

MISES, LUDWIG VON. "Economic Calculation in the Socialist Commonwealth," in FRIEDRICH VON HAYEK, ed., 1935, pp. 87–130.

——. *Human action: A treatise on economics.* 3rd rev. ed. Chicago: H. Regnery Co., 1966.

——. *Notes and recollections.* South Holland, IL: Libertarian Press, 1978.

MURRELL, PETER. "The Transition According to Cambridge, Mass.," *J. Econ. Lit.,* Mar. 1995, *33*(1), pp. 164–78.

NEURATH, OTTO. *Empiricism and sociology.* Eds: MARIE NEURATH AND ROBERT S. COHEN. Dordrecht, Holland: D. Reidel, 1973.

POLANYI, KARL. *The great transformation.* New York: Farrar & Rinehart, 1944.

RAE, JOHN. *Contemporary socialism.* 2nd ed. New York: C. Scribner's Sons, 1891.

RANSOM, GREG. "Insuperable Limits to Reduction in Biology." Manuscript. Apr. 1992.

——. "The Significance of Myth and Misunderstanding in Social Science Narrative: Opening Access to Hayek's 'Copernican' Revolution in Economics." Manuscript, June 1996.

ROEMER, JOHN E. "Can There Be Socialism after Communism?" in PRANHAB K. BARDHAN AND JOHN ROEMER, eds. 1993, pp. 89–107.

——. *A future for socialism.* Cambridge, MA: Harvard U. Press, 1994.

——. "An Anti-Hayek Manifesto," *New Left Review*, May-June 1995, *211*, pp. 112–29.

SALERNO, JOSEPH. "Ludwig von Mises as Social Rationalist," *The review of Austrian economics*. Vol. 4. Eds.: MURRAY N. ROTHBARD AND WALTER BLOCK. Dordrecht and London: Kluwer Academic, 1990, pp. 26–54.

SCHUMPETER, JOSEPH. *Capitalism, socialism and democracy*. 3rd ed. New York: Harper & Row, [1942] 1950.

SENT, ESTHER-MIRJAM. "Bounded Rationally on the Rebound." Manuscript, 1997.

SHEARMUR, JEREMY, *Hayek and after: Hayekian liberalism as a research programme*. London: Routledge, 1996.

——. "Hayek, Keynes and the State." *Hist. Econ. Rev.*, Winter 1997, *26*, pp. 68–80.

STEELE, DAVID RAMSAY. *From Marx to Mises: Post-capitalist society and the challenge of economic calculation*. La Salle, Il: Open Court, 1992.

STIGLER, GEORGE. *Memoirs of an unregulated economist*. NY: Basic Books, 1988.

STIGLITZ, JOSEPH. *Whither socialism?* Cambridge, MA and London: MIT Press, 1994.

THOMSEN, ESTEBAN F. *Prices and knowledge: A market process perspective*. London and New York: Routledge, 1992.

VANBERG, VIKTOR. *Rules and choice in economics*. London: Routledge, 1994.

WEBB, SIDNEY AND WEBB, BEATRICE. *Soviet communism: A new civilization?* London: Longmans, Green, 1935.

WEBER, MAX. *Economy and society: An outline of interpretive sociology*. Eds.: GUENTHER ROTH AND CLAUS WITTICH. Berkeley: U. of California Press, 1978.

WERSKEY, GARY. *The visible college: A collective biography of British scientific socialists of the 1930s*. New York: Holt, Rinehart and Winston, 1978.

WOOTTON, BARBARA. *Freedom under planning*. Chapel Hill, NC.: U. of North Carolina Press, 1945.

YEAGER, LELAND B. "Mises and Hayek on Calculation and Knowledge," *Rev. Austrian Econ.*, 1994, *7*(2), pp. 93–109.

——. "Salerno on Calculation, Knowledge, and Appraisement: Rejoinder," *Rev. Austrian Econ.*, 1996, *9*(1), pp. 137–39.

47

HAYEK ON GOVERNMENT

Two views or one?

Chris Guest

Source: *History of Economics Review* 26 (Winter–Summer 1997): 51–67.

Introduction

In 1975, Margaret Thatcher, then Leader of the Conservative Party Opposition, met with the Party's Research Department. The meeting was to consider a policy paper which argued a pragmatic middle way between the extremes of Right and Left. However, a middle way was unacceptable to Thatcher. Before the presentation of the paper had finished, she produced a copy of Hayek's *The Constitution of Liberty* (1960). "This is what we believe" she said, as she slammed the book on the table (Cockett, 1995, 174).

Thatcher, and the principal modern critics, Brittan (1983) and Gray (1989), regard Hayek as having one view of government. This is a government whose purpose is to support the liberal order by confining its activities. The thesis of the paper is that there were two Hayeks on government. The paper supports the criticism by Keynes of Hayek on the role of government in *The Road to Serfdom* (Keynes, 1944, in Cockett, 1995, 89), and finds further evidence for Keynes' criticism in Hayek's later works on policy, *The Constitution of Liberty* (1960), and *Law, Legislation and Liberty* (1976)[1].

One Hayek on government dated from the rise of Nazi and Soviet totalitarianism in Europe, and the interventionist role of government contained in the 1942 Beveridge proposals for social security in England (see Cockett, 1995, 59–60 and 78–79). For this Hayek, there was no middle road between liberalism and totalitarianism. Any move beyond a minimum role of government would be inexorably the "road to serfdom". Government must be confined to constructing a stable framework of the rule of law to promote individual liberty. Government's only monopoly was the power of coercion, which was limited to enforcing the rule of law, collecting taxes and ensuring external security. All else was determined by the competitive market. The role of policy was to make the market as competitive as possible. This is the Hayek on government Thatcher, Brittan and Gray understood.

A thorough examination of Hayek's policy positions reveals another Hayek on government. This Hayek recognised the duty of government extended beyond policies which underpin and improve the competitive market. These exceptions and qualifications to laissez-faire were guided by considerations of social welfare, an appreciation of the failures of the competitive market and changing ideas about policy. Hayek tried to show that the way is open for government to do more than support the competitive market, by following rules that are consistent with the liberal order. However, the paper argues that Hayek's attempt to make these exceptions and qualifications to laissez-faire consistent with a government bound by the rule of law was unsuccessful, because Hayek violated his own rules and because the rules themselves were flawed. The result of advocating policies to correct the failings of laissez-faire was a second, unintended, view of the role of government.

Hayek's advocacy of a minimum, active government was supported by an integrated system of thought comprising the value of liberty, the rule of law as the political prerequisite to liberty, and the competitive market as the economic prerequisite to liberty, which provided the only efficient means of dealing with the knowledge problem. This system is presented in Section 1. The rules for government policy which Hayek proposed to ensure a liberal order are presented in Section 2. The policy roles Hayek assigned to government are discussed in Section 3. The conclusion emphasises the inconsistency of Hayek's "constitution of liberty" with his policy position (Section 4).

1. Hayek's system

Values

Hayek's central value was liberty, by which he meant that "the coercion of some by others is reduced *as much as is possible* in society" (*CL*, 11 – emphasis added). Liberty is not the freedom *to do* certain things, but freedom *from* the will of others. Liberty is being able to "decide what use we shall make of the circumstances in which we find ourselves" (*CL*, 19). It is being able "to order our own conduct in the sphere where the material circumstances force a choice upon us" (*RTS*, 157). For Hayek the individual's material circumstances are irrelevant to his liberty. One may be rich and subject to coercion, or poor and free (*CL*, 17). Liberty is freedom from the "arbitrary will of another" (Hayek, 1962, 229). No one has the moral right to impose their values or will on anybody else. That would be coercion, which is "bad because it prevents a person from using his mental powers to the full and consequently from making the greatest contribution that he is capable of to the community" (*CL*, 133–134).

Although for Hayek freedom was "desirable for itself on ethical grounds" (*LLL*:2, 71, and see also *CL*, 68), its primary justification was as a means. According to Hayek, following Kant, "welfare has no principle ... it depends on the material content of the will, which is dependent on particular facts and is therefore incapable of a general rule" (quoted in *FC*, 73). There were two arguments for freedom in Hayek's interpretation of Kant's view. One was that people have different values (*RTS*, 45). There is no "complete ethical code" in which "all different human values are allotted their due place" (*RTS*, 43). Hayek's solution to the problem of competing values was to avoid the issue of value choices, by giving people the freedom to decide for themselves "as much as is possible" what they want. The second argument was the "inevitable ignorance of all of us concerning a great many of the factors on which the achievement of our ends and welfare depends" (*CL*, 29). The individual can only use "all his unique combination of information, skills and capacities which nobody else can fully appreciate" if he is free (Hayek, 1962, 233). In so far as society is controlled or directed, it is limited to the powers of the individual minds which control or direct it (Hayek, 1945a, 32). Because we do not know how people will use their freedom, we do not know who will do things of benefit to society, so everyone must have freedom (*CL*, 32 and Hayek, 1945a, 15).

The rule of law

Freedom can only be exercised if people subject their behaviour to restraint. Restraints limit what people can do, but Hayek argued there is no freedom without rules of law and conduct (*LLL*:3, 163, Hayek, 1945a, 11 and 24, note 23). The rules must be known beforehand, embody abstract, normative principles, and have uniform application.

Rules must be known in advance so that they constitute data in relation to which men can plan (*CL*, 153 and *RTS*, 60). Rules then become an "instrument of production" (*RTS*, 55). The rules are like the laws of nature: if they are known beforehand, the individual can use his knowledge of the rules to achieve his aims, just as he can use his knowledge of the laws of nature (*CL*, 142). For Hayek, known rules enable the individual "to make the fullest use of his knowledge". This is because the "law tells him what facts he may count on and thereby extends the range within which he can predict the consequences of his actions" (*CL*, 156–157). Rules that are known beforehand are not coercive, because the individual can avoid putting himself in a situation where he would be subject to the rule (*CL*, 142).

The rules must express abstract, normative principles. They should not have "concrete ends" or apply to "particular sets of circumstances"

(*LLL*:3, 20). Their effect on particular individuals cannot be foreseen at the time they are laid down (*CL*, 153–159 and *LLL*:3, 112). By not serving particular ends, abstract rules serve values, or the preservation of a kind of order (*LLL*:2, 15). They will eliminate certain choices for the individual, but will not limit the choice to some specific action that somebody else wants him to take. In this way, rules give people the freedom to make the greatest use of their knowledge, because the rules have nothing to say about the particular circumstances of time and place (*RTS*, 56–57). Such rules are not coercive (*CL*, 154–155).

The content of the abstract principles must be "deeply ingrained moral beliefs" which command agreement among men (*CL*, 62). The content of rules requires time-honoured social agreement, which is more than a matter of majority voting. Social agreement will only be possible for general principles, for agreement is more difficult the more specific is the issue (*LLL*:3, 17). Agreement to the rules is critical because coercion can only be a minimum if individuals can be expected to conform *voluntarily* to the abstract rules (*CL*, 62).

Finally, rules must have uniform application. The rule must be the same for everyone. This is equality before the law, which is Hayek's notion of justice. The rules of law and conduct are just if they are the same for all. Rules are not coercive when they apply equally to all (*CL*, 154–155). Discriminatory rules, specific commands or the granting of certain privileges for particular individuals are all inconsistent with justice (*LLL*:3, 100). Justice will produce unequal outcomes, because people are different. However, to have rules which aim to do the reverse, that is, produce equal outcomes, requires discriminatory rules. This would be inconsistent with freedom (*CL*, 275). So the consequence of the rule of law is economic inequality (*RTS*, 59).

The idea of the market

The starting point of the economic problem is that all the individual members of the economic system have some knowledge about their skills, opportunities and values. Much of this knowledge is tacit or unconscious. Thus, it often cannot be communicated as knowledge others can use. Freedom gives individuals the scope to use this knowledge and take account of their knowledge. This means more information is used, because more questions are asked and more answers found (*LLL*:2, 9 and *FC*, 77).

The market provides the means for this knowledge to be disseminated. Market prices are generated by people acting on their plans through exchange. Prices summarise the knowledge of individuals about their values and the costs of production. As such, they communicate a great deal of knowledge. Prices summarise more knowledge than any individual can acquire. Prices allow the individual to use tacit knowledge in decisions about values and costs and to take advantage of the knowledge of others, without having that knowledge. Price provides "a readily intelligible yardstick" by which to make informed choices (Hayek, 1968, 187 and *LLL*:2, 72). Decisions about production and consumption taken in relation to price can be made without self-examination in relation to values and in ignorance of the events affecting the market (*LLL*:3, 162). The feature of the market is that people need not know very much to make good decisions, if they rely on price signals (Hayek, 1945b, 86).

Prices are a communication system, with positive and negative feedback loops, because they communicate information about opportunities and errors. The difference between expected prices and the costs of provision provides information to entrepreneurs about the value to society of resource allocation. Prices reveal where the market (and society) believes benefits lie. Costs reveal the values that must be given up. If there is a positive difference, it indicates an improvement in the use of resources is possible. By performing this guidance function, prices lead producers to serve unknown consumers with unknown ends, ends that the producer does not need to know, and which are irrelevant to the decision he makes about what to do (*FC*, 59 and 100). The knowledge society has about least cost methods of production and about consumer values is *created* by the market process. Without competition they would not be known (*LLL*:3, 75). It is because of the market "that people know at least as much about possibilities and opportunities as they in fact do" (Hayek, 1946, 106).

Society requires a means of adapting to change successfully if it is to survive and prosper. Change can only be resisted at the cost of falling income. The market is the most effective means of adaptation because it relies on decentralisation, so individuals, who are best placed to make decisions about themselves, can make decisions about how to adapt. Change will only be known to some (and even for them, knowledge may only be partial, for the adaptation to the unknown unfolds slowly). The market spreads this knowledge by prices, and shares the consequences. The adaptation may not be perfect, but it is the best there is. This ability to adapt is why the market societies survive and prosper (*FC*, 76), even though usually no one will know how the necessary adaptations will be brought about (*CL*, 400). The adaptation to unforeseen events will always mean someone is hurt (*LLL*:1, 63). Competition discovers which plans are "false" (*LLL*:2, 117), which disappoints or defeats some expectations or intentions (Hayek, 1968, 180). However, it is in the "permanent interest of all" that some be forced to do something they do not like, such as changing jobs or accepting a lower income (*LLL*:3, 94).

The outcome of market competition is material progress (*CL*, 394), which generates a level of real income in which the share of each individual is "as large as we know how to make it" (Hayek, 1968, 186). The maximum aggregate real income was for Hayek the only meaningful economic welfare objective (*LLL*:1, 121 and Hayek, 1966, 173). Progress constitutes the "general good" arising from "the facilitation of the pursuit of unknown individual purposes" (*LLL*:2, 1). However, the essence of freedom is that its benefits are "unknown and uncertain" (*CL*, 68). Freedom does not guarantee progress, rather it is *more likely* to generate progress than any alternative.

Progress is generated by market competition, which in turn requires freedom, Hayek's central value. This is a critical step in Hayek's argument. It marries the idea of the market as a knowledge generator and disseminator with the design of the liberal order. The market is politically desirable because it is the means of minimising coercion and economically desirable because of its knowledge qualities. An efficient market requires freedom, and freedom is the purpose of the liberal order. Thus, the rules of a liberal order must also be the rules of a competitive market, and these are the rule of law.

2. The rules for government in a liberal order

The coercive role of government

For Hayek, the aim of policy in a society of free men cannot be a maximum of foreknown results, but only an abstract order:

> The aim of policy in such a society would have to be to increase equally the chances for any unknown member of society pursuing with success his equally unknown purposes, and to restrict the use of coercion ... to the enforcement of such rules as will, if universally applied, tend in this sense to improve everyone's opportunities.
>
> (*LLL*:2, 114)

There is no good alternative to improving the competitive market due to its effectiveness in marshalling knowledge and co-ordinating the different plans people have. Government policy is constrained by ignorance and the need to select a single value or hierarchy of values, when no substantive value can be "correct". Government can only assist or make possible the formation of an abstract pattern or structure in which the expectations of individuals approximately match each other, through making each observe rules which are independent of particular purposes (*LLL*:3, 139). The principal benefit of such rules is that they reduce coercion as much as is possible (*FC*, 63 and *LLL*:3, 146).

The role of government is to identify and promulgate the rules necessary for the abstract order, whose economic dimension is the competitive market. Thus government economic policy must be known, general and uniform, because policy of this kind fosters the competitive market. Government may only use coercion to enforce rules of this kind (*CL*, 284). Government must have a monopoly of coercion for the purposes of enforcing the rule of law, collecting taxes and ensuring national security, and this must be its only monopoly (*CL*, 210 and *LLL*:3, 42).

The rationale for coercion by government was that it prevents more severe coercion by others (*CL*, 144). Government was to do this by designing the rule of law to create a private domain within which the individual was free. This required private property rights (*CL*, 20) and contract law (*CL*, 141). For Hayek the real issue for the role of government was "whether the state ought to confine its coercive action to enforcing these rules [of private property] or go beyond this" (*CL*, 145). Hayek's view was that the coercive activities of government must be "strictly limited" (*CL*, 257). As the justification for coercion by government was to prevent coercion by others, and the means to do this was the private domain, it would follow that government coercion should be limited to enforcing the rule of law to protect the private domain through property rights (*CL*, 144–145). Thus, the protection of liberty "requires that coercion be used only to enforce the universal rules of just conduct *protecting the individual domains*" (*LLL*:3, 111 – emphasis added). Measures to ensure the competitiveness of market relations, principally the free flow of information and low barriers to entry (Hayek, 1966, 174), assist the individual's freedom in the private domain by allowing property rights to be exercised as widely as possible. The provision of information must be funded by coercive taxation, while ensuring low barriers to entry required a coercive legal framework.

The non-coercive role of government

Government may do things other than identify and enforce the known, abstract, just rules necessary for the abstract order, collect taxes and secure peace. Hayek stressed that no role is *necessarily* excluded from government, although competition is always preferable if it is possible (*RTS*, 27, Hayek, 1947, 110, *LLL*:3, 42 and *HOH*, 113). Government has a role where effective competition cannot be created for the provision of "valuable" output. Thus, *The Road to Serfdom* supported a significant number of exceptions and qualifications to laissez-faire. These exceptions were the source of Keynes' criticism of *The Road to Serfdom* (quoted in Cockett, 1995, 89–90). According to Keynes, Hayek was arguing that "as soon as one moves an inch in the planned direction you are necessarily launched on the slippery path which will lead you in due course over the precipice". At the same time, Keynes said, Hayek admitted that the practical matter is one of knowing where to draw the line (see *RTS*, 61), because the extreme position is not possible. Keynes concluded that this admission means Hayek is "done for", because the argument is then about where to draw the line.

In his later work, principally *The Constitution of Liberty*, Hayek set out rules for the exceptions to laissez-faire. The rules were designed to ensure that these roles of government were consistent with the liberal order. Each role must meet four requirements: it must follow the rule of law (*CL*, 221), which means it is compatible with the competitive market, and does not replace the market with planning; second, although consistent with the rule of law, the role must be non-coercive (*CL*, 257 and 284); third, where possible, the role should be *outside* the market (Hayek, 1976a, 306); finally, government must not claim a monopoly of provision (*CL*, 223 and *LLL*:3, 47). If the role can be provided in a way that satisfies these four requirements, whether government should perform the role is then dependent on its "expediency", or whether the "benefits are worth the cost" (*CL*, 222, and see also *RTS*, 28).

3. The roles of government

According to Gray (1989, 141), Hayek assigned government two policy roles: "the refinement of the institutions and legal arrangements which shape the market process", and "the provision of the goods and services the market will not provide". Further, says Gray, these two roles were justified by Hayek, not on utilitarian grounds, but by their contribution to the working of competitive processes and the prospects of people to participate in market activity. The discussion of this Section finds that some government roles and reforms do fit Gray's first category. The roles are designed to contribute to the competitive effectiveness of the market, and they are consistent with Hayek's rules for the role of government. This group comprises the "private law", competition and stabilisation policies. These also tend to be the cases where Hayek was most clear and consistent about what he believed government should do. There is much less evidence for Gray's view that the provision of goods and services the market will not provide is to contribute to the competitiveness of the market. There is *some* evidence, in relation, for instance, to the role Hayek assigned government in information provision (see *CL*, 223). However, it cannot be said to be Hayek's rationale for the wide-ranging roles he advocated.

Brittan argues that "[c]ontrary to popular belief Friedrich Hayek has not provided any recognisable economic criteria for recognising state intervention of the harmful type" (Brittan, 1983, 63). The criteria are recognisable: they are Hayek's rules for the role of government. The problem for Hayek is that a number of his policies are *inconsistent* with his own rules and the rules are *flawed*. This group of policies includes an income maintenance scheme, collective goods, education, and town

71

planning. These tend to be the roles where Hayek's proposals were not always clear, and reveal the impracticality of his view about reconstructing the evolutionary tradition to reveal policy needs (*FC*, 69). These are also roles about which Hayek tended to change his position.

"Private law"

The most important task of the government is to "articulate, interpret and develop" what Hayek called the "private law". Private law comprises private property rights, protection from force and fraud, the rules of contract, and the liability for damages caused to another. Private law defines the individual domain, ensures the performance of promises and the justice of exchange, gives people the freedom to produce and price at whatever level they choose, and makes people take account of the impact on others of what they do (*CL*, 145, Hayek, 1966, 167, *LLL*:1, 103, and *LLL*:2, 40). For Hayek the rights established by private law are artefacts, not natural rights. They are protected because they are an effective means of securing the freedom necessary for a market: The "recognition of private property is an essential condition for the prevention of coercion, though by no means the only one" (*CL*, 140), because private property provides *autonomy*. With his private property rights protected, man is free from coercion (*CL*, 20). Private property is also an "inducement" to the individual to contribute as much as possible to the need of all others (Hayek, 1945a, 13).

The content of private law is to be defined and revised as required by the needs of competitive system (*CL*, 229). The most important reform for Hayek was the removal of the special legal position of trade unions (Hayek, 1947, 117). Hayek believed trade unions had become "the only important instance in which governments signally fail in their prime function – the prevention of coercion and violence" (*CL*, 267). Unionism can produce a *de facto* authority which replaces market competition (*CL*, 270–3). Hayek also believed patents and copyright unduly extended private property rights and fostered the growth of monopoly (Hayek, 1947, 113–115). Copyright may not be an effective stimulant to effort, and should be confined to "exceedingly useful works" such as dictionaries and textbooks, which "could not be produced if, once they existed, they could be freely reproduced" (*FC*, 36–37). Hayek also advocated the reform of corporation law, which he believed had tended to encourage the expansion of the modern corporation beyond what is justified by technology (Hayek, 1947, 116 and Hayek, 1960a). The problems of corporations are problems of the special conditions which the law has created and the law can change.

"Fugitive resources", which include game, fish, water and oil, raise problems for defining property rights. The problem is that no one has an incentive to conserve these resources, since what one does not take another will. The problem is that "private property cannot exist" or private property is only beneficial if it is given exclusive control of the resource (*CL*, 369). However, Hayek favoured a system of private property rights rather than "social control". Hayek was never explicit about the way a system of private property rights could be implemented. His argument was confined to the merits of private property and the market compared with government control. Hayek acknowledged there is an "act of faith" required to accept market authority (*CL*, 369).

Hayek also identified important exceptions to the inviolability of private rights. Private property rights may be suspended in times of emergency, like wars and natural disasters (*LLL*:3, 54). These are examples of "necessary infringements of private sphere". They must be cases where the public gain is greater than harm done by the disappointment of normal expectations, the exceptions must be defined by rule, and full compensation must be paid (*CL*, 217–8). However, these conditions do not satisfy Hayek's rules for the role of government. The first, the excess of public gain over private harm, is a consideration of expediency, which on Hayek's account cannot justify coercion. The second constitutes a break with the generality of rules requirement of the rule of law. The third is a new consideration, nowhere raised by Hayek in relation to the rule of law. The idea that compensation can be paid to offset a violation of property rights sits uncomfortably with Hayek's stress on the importance of property rights to liberty.

Competition

Hayek was critical of competition policy which focussed on market *performance*. This follows from his idea of the market as a means of discovery: "If we do not know the facts we hope to discover by means of competition, we can never ascertain how effective it has been in discovering those facts that might be discovered" (Hayek, 1968, 180). This kind of competition policy requires knowledge that authorities are unlikely to have (*LLL*:3, 85). Its premise is inconsistent with the rationale for adopting competition for resource allocation. This is the argument for competition: we do not know beforehand who will do best nor what is best. It is a discovery procedure for this purpose, and it does so in a way that is consistent with the rule of law. By contrast, competition policy commonly entails discretionary powers, which infringe the rule of law and so are inconsistent with the prerequisites of the free market (*CL*, 265).

There is a role for another kind of competition policy. The correct focus of competition policy is to ensure that the market *process* is as competitive as possible (*LLL*:3, 68). There are two requirements for a competitive market. There must be no impediments to the flow or transmission of knowledge and there must be low barriers to entry (Hayek, 1966, 174). Barriers to entry must be low enough for there always to be the threat of entry. The threat is sufficient to ensure that existing firms are under competitive pressure (Hayek, 1940, 196). Thus, it is not monopoly as such which is undesirable, but the prevention of competition (*LLL*:3, 83).

Monopolies are caused by economic superiority, government policy and collusive behaviour. There is no role for policy where monopoly is due to economic superiority. This result is simply the market doing what it does best, discovering how to do things efficiently. Although it would be better not to have monopolies, they are an inevitable part of an economy (*CL*, 265). The power to determine price or quality is a consequence of private property, and cannot be eliminated without abandoning private property. Neither size nor ability to set prices is a measure of harmful economic power. There is no economic standard for determining if a firm is too large (*LLL*:3, 77). Much enterprise monopoly is the result of better performance. Sometimes competition has done its best when it yields a monopoly (*LLL*:3, 73). So we must allow the monopolist the possibility of a monopoly profit. If there is no entry in these circumstances, this suggests that the monopolist is performing better than any potential entrant could. However, where monopoly is due to a government policy, then that policy should be changed to remove its monopoly result. The most effective policy is to deprive government of the power of benefiting particular groups or interests (*LLL*:3, 82). This would occur if government were bound by the rule of law.

The situation is different where market power is used to prevent others from serving customers better (*LLL*:3, 72). What is harmful is the ability of a monopolist to preserve its position after its source of superiority has gone (*LLL*:3, 84). The problem Hayek identified was collusive action (*LLL*:3, 90). Hayek suggested a number of ways for government to check collusion. One is the dissemination of information, for the "real issue is how we can best assist the optimum utilisation of the knowledge, skills and opportunities to acquire knowledge" (*LLL*:3, 68), for "there is no doubt that the utilisation of knowledge can be greatly increased by deliberate efforts" (*CL*, 376). His proposed reform of patents and copyright arrangements were relevant here, as well as the information responsibilities assigned to government in relation to collective goods (see below). Potential competitors could be used as watchdogs on performance by being given a remedy against price discrimination, such as a claim of multiple damages, and all agreements in restraint of trade could be declared invalid (*LLL*:3, 85–87).

There may be cases of what Hayek called "inevitable" monopoly, such as railways, road and air transport, and the supply of gas and electricity (*RTS*, 146). The policy issue is then a choice between the freedom of a market with no legal monopoly rights and the greater abundance of a market supplied by a producer with legal monopoly rights. The interesting feature of Hayek's discussion is that it was not conducted in terms of the undesirability of a monopoly, because of its reduction of market freedom and its inconsistency with the rule of law, but in terms of a social judgement to be made on the merits of the alternatives. Where society chooses to confer monopoly rights, Hayek's preference was for government supervision of private monopolists. Private monopoly is "scarcely ever complete and even more rarely of long duration or able to disregard potential competition" (*RTS*, 146). By contrast, government monopolies make competitive experimentation impossible and so prevent selection by evolution (*FC*, 103). Hayek expressed a preference for the control of monopolists through "stringent price control". He expected that this would make monopoly unattractive to entrepreneurs, who "will rediscover their taste for the bracing air of competition!" (*RTS*, 147). This expectation sits uncomfortably with his concern about the tendency to collusive action (*LLL*:3, 90).

Stabilisation

The focus of Hayek's work on stabilisation policy was that a market economy will always generate unemployment as a consequence of change, which may impact on industries or regions, as well as the investment and consumption goods sectors (Hayek, 1933, 1925 and 1950). Economic change leads to a discrepancy between the distribution of resources and the distribution of demand. So the problem is one of inappropriate relative prices and wages: "Economic activity is not guided by totals but always by relations between different magnitudes, and the practice of always thinking in 'global' totals can be very misleading" (Hayek, 1952, 347). In those cases, additional expenditure may not create additional employment. Only a reallocation of resources in response to revised prices and wages solves the problem in a free economy (Hayek, 1950, 271–2 and Hayek, 1972, 201). Here the idea of the market re-emerges. The only way to secure full employment is for the distribution of labour to be consistent with the needs of the market, and this cannot be known beforehand. It is something to be discovered by letting the market do its job (Hayek, 1950, 275).

The structural unemployment that change produces is due to the freedom of workers. So long as workers have the freedom to choose their work, there will be delays in the adjustment process and so some unemployment. Workers will initially exercise their freedom by resisting the change, and this will lead to some of them becoming unemployed. A monetary expansion can serve to keep some in their jobs for longer than they otherwise would be. However, in the long run it becomes self-defeating and serves only to hold up the reallocation of labour made necessary by the changes in the market. The result is lower labour productivity and an increase in "the proportion of the working population which can be kept employed at present wages only by artificial means" (*RTS*, 154). The policy dilemma is that if credit expansion stops, unemployment would be greater than it would otherwise have been (Hayek, 1950, 273).

The major shift in Hayek's position was in relation to his views on monetary policy. In *The Road to Serfdom* Hayek had endorsed the use of monetary policy and (more cautiously) public works to combat unemployment (*RST*, 90–91). Six years later, he expanded on this simple endorsement by arguing that where there is general unemployment in the sense that resources of all kinds are unemployed, then monetary expansion is beneficial (Hayek, 1950, 271–2). In the *Constitution of Liberty* his position was that government should try to reduce cyclical unemployment as much as possible by monetary policy (*CL*, 302). This would preserve the impersonal method of market adjustment where people can choose their occupation. However, government should retain control of monetary policy, because business has come to rely on existing forms of money and credit, and monetary policy can reduce unemployment (*CL*, 324). The best monetary policy is one which follows a mechanical rule set according to long run considerations (*CL*, 333). The objective of monetary policy should be a stable price level, which is the best means to a high and stable level of employment (*CL*, 337).

Hayek's final position was to argue for the denationalisation of money combined with a fixed exchange rate, a position he had first suggested in a footnote in *The Constitution of Liberty* (*CL*, 520, note 2). Hayek proposed that governments should give up the monopoly of their own currencies in regard to legal tender, and should allow private contracts to be made in terms of any other currencies. Government had abused the monopoly power of issuing money, and a competitive market of private moneys would be a more effective check on inflation, because people would seek out the most inflation proof currency (Hayek, 1991). Hayek's argument for fixed exchange rates was that they constitute a "discipline on governments" (*HOH*, 150). The monetary rule Hayek proposed in *The Constitution of Liberty* represented an effort to find a rule of law for the market. Hayek felt the monetary rule had failed because it was too vulnerable to discretionary abuse by government. It was preferable to remove the monopoly of the issue of money from government to eliminate discretionary abuse.

Minimum income scheme

Hayek advocated an income maintenance scheme which provided "a constant minimum for everybody who cannot earn more than that minimum in the market" (*HOH*, 149). This minimum should be "more than is absolutely necessary to keep alive and in health" (*CL*, 285). It should be available to anyone who experiences misfortune from the risks "which are common to all". A minimum income scheme is a "clear moral duty" (*LLL*:2, 87), and a "necessary part of the Great Society". It is necessary in a large society where people do not have the private help of others, and it is possible in a prosperous community (*LLL*:3, 55). The level of protection depends on community prosperity, that is, the ability of the community to pay (*CL*, 101). Because of the uncertainty of "the common hazards of life", "few individuals can make adequate provision" against them, a problem of market failure. Insuring against these risks does not generate problems of moral hazard, so there is a very strong case for government "helping to organise a comprehensive system of social insurance" (*RTS*, 90). As a "recognised duty of the public", insurance would have to be compulsory (*CL*, 286). In addition, Hayek justified coercion on the basis that otherwise non-payers would become a charge to the public and because it forestalls greater coercion of the individual by those suffering "extreme misery" (*CL*, 286).

Hayek rejected any "deliberate redistribution beyond" the provision of a safety net (*HOH*, 149). Such a policy would require unequal treatment of people, because it represents particular benefits for specific individuals, which can never be just, and is inconsistent with the rule of law (*LLL*:2, 142). By requiring discretionary judgement by authority, it "suspends" the market (*LLL*:2, 87), which has "brilliantly" reduced absolute poverty: relative poverty must always exist outside of any completely egalitarian society (*LLL*:2, 139). In addition, the poor have no moral claim for a greater share of the wealth of society. The wealth of a community "may set a standard for what some ought to be willing to give, but not for what anyone can demand" (*CL*, 101). Finally, increasing the security of one group necessarily reduces the security of the rest, because the share of fluctuations they bear must increase, and "the essential element of security which the competitive system offers, the great variety of opportunities, is more and more reduced" (*RTS*, 95). In Hayek's view, the market game increases the chances of all of a high real income, and this, plus the assurance of a minimum income *outside* the market, "leaves no moral justification for a use of force to determine relative incomes" (*LLL*:3, 142). Hayek distinguished the minimum income scheme from any deliberate redistribution "beyond that" on the basis that his scheme was outside the market, whereas other schemes distorted the market (*LLL*:2, 87).

There are two sets of issues in relation to the scheme. The first is whether the scheme is consistent with Hayek's rules for government, and the second is what the scheme reveals about the rules. The scheme could be seen as being consistent with the rule of law, because it provides a known, general and uniform kind of safety net. The content of the rule could be seen as a "recognised duty of the public", recalling Hayek's notion of the "ingrained moral tradition". On this basis, the government would be justified in using coercion to enforce the scheme, if the scheme meets Hayek's requirement that it is necessary for the abstract order by identifying and protecting the private domain. However, the interesting feature of Hayek's presentation of the scheme is that it was not justified for its contribution to the competitive order. In fact, Hayek acknowledged that people are prepared to give up some freedom, rather than bear "too great" a risk (*RTS*, 99). If the scheme is not necessary for "protecting the individual domains" (*LLL*:3, 111), then the use of coercion is not justified. Hayek's case for coercion was a concern for the viability of the scheme and the protection of society from those in "extreme misery". Neither of these concerns is related to Hayek's insistence on limiting coercion to the enforcement of the rule of law.

It is not clear that an entitlement to a minimum income in the event of misfortune is "outside" the market; whereas any other income entitlement in specified circumstances "beyond that" is "inside" the market and a distortion of the market. Nor is it clear that Hayek was correct in expecting that "suitable" private institutions could evolve, so avoiding a government monopoly (*CL*, 287–288). The importance of benefits "based on need" (*CL*, 293), and problems of moral hazard and adverse selection would make viable private insurance arrangements unlikely.

The scheme reveals some fundamental weaknesses in Hayek's rules for the role of government. Hayek's discussion of the moral duty of the community to those who suffer misfortune reveals the problem of knowing what an "ingrained moral tradition" is. The community has a moral duty to provide "more than is absolutely necessary", while the poor have "no moral claim for a greater share of the wealth of society". Where is the line drawn between the moral duty of society and the moral claims of the poor? The recognition of a moral duty does more than simply supply the content of the rule of law, because it affects the amount of freedom. Hayek here implicitly advocated the sacrifice of an amount of freedom for a gain in social welfare, a trade-off he was not prepared to consider when arguing the case for freedom. Second, it is not clear that a rule, which specifies people's eligibility according to certain misfortunes, is general whereas a rule which specifies people's eligibility according to other defined events, like "structural adjustment", is not. Hayek's notion of the generality of a rule is a fiction, because it did not recognise the need for policy to specify the categories of people and circumstances to which the policy rule is to apply.

Collective goods

Hayek recognised that there are goods the market may not provide at all or not provide in sufficient quantities. He called these goods collective goods. Hayek's understanding of what constituted collective goods changed markedly. In the 1944 work, *The Road to Serfdom*, he identified the need for collective goods as occurring where there is an "important" *"divergence between the items which enter private calculation and those which affect social welfare"* (*RTS*, 29 – emphasis added). The problem is the absence of property rights in external benefits and costs. In these cases, "some other method than competition may have to be found." Hayek's examples of this Pigovian concept were signposts, roads, deforestation, some methods of farming, smoke, and noise (*RTS*, 29), and knowledge, information and mobility (*RTS*, 71).

In the 1960 work, *The Constitution of Liberty*, Hayek shifted the emphasis of the concept of collective goods. There he argued, following the concept of public goods introduced by Samuelson and Musgrave, that it is "essential for government to provide all those services which are clearly desirable, but would not be provided competitively because it is *impossible or difficult to charge the beneficiary for them*" (*CL*, 223 – emphasis added).

The examples Hayek cited were sanitary and health services, construction and maintenance of roads, municipal urban services, public works, military preparations, and the advancement of knowledge; things which facilitate the acquisition of reliable knowledge about facts of general significance, including a "reliable and efficient" monetary system, standards of weights and measures, surveying, land registration, and statistics (*CL*, 223). There is another group of cases as well, comprising natural parks, museums, theatres and sports grounds. According to Hayek, "there can be no objection to the government providing such amenities ... so long as the community approves this, in full awareness of the cost, and realises that this is one aim competing with others and not a unique objective overrding all other needs. If the taxpayer knows the full extent of the bill he will have to foot and has the last word in the decision, there is nothing further to be said about these problems in general terms" (*CL*, 375).

In *Law, Legislation and Liberty* (1976) the concept of collective goods changed again, as did the examples. For the first time Hayek used the term collective goods synonymously with public goods (*LLL*:3, 44). The discussion of collective goods emphasised the difficulty of confining benefits to those willing to pay for their costs (*LLL*:3, 43). There was also the problem of consumer ignorance, reducing the demand for knowledge below what would be socially beneficial. There is a case on this ground, and the low cost of the reproduction of information, for information to be free (*LLL*:3, 60). The government's monopoly on the issue of money was removed from the category of collective goods (*LLL*:3, 148). Long distance roads, on which tolls could be levied, were excluded as collective goods, but quality certification was included (*LLL*:3, 44), as were some "public institutions", which were close to being merit goods:

> Building regulations, pure food laws, the certification of certain professions, the restrictions on the sale of certain dangerous goods (such as arms, explosives, poisons and drugs), as well as some safety and health regulations for the processes of production and the provision of such public institutions as theatres, sports grounds, etc., certainly assists intelligent choice and sometimes may be indispensable for it. . . . All that is required for the preservation of the rule of law and of a functioning market order is that everybody who satisfies the prescribed standards has a legal claim to the required certification, which means that the control of admissions authorities must *not* be used to regulate supply.
>
> (*LLL*:3, 62)

The provision of a collective good was subject to two criteria. The first was a consistent position of Hayek: the collective good must be supplied subject to the rule of law. Hayek's first preference was for government to fund provision but to leave supply to the private sector (*CL*, 224). Second, in *The Road to Serfdom* and *The Constitution of Liberty*, the benefit of the collective good must exceed its cost. This is the test of "expediency" (*RTS*, 28 and *CL*, 222). In *Law, Legislation and Liberty*, this criterion was replaced by a test of whether the good itself satisfies the defined requirements of a collective or public good (*LLL*:3, 43–44). The term "expedient" took on a pejorative meaning in *Law, Legislation and Liberty*, where it was used to describe the practice of making decisions based on the merits of the case, and thereby sacrificing the principle of freedom (*LLL*:1, 56). This change left open the question of how decisions would be made about which public goods to supply, and in what quantities. However, Hayek's concept of the test of "expediency" was consistently vague.

Expediency was a matter of whether "it is thought worthwhile". For instance, Hayek cautioned against regulating the method of production, because such rules limit experimentation and raise the cost of production. "But if this effect on cost is fully taken into account and it is still thought worthwhile to incur the cost to achieve a given end, there is little more to be said about it" (*CL*, 224). Similarly, while the rule of law excludes government from making decisions about who will produce, and at what prices and quantities, it does not exclude admitting to certain occupations only those with specified qualifications (*CL*, 227). The practical problem is that of determining what those qualifications should be without making a judgement about merit, which would violate the generality condition of the rule of law. However, a decision about qualifications does require that the categories of acceptable qualifications be specified. Interestingly, the examples of this entry restriction in *The Constitution of Liberty* were the control of the *sellers* of poisons and firearms, which in *Law, Legislation and Liberty* was a matter for the restriction of *sales* (*LLL*:3, 62).

The provision of collective goods entails coercion, because they must be funded by taxation, but they are not equally available to all, and so are "unjust" in Hayek's sense (*LLL*:1, 139), and therefore inconsistent with the rule of law. Significantly, Hayek did not use this inconsistency as a ground to argue against collective goods. His solution was that so "long as each may expect to get from this common pool services which are worth more to him than what he is made to contribute, it will be in his *interest to submit to the coercion*" (*LLL*:3, 45 – emphasis added. See also *LLL*:2, 6–7).

Hayek's endorsement of coercion violated the limits of the liberal government, because it was not justified by the need to enforce the rule of law, and sits uncomfortably with the central value of freedom. As with the minimum income scheme, Hayek justified the use of coercion on practical grounds, and did not confine coercion to the policies meeting the requirements of the rule of law.

Education

Market intervention in relation to education is required for two reasons. The first is the problem of consumer ignorance. Children cannot make informed decisions and parents may not make decisions in the children's best interests. For adults, education may awaken capacities they did not know they had (*LLL*:3, 61). Hayek advocated compulsory general education for all. The case for coercion is that the catallaxy is stronger if everyone shares some basic knowledge and values (*CL*, 377). If all families are compelled to send their children to school, then the community should pay for those families for whom the "cost would be a severe burden" (*CL*, 378). The period of compulsory, publicly funded education depends on the prosperity of the community, the character of the economy, and the "climatic conditions affecting the age of adolescence" (*CL*, 382). Hayek supported a voucher system to avoid a government monopoly of the provision or control of the content of education, which would be dangerous for freedom due to its power over men's minds (*CL*, 380–381). He suggested that government schools could be confined to cases of small isolated communities where the numbers of children are too small for the economic provision of private education (*CL*, 381).

Hayek's presumption was that higher education should focus on a "comparatively small elite" (*CL*, 382). Advances in knowledge depend on research, and increasingly, Hayek felt, fewer universities were doing this. This was due to the universities' "utilitarian bias" for conferring professional qualifications, and the "democratic preference" for better material opportunities for large numbers over the advancement of knowledge. In order to advance knowledge, universities should not provide what customers demand (*CL*, 389). Hayek proposed subsidy assistance for general education and cases where the contribution education generates becomes freely available to all, and is not reflected in the price scientists and scholars receive for their services. This, therefore, excludes vocational and professional training from subsidies, which the individual can fund by loan arrangements, despite their practical difficulties (*CL*, 382–383).

The entry of students to higher education should not be by the "subjective merit" of "effort and sacrifice", but capacity and aptitude (*CL*, 385). Those who display the greatest ability should be allowed to develop their talent irrespective of family means, though how ability is to be determined is extremely unclear (*CL*, 386). This means certain advantages are to be limited to some, which may be "unfair", but making the best use of the "accidents of the environment", which includes some having more ability than others, is the source of the "growth of civilisation" (*CL*, 385). Having all start with the same chances is "literally impossible to realise" (*CL*, 385), and undesirable, because it would tend to repress the ability of people to take advantage of their "unfair natural gifts" and "opportunities", which are the source of progress (*CL*, 388).

Hayek on education raises two issues. First, his views on higher education represent a significant qualification to his idea of the market as the best means of determining resource allocation. His recognition of consumer ignorance in relation to education, but not in other areas like health (*CL*, 299), seems arbitrary, Second, Hayek's rejection of equality of opportunity, because it requires unequal treatment of people, and his desire to encourage those with ability to develop their talent irrespective of family means (*CL*, 386), seems inconsistent. More fundamentally, the inconsistency reveals the ambiguity of the requirement that government policy have a uniform application. The uniformity needs to be specified in relation to selected circumstances. This selection requires other, unspecified, criteria.

Town planning

The first recognition by Hayek that competition does not "adequately solve" the problems created by a town was in *The Road to Serfdom* (35), and developed in greater detail in *The Constitution of Liberty*, where it was recognised that a significant number of the costs of city life are "communal" (341). Whereas with "mobile property" the advantages and disadvantages accrue to the owner, the use of land "often necessarily affects the usefulness of neighbouring pieces" (*CL*, 349). The value of land reflects the uses of neighbouring land and the services and regulations of authorities, and economic decisions require that these effects be taken into account (*CL*, 349). Hayek's argument was that the market should be retained, because of its effectiveness in mobilising private initiative and dispersed knowledge and foresight, but that a more detailed "framework of rules" is required (*CL*, 350). Town planning establishes the "general conditions to which all developments of a district or neighbourhood must conform, but which, within these conditions, leaves the decisions to the individual owner [and makes] the market mechanism more effective" (*CL*, 350). Essentially, Hayek's approach was to internalise the externalities by increasing the size of the planning unit from the private property owner to the community" (*CL*, 351–352).

The problem of town planning is that planning measures will increase the values of some property and reduce others. To ensure a measure is beneficial, gains must exceed losses. The practical problem is to measure the costs and benefits. Hayek accommodated this problem by making the planning authority responsible for the gains and losses, so that it could capture the benefit of increases in value and compensate those whose property value has suffered. The means is the power to expropriate at "fair market value" from those who oppose the measure. So long as this is the only coercive power, it is acceptable because of the obligation to compensate at "fair market value", and provided disputes are only settled by "independent courts", meaning that planning authorities have no discretionary power (*CL*, 351).

Once again, compensation was used to justify coercion, even though such compensation was not part of Hayek's general rules for the role of government. Hayek ignored the practical difficulty of determining the impact of a planning measure on property value, even though a recognition of this kind of problem was part of his strong attack on the British Town and Country Planning Act (Hayek, 1949a, 334). In any event, coercion is not justified in relation to Hayek's rules for government. The problem Hayek addressed was the impact of changes to land use plans. Changes cannot be known in advance, so land use planning does not satisfy the requirement of the rule of law that the policy be known in advance.

Taxation

Taxation is an allowable coercion by government, providing it is exercised in accordance with the rule of law. However, Hayek was strongly critical of progressive income taxation. There were four elements to this view. First, progressive taxation abandons the principle of equality before the law (*CL*, 310). It constitutes an invalid coercion of the rich, even though the rich can "survive" under progressive taxation, which would suggest that on Hayek's test of coercion that progressive taxation is not coercive (*CL*, 136). For Hayek progressive taxation was a distributional decision imposed by a majority, which violates the rule of law (*CL*, 311). Second, it interferes with the working of the market. Progressive taxation limits the ability of successful people to accumulate a fortune. This impacts adversely on investment and technical progress, the allocation of resources, incentives, and reduces social mobility by making it "practically impossible" for a successful man to rise by accumulating a fortune (Hayek, 1947, 118 and *CL*, 308). Third, it eliminates an important part of a free society, the man of independent means (Hayek, 1947, 118). Fourth, the "scientific" argument in favour of progressive taxation, the decreasing marginal utility of consumption, is flawed. This is due to the difficulty of comparing utilities between people, and because it is doubtful whether the concept of decreasing marginal utility has any meaning, if "we count as income all the advantages a person derives from the use of his resources (*CL*, 309).

Hayek advocated proportional income taxation. It is consistent with the rule of law because all are treated equally. It is also a rule on which all people, "those who will pay absolutely more and those who will pay absolutely less", are likely to agree (*CL*, 314). There are three difficulties with Hayek's proposal, which also relate to his criticisms of progressive taxation. As a longstanding system of taxation, progressive taxation may be said to constitute an "ingrained moral belief", in which case it is arguably an appropriate abstract principle for the rule of law to embody. Second, progressive taxation is consistent with Hayek's rule of law, interpreted in the sense in which he uses the concept in cases like control of occupational entry – there may be a different rule for a group with special features. Finally, there is the problem of the incompatibility of Hayek's objections to progressive taxation and his support of a minimum income scheme and government funding of general education. The funding principle of the income scheme and education was the community's ability to pay. Their rationale was vertical equity, by providing specific assistance to those who suffer misfortune under the minimum income scheme and assisting families not able to pay for compulsory education.

4. Conclusion

Hayek's system comprised the value of liberty, the idea of the market as an efficient means of solving the knowledge problem, and the position that freedom and the market are best promoted by a government which identifies and enforces the rule of law, and is itself bound by the rule of law. This is Hayek on a minimum, but active, government. And yet, as this chapter has shown, Hayek advocated a significant set of policies which went beyond what was necessary for a properly functioning competitive market.

Hayek on policy often discarded elements of his "constitution of liberty", depending on the merits of the situation. In some cases, like income maintenance, values other than freedom constituted the goal of policy. The commutative justice of the market, which Hayek argued strongly was a consequence of freedom and necessary for the efficiency of the market (Hayek, 1940, 203, 1946, 21–22, and 1963, 258), was qualified by a scheme which cushions people against errors and misfortune. In others, like education, ignorance by consumers justified regulating the market by making schooling compulsory. The work of universities should not be driven by the market, despite Hayek's view that the market is the source of information about social value. The notion of collective goods was broadened considerably by Hayek in a way that reflected the development of the ideas of public goods from Pigou to Musgrave. However, adoption of a Musgravian notion of public goods funded by taxation created difficulty for Hayek's concept of coercion. Hayek's choice between extending public goods, or limiting public goods and preserving the rule of law, was to choose the former and change the justification of coercion.

Keynes' observation, that for Hayek the practical issue of policy was where to draw the line, leads to the idea presented in this chapter there were two Hayek's on government. The presence of two views on government constitutes an inconsistency in Hayek's position. It also reveals the difficulty of designing a "constitution of liberty" which provides a workable policy framework. Hayek's policy views show the problems of confining policy by a permanent set of rules. Contrary to Hayek's purpose, his policy position revealed the impacts of values other than freedom, historical circumstances, an awareness of the problems of market failure, and a reliance on comparisons of costs and benefits in policy making. These are elements of time and place, and judgements about merit, which elude efforts to confine policy to a set of rules for government.

Acknowledgement

I gratefully acknowledge the advice of Peter Groenewegen.

Note

1 The following abbreviations are used for the most commonly cited Hayek texts.

> *Hayek on Hayek*: HOH
> *Law, Legislation and Liberty*: LLL
> *The Constitution of Liberty*: CL
> *The Fatal Conceit*: FC
> *The Road to Serfdom*: RTS

References

Brittan, S. 1983. *The Role and Limits of Government: Essays in Political Economy.* Temple Smith, London.

Cockett, R. 1995. *Thinking the Unthinkable: Think-Tanks and the Economic Counter-Revolution, 1931–1983.* Fontana Press, London.

Gray, J. 1984. *Hayek on Liberty*. Basil Blackwell, Oxford.

Gray, J. 1989. Hayek on the Market Economy and the Limits of State Action, in D. Helm (ed.) 1989. *The Economic Borders of the State*. Oxford University Press, Oxford.

Hayek, F.A. 1933. *Monetary Theory and the Trade Cycle*. Augustus Kelley, New York.

——, 1935. *Prices and Production*. 2nd edition, Augustus Kelley, New York.

——, 1940. Socialist Calculation: The Competitive Solution, in Hayek, 1949.

——, 1944. *The Road to Serfdom*. Routledge, London.

——, 1945a. Individualism True and False, in Hayek, 1949.

——, 1945b. The Use of Knowledge in Society, in Hayek, 1949.

——, 1946. The Meaning of Competition, in Hayek, 1949.

——, 1947. Free Enterprise and Competitive Order, in Hayek, 1949.

——, 1949. *Individualism and Economic Order*. Routledge & Kegan Paul, London.

——, 1949. The Economics of Development Charges, in Hayek, 1967.

——, 1950. Full Employment, Planning and Inflation, in Hayek, 1967.

——, 1952. Harrod's Life of Keynes, in Hayek, 1967.

——, 1959. Unions, Inflation and Profits, in Hayek, 1967.

——, 1960. *The Constitution of Liberty*. Routledge, London.

——, 1960a. The Corporation in a Democratic Society, in Hayek, 1967.

——, 1962. The Moral Element of Free Enterprise, in Hayek, 1967.

——, 1963. The Economy, Science and Politics, in Hayek, 1967.

——, 1966. The Principles of a Liberal Social Order, in Hayek, 1967.

——, 1967. *Studies in Philosophy, Politics and Economics*. Routledge & Kegan Paul, London.

——, 1968. Competition as a Discovery Procedure, in Hayek, 1978.

——, 1972. The Campaign Against Keynesian Inflation, in Hayek, 1976.

——, 1976. *Law, Legislation and Liberty*. Routledge, London.

——, 1976a. Socialism and Science, in Hayek, 1978.

——, 1978. *New Studies in Philosophy, Politics, Economics and the History of Ideas*. Routledge & Kegan Paul, London.

——, 1988. *The Fatal Conceit: The Errors of Socialism*. Routledge, London.

——, 1991. *Economic Freedom*. Basil Blackwell, Oxford.

——, 1994. *Hayek on Hayek: An Autobiographical Dialogue*, edited by Kresge, S. and Wenar, L., Routledge, London.

Knight, F. 1967. Laissez Faire: Pro and Con. *Journal of Political Economy* 75:782–792, in Wood, J. C. and Woods, R. N. 1991. Vol 2.

Machlup, F. (ed.) 1977. *Essays on Hayek*. Routledge & Kegan Paul, London.

Viner, J. 1961. Hayek on Freedom and Coercion, in D. A. Irwin (ed.) 1991, *Jacob Viner: Essays on the Intellectual History of Economics*. Princeton University Press, New Jersey.

Wood, J. C. and Woods, R. N. (eds) 1991. *Friedrich A. Hayek: Critical Assessments*. Routledge, London.

48

HAYEK, KEYNES AND THE STATE

Jeremy Shearmur*

Source: *History of Economics Review* 26 (Winter–Summer 1997): 68–82.

1. Introduction

In this chapter, I discuss some aspects of the inter-relations between Hayek and Keynes, as a way of raising some questions about Hayek's ideas concerning the state. Hayek sent Keynes a copy of *The Road to Serfdom* (Hayek, 1944) on its publication. In the course of a letter to Hayek in response, Keynes raised a problem about how Hayek would demarcate between legitimate and illegitimate forms of state activity. In my view, Hayek had, in *The Road to Serfdom*, already implicitly furnished a fairly clear answer to this question. But it may have been an answer about which he became uneasy – not least, perhaps, because of the respects in which Keynes, himself, might seem to have embraced these very ideas, and the kind of interpretation which he gave to them.

Whatever, historically, may have motivated Hayek,[1] he subsequently – as I here document, from archival materials – returned to what looks very much like the question which Keynes had put to him. Hayek then develops a distinctive answer to that question; one which is by no means obviously the same as that which may be extracted from *The Road to Serfdom*. It is a view which sees the legitimate sphere of the activity of the state as being given by what is compatible with the rule of law, as interpreted in the *Rechtsstaat* tradition. (That is to say, of a tradition in which law is seen as universal in its form, government is seen as itself subject to the law, and in which the formal requirements which are imposed on the law are seen as endowing it with a content that echoes Kantian themes within moral philosophy (compare Hayek, 1955; Shearmur, 1996a).)

Now, the ideal of the rule of law (which I discuss later) is to be found in *The Road to Serfdom*; and Hayek there uses it as a critical weapon against central economic planning. What he does not do there is to consider how it applies to his own views. My argument, in this chapter, is that subsequent to Keynes' letter to him, he gives a central position to this ideal. Hayek suggests that it offers the basis upon which one can demarcate between legitimate and illegitimate forms of state activity. Clearly, however, if he takes this view, he needs to show that his own account of the legitimate activities of the state is, itself, compatible with this ideal. And this, indeed, is his concern in the sections of *The Constitution of Liberty* (Hayek, 1960) which deal with problems of governmental policy.

I suggest that this leads Hayek to an interpretation of liberalism which contrasts with that of Keynes. (I here argue against a strand of argument in the recent work of Andrew Gamble (Gamble, 1996), which suggests that their views were, in fact, closer than is often supposed.) However, I also tentatively question the adequacy of these views of Hayek's, to the concerns that he developed in *The Road to Serfdom*. (A full appraisal of this issue would require an assessment of Hayek's treatment of both the form and the scope of governmental activity in *The Constitution of Liberty*; a task which I cannot undertake here.)

If I am correct in this judgment about the adequacy of Hayek's views, this poses the problem: can forms of governmental activity which would *not* be compatible with Hayek's ideas about the rule of law be reconciled with his concern for individual liberty? I conclude the paper by suggesting that they can, referring briefly to some suggestions which I have discussed more fully elsewhere (Shearmur, 1996a).

2. Hayek and Keynes

Hayek was in disagreement with Keynes both about the theoretical approach that one should take to the understanding of trade cycles, and also with regard to the kinds of policy measures that were appropriate to the situation in which Britain found itself in the 1930s. However, he did not engage with Keynes, in response to Keynes' *General Theory* (Keynes, 1936). In his old age, Hayek was to return to the criticism of Keynes, both in respect of what he claimed to be the inflationary consequences of 'Keynesian' economics, and also because of the critical attitude towards traditionally accepted moral rules which he saw Keynes as having adopted, under the influence of G. E. Moore.

In his 'Introduction' to *Contra Keynes and Cambridge* (Hayek, 1995), Bruce Caldwell reviews in some detail the history of the interactions between Hayek and Keynes. In particular, he recounts the story of how, from the 1930s through into the period just after the Second World War, Hayek's programmatic approach within economics lost influence to that of Keynes. The collapse was dramatic. From Hayek's being a key figure within economics in England, especially in London, things changed such that, by the end of this period, virtually only Lachmann and Hayek remained proponents of Hayek's approach.[2] And even Hayek was soon to give up on technical work within economics in order to pursue issues in the field of social philosophy, methodology and the history of ideas.

Andrew Gamble has recently argued (Gamble, 1996, chap 7) that while Hayek depicted Keynes as a proponent of 'false' individualism, they were in fact both attached to the British tradition of liberalism; to Hayek's 'true' individualism. However, Gamble suggests, they took different views of what ailed it. Gamble writes (Gamble, 1996, p. 159): 'For Hayek, ... it is an inheritance which is in danger of being lost because of intellectual error; whereas for Keynes, it is a living reality which is in danger from ossi-fied forms of thought and stupidity, and can be preserved only through creative political action'. Gamble argues that they were also similar in their political elitism – although, on this, he suggests that Hayek was more of a democrat than was Keynes. I will return to the charge of elitism at the end of this chapter. My main concern here, however, is rather different; it relates to Keynes' reaction to Hayek's *Road to Serfdom*. To appreciate this, it might be useful to start by saying something about that book.

The Road to Serfdom is, in my view, best understood as having two, related, roots. On the one side, it comes out of Hayek's work on the prob-lems of economic calculation under socialism (see, notably, Hayek (1948)). This was of key significance in the development of Hayek's thought, in the sense that it was a source not only of some of his major ideas within eco-nomics (notably, his interest in the information-transmitting characteristics of prices, and his shift away from an economics that was centered upon general equilibrium theory (Caldwell, 1995; Shearmur, 1996a)), but also of his ideas on social theory. As I have argued elsewhere (Shearmur, 1996a) Hayek's view of society was of an extended market order, his conception of which was informed by his understanding of the economic calculation debate. That is to say, Hayek's view of the social order within which his (Western) readers are living, is of it as an extended market-based society, within which people practise the division of labour. Their actions, taken on the basis of knowledge which is, essentially, socially distributed, are coordinated by means of their acting on the basis of prices, within the ambit of the rule of law. Further, such a society is characterized by the fact that, within it, people cannot be – and do not need to be – conscious of the full ramifications of their actions. Indeed, on Hayek's account, prices supply to them a composite summary (based on what has happened in the immediate past) of other people's evaluations of their possible activities and uses of resources, disaggregated action on the basis of which attunes each individual to such evaluations.

On the other side, there is Hayek's interpretation of the character of Nazi Germany and, more generally, of totalitarianism. These, he argued, were the products of an attempt at central economic planning.[3] Not only, on this score, was Nazism not to be understood as the antithesis of communism,[4] but the respects in which the regimes of Hitler and of Stalin resembled one another were, in his view, to be explained by the fact that they each departed in a similar way, in their favored forms of economic organization, from the characteristics of a systematically market-based society.[5]

Hayek's *Road to Serfdom*, itself, seems to me best understood as offering an argument that a loss of freedom, and many of the unlovely features of regimes such as those of Hitler and of Stalin, will follow, as an unintended consequence, if the aims of economic planners are systematically pursued. It was not so much a prophecy that things will happen, as a warning that they will, *if* certain things are done.[6] On my understanding, Hayek's own view was that things which could have posed a serious threat to liberty did, indeed, subsequently occur in the United Kingdom, as a consequence of the regulations which were introduced to foster economic planning.[7]

It would, however, be a mistake to read *The Road to Serfdom* as consisting simply of such a warning. For, in it, Hayek also put forward some positive political ideas of his own: *The Road to Serfdom*, in effect, also sets out to offer a restatement of a vision of the liberalism that he favours. From the point of view of this chapter, it is significant to note that his account has two features. First, he stresses the importance, for a free society, of the rule of law. Second, he is not a proponent of laissez faire; rather he is concerned that governmental intervention in the economy shall take place in ways that do not threaten that market-based social order which, in his view, is of such importance for both the liberty and the well-being of citizens.

3. Keynes and *The Road to Serfdom*

Despite their disagreements over economic issues, Hayek had got to know Keynes personally, notably when the L.S.E. was in exile in Cambridge, and they seem to have had good personal and professional relations (Hayek, 1994, p. 91). It was, in consequence, no surprise that Hayek was to send Keynes a copy of *The Road to Serfdom*. In a well-known letter that Keynes sent to Hayek in response, he took what was in some ways a surprisingly positive attitude towards the book. But he also offered some criticism. The heart of his criticism – which Gamble broadly endorses in his book – is conveyed by the following.

Keynes had noted that, in this work, Hayek is critical of 'laissez faire'. But he commented to Hayek, in relation to what activities government should undertake (Keynes, 1980, pp. 386–7): 'You admit here and there that it is a question of knowing where to draw the line. You agree that the line has to be drawn somewhere, and that the logical extreme [i.e. laissez faire] is not possible. But you give us no guidance as to where to draw it.' Keynes then goes on to argue that: '. . . as soon as you [Hayek] admit that the extreme is not possible, and that a line has to be drawn, you are, on your own argument, done for, since you are trying to persuade us that as soon as one moves an inch in the planned direction you are necessarily launched on the slippery slope which will lead you in due course over the precipice.'

In my view, Keynes' criticism misses the mark, and rather badly. For it seems to me to misunderstand, in a significant way, the thrust of Hayek's argument. For Hayek is not, in *The Road to Serfdom*, arguing that *all* governmental activity in the economy represents steps on 'the road to serfdom'. Rather, what he is doing is to argue that there are dangers in some *forms* of governmental activity, and in effect, he sets out to tell us what it is, and what it is not, in order for the government to do.

The heart of Hayek's case is fairly simple. He wishes to argue, first of all, that the central direction of the economy – so-called 'economic planning' – is a disaster. It will not, Hayek argues, accomplish what its proponents want from it; and it will, indeed, if attempts are made to implement it, lead to the kinds of problem that he highlighted in his *Road to Serfdom*. He also wishes to argue, however, that if one has a market-based society, then there are some things which one cannot at the same time achieve; for example, outcomes of market-based economic relations that also fit some pattern of 'social justice'. And, he cautions us that if it is attempted to *make* the mechanisms of a market-based society deliver such outcomes, the result will be a gradual move to a centrally-planned society, and to serfdom.

All this, emphatically, does not mean that Hayek is a proponent of laissez faire. Indeed, Hayek has, in *The Road to Serfdom*, what could be described as a fairly full agenda for governmental action. In broad terms, he looks to the government to perform the following functions.

First, Hayek wishes that government should provide a framework within which economic activity and other forms of voluntary cooperation between people can take place. This is not a matter of simply accepting institutions as they are, but also of improving upon them; indeed, as Hayek says (Hayek, 1944, p. 17), of: 'deliberately creating a system in which competition will work as beneficially as possible'. He elaborates upon this point, when he says (Hayek, 1944, p. 36) that: 'in order that competition should work beneficially, a carefully thought-out legal framework is required ... [adding that] neither the existing nor the past legal rules are free from grave defects'. It is important, in this connection, to note that he refers not just to the initial setting-up of a framework of activity, but also to 'an intelligently designed and *continuously adjusted* legal framework' (italics mine) (Hayek, 1944, p. 39).

Second, he took the view that the government should provide various things which he thought important for the working of a market-based economy, but which he did not think that markets could themselves provide; what he referred to as the 'positive requirements of a successful working of the competitive system' (Hayek, 1944, p. 38). These, he explained, included the 'adequate organization of certain institutions like money, markets and channels of communication'; and also 'the prevention of fraud and deception (including exploitation of ignorance)' (Hayek, 1944, p. 39).

Third, there was what one might, more generally, call governmental action to address a list of market failures. Hayek offers examples, in this context, of such things as the provision of signposts and indeed of roads; of the need to address externalities created by deforestation and certain kinds of farming, and, in addition, problems – like those in modern towns – 'caused by close contiguity in space' (Hayek, 1944, p. 39 and, for the quotation, p. 48). He also considers as legitimate objects of state action such issues as the control of weights and measures, the need for building regulations and factory laws (although he clearly has misgivings about the wisdom of some specific examples of these), and in addition wishes the state to have a role in the spreading of knowledge and information, in order to assist mobility (Hayek, 1944, pp. 81 and 95). Further, where monopoly is inevitable, he favours state regulated private enterprise; that is to say, something like the American model (Hayek, 1944, p. 198).

Finally, Hayek favours welfare measures of various kinds. He discusses, in this context, such things as the provision or facilitation of sickness, accident and social insurance; of insurance for earthquakes and floods, and the taking of actions to handle the welfare consequences of fluctuations of economic activity and employment. As remedies for unemployment, he discusses as alternatives monetary policy and a program of public works; and, while he would clearly welcome it should the former prove sufficient, he does not rule out the need for the latter (Hayek, 1944, pp. 120–2). In the course of its discussion, however, he writes (Hayek, 1944, p. 122): in experiments in this direction [i.e. in tackling such problems by way of public works], we shall have carefully to watch our step if we are to avoid making all economic activity progressively more dependent on the direction and volume of governmental expenditure'.

At the same time, he explicitly states that such governmental activity does not amount to a form of planning which 'constitutes ... a threat to our freedom'. (Indeed, it is striking that, in his unpublished *Postscript to The Road to Serfdom* (1948), Hayek draws attention to the fact that he had made this point in his book, and explains that while he dissents from 'Keynesian' views, his reasons for doing so are not related to the main argument of the book. Indeed, he goes out of his way to stress that his own views, while differing from those of Keynes, would call for government to pursue an active monetary policy.[8]) Hayek also accepts what might seem to be quite vigorous forms of intervention, with an eye to handling problems of welfare, writing that: 'adequate security against severe privation, and the reduction of the avoidable causes of misdirected effort and consequent disappointment will have to be one of the main goals of policy' (Hayek, 1944, p. 132).

Now, if we consider all this material, it is clear that Hayek can, in no sense, be described as a proponent of laissez faire; indeed, it is in some ways surprising that he should have been taken, by his critics, to hold such views. It is understandable that his work was found upsetting by some, as the kind of planning of which he was critical was dear to the hearts of many people at the time. In respect of his argument against that, Hayek was, surely, correct. The problem about Hayek's argument, rather, was that he *might*, indeed, seem to have fallen into exactly the difficulty that Keynes had highlighted; namely, was he not arguing that governmental intervention led us onto the 'road to serfdom', while – as we have seen – himself being willing to advocate a fairly full program of just such action? I have already stated that I do not think that Keynes was, here, quite right. Let me now turn to explain why.

4. Hayek and the state in *The Road to Serfdom*

It seems to me that Hayek has a fairly simple response to Keynes' criticism available to him. It is that the entire thrust of his book was not against governmental action, but instead, that it explicitly addressed the issue of what government should and should not do. He argued, first, that there were some things that looked attractive to people of goodwill (for example, a planned economy), but which would prove a disaster, if attempts were made to implement them. Second, he argued that some other goals, if pursued directly by way of governmental intervention in the economy, would also lead to dire results. Third, there were some matters – such as, say, the regulation of working hours – which he argues to be problematic not in principle, but as a matter of degree.[9] Fourth, and more positively, his argument was that we should appreciate the role played by markets and other forms of spontaneous order, and both foster them, and make sure that we pursue our other goals in ways that are complementary to, rather than disruptive of, both them and, more generally, a market-based social order.

Indeed, there is a sense in which this final message of Hayek's might be seen as summed up in something that *Keynes* wrote to Hayek when he first received *The Road to Serfdom*. It was written prior to the well-known letter, to which I have earlier referred. Keynes wrote in an appendix to a letter which he wrote to Hayek on matters connected with *Economica*, of which Hayek was then the editor:[10]

I have still to thank you for kindly sending me 'The Road to Serfdom'. I only glanced at it at present, but am taking it away to read over Easter. It looks fascinating. It looks to me in the nature of medicine with which I shall disagree, but which may agree with me in the sense of doing me good. Something to be kept at the back of one's head rather than at the front of it. But it is just as serviceable a public act to get the right packings in the back of people's heads as the right impulse to action in the front of them.

What I had in mind, in commenting that this could be seen as summing up one lesson from Hayek's work, is that Keynes is here suggesting that a lesson to be learned from Hayek's work is – in large measure – one that those involved in the design and implementation of policy should internalize; namely, that they should not do things which would serve to damage a market-based social order. From this point of view, many of Keynes' further reactions, in his later and well-known letter, serve to elaborate much the same point. He clearly sees himself in a measure of disagreement with Hayek, in the sense that he thinks that more by way of planning can safely be done than Hayek would countenance. But he also says (Keynes, 1980, pp. 386–7): ' ... planning should take place in a community in which as many people as possible, both leaders and followers, wholly share your moral position. Moderate planning will be safe if those carrying it out are rightly oriented in their own minds and hearts to the moral issue'.

By this, however, Hayek was horrified. But on what grounds? In part, it is, clearly, that he did not agree with Keynes that 'moderate planning' was acceptable, if this meant the kinds of things against which he had argued. But there was another sense in which Hayek seems to have been alarmed; namely, by Keynes' stress upon what can reasonably be interpreted as discretionary activity on the part of an elite. (It is also possible that, reflecting on these issues, and, more generally, on the critical reception of *The Road to Serfdom*, Hayek is led to consider that his own approach, in *The Road to Serfdom*, has been problematic, in that he has criticized others on the grounds of the incompatibility between their favoured approach and the rule of law, but has not examined whether his own views would also pass such a test.) At any rate, from this point onwards Hayek places emphasis upon a strand of thought which is distinctive – and which may be contrasted with the approach which is to be found in his *Road to Serfdom*. It is a view which places greater and greater emphasis upon a particular interpretation of the idea of the rule of law and which, in the end, offers a response to Keynes' question about the demarcation between legitimate and illegitimate governmental activity in terms of the ideal of the rule of law. This approach is not quite the same as that which was set out in *The Road to Serfdom*; for there, as I have indicated, he implicitly offered a response to the problem that Keynes posed in terms of Hayek's own economic and social theories about the character of a market-based society. And it is by no means obvious that all the activities of government, to which Hayek referred there, could be accomplished in ways which are compatible with his understanding of the rule of law.

In *The Road to Serfdom*, and elsewhere, Hayek offers a distinctive account of liberalism. It is one in which stress is placed upon individual freedom and a market economy, where these are united with a particular account of the state. The liberal state is presented by Hayek as a *Rechtsstaat*, operating under the rule of law. This idea is set out already in *The Road to Serfdom*. For example, democracy is to be understood not just in terms of the pursuit of shared purposes, but also as operating under fixed rules (Hayek, 1944, p. 71): 'If democracy resolves on a task which necessarily involves the use of power which cannot be guided by fixed rules, it must become arbitrary power.' And he there elaborates on the way in which the idea of the rule of law (which is to be interpreted not in a purely formalistic sense, but in line with the Continental *Rechtsstaat* tradition; a point which is best clarified in his *Political Ideal of the Rule of Law* (Hayek, 1955)), is of significance because it allows for individual freedom, choice, and the use of socially divided knowledge (Hayek, 1944, pp. 75–6). The key issue, is that the individual can foresee the actions of the state in advance (Hayek, 1944, p. 81), and Hayek admits that this will have the consequence that the specific *effects* of state action will, then, be unpredictable (Hayek, 1944, p. 76).

However, while these ideas are set out in *The Road to Serfdom*, and while he uses them there as a stick with which to beat the proponents of economic planning, he does not, there, discuss how these ideas relate to his own views about governmental action. The latter, rather, could be taken – as Keynes was to interpret them – as suggestions addressed to an elite, as to how they should steer the ship of state.

His ideas about the rule of law come, with the passing of time, to play a particularly important role in Hayek's work. Already in a talk that Hayek gave about *The Road to Serfdom* in the United States, in 1945 (a transcription of which is held in the Hayek Archive at the Hoover Institution), he referred to the need for a clear set of principles to distinguish between the legitimate and illegitimate fields of governmental activities, and describes himself as having addressed that task, in his book.[11] At the same time, there is a note of ambivalence in Hayek's account, in that he also indicates that this is a task which is still to be undertaken.

I would take the task which is still to be undertaken as his showing that his own account of the legitimate role of state action is compatible with his ideas about the rule of law. It is important, in this context, to note that Hayek's account is still implicitly addressed to a decision-making elite. But he wishes to show that the policies which he wishes them to implement are compatible with the rule of law. For Hayek, compatibility with the rule of law is a necessary (but not sufficient) condition for policy to be in order:

he still, from time to time, refers to policies which would be permissible on this basis, but which he thinks would be unwise. At the same time, the ideal of the rule of law has, in his view, the dual characteristic of safe-guarding people's freedom of action (as argument for which he develops at length in *The Constitution of Liberty* (Hayek, 1960), and of being incompatible with a centrally planned economy.

This very task, I would like to conjecture, then becomes the agenda that Hayek addresses, in his writings on political issues during the late 1940s and 1950s. Indeed, if I am right, one could see all of this work of Hayek's as offering a response to the criticism that Keynes had made of his work, in the material quoted in section 3, above. A full argument to this effect would take more time – and underlying research – than it is possible for me to undertake in the present paper. But I would like to suggest that this view is plausible, on the basis of a limited amount of additional evidence from unpublished materials in the Hayek Archive.

My first port of call is the *Postscript to The Road to Serfdom* (1948), to which I have already had occasion to refer. In this connection, after briefly discussing his ideas about monetary policy, Hayek states that he attaches great importance to the idea that monetary policy should be guided by known rules, and he is sharply critical of a discretionary approach.[12] That is to say, he is indicating that his own favoured response to problems of trade cycles needs to be compatible with the rule of law.

Second, there is a paper of Hayek's, dated 1950, entitled 'The Meaning of Government Interference'.[13] In this, Hayek raises the question of what kind of governmental action is legitimate, and answers it in terms of the idea of equality before the law. He stresses again – as was done in *The Road to Serfdom* (and also in the unpublished 'Postscript') – that in saying this, he does not mean that all action that is on this basis permissible, will be wise. And he also goes out of his way to argue that if such a restriction is imposed, it may mean that we prevent government from doing things which we would judge to be good. The advantage, to Hayek, of the argu-ment that he is offering, is that it would seem to him to be incompatible with economic planning of the kind of which he is critical, and that it would be incompatible with the discretionary granting of licenses, permits, and allocations, and with price fixing, as well as with most forms of quotas and subsidies (unless the latter were offered to anyone who wished to undertake the activities in question). He again recognizes that some arrangements which would pass his test nevertheless might well be prob-lematic even if formally in order (e.g. if a legislature were to keep chang-ing the character of such restrictions, on a frequent basis), and he argues that rules should be kept stable, for extensive periods of time.[14]

Third, there is a paper, 'Planning and Competitive Order', which is not dated, but which I would judge to stem from much the same period.[15] Within it, Hayek poses directly the question of how to distinguish between

those kinds of governmental action which are compatible with a free economic system, and those which will lead to a planned economy, and
answers the question in terms of the rule of law. He mentions that this
may well only be an ideal that we can approach, rather than something
that can be fully realized. When discussing its characteristics, he writes of
government as laying down rules of behaviour, enforcing them, and also
being limited by them itself. The rules would apply equally to all people,
and they are also intended to remain the same, over long periods.

It is obvious enough how all this relates to Hayek's subsequent concern
with the development of the ideal of the rule of law in his *Political Ideal of
the Rule of Law* (Hayek, 1955), and, further, to his discussion of the rule of
law in *The Constitution of Liberty* (Hayek, 1960). What is worth spelling
out, is that the ideal of the rule of law turns out to play a remarkable role
in Hayek's work after *The Road to Serfdom*. For, at once, it serves two
functions. On the one side, it offers a clear-cut answer to Keynes, in that,
as Hayek's account develops, it is by reference to the ideal of the rule of
law (interpreted in the light of *Rechtsstaat* ideas), that he offers a demarcation between those kinds of governmental activity that are permissible
(although not necessarily wise), and those that are not. On the other, it
turns out also to be just what is required by Hayek's account of individual
liberty, too. For as he develops this in *The Constitution of Liberty*, it turns
out that freedom, for Hayek, is preserved, if people are faced with laws
which are universal in their form. Indeed, the reader might well think that
this is all too good to be true. I would share his suspicions.

First, while I am not in a position to undertake such an analysis in the
present paper, there would seem to be reason for suspicion as to whether
the agenda for governmental action as set out in *The Road to Serfdom* can,
in fact, be undertaken within the compass of the rule of law as set out in
Hayek's later writings. My reason for not addressing this issue here, is that
it would require a detailed analysis of Hayek's extensive proposals for how
policy issues are to be addressed in *The Constitution of Liberty*, and a comparison of the results with the ideas about governmental action, as set out
in *The Road to Serfdom*.[16]

My reason for suspicion is that, as I have suggested earlier, the agenda for
action that Hayek set out in *The Road to Serfdom* related to his economic
ideas about the character and functioning of a market-based economy, and
to what was compatible and what was incompatible with these. And while
there are, indeed, close relations between Hayek's economic and political
ideas – this is why his ideas are in some ways so interesting – there would
seem no reason to believe, *prima facie*, that there should be such a close link
that the ideas developed on the basis of his economic analysis should all turn
out to be compatible with his ideas about the rule of law.

Second, it seems to me that Hayek himself eventually came to have
some misgivings about the views about this synthesis that he set out in *The

Constitution of Liberty. With regard to liberty, Hayek, in *Law Legislation and Liberty* (Hayek, 1973–79), in effect accepted arguments that had been offered earlier by Hamowy (1961) and by Watkins (1961), that the formalism of his earlier approach to liberty was defective. While, under the impact of Leoni, and influenced by an 'evolutionary' line of thought which became more pronounced with the passing of time, Hayek seems (at least at times) to turn his back not just upon legislatures, but on the programme of the critical re-shaping of inherited institutions upon which he had earlier been so insistent in *The Road to Serfdom* (see, for discussion, Shearmur 1996a).

I will not, at this point, pursue Hayek any further into the ideas of his old age. Instead, I will turn back to Hayek and Keynes, and to some of the differences between their views of government.

5. Hayek, Keynes and 'governmentality'

In the course of his 'Governmental Rationality: An Introduction' (Gordon, 1991), which offers an introduction to Foucault's ideas about 'governmentality', Colin Gordon comments upon a distinction, which can be found within early liberalism, between the approaches of Adam Smith and of Sir James Steuart. Steuart, he comments (drawing on Hirschman, 1977), compares a modern economy to the mechanism of a watch which is upset if it is handled by other than the most delicate hand, but which, at the same time, stands in need of frequent corrective moves by an expert 'statesman'. Smith, by way of contrast, is depicted as concerned more with setting limits on governmental ineptitude. In the light of recent work by authors as otherwise diverse as Winch (1978) and Haakonssen (1981) which have stressed the roles played by politics and the 'statesman' in Smith, the distinction is perhaps overdrawn (although compare the final section of Shearmur, 1996c for some reservations). But if one thinks back to the approaches of Keynes and of Hayek, it would seem to me that there is something suggestive about it.

For, seen in this light, there is a real difference between the interpretations of liberalism offered by Keynes and by Hayek – at least, *after* Hayek's *Road to Serfdom*. They are both liberals, both in respect of values (although there are differences with respect to how they interpret these[17]), and also in terms of their espousal of a market-based form of social organization. Further, as Gamble has argued, Keynes can, on occasion, even be found voicing arguments drawn from Burke.[18] But there is, nevertheless, a significant difference between them. For Keynes, liberalism depends upon the discretionary intervention of an elite, armed with theoretical knowledge; while Hayek's vision of liberalism becomes one of individual action which can take place freely, under general laws by which the government itself is also bound. It is in the context of *his* interpretation of liberalism that, as I have already suggested, Keynes interprets the message of Hayek's *Road to Serfdom*; namely, as supplying an important warning, that should be kept in the back of their minds by the elite who are playing an activist role within a Keynesian liberalism.

But what of Hayek? As I have suggested, as Hayek's views develop over time, he places increasing stress upon the rule of law as giving a form within which governmental action should take place. Just as in Keynes, there is theoretically-informed intervention – both in the construction and the improvement of a constitutional and legal framework, and in policy measures within it. But formal limits are placed upon all this, which relate to Hayek's analysis of individual freedom. All this, however, seems to me to lead to two problems relating to his work.

The first is that, as we have seen, in *The Road to Serfdom*, Hayek allows government a fairly extensive agenda; further, his key concern there would seem to be simply that, when government is acting in order to do the kinds of things that he favours, it does not act so as to foul up the workings of a market-based social order which Hayek thinks so important for people's well-being and also for their liberty. The key problem, however, is whether government can, in fact, accomplish what Hayek wishes it to do in *The Road to Serfdom*, while limited to actions undertaken in accordance with the rule of law as he subsequently interprets it. As I have explained, I am not in a position to examine this issue in detail in the present paper. But it would seem to me that this is, in effect, the agenda of the discussion of policy issues in his *Constitution of Liberty*; although, as I have indicated, he changes his position yet again, in his subsequent writings. This work is impressive, but it would seem to me that in it – and with the passage of time – Hayek becomes less interventionist than he is in *The Road to Serfdom*.[19] And indeed, a key problem that faces someone attracted to the argument of *The Road to Serfdom* is: can government in fact accomplish what Hayek there wishes that it should do, if it is limited to acting on the basis of general rules? It is striking, in this context, to recall that Hayek in *The Road to Serfdom* referred to the way in which the effects of the actions of a state, limited to acting on the basis of general rules, would be unpredictable (Hayek, 1944, p. 76). But, at least on the face of it, some of the kinds of action to provide specific services, which he envisages the state as undertaking in that very book, would require its acting in ways that *can* be predicted, in detail.

Hayek's attachment to the rule of law would seem also to pose some more general problems for his approach. Hayek's work is distinctive among those who come to political thought from a background in economics, in treating people as acting on the basis of specific rules and habits, rather than for addressing the actions of 'rational economic man'. This leads him – as in 'Individualism: True and False' – into a kind of cultural conservatism. But clearly, insofar as what Hayek has dubbed 'false individualism' becomes influential – which is one of his worries – there is a problem. For one consequence of his approach, is that his view of liberalism seems to require people with particular characters, as its starting point. And if one is led to agree with Hobbes that: 'Man is not fitted for society by nature, but by discipline',[20] this poses a problem for a Hayekian approach as to whether government can have any legitimate role in the creation or even the maintenance of the characters needed for liberalism, on the part of those people who live within liberal regimes.

The second problem relates to the connection between Hayek's argument and the actual processes of action on the part of the state. *What* government should do, for Hayek, needs to be informed by *his theories*. What Hayek offers in *The Road to Serfdom* is an argument about the character of a desirable social order. It is theoretical in its character, and it is, as it were, pitched to a benevolent despot who would be moved to action by truths about what is in the public interest, and who is, in effect, assumed to act upon the truths that are to be found, relating to such matters. This leads to three difficulties. First, as I have already argued, it is not clear why these specific requirements should necessarily be compatible with the requirments of the rule of law. The second of these, to which I have also already referred, was pressed upon Hayek by Leoni (Shearmur, 1996a), and could subsequently be reinforced by considerations drawn from public choice theory. It is that it is not clear that government, when seen as consisting of real-life legislatures, to say nothing of the impact upon them of various interacting bodies of people with specific, and sometimes highly self-interested, motivation, can be depended upon to act as Hayek would have it do. There is a sense in which a philosopher-king, or a benevolent despot, might at least be able to listen to, and to appreciate, Hayek's argument; whereas it is not clear how it can even be addressed to the diverse figures involved in the actual policy-making process within liberal democracies. (We must here bear in mind that it is also the actual political process that would be responsible for the legislation that Hayek commends to us when, in his work, he discusses the ideal of the rule of law.)

Third, Hayek himself, in his later writings, responds to these very problems about the political process by suggesting a revision of our political institutions and, in the end, by proposing that there should be a division between an upper and a lower chamber, both elected, but one imposing rules under which the other operates (Hayek, 1973–79, volume 3). While some of the details of Hayek's account are a little strange, and while one may have some doubts about the practicability of any such arrangements, the overall thrust is clear enough. For it offers us a model in which the rules under which government in the more regular sense operates, are set by a democratic body which stands outside of the political process, as ordinarily conceived, and which lays down general rules with which the conduct of government must then comply. (One has here, as in some other ways – not least their legal formalism and its supposed link with freedom – an interesting parallel between Hayek and the Rousseau of the *Social Contract*.) One key problem about Hayek's approach, however, would seem to be that there is no reason why the general rules to which an elected body would agree, would be informed by the theoretical ideas of Hayek's liberalism.

Indeed, to sum all this up, there seems room for scepticism about the way in which Hayek's ideas developed after *The Road to Serfdom*. For while it is understandable that he found attractive a view which seemed to resolve the problem of the agenda and non-agenda of governmental action, and the problem of individual freedom, in one single move relating to the ideal of the rule of law as set out in the *Rechtsstaat* tradition, it is not clear that such a government could in fact accomplish what Hayek himself would require of it.

What, then, is to be done? The first issue that needs to be addressed, is the charge of 'elitism' that was leveled against both Keynes and Hayek by Gamble. In this connection, Gamble quotes Keynes as follows (Gamble, 1996, p. 157, quoting Keynes, 1972, p. 295):

> I believe that in the future, more than ever, questions about the economic framework of society will be far and away the most important of political issues. I believe that the right solution will involve intellectual and scientific elements which must be above the heads of the vast mass of more or less illiterate voters.

Now, Keynes here puts things bluntly; and it is surely possible to modify his views, in the light of a recognition of the fallibility of human knowledge, by saying that, in principle, the judgments of experts should be open to criticism by anyone (compare Shearmur, 1996b). But be this as it may, both Keynes and Hayek offer arguments to the effect that there are considerations which pertain to those arrangements which will best secure human well-being and freedom, which cannot, realistically, be made transparent to the understanding of all citizens. It is not enough merely to deplore their elitism, as does Gamble; rather, in order to criticize them, one needs to meet their argument. I am sceptical as to whether this could be done.

What conclusion should, then, be drawn from the argument of this chapter? Is it that, in the end, it was Keynes rather than Hayek who was right, and that when Gamble indicates that Hayek was more of a democrat than was Keynes, it was Keynes who got the better of the argument? To this I wish to respond, although my personal interest is not so much in democracy as in individual liberty. I think that ideas about the significance of criticism in a public forum, and the discursive redeemability of our factual, normative and aesthetic claims are important. I also think that there are advantages to being able to get rid of governments by votes rather than by force, and that insofar as we have to make collective decisions, it is best done by voting. But, personally, my preference is for forms of social and political order which limit to the greatest possible extent the need for collective decisions (for example, by restricting these to minimal) 'rules of the game', thus allowing people, within them, to make what choices they wish). Such ideals, however, would seem also to be hit by Keynes' argument. How is the libertarian to respond to the argument that, without Keynes and his ilk ruling over them, or Hayek and his ilk, they cannot enjoy the benefits of a liberal social order?

In my view, there is no necessary incompatibility between liberty, and the rule of an elite (subject, say, to 'Popperian' critical constraints). There is, further, no necessary incompatibility between liberty and discretionary governmental action, or, even, with government's shaping our characters by means of various disciplines, so as to produce the kind of order within which we wish to live. For such 'government' may, itself, be a matter of *individual choice*, in the sense that it may be seen as the product not of majority voting, or of the interplay of interest groups within a pluralistic regime, but, instead, as something the character of which we can *each* choose, on a voluntary basis.

Indeed, as I have argued in my *Hayek and After*, I think that Hayek's ideas about an interventionist government within a *Rechtsstaat* – to say nothing of his later ideas about new constitutional arrangements – were not, in the end, a fruitful way of developing his insights. Rather, not only may 'Keynesian' – in the sense of elitist and discretionary, rather than of his specific economic theories – elements with regard to the activities of government well be required if liberal regimes are to flourish, but regimes allowing for the use of these, or a regime dependent on at times abstruse theoretical ideas (as would be Hayek's), can only be combined with individual liberty if their activities are seen not as those of government in the regular sense, but as those of something the membership of which an individual can choose from within a *minimalist* governmental structure. All told, it thus seems to me that the problem of the state opened up by Hayek's work, and by Keynes' comments upon it, is best answered by ideas similar to those to be found in the 'utopia' section of Robert Nozick's *Anarchy, State and Utopia* (Nozick, 1974). It is a minimal state – but one which offers the possibility of voluntary choices, within it, for something more substantive, including, if people find the prospect attractive, rule by a Keynesian or a Hayekian elite – which seems to me to offer the best prospects for the flourishing of a Hayekian liberalism.

Notes

* I would like to thank the Social Philosophy and Policy Center at Bowling Green State University for the academic hospitality and support which enabled me to write this chapter; the Australian National University for its award of a Faculties Research Fund grant in 1995, which enabled me to consult the Hayek Archive at the Hoover Institution, and in that connection to locate unpublished Hayek materials upon which I draw in this chapter, and James Taylor and especially Bruce Caldwell, for their comments on an earlier version of the paper.

1 Although I should stress that as I have no specific evidence that Hayek was motivated, in what I suggest to be these changes in his views, by a wish specifically to respond to Keynes' letter, I would not wish to claim that I can show that it played a causal role in the development of Hayek's thought. At the same time, it does seem to me that these changes do offer a specific answer to the question that was put by Keynes to Hayek, as distinct, for example, from requests that were put to him by others to say more about his own more positive views. (Bruce Caldwell, whose queries have prompted me to spell this out, refers in the latter connection to a review by H. D. Dickinson of (Hayek, 1939).)

2 It is, though, striking that Durbin, while a socialist, continued to work within a Hayekian research program in respect of his ideas on the theory of capital and the trade cycle.

3 There are two unpublished essays in the Hayek Archive at the Hoover Institution on the theme of the character of Nazi Germany. Hayek also tells us that he wrote a memo on this general theme for Beveridge, the Director of the L.S.E. (see 'The Economics of the 1930s as seen from London', in Hayek (1995), p. 62). Hayek then published an article (Hayek, 1938), which was subsequently expanded into a pamphlet (Hayek, 1939), and which was, in turn, expanded as (Hayek, 1945).

4 Hayek comments on the contrast between his view of National Socialism and that of some of his colleagues at the L.S.E. in the following terms. 'They ... tended to interpret the National Socialist regime of Hitler as a sort of capitalist reaction to the socialist tendencies of the immediate post-war period, while I saw it rather as the victory of a sort of lower-middle-class socialism...'. See 'The Economics of the 1930s as seen from London' in (Hayek, 1995), p. 62.

5 This would not be the appropriate place to discuss the merits of Hayek's ideas on this score; but whatever the pros and cons of his approach, he was at least attempting what would be required of a *theory* of totalitarianism; namely, trying to *explain* why regimes which, prima facie, would seem to be the antithesis of one another nevertheless had certain key characteristics in common. It seems to me a mark of the quality of much work on this theme within political science, that approaches like that of Hayek were ignored, while, instead, people seemed satisfied with putting forward what amounted to little more than classificatory schemas and *lists* of features that the different regimes were supposed to have in common – as if these constinuted an explanatory theory.

6 On the distinction, compare Karl Popper's 'Prediction and Prophecy in the Social Sciences', in (Popper, 1963).

7 See, on this, his 'Foreword' to the republication of the American edition of *The Road to Serfdom* (Hayek, 1956), also published as 'The Road to Serfdom *after Twelve Years*', in (Hayek, 1967). Compare also Hayek to Durbin 17/2/48 (Durbin 3/10, L.S.E. archives) in which Hayek comments that what has taken place in the last three years has exceeded his worst apprehensions, and, for his

most detailed argument the first section of his (incomplete) 'Postscript to The Road to Serfdom (1948)' in the Hayek Archive in the Hoover Institution Archive. (Box 93, accession number 86002-8M.40; the material is included in the brown folder inscribed 'Road to Serfdom'. N.B. this is among the Hayek material that has not yet been processed, and so does not have a regular Hoover Archive identification.) Hayek drew on some of the material from this projected Postscript, in writing his foreword to the (new) American edition.

8   See Hayek. 'Postscript to The Road to Serfdom (1948)', pp. 11–12. In response to a query from Bruce Caldwell, I should stress that the word 'active' in the text is mine; but I would wish to suggest that it is justified by Hayek's argument, which is that the existing monetary and credit mechanism contains disequilibrating forces which ought, Hayek suggests, to be counteracted by a sensible monetary policy. We will note later that Hayek in this Postscript also emphasises that he wants this policy to be guided by known rules.

9   See, for a particularly clear statement of this, the transcription of a radio discussion of *The Road to Serfdom*, in (Hayek, 1994, p. 112).

10 Archives, British Library of Economic and Political Science, Misc. 600. Keynes to Hayek, April 4, 1944. N. B. Unpublished writings of J. M. Keynes copyright The Provost and Scholars of King's College, Cambridge, 1997.

11 See 'The Road to Serfdom', Address Before the Economic Club of Detroit, April 23, 1945. Hayek Archives, Hoover Institution, Box 94, [folder 38]; see pp. 6–7. (This is among the material that has not yet been processed and so does have not a standardized archive location.) The paper is a transcript of Hayek's talk taken by a shorthand reporter.

12 'Postscript to The Road to Serfdom (1948)', pp. 12–13.

13 Hayek Archive, Hoover Institution, Box 94, folder 46. (Again, this is among the 'not yet processed' material in the Archive.)

14 Those interested in the development of Hayek's work might note that this suggests that Hayek was at this early stage already open to the argument that Leoni was later to press against his preference for legislation (i.e. that the problem with legislatures was that they as a matter of fact could not be depended upon to leave such things alone and thus to provide stability); a development which in turn led to the change of Hayek's legal views in *Law, Legislation and Liberty* (Hayek, 1973–79). (See for discussion of the impact of Leoni (Shearmur, 1996a).)

15 'Planning and Competitive Order', Hayek Archive, Hoover Institution, Box 108; the folder in which this is held is labeled 'Planning and Competitive Order'; it is again among the unprocessed material. In the first section of the lecture, Hayek explains that this was the first of three lectures, the second of which dealt with why in a planned economy the rule of law could not be preserved, while the third lecture would be concerned with the planning of a legal order such that, within it, the free decisions of individuals would contribute as much as possible to the welfare of the society as a whole. (At the same time, the second and third sections of the paper themselves deal briefly with the topics announced for the other lectures, so it is difficult, without more information than is currently available to me, to judge whether we may not, here, have some version of the text of all three lectures.)

16 At the same time, it seems to me important that one identifies what Hayek's problematic actually was; something concerning which one needs to note changes over time. The dangers of not doing so are, I believe, illustrated by Kley's recent *Hayek's Social and Political Thought* (Kley, 1994). This, while discussing Hayek's ideas in some detail, seems to me to misunderstand what

Hayek was attempting to do, because it tries to relate his ideas about government to general notions about spentaneous order, rather than to the specific agenda which he was setting himself, and its transformations over time of the kind which I have discussed here.

17 On this, Hayek, in his 'Individualism: True and False', in his *Individualism and Economic Order* (Hayek, 1948), and in his 'Three Sources of Human Values' (available, for example, as the Appendix to volume three of (Hayek, 1973–79)), would seem to me to protest too much, in that the role of traditional morality, for him, is functional rather than something of intrinsic significance. It is not clear that his view that we should take an uncritical attitude towards it is adequate, given that it also contains elements which, as Hayek elsewhere admits, are hostile to a liberal market order.

18 (Gamble, 1996, p. 159.) Gamble's case is perhaps weakened by the fact that the material that he quotes is an argument for a focus on the short run.

19 Bruce Caldwell has drawn my attention to the fact that Hayek himself, in his 1976 Preface to a new edition of *The Road to Serfdom*, says that when he wrote the original book, he 'had not wholly freed [himself] from all the [then] current interventionist superstitions, and in consequence made concessions that [he] now think[s] unwarranted' (Hayek, 1976, p. xxi).

20 Thomas Hobbes, *De Cive*, 1.1; quoted by Gordon (1991), p. 14.

References

Caldwell, Bruce. 'Introduction' to (Hayek, 1995), pp. 1–48.

Gamble, Andrew. *Hayek: The Iron Cage of Liberty*, Cambridge: Polity, 1996.

Gordon, Colin. 'Governmental Rationality: An Introduction', in Graham Burchell and others (eds) *The Foucault Effect*, Chicago: University of Chicago Press, 1991.

Haakonssen, Knud. *The Art of the Legislator*, Cambridge: Cambridge University Press, 1981.

Hamowy, Ronald. 'Hayek's Concept of Freedom: A Critique', *New Individualist Review*, 1, 1961, pp. 28–31.

Hayek, Friedrich, A. 'Freedom and the Economic System', *Contemporary Review*, April 1938.

Hayek, Friedrich, A. *Freedom and the Economic System*, Chicago: University of Chicago Press, 1939.

Hayek, Friedrich, A. *The Road to Serfdom*, Chicago: University of Chicago Press, 1944.

Hayek, Friedrich, A. *Individualism and Economic Order*, Chicago: University of Chicago Press, 1948.

Hayek, Friedrich, A. *The Political Ideal of the Rule of Law*, Cairo: National Bank of Cairo, 1955.

Hayek, Friedrich, A. *The Road to Serfdom* (American paperback edition), Chicago: University of Chicago Press, 1956.

Hayek, Friedrich, A. *The Constitution of Liberty*, Chicago: University of Chicago Press, 1960.

Hayek, Friedrich, A. *Studies in Philosophy, Politics and Economics*, Chicago: University of Chicago Press, 1963.

Hayek, Friedrich, A. *Law, Legislation and Liberty*, Chicago: University of Chicago Press. 1973–9.

Hayek, Friedrich, A. *The Road to Serfdom* (with new Preface, 1976), Chicago: University of Chicago Press, 1976.

Hayek, Friedrich, A. *Hayek on Hayek*, ed. Stephen Kresge and Leif Wenar, Chicago: University of Chicago Press, 1994.

Hayek, Friedrich, A. *Contra Keynes and Cambridge, Collected Works volume 9*, ed. Bruce Caldwell, London, Routledge; Chicago: University of Chicago Press, 1995.

Hirschman, Albert, O. *The Passions and the Interests*, Princeton: Princeton University Press, 1977.

Keynes, John, M. *The general theory of employment, interest and money*, New York: Harcourt, Brace, 1936.

Keynes, John, M. *Essays in Persuasion: Collected Writings volume 9*, London: Macmillan, 1972.

Keynes, John, M. *Activities 1940–46: Collected Writings volume 27*, ed. D. Moggridge, London: Macmillan, 1980.

Kley, Roland. *Hayek's Social and Political Thought*, Oxford: Clarendon Press, 1994.

Nozick, Robert. *Anarchy, State and Utopia*, New York: Basic Books, 1974.

Popper, Karl. *Conjectures and Refutations*, London: Routledge, 1963.

Shearmur, Jeremy. *Hayek and After*, London & New York: Routledge, 1996(a).

Shearmur, Jeremy. *The Political Thought of Karl Popper*, London & New York: Routledge, 1996(b).

Shearmur, Jeremy. 'From Divine Corporation to a System of Justice', in P. Groenewegen (ed.) *Economics and Ethics*, London & New York: Routledge, 1996(c).

Watkins, J. W. N. 'Philosophy', in A. Seldon (ed.) *Agenda for a Free Society*, London: Hutchinson, 1961.

Winch, Donald. *Adam Smith's Politics*, Cambridge: Cambridge University Press, 1978.

49

THE VARIETIES OF SUBJECTIVISM

Keynes and Hayek on expectations

William N. Butos and Roger G. Koppl

Source: *History of Political Economy* 29(2) (1997): 327–359.

1. Introduction

The relationship between J. M. Keynes and Friedrich Hayek, as John Hicks (1967, chap. 12) notes, is curious. Despite profound differences in their positions on policy questions, Keynes and Hayek held similar views on important matters in other areas. It is widely, though not universally, accepted in modern Austrian and post-Keynesian circles that Keynes and Hayek both embraced subjectivism (see Boehm 1989). Their theories of the business cycle (at least of the early Keynes) built on Wicksellian foundations and their analyses of the downswing had certain features in common (see O'Driscoll 1977, Mason 1996, 154–56). On these grounds a kind of synthesis between Keynes and Hayek might appear both plausible and desirable.[1]

Notwithstanding areas of commonality, the fact remains that serious tension, perhaps antagonism, characterized Keynes's and Hayek's professional relationship.[2] Moreover, many players on the sidelines during the 1930s felt the need to choose between their theories, a choice many of their present-day followers find necessary to make as well.

We believe the attempt to integrate the subjectivist ideas of Keynes and Hayek entails difficulties not widely recognized. These difficulties help to explain why Keynes and Hayek were rivals on more than just policy in the 1930s. The difficulties concern the differences in the philosophical groundings each thinker presumed in his economics. In this chapter we argue that the philosophical bases of their economic ideas are fundamentally opposed and that these different groundings contribute to their different views of the market process. Any attempt to integrate the ideas of Keynes and Hayek must somehow engage these strong philosophical differences.

Those who would place Ludwig Lachmann and G. L. S. Shackle at the center of the neo-Austrian movement should recognize that the subjectivisms of Keynes and Hayek are distinct species within a genus.

This chapter may also serve as a reminder that the undercurrents connecting and distancing the great thinkers of economics are typically complex and subtle. Although we make no claim that our discussion captures all the relevant ways Keynes and Hayek might be linked, we do hold that the differences in their philosophical views are germane to understanding their differences in economics. We will not try to show that the philosophical vision of either thinker logically implies his market theory. We will argue, however, that the respective philosophical positions of Keynes and Hayek conduce toward their market theories. Because we wish to establish and contrast the connections between each thinker's philosophy and economics, we will neglect other reasons for differences in their market theories.

The purpose of this chapter, then, is to identify and explain the main differences between the subjectivisms of Keynes and Hayek. In section 2 we compare the underlying philosophical notions of the two by examining Keynes's epistemology and Hayek's theory of mind. In section 3 we discuss how these different starting points contribute to divergent views of the market process. Finally, in section 4 we appraise the two theories and draw out the perhaps surprising implication that it was Hayek who pointed the way to a more general theory of the market process. Hayek's theory, not Keynes's, allows us to say when markets will behave in the way Keynes described and when they will instead behave in more coordinated ways. We claim, in short, that a Hayekian theory is needed to understand a Keynesian world.

2. Keynes and Hayek: philosophical ideas

2.1. Keynes's rationalist epistemology[3]

Keynes's appeal to "animal spirits" and his judgment that long-term expectations are unconnected to underlying economic realities reflect his epistemology. We will show below (section 3.1.2) how Keynes relates his ideas about expectations to his theory of probability. First, though, we need to discuss Keynes's epistemology.

The standard definition of knowledge is, as Skidelsky notes, "justified true belief" (1992, 83), a view Keynes follows in *A Treatise on Probability* (CW 1973b, 10–11). Keynes principally took a rationalist approach to justification. He distinguished two types of knowledge, "direct knowledge" and "indirect knowledge" (12). Indirect knowledge of propositions is gotten by "argument" from direct knowledge and indirect knowledge previously acquired. Direct knowledge of propositions—the "objects of knowledge and belief" (12)—is obtained from "direct acquaintance" with things. Direct acquaintance is of three kinds: (1) direct acquaintance with one's own "sensations" is "experience," (2) direct acquaintance with "ideas or meanings" is "understanding," and (3) direct acquaintance with the features of meanings and sense-data and with the relations among them—including the principles of logic—is "perception."

To "argue" is to "pass to knowledge about one proposition by the contemplation of it in relation to another proposition of which [one has] knowledge—even when the process is unanalysable" (CW 1973b, 13–14). Notice that "argument" has nothing to do with rhetoric or discourse. It is a private monologue, not a public dialogue.[4] Keynes is willing to accept indirect knowledge that is gotten by "arguing" or "passing" from prior knowledge even when the passageway (that is, the principles of logic by which the passing gets done) is unknown. Thus he allows intuition to play a role in our reasoning that Rene Descartes's principle of clear and distinct ideas forbids. In this particular regard, Keynes is not a Cartesian. According to Keynes, however, you can start with the objects of direct acquaintance. From them you will attain a justified and certain belief in many true propositions. Now pass by "argument" from these "propositions" to others not known directly. From this expanded set of propositions that are true, certain, and justified beliefs of yours, pass by further "argument" to others still. Keep at it long enough and you will fill volumes with genuine knowledge.

Keynes's treatment of the fundamentals of epistemology is a variety of rationalism. Hayek (1978, 288) suggests that Keynes shared "the peculiar brand of rationalism which dominated [his] generation." R. M. O'Donnell (1989) argues that Keynes's phrase "Cambridge rationalist" fits Keynes himself (81), that "Keynes's philosophy is a form of foundationalism or justificationalism" (93), and that his "epistemology remained essentially constant throughout his life" (209). His rationalism consisted, O'Donnell argues, principally in granting to intuition a central role in transforming experience into knowledge (93). O'Donnell observes that "while agreeing with empiricism that experience is a precondition of knowledge, [Keynes's epistemology] passed beyond it in maintaining that much knowledge is impossible without a priori reasoning or intuition" (93).

A. M. Carabelli (1988) argues that Keynes's *Treatise on Probability* was "a sort of anti-*Discours de le méthode*" because of its emphasis on intuition and uncertainty (149). We do not agree with Carabelli,[5] however, that Keynes stood at any great "distance from the rationalist faith." On the contrary, as O'Donnell (1989, 149) shows, despite its various qualifications and hedges, Keynes's "My Early Beliefs" is a reaffirmation of his early rationalism. That his theory of probability should emphasize intuition does not weaken, but strengthens, the claim that Keynes was a rationalist. That it emphasized uncertainty is hardly surprising. All theories of probability, by definition, emphasize uncertainty.[6]

The rationalism to which Keynes swore allegiance was essentially the "constructivist" or "Cartesian" rationalism at whose feet Hayek has laid the blame for the sins of modernism. Hayek has cited Keynes as exemplar of the "constructivist" rationalism he rejects in favor of "critical" rationalism (1967, 89–90). Keynes accepted the essential tenets of constructivism or Cartesianism, as Hayek describes them. The "dominant characteristic" of the constructivist "movement" started by Descartes was, Hayek argues, the "rejection as 'mere opinion' of all that could not be demonstrated to be true" by reason. According to Hayek, constructivism requires that such demonstrated truths had to be "logically derived from explicit premises that were 'clear and distinct,' and therefore beyond possible doubt" (1973, 10). What, in this description, needs to be "clear and distinct" are the *premises* from which reason works. In this regard, Keynes was a good Cartesian despite his willingness to "argue" by principles intuited but unknown. Keynes's reasoning begins, as O'Donnell notes, with "intuitions (or direct knowledge) [that] eliminate infinite regresses through providing putatively true knowledge incapable of further proof" (1989, 93).

In "My Early Beliefs," Keynes describes the comical results that a cleavage to this epistemology produced in his circle of friends and colleagues at Cambridge during the years before World War I. Knowledge of the good, said Keynes, "was a matter of direct inspection, of direct unanalysable intuition about which it was useless and impossible to argue" (CW 1972, 437). Such a doctrine disinclines one to dialogue. If two seemingly reasonable persons should disagree, an explanation of the disagreement was needed. Two official explanations were generally recognized in Keynes's circle. First, the disputants, perhaps, "were not really talking about the same thing" and if their intuitions were trained on different objects, howsoever similar the objects might be, then "by virtue of the principle of organic unity, a very small difference in the object might make a very big difference in the result" (437).

The second explanation appealed to differences in discernment. After all, Keynes maintained, "just as some people can judge a vintage port and others cannot" so too "some people had an acuter sense of judgment" in intellectual matters (CW 1972, 437). These were the official explanations. However, "in practice, victory was with those who could speak with the greatest appearance of clear, undoubting conviction and could best use the accents of infallibility" (437–38). And the master, Keynes reports, was G. E. Moore, who would answer you "with a gasp of incredulity" and ask "*Do* you *really* think *that*" with an expression that "reduced him to a state of wonder verging on imbecility, with his mouth wide open and wagging his head in the negative so violently that his hair shook. *Oh!* he would say, goggling at you as if either you or he must be mad; and no reply was possible" (438). Keynes and his colleagues regarded "all this as entirely rational and scientific in character" because it was "nothing more than the application of logic and rational analysis to the material presented as sense-data" (CW 1972, 438–39). They thought one's "apprehension of good" to be "exactly the same" as one's "apprehension of green" and they "purported" to use "the same logical and analytical technique" in both cases. "Indeed," Keynes relates, "we combined a dogmatic treatment as to the nature of experience with a method of handling it that was extravagantly scholastic. Russell's *Principles of Mathematics* came out in the same year as *Principia Ethica*; and the former, in spirit, furnished a method for handling the material of the latter" (438–39). Keynes's justificationism was not an empty reflection of the reigning Official Methodology, but a daily fact of social life.

Keynes's rationalism led him to reject tradition. In "My Early Beliefs," Keynes reports that in his youth he and his friends "entirely repudiated a personal liability on us to obey general rules. . . . We were, that is to say, in the strict sense of the term, immoralists" (CW 1972, 446). When Keynes claimed the right to judge each case on its merits, he also claimed the power to do so. "Ought" implies "can." His was the rationalist view of knowledge as justified true belief emergent from the sort of "argument" that one can carry out like Descartes in his "closet," that is, alone and isolated from the inhibitory force of common opinion. And it was this view of knowledge that made the binding force of externally imposed rules seem irrational and objectionable to him.

2.2. Hayek's theory of mind[7]

Keynes's was a rationalist. As we shall argue below, his theory of long-term expectation, based on that rationalism, claims that there can be little correspondence between expectations and economic events. Hayek, as we shall see, took quite the opposite approach. In Hayek's theory, economic expectations have a coherence not possible within Keynes's system. This coherence of economic expectations is largely a reflection of his deeper philosophical views regarding epistemology and the philosophy of mind. Hayek rejected rationalism in favor of an evolutionary epistemology according to which "man is as much a rule-following animal as a purpose-seeking one" (1973, 11).

That fundamental uncertainty requires a Keynes-like theory of expectations hinges on the particular conception of subjectivism employed. Keynes's approach to economic expectation represents just one variety of subjectivism within the panorama of available subjectivist theory. We find in Hayek a kind of subjectivism that entails no mass psychology guiding individual behavior and implies no systematic discoordination of economic activity.[8]

Knowledge for Hayek is not justified true belief and it is not obtained from "immediate experience or observation, but in the continuous process of sifting a learnt tradition" (1988, 75). An evolutionary selection process, working on "irrational, or, rather, 'unjustified' beliefs" induces in us habits and routines that embody more information than we can know. "The process of selection that shaped customs and morality could take account of more factual circumstances than individuals could perceive, and in consequence tradition is in some respects superior to, or 'wiser' than, human reason" (1988, 75). Hayek begins from a different starting point than Keynes and ends up with a different conclusion.

Hayek's view of knowledge as practice is quite different from what is perhaps the more standard view of knowledge as justified true belief.[9] But it is not without precedents. Hayek quotes John Locke favorably in this connection as one who defined "reason" as "certain definite principles of action from which spring all virtues and whatever is necessary for the proper moulding of morals" (Locke, as cited in Hayek 1967, 107, n. 2). Karl Popper, to whom Hayek dedicated *Studies in Philosophy, Politics, and Economics*, criticized the "bucket theory of mind" as falsely equating knowledge with belief states (Popper 1979, 60–63). Hayek cites Popper as a seminal figure in the "critical rationalist" school with which he identified himself (Hayek 1967, 94).

For Hayek, knowledge is practice; it is "knowing how" rather than "knowledge that" (Ryle 1949). Knowledge is a set of dispositions to act or not act in certain kinds of ways given various contingencies. According to Hayek in "The Primacy of the Abstract" (1978), the mind's interpretation of "sensations and perceptions are these dispositions which they evoke" so that "all the 'knowledge' of the external world which such an organism possesses consists in the action patterns which the stimuli tend to evoke" (40, 41). Because, as we will discuss below, Hayek conceives of cognition as rule-governed classification, "what we call knowledge is primarily a system of rules of action" (41). Moreover, because Hayek does not equate the mental realm with consciousness, these rules, especially in the higher cognitive functions, will be tacit and function in ways that cannot always be made explicit (Hayek 1952, chap. 6).[10] For Hayek "all sensory experience, perceptions, images, concepts, etc., derive their particular qualitative properties from the rules of action which they put into operation" (42).

It is important that Hayek sees knowledge as a structure of rules embodied in social practice. Knowledge is thus more habit than belief. Some habits have evolved biologically and are common to the species. Others have evolved socially and may vary from one group to another. Finally, some are idiosyncratic products of an individual's personal history. In any event, in Hayek's system, all knowledge is a fallible interpretation of experience, an interpretation manifested in one's habits of action. For most of us, it is probably more natural to think of knowledge as a belief state than as a way of acting. Hayek, however, claims that "what we call [man's] understanding is in the last resort simply his capacity to respond to his environment with a pattern of actions that helps him to persist" (1973, 18).

Hayek's defense of this claim is based partially on a factual proposition, namely, that design and precognition have played only a small role in the creation of social order. Social order results primarily from individuals obeying rules of conduct. These rules were not at first designed nor even consciously known. The order-giving rules of social life were not the product of reason, for language and the capacity to reason that followed its appearance are themselves products of such rule-generated order (1973, 8–21). Thus, the knowledge that made society possible in the first place consisted in rule following, not belief states. Hayek's theory of mind gave him other reasons to equate knowledge with a set of dispositions to act.

Hayek's theory of mind, as developed in *The Sensory Order*, is an attempt to explain how the operations of the central nervous system could create a mind. It is an investigation of the mind-body problem. He attempts to explain in detail "how the physiological impulses proceeding in the different parts of the central nervous system can become in such a manner differentiated from each other in their functional significance that their effects will differ from each other in the same way in which we know the effects of the different sensory qualities to differ from each other" (1952, 1). His solution is used to explain, in less detail, all mental activity, including abstract thought (142–46).

Hayek, then, has a theory about how people come to live in a sensory order created by the operation of the central nervous system. He finds the outlines of his theory adequate to explain also consciousness and conceptual thought. This story tells him that thought and emotion are dispositions to act and that all mental activity is a product of rules governing the operation of the brain in its capacity to classify sensory inputs. The emotions are "a temporary bias or preference for certain types of responses towards any external situation" (1952, 99). Abstract thought is a more complex matter; nevertheless, "all the 'higher' mental processes may be interpreted as being determined by the operation of the same general principle" used to explain lower forms of mentation (146). Thinking and acting are rule-governed phenomena in Hayek's system, and even the most abstract and "rational" thought is, in the end, a patterned behavioral response to environmental stimuli.[11]

To equate knowledge with a disposition to act is not to deny mental activity or reduce it to a stimulus-response mechanism. In the description and explanation of such dispositions one must use mental terms. One must refer to what the actor is thinking and feeling. Hayek, in other words, is no behaviorist. (Behaviorism and Hayek's relation to it have little bearing on the issues raised in this chapter. We think it important for the interpretation of Hayek in this chapter, however, to warn the reader against seeing him as a behaviorist; hence this and the following paragraph.)

Behaviorism is the conviction that no particular limits exist to our ability to discard those descriptions and explanations of behavior that use mentalistic language in favor of those that refer only to environmental factors and objective behavior. Hayek rejects this conviction using an argument analogous to Georg Cantor's famous "diagonal argument," according to which the number of elements of a set is always less than the number of elements of the set composed of all its subsets. Hayek concludes that we can "reduce" mental phenomena to physical phenomena only "in principle." But "any attempt to explain particular mental processes must," of necessity, "contain references to other mental processes and will thus not achieve a full reduction to a description in physical terms" (1952, 190).[12] Thus, even though Hayek explained knowledge as a disposition to act and mind as matter in motion, he was a defender of *verstehende* psychology (191–94).

As important, Hayek's claim concerning the limits of reductionism instantiates his more general point that there always exist definite constraints on knowledge. First, as we will discuss below, Hayek claims that perception necessarily is selective as a consequence of the classificatory operation of mental activity; thus only some but not all properties of the external world are perceived. Second, Hayek held that precise though unspecifiable limits on knowledge exist because "any apparatus of classification must possess a structure of higher complexity than is possessed by the objects which it classifies," which implies that the "brain can never fully explain its own operations" (1952, 185). Thus, for Hayek, ignorance is an essential implication of his cognitive theory and not simply a consequence of individuals gazing into a future that is unknowable until it has occurred.

Hayek, as discussed earlier, equated knowledge with practice. This matters for our argument because social practice is largely the product of *blind* evolution. From a Hayekian perspective, we shall argue, the reliability of our knowledge of the future, of our long-term expectations, does not depend so much on the rationality of our projections as on the properties of the economy's selection processes. If Hayek's view holds water, it undercuts the sort of general epistemic critique attempted by Keynes, Shackle, and Lachmann. Alternatively, if Keynes's views on knowledge are substantially correct, then Hayek's faith in the efficacy of social evolution was misplaced.

Our most basic knowledge of the external world is the product of biological evolution.[13] According to Hayek, in the higher species this process has generated a central nervous system consisting of fibers that carry impulses from external and internal receptor sites to the brain. The brain then classifies the impulses coming to it along these fibers.

The impulse coming up a given fiber will be classified in one way or another depending on what other impulses are coming in from other fibers, what other impulses have lately arrived, and the prior existing structure of cognitive relations the organism possesses. In this way, the brain partitions the set of possible impulse clusters into equivalence classes according to certain, but not necessarily all, perceived characteristics of those impulses. The simplest version of a central nervous system matching this description would put any impulse cluster into one of two boxes. We might think of one box as carrying the label "go right" and the other "go left." Biological evolution would tend to select, from among such simple organisms, those whose central nervous systems tended to say "go left" when more nourishing environments existed to the left and "go right" when more nourishing environments existed to the right. Natural selection would tend to favor those spontaneous variations that generated more complex responses ("go left then right") to environmental stimuli. Emergent species would, then, tend to have ever more receptor sites, ever more nerve fibers, ever larger brains, and, in consequence, ever more complex ways of classifying and responding to incoming signals.

In *The Sensory Order* Hayek argues that the work of perception performed by the central nervous system is a work of classification and thus of interpretation. By denying that some impulses intrinsically have, in themselves, a significantly different "quality" from others (1952, 8–12), Hayek is led to conclude that the differentiations that the system makes among incoming impulses can only be based on their being or not being accompanied or preceded by other impulses traveling on other fibers. On this reading, the essential activity of the central nervous system is to construct a good taxonomy of nerve impulses. Such a taxonomy partitions impulse clusters into equivalence classes that will tend to ensure the survival and reproductive success of the organism. But this, in turn, implies that the properties of the external world perceived by an organism are properties of the operation of its central nervous system. As we put it in an earlier article, "what we think of as a property of things is, in the first instance, a property of the mind's taxonomic framework" (Butos and Koppl 1993, 307–8).

The taxonomic framework created by the operation of the central nervous system interprets signals according to the mind's existent classificatory apparatus. For Hayek, such signals only attain meaning because they can be so arranged. Thus, whereas experience is the source of perception, all experience in Hayek's system is perceived and made meaningful only because it can be ordered into pre-existing (or a priori) "categories" of the mind. These categories, in turn, may be affected and themselves reorganized or displaced by experience.[14] In this way classification constitutes an interpretation of experience. This now brings us to the central insight that drove Hayek to write on the theory of mind in the first place: "we do not first have sensations which are then preserved by memory, but it is as a result of physiological memory that the physiological impulses are converted into sensations. The connexions between the physiological elements are thus the primary phenomenon which creates the mental phenomena" (1952, 53).

In the introduction to *The Sensory Order*, the physiological psychologist H. Kluever identified Hayek's "most important and original contributions" with his demonstration of the complexity of the relations between "the factor of 'experience' " in perception and "the conditions, structures, or presuppositions which make experience possible" (xx). The former are the "sensations" common to many empiricist epistemologies, the latter are the "categories" emphasized in Kantian epistemologies. The contribution Kluever attributes to Hayek is that neither element in perception is stable or "given."

Sensations are variable interpretations. To perceive an event in the world is to attribute a meaning to sensory impulses. The meaning given depends on the taxonomy used. Because experience alters the taxonomy used, the "givens" of sensory experience, the basic phenomena of perception, are variable and not constant (Hayek 1952, 173–76). Similarly, Kluever's "conditions, structures, or presuppositions" of experience are variable. In even pre-human perception there is a kind of Kantian "synthetic a priori" or metaphysical taxonomy to organize data. Hayek's theory implies that, *pace* Kant, this synthetic a priori is not constant and eternal. It is the variable product of experience, a result of the interplay of action, based on a given structure of experience, with the consequences of action. Some elements of this structure, those "hardwired" by biological evolution, are relatively stable; others less so. As Kluever observes, "Dr. Hayek, therefore, does not take a static view of either the 'elements' or the 'relational' structure involved in the sensory or any other kind of order" (xx).

If none of the elements of perception are perfectly static, all knowledge is subject to revision. But then all knowledge is fallible. All knowledge is a fallible interpretation of a world we cannot know directly, but only through the filter of our perceptions. Whereas the rules governing the classificatory functioning of cognitive activity are in principle finite, the various permutations of interpretation that can be constructed are limitless. This means that the mind can not only reorder its perceptions of reality, but also create new theories about reality. The mind, for Hayek, is thus an instrument of learning and creativity. And this functioning, according to Hayek, accomplishes this by "representing both the actual state of the environment" as it is perceived and "the changes to be expected in that environment" so that individuals actually live "as much in a world of expectation as in a world of 'fact' " (1952, 118, 121). Thus Hayek is completely at odds with the rationalist tradition that would seek to find *some* constant and reliable center in thought and perception. In this regard, as in others, Hayek is a vigorous anti-Cartesian.

In order to bring the discussion of Hayek's theory of mind into contact with the issue of economic expectation, it is necessary to discuss his ideas on social evolution. The social processes shaping our knowledge and actions are similar to the biological process discussed in *The Sensory Order*. This similarity permits many of the conclusions of Hayek's theory of mind to be carried over to a discussion of economic expectations.

In the human species, according to Hayek (1988), biological evolution has been superseded by cultural evolution. The principles of biological and cultural evolution are pretty much the same. Each is a process of variation, selection, and retention. In cultural evolution, however, the things getting varied, selected, and retained are not genes or organisms, but ways of acting. Cultural evolution is Lamarckian, not Darwinian, because the acquired characteristics of people can be passed on.

The central mechanism in Hayek's theory of cultural evolution is group selection.[15] Rules that induce success among groups are preserved through cultural traditions that permit cooperation among large numbers of persons; these traditions contend with and supersede the innate rules generated by biological evolution.[16] Hayek argued that language, morality, and the basic achievements of civilization, namely an abstract system of justice and a refined division of labor, were all the products of cultural evolution driven largely by group selection. The main phenomenon explained by group selection, as opposed to the more general phenomenon of cultural evolution, is the transition to civilization. Hayek emphasized that "the cultural selection of learnt rules" served to "repress some of the innate rules which were adapted to the hunting and gathering life of the small bands of fifteen to forty persons, led by a headman and defending a territory against all outsiders" (1979, 160–61). The passage from small groups to what Hayek called "the extended order" requires an explanation free of design elements; group selection provides such an explanation.

3. Implications for market theory

3.1. Keynes on the subjectivism of expectations

Keynes believed that economic expectations are subjective. The subjectivity of expectations, however, has more portentous consequences for long-run expectations than for short-run expectations. Short-term expectations are tightly moored to realized values. Long-term expectations are not shaped by rational calculation; they rest on no "adequate or secure foundation" (Keynes 1937, 218).

3.1.1. Short-term and long-term expectations distinguished

Keynes distinguishes sharply between short- and long-term expectation. Short-term expectation "is concerned with the price which a manufacturer can expect to get for his 'finished' output" given his general productive capabilities. It is thus very different from long-term expectation, which "is concerned with what the entrepreneur can hope to earn in the shape of future returns if he purchases ... 'finished' output as an addition to his capital equipment" (CW 1973a, 46–47). From these definitions Keynes draws the inference that a firm's "daily output will be determined by its short-term expectations" (47; emphasis deleted), whereas investment in new capital is a function of long-term expectations. As Keynes explains in chapter 5 of *The General Theory*, there is a feedback mechanism working to keep short-term expectations in close conformity with the underlying realities of supply and demand. Thus "it will often be safe to omit express reference to short-term expectation" (50). No such feedback mechanism operates to constrain long-term expectations. Therefore "express reference to current long-term expectations can seldom be avoided" (50).

Keynes noted that it would be "too complicated" for entrepreneurs to recalculate short-term expectations *de novo* from day to day. Besides, "circumstances usually continue unchanged from one day to the next," so it would also be "a waste of time" (51). Entrepreneurs wisely choose to assume that present conditions will continue "except in so far as there are definite reasons for expecting a change" (51). In practice, "producers' forecasts are more often gradually modified in the light of results than in anticipation of prospective changes" (51). In other words, a stable negative feedback loop keeps short-term expectations close to underlying real values.[17] Because this loop operates quickly, we may safely substitute realized results for expected outcomes.

No such feedback mechanism keeps long-term expectations in line with realized values. "It is in the nature of long-term expectations that they cannot be checked at short intervals in the light of realized results" (51). Because long-term expectations concern relatively far-off events, a negative feedback loop cannot operate. Too much time and too many changes intervene between choice and outcome for such a mechanism to work. "Thus the factor of current long-term expectations cannot be even approximately eliminated or replaced by realized results" (51).

3.1.2. Why long-term expectations cannot be rational

Keynes could have avoided "express reference to current long-term expectations" by taking a weighted average of possible outcomes. But he did not believe that entrepreneurs could simply make a list containing every possible future outcome, assign a probability to each item on the list, and then calculate an expected value. That entrepreneurs cannot form such a Benthamite calculation of long-term values is the point of chapter 12 of *The General Theory*. In this chapter Keynes says that "our existing knowledge does not provide a sufficient basis for a calculated mathematical expectation" (CW 1973a, 152).

Keynes's argument is an openly philosophical one concerning the bases of rational action. One might say that, though a calculated *mathematical* expectation of long-term values cannot be gotten, rational forecasts of expected values can be. However inadequate such forecasts may be, a rational mind can make them. This way of speaking is not ruled out by Keynes's theory, but such rational claims as can be made about future values are so vague and dubious that no rational action can be based on them.[18] It is in this sense that we may call rational forecasts of future values "impossible."

Tony Lawson argues that in Keynes, convention-following propelled by animal spirits is "rational in the sense that there are known good reasons for the particular actions undertaken" (1993, 175). We find little to object to in Lawson's analysis except his use of the word "rational." In Keynes's system "the probable is the hypothesis on which it is rational to act" (CW 1973b, 339). As one of us has said in the past, "People who are propelled by animal spirits are not guided by estimates of more and less probable; in that sense, their actions are irrational" (Koppl 1991, 205).

Keynes recognizes that economists might feel that a "general, philosophical disquisition on the *behavior* of mankind is somewhat remote" from the economic theory of investment. "But," he opines, "I think not." He accuses the "classical" theory, which he claims emphasized the mathematical calculation of expected values, of falling prey to "market place idols." It is "one of these pretty, polite techniques which tries to deal with the present by abstracting from the fact that we know very little about the future" (Keynes 1937, 215; emphasis added). Thus, although one might think it somehow philosophical to emphasize man's ignorance of the future, the failure to do so tends to lead economists down the primrose path toward false market idols.

The argument of *The General Theory*'s chapter 12 comes in two parts. The first part tells us why it is impossible to make a calculated mathematical expectation of long-term values. The second part tells us how entrepreneurs formulate their (irrational) expectations given this impossibility of rational forecasting. How entrepreneurs formulate their expectations depends on the stage of capitalism. One story applies to the days before the advent of the stock market, the other to the days after.

Why are entrepreneurs unable to make rational forecasts of long-term values? Below we identify five conditions that Keynes claimed are necessary for the reliable calculation of expected values and, hence, for rational behavior. In the *Treatise on Probability*,[19] Keynes identified three conditions for the application of the standard probability calculus (the principle of indifference, measurability, and atomic uniformity). Two others (limited independent variety and weight of argument) refer to the problem of induction and the confidence we may have in probability statements. These conditions, Keynes argued, fail in most applications to social life, thus spelling trouble for rational action. If these conditions were satisfied, according to Keynes, individuals would not necessarily be driven by animal spirits and could invoke the probability calculus in forming their long-term forecasts. Their expectations and behavior would then be based on rational (Benthamite) calculations of expected value. Let us consider Keynes's reasons why such rational calculations are not possible.

3.1.2.1. MEASURABILITY

Application of the probability calculus requires that probabilities be measurable. In the *Treatise on Probability*, Keynes denied that all probabilities are numerically measurable or even capable of being ranked on a uniform scale of greater and less. Keynes argued in "The General Theory of Employment" that the probabilities relating to the relatively distant future are not measurable, claiming that matters such as "the prospect of a European war" or "the rate of interest twenty years hence" were so uncertain that "there is no scientific basis on which to form any calculable probability whatever. We simply do not know" (Keynes 1937, 213–14). The probabilities of events affecting the value of current additions to capital are not measurable. Therefore, the present value of current investment cannot be calculated.

3.1.2.2. THE PRINCIPLE OF INDIFFERENCE

Application of the probability calculus requires that the principle of indifference (defined presently) holds. When it does, probabilities can be assigned. Thus the inapplicability of this principle of indifference counts as another reason why the probability calculus cannot be used for social phenomena.

The principle of indifference asserts that "*equal* probabilities must be assigned to each of several arguments, if there is an absence of positive ground for assigning *unequal* ones" (CW 1973b, 45). This implies that the principle succeeds if legitimate grounds exist for assigning some particular set of unequal weights. If no such grounds exist for assigning unequal weights, the principle of indifference requires that we assign equal weights.

This principle can be applied, Keynes insisted, only when you are reviewing "*indivisible* alternatives" (CW 1973b, 65). An alternative is "divisible" if it is the disjunction of two or more mutually exclusive possibilities. An alternative is thus "indivisible" when it is not the disjunction of

120

two or more exclusive possibilities. You cannot apply the principle of indifference if one of your alternatives "is capable of being further split up into a pair of possible alternatives" (66).

Keynes's qualification is severe. It is, he noted, "fatal to the practical utility of the Principle of Indifference" in all those cases "in which it is possible to find *no* ultimate alternatives" in terms of which one may describe the phenomena in question (CW 1973b, 62).

In *The General Theory* Keynes rejected the view that future events in the social world can be reduced to any list of indivisible alternatives. We cannot "rationalize our behavior," he explains, "by arguing that to a man in a state of ignorance errors in either direction are equally probable, so that there remains a mean actuarial expectation based on equiprobabilities." It "can easily be shown," Keynes asserted, that arguing from the "assumption of arithmetically equal probabilities based on a state of ignorance leads to absurdities" (CW 1973a, 152). The principle of indifference is inapplicable to social and economic phenomena. Therefore it cannot be applied to the formation of rational calculations of long-term values by entrepreneurs.

3.1.2.3. ATOMIC UNIFORMITY

The condition of atomic uniformity requires that causes work additively rather than organically. In classical mechanics forces interact additively; their net effect is the vector sum of their separate effects. When the principle of atomic uniformity holds, the net result of any complex of causes interacting simultaneously can be inferred from a knowledge of the several effects of the causes as they occur when isolated. You just add up these separate effects, and the sum is the joint effect of the simultaneous operation of the different causes.

Keynes uses the term *atomic* uniformity because he believed the principle works when the phenomena being studied consist of "*legal atoms*, such that each of them exercises its own separate, independent, and invariable effect." When you have such atoms, any changes in the "total state" of things is "compounded of a number of separate changes each of which is solely due to a separate portion of the preceding state." In such a system, each of the "legal atoms" of which the system is ultimately composed can "be treated as a separate cause and does not enter into different organic combinations in each of which it is regulated by different laws" (CW 1973b, 276–77).

When the condition of atomic uniformity does not apply, there is some measure of "organic unity" and we may speak of the Principle of Organic Unity. Today, a special case of the principle of organic unity is well known in the mathematics of chaos, namely the extreme dependence on initial conditions, or the "butterfly effect." In his essay on Francis Edgeworth,

Keynes (CW 1972, 262) upheld the principle of organic unity in the sphere of "psychics." He thus rejected the condition of atomic uniformity for social phenomena.

3.1.2.4. LIMITED INDEPENDENT VARIETY

The condition of "limited independent variety," Keynes argued, is necessary if we are to draw inductive conclusions from experience. The condition amounts to the requirement that the relevant structural characteristics of the system at hand be identical to those of an axiom system (in the modern sense) whose axioms and undefinables are finite in number.

Keynes (CW, 1973b, 279) holds that when you are studying some "system of facts or propositions" the number of such facts will generally be larger than the number of "ultimate constituents or indefinables of the system." Moreover, there will be "certain laws of necessary connection" among the propositions of the system. The "truth or falsity of every member [of the system] can be inferred" from a knowledge of these laws "together with a knowledge of the truth or falsity of some (but not all) of the members" (CW 1973b, 279).[20] The independent variety of a system is the number of "ultimate constituents" plus the number of "laws of necessary connection" operative in the system. When this number is finite, induction is possible and the system is characterized by "limited independent variety" (see CW 1973b, 279–94).

That Keynes rejected the applicability of the assumption of limited independent variety may be inferred from his emphasis on our ignorance of the "*character*" of future changes (Keynes 1937, 214) and his insistence throughout chapter 12 of *The General Theory* that market instabilities arise from endogenous and psychological causes.

3.1.2.5. ON THE WEIGHTS OF ARGUMENT

Even when numerically precise, a probability judgment may be based on scanty evidence. In such cases, our confidence in the probability judgment will be low. The "weight" of an argument is the degree of confidence we may place in it, as determined by the sufficiency of our evidence. The argument that one-sixth is the probability of a seven at the Las Vegas craps tables has an extremely high weight. The argument that one-sixth is the chance of an economic recovery by year's end has considerably lower weight. "The weight, to speak metaphorically, measures the *sum* of the favorable and unfavorable evidence, the probability measures the *difference*" (CW 1973b, 77).

Keynes's concept of the weight of an argument makes an explicit appearance in *The General Theory* (see Runde 1990). "It would be foolish," he says, "in forming our expectations, to attach great weight to matters which are very uncertain" (148). And in a footnote he explains that, "By 'very uncertain' I do not mean the same thing as 'very improbable'. *Cf.* my *Treatise on Probability*, chap. 6, on 'The Weight of Arguments' " (CW 1973a, 148).

3.1.2.6. THE FIVE CONDITIONS: CONCLUSION

Keynes's discussion of measurability, the principle of indifference, atomic uniformity, limited independent variety, and the weights of argument add up to an argument that it is impossible to make rational economic calculations of long-term values. Keynes believed that we cannot formulate a rational forecast of future values because we are ignorant of the future. We lack and cannot obtain at any price the knowledge necessary to calculate expected present values. Instead of letting ourselves be paralyzed by the inability to make reliable guesses about the consequences of our actions, Keynes argued, we let ourselves be driven by animal spirits.

3.1.3. Animal spirits: formation of long-term expectations

For the reasons we have just reviewed, Keynes believed business calculations are profoundly unreliable: "The outstanding fact is the precariousness of the basis of knowledge on which our estimates of prospective yield have to be made" (CW 1973a, 149). The incompetence of long-term expectations posed no fundamental difficulty for capitalism in the halcyon days when enterprises could not be "floated off on the Stock Exchange at an immediate profit" (151). In those days, the decision to invest in a business was "largely irrevocable, not only for the community as a whole, but also for the individual" (150). This marriage of the entrepreneur to his capital might seem, when present values cannot be calculated, to be a drag on investment. But enterprises were not undertaken "merely as a result of cold calculation" (150). Rather, entrepreneurs "embarked on business as a way of life" (150). Thus the irrational element in human action worked to good effect. Animal spirits prompted men to act in a socially useful way by inducing them to invest.[21]

Then came the stock exchange. "With the separation between ownership and management ... which prevails today and with the development of organized investment markets, a new factor of great importance has entered in, which sometimes facilitates investment but sometimes adds greatly to the instability of the system" (150–51). The new factor is speculation. The speculator attempts to assess not present values, but near-term stock prices. Because present value calculations are largely spurious, the speculators' estimates can have no foundation in any supposed underlying market reality. Even if some speculator were mysteriously granted reliable knowledge of "true" present values, he would not be able to put it to good use: "It is not sensible to pay 25 for an investment of which you believe the prospective yield to justify a value of 30, if you also believe that the market will value it at 20 three months hence" (155). The professional trader needs to know, Keynes insisted, imminent changes in current asset prices, not long-term values.

When equity shares are liquid, "speculation" dominates "enterprise." The irrational element in human action is no longer directed to a salutary end, investment. It is instead pointed in an unfortunate direction, toward destabilizing speculation. The very animal spirits that were once a counterweight to the precariousness of our knowledge of the future now exacerbate the instabilities implicit in our fundamental inability to "defeat the dark forces of time and ignorance" (157).

In the old days, the illiquidity of equity shares ensured first that such limited "real knowledge" (153) about capital values as existed was put to use, and second that changes in economic expectations could not be translated into large fluctuations in economic activity. When equity shares became liquid the situation reversed. The knowledge upon which investment decisions were based was detached completely from honest appraisals of underlying scarcities. The expectations underlying investment decisions became volatile. Simultaneously, change in expectations became a powerful force in determining the level of economic activity. In the stock market, a process of mass psychology induces waves of optimism and pessimism; these shifts, in turn, cause the trade cycle (see CW 1973a, chap. 22).

Long-term expectations are subjective in Keynes's theory. And they are fundamentally exogenous to the economic process.[22] The process of mass psychology that generates them is mostly self-referencing and not causally dependent upon other economic processes. For Keynes, long-term expectations do not and cannot bear any systematic relationship to underlying economic reality.

Keynes's doubts about the stability of markets depend on such matters as whether or not market institutions marry entrepreneurs to their capitals. But his doubts also vitally depend on his epistemology. Keynes was a Cartesian rationalist who saw about him a non-Cartesian social world. In such a world action cannot be rational; it must spring from an irrational source, animal spirits (Koppl 1991, 1992). A Cartesian rationalist may be glad for the impulse to action that animal spirits provide, but he cannot have much faith that the actions so motivated will very often turn out as intended. Keynes's fundamental economic ideas as expressed in chapter 12 of *The General Theory* are strongly driven by the contrast between the Cartesian canons of reason and the non-Cartesian structures of the social world.

3.2.1. A Hayekian theory of expectations

Hayek's ideas about knowledge and the evolution of rules of conduct suggest a theory of expectations. Yet, he did not develop such a theory very explicitly or in much detail. Indeed, in the conclusion to his famous essay "Economics and Knowledge," Hayek denies that his discussion of the role of knowledge in the market process should lead to any fundamental changes in economic theory. He seems never to have thought it necessary to develop anything labeled a "theory of expectations." In an earlier work (Butos and Koppl 1993), however, we identified four essential features of a theory of expectations consistent with Hayek's cognitive and philosophical work. First, as noted in section 2.2 above, all knowledge in Hayek's view is fallible interpretation. Thus "expectations are formed in the context of ignorance about reality" (314). Second, an individual's knowledge and, therefore, expectations "derive from a mental classificatory apparatus," the taxonomy induced by the operation of the central nervous system. Third, this taxonomy is "a mechanism of adaptation" and the changes it undergoes are governed by a goodness-of-fit criterion. Finally, the knowledge and expectations governing an individual are endogenous to its environment (315).

Of these four features of a Hayekian theory of expectations, the last, endogeneity, is perhaps the most important in the current context. In the original biological context of Hayek's theory of mind, it is clear that knowledge and expectation are endogenous. What the individual can know is a function of the taxonomic framework of its central nervous system. The structure of that framework, in turn, is produced by the experience of the organism and its species in its environment. The synthetic a priori categories of experience are a product of the environment they are used to interpret.[23]

A parallel insight applies to the knowledge created by social experience. Our expectations about social and economic events are embodied in our habits of action. These habits, in turn, are endogenous to that same social and economic environment.[24] It follows from Hayek's view of knowledge that the evolutionary conditions of the economic environment influence the reliability of economic expectations. Hayek adopts such a perspective in his general defense of property (1973, 107–10) and in his critique of socialism (1988, chap. 5). He was not, however, very explicit on this point nor, as we have said, did he attempt to develop a separate theory of expectations. It is clear, though, that Hayek did not view the absence of "rational calculation" as a reason for discoordination. Indeed, for Hayek, economic theory "is based not on the assumption that most or all of the participants in the market process are rational, but, on the contrary, on the assumption that it will in general be through competition that a few *relatively* more rational individuals will make it necessary for the rest to emulate them in order to prevail" (1979, 75; emphasis added). And what the emulators will have to adopt are more "rational *methods*" (75; emphasis added). In this way, competition tends to breed commercial traditions of rational procedure. Hayek tells us that competition induces such rational habits and procedures even though the great majority of those who are forced to adopt them do not understand why they are useful.

In arguing that competition breeds rationality, Hayek is claiming that the filter of profit and loss weeds out those whose habits tend to generate inappropriate responses to market signals, that is, those with inappropriate propensities to act. Losses tend to filter out inferior expectations. For instance, traders in the stock market who study tea leaves are likely to lose money and be removed from the market. Those with techniques to project earnings may do better. Profits will go to those with better ways of projecting earnings whether or not they understand why their forecasting procedures are better.

We have seen Hayek argue that "the process of selection that shaped customs and morality could take account of more factual circumstances than individuals could perceive, and in consequence tradition is in some respects superior to, or 'wiser' than, human reason" (1988, 75). Hayek's position suggests something similar for the market place. The home-grown traditions bred by market competition are shaped by more factual circumstances than market participants can perceive, and consequently tried and true business practices may sometimes embody greater wisdom than rational calculation can achieve. In short, as Walter Weimer (1980, 169) notes, Hayek advances a "rational theory of tradition."

More work is needed to explore whether Hayek's confidence in market coordination is strongly driven by his theory of mind in the way that Keynes's doubts about coordination are strongly driven by his Cartesianism. In any event, there are close parallels between Hayek's theories of mind and market. These parallels suggest at least a kind of "weak driving" of his market theory by his philosophy. As we have noted in the past, Hayek's treatments of mind and market share as central concerns "the role of mechanisms for the transmission of knowledge, the necessity of and dependence on abstract rules, and the self-regulative or adaptive character of the process" (Butos and Koppl 1993, 306). In short, in both domains of inquiry, Hayek is studying a spontaneous order.

Whereas Keynes saw the market as a field of action in which rational calculation had to cede much ground to animal spirits. Hayek saw the market as the principal cause for what little rationality animates men's actions. It is "in general not rationality which is required to make competition work, but competition, or traditions which allow competition, which will produce rational behaviour" (Hayek 1979, 76). Hayek's position is not the strict logical negation of Keynes's, but on the relation of rationality

126

and competition and on the orderliness of markets, the two great subjectivists hold divergent views.[25]

Here the issue is joined. How is knowledge produced and distributed in society? In Keynes's view, knowledge is justified true belief. This rationalist view leads him to see economic expectations as exogenous to the market process and, sometimes at least, volatile. In Hayek's view, knowledge is a propensity to act. This anti-rationalist view leads him to see economic expectations as endogenous to the market process and, potentially at least, coordinative.

This contrast between Keynes and Hayek goes beyond the likelihood of market discoordination. It is a matter of the sources of order and disorder in markets. Keynes's vision of Cartesian rationality afloat in a non-Cartesian social world encouraged him to the view that the liquidity of assets makes market disorder inevitable (CW 1973a, 155, 157). Hayek had more confidence in market order in part because his anti-Cartesian philosophy suggested competitive evolutionary processes as the main sources of social order (Hayek 1988). In each case, philosophical ideas about knowledge conduce to economic ideas about markets. These connections between philosophy and economics are important and constitute a difficult set of problems any satisfactory integration of post-Keynesian and Hayekian themes would have to resolve.[26]

4. Conclusions

Both Keynes and Hayek take up subjectivist positions. But they represent different varieties of subjectivism.[27] The differences in their theories of subjectivist expectations stem from differences in philosophy. Keynes was a Cartesian of sorts. He was a "constructivist" in Hayek's sense who believed that knowledge is justified true belief. For Keynes, expectations are a belief state and cannot be formulated by "rational calculation." For Hayek, expectations are implicit in the practices, rules, and reaction patterns governing action. These differences in philosophy help to explain the differences in their approaches to subjective economic expectations.

For Keynes, expectations of the future are belief states. If these belief states are to guide action reliably, they must embody reliable knowledge. But reliable knowledge of the future cannot be had. We cannot make any "calculated mathematical expectation[s]" of future values (CW 1973a, 152). In a world where people plan for the future, then, most action is irrational action. "Most, probably, of our decisions to do something positive," Keynes believed, "the full consequence of which will be drawn out over many days to come, can only be taken as a result of animal spirits, a spontaneous urge to action rather than inaction" (161). Full vent is given by Keynes to behaviors struggling against the dark "forces of time and our ignorance of the future" (157). Thus, according to Keynes, on modern asset markets speculators' long-term expectations create an atmosphere that tends to generate ex nihilo waves of pessimism and optimism and thus waves of greater and lesser investment spending. Though the economy suffers from "severe fluctuations" in output and employment, "it is not violently unstable" (249). Instead, Keynes held that the system "may find itself in a stable equilibrium ... below full employment" (30). The expectations that underpin liquidity preference and the inducement to invest have resulted in interest rates that are too high and prospective yields on capital that are too low. But these expectations are not revisable via rational calculation because an unknowable future nullifies the force of Cartesian reason. Thus, endogenous mechanisms cannot be relied upon to extricate the system from unemployment equilibrium. Keynes, despite dismissing the applicability of Cartesian rationalism as a force from within the system, still retains it as an epistemological authority. But now such authority enters as an exogenous constructivist element in the form of government intervention.[28]

A Hayekian theory of expectations is notably different from Keynes's theory. Hayek avoids casting expectations as "rational" or "nonrational" by rejecting the Cartesian foundations that often underlie such distinctions. Instead, Hayek builds on a cognitive theory that implies essential and inherent constraints on what individuals can know. For Hayek, defining knowledge according to Cartesian (justificationist) criteria errs by assuming the existence of an infallible epistemological authority. The argument of *The Sensory Order* is that no such authority exists.

For Hayek, expectations are embodied in habits, practices, norms, and traditions. Expectations, in other words, are embodied in the rules governing action. These rules are a product of social and, as in the case of the sensory order, even biological evolution. In this evolutionary view there is no reason to see in the uncertainty of the future a special cause for discoordination of actions. Expectations, on the contrary, have a tendency toward coherence and coordination. The evolutionary selection processes at work among thoughts and actions tend to select "fit" expectations and to weed out "unfit" expectations. Hayekian expectations, in sharp contrast to Keynes's long-term expectations, are inextricably linked to the market process.

Connecting expectations to the market process carries advantages that are not available when expectations are made exogenous.[29] As we have shown elsewhere (Butos and Koppl 1993), the orderliness of market processes depends on the institutional context within which individuals function. Individuals' expectations (whether they are understood as "belief states" as in Keynes or as "dispositions to act" as in Hayek) and the plans they induce will generate varying degrees of coordination depending on the extent to which the institutional context satisfies certain conditions. When the context is "competitive" (in the sense of Kirzner

1973) and participants are constrained by stable rules, the correspondence between expectation and realization is likely to be close; markets will exhibit outcomes through time that reasonably approximate planned coordination. Alternatively, when the context facing individuals is dominated by "Big Players"—in other words, participants whose discretionary actions have a disproportionate effect on the market—individuals' expectations are more likely to generate perverse and incoherent outcomes (see Koppl and Yeager 1996). Under the influence of Big Players, markets will display characteristics similar to those Keynes describes in chapter 12 of *The General Theory*. Thus it is possible to use Hayek's theory of expectations to indicate when coordination is and is not likely to emerge. Because Keynes's theory deals only with coordination failures, it can be claimed that Hayek's is the more general.

The differences between Keynes and Hayek appear to run deep. These differences present a difficult set of problems for those who would try to integrate the economic ideas of these two thinkers. The fact that they are both subjectivists should not lead us to ignore their differences. We have attempted to identify elements of such differences and to suggest that they can contribute to explaining Keynes's and Hayek's divergent market theories. Arguably, much work remains in order to demonstrate more robustly the kinds of linkages connecting their epistemological positions with theories of the market process. This, we believe, may be especially true for Hayek. Although much work on Hayek has appeared recently,[30] to our knowledge a full reckoning of the relationship between his cognitive theory and his theory of markets has yet to be undertaken.

Acknowledgments

We gratefully acknowledge useful comments on earlier drafts from Peter Boettke, Sean Keenan, Gary Mongiovi, Mario Rizzo, participants of the New York University Austrian Economics Colloquium, participants in the August 1995 Post-Keynesian Theory Seminar given on the Internet (a transcription of which can be found at http://csf.colorado.edu/econ/ aug95sem.html), and two anonymous referees. The usual caveat applies.

Notes

1 A synthesis of Keynesian and Austrian ideas has been proposed more than once. See, for example, O'Driscoll 1977, 113. The title of O'Driscoll and Mario Rizzo's book, *The Economics of Time and Ignorance* (1995), alludes to Keynes's remark that the "social object" of investment should be to "defeat the dark forces of time and ignorance that envelope our future" (CW 1973a, 155). They say that "it is evident that there is much common ground between post-Keynesian and Austrian subjectivism" (O'Driscoll and Rizzo 1995, 9). Lachmann, to whom O'Driscoll and Rizzo dedicated their book, was famous

for his admiration of Keynes's treatment of expectations (Lewin 1994, 246). The economics of Shackle and of Lachmann have long appealed to both Austrians and post-Keynesians.

O'Driscoll and Rizzo favorably quote Paul Davidson to the effect that post-Keynesians put economic events in real time, recognize the importance of expectations in a world of uncertainty, and recognize the importance of economic and political institutions (1995, 9; see Davidson 1980, 158–64.) This chapter goes along way toward explaining why "cross-fertilization between these two schools is" nevertheless "exceedingly rare" (O'Driscoll and Rizzo 1995, 9). For strikingly different views on the affinity between Austrian economics and post-Keynesian versus neoclassical economics by leading contemporary Austrians, see the "Afterword" essays by Rizzo and White in Caldwell and Boehm 1992. Karen Vaughn (1994) provides an insightful discussion of these matters.

Finally, Burczak (1994), writing from a postmodernist perspective, claims it is possible to "integrate the subjectivist post-Keynesian understanding of the potential for macroeconomic disorder with Hayek's concepts of constituted creative choice and market process" (55). According to Burczak, Keynes and Hayek are both hermeneutical subjectivists. Our argument that Keynes is a rationalist obviously disputes Burczak's claim. Although hermeneutics falls within the anti-rationalist tradition and on that account might be more closely associated with Hayek, Caldwell (1994) points out that Hayek's methodological writings after 1942 reflect his "unwillingness to take the interpretive turn" and that "it is probably better to characterize Hayek as a non-hermeneut rather than as an anti-hermeneut, to indicate a path that he chose not to follow rather than as one that he vigorously opposed" (308). Caldwell argues that Hayek wished "to provide a scientific foundation for subjectivism" and that Hayek thought this had been achieved in *The Sensory Order*; thus "hermeneutics was an unnecessary supplement" for Hayek (311). Although we are in basic agreement with Caldwell's interpretation, the question of whether Hayek is a hermeneut falls outside the scope of this chapter.

2 Keynes and Hayek sparred vigorously in the early 1930s, beginning with Hayek's scathing review of the *Treatise on Money*. See Butos 1994 for an overview of these exchanges: see also Gilbert 1982; Fletcher 1987.

3 Skidelsky (1992, 74–89) provides an excellent review of the issues and literature (up to about 1991) on Keynes's philosophy and its relation to his economics.

4 Following McCloskey (1985), Keynes's view is "modernist."

5 Davis (1994) takes a position similar to Carabelli's.

6 Carabelli's reference to uncertainty may have been an allusion to Keynes's discussion of the weights of argument. If so, it is not clear how Keynes's discussion of weights puts him beyond the pale of rationalism.

7 Hayek's theory of cognition has received little attention by economists. An important exception is Streit (1993; see also Horwitz 1994). This is surprising given that Hayek's "knowledge papers" of the 1930s and 1940s have a distinct epistemological flavor. From outside economics, however, aspects of Hayek's *Sensory Order* have been treated recently by de Vries (1994) and Smith (1995) and somewhat earlier by Agonito (1975). The rehabilitation of interest in Hayek's cognitive theory must be credited to Walter B. Weimer, whose 1982 essay still remains the single best treatment of Hayek's cognitive psychology.

8 Hayek's treatment of the individual's "choice-theoretic" problem may be unique in that other theories, like Herbert Simon's "bounded rationality" and Keynes's approaches, emphasize the complexity of the external world con-

fronting the individual and not the cognitive complexity of the acting agent. For Hayek, the mind—like the market, law, and language—is a complex phenomenon.

9 For a critique of justificationism, see especially Bartley 1984 and Weimer 1979. It is worth noting that many non-justificationist philosophers of science, such as Bartley, Weimer, and Popper, have acknowledged Hayek's influence on their own work.

10 Also see Agonito 1975; Weimer 1979, 1982.

11 Ronald Heiner (1983) explains how rules emerging as a consequence of the constraints on knowledge can generate predictable behavior. For Hayek, of course, such prediction would be of "patterns." According to Hayek, rule-governed cognitive activity operates at both the conscious and supraconscious (tacit) levels. See Hayek 1952, chap 6; Agonito 1975; and Weimer 1980, 1982.

12 See Hayek 1952, 25–30, for further criticisms of behaviorism.

13 It is, of course, notoriously difficult to say what the term "external world" might mean. Hayek's theory turns out to imply that an "external world" does exist. In saying that such a world exists, however, Hayek is "merely stating that it is possible to construct an order ... of events ... which enables us to give a more consistent account of the behaviour of the different events in that world" (1952, 173).

14 See Nishiyama 1984, xlvi–l, on Hayek's synthesis of the a priori and the a posteriori. Nishiyama calls this the "most unique significance of his contribution" and "worthy of the name 'Hayekian revolution' " (xlviii).

15 Viktor Vanberg (1986) provides a thoughtful criticism of Hayek's theory of group selection. We do not address here the issue of whether Hayek's theory violates precepts of methodological individualism.

16 Hayek's ideas thus suggest a sophisticated theory of alienation. From a Hayekian perspective, feelings of "alienation" cannot be eliminated except by abolishing civilization altogether.

17 We thank Roger Garrison for this interpretation of Keynes on short-term expectations.

18 Compare Geoffrey Hodgson's claim that "according to Keynes, human beings are rational but they live in a world where widespread uncertainty places severe limits on the capacities of individuals to make detailed, rational calculations about the future. These constraints derive not from the limited rationality of individuals but from the ubiquitousness of uncertainty" (1985, 13).

19 The fact that we can use Keynes's ideas from the *Treatise on Probability* to organize a discussion of his ideas concerning long-term expectations is evidence that these probability notions may have been at the root of his ideas on expectations. For arguments that Keynes's philosophical ideas, especially those relating to probability, were indeed the basis for his economic theory of expectations, see O'Donnell 1989, 247–72; and Carabelli 1988. See also Shackle's discussions of probability in *Epistemics and Economics* (1972).

20 The *Treatise on Probability* was written under the influence of Russell and Moore. An earlier version was completed in 1908, and the final version was published in 1922. It could not, therefore, have taken into account Kurt Gödel's famous 1931 theorem proving the incompleteness of any consistent axiomatic foundations of mathematics. We are not aware of any evidence that Keynes seriously reconsidered his arguments in probability theory or epistemology in light of Gödel's theorem. Kyburg's (1995) analysis of the logic of *The Treatise on Probability* includes a discussion of its relation to the mathematics of Russell and Whitehead.

21 Keynes thought that, without the impulse of animal spirits, investors would be paralyzed into inactivity like Shakespeare's Hamlet or John Buridan's ass. See Koppl 1991.

22 John Hicks (1969, 313) argues that "expectations do appear in *The General Theory*, but (in the main) they appear as *data*; as autonomous elements that come in from outside, not as elements that are moulded in the course of the process that is being analyzed." That Keynes's treatment of long-term expectations in *The General Theory* leads to odd results is evidenced in his theory of liquidity preference. The speculator, Keynes holds, is driven to hold money or buy consols based on the current level of interest (or price of consols) relative to a "critical rate of interest" toward which the speculator believes the market interest rate must gravitate. This "critical rate of interest," however, appears as a fully exegenous and non-revisable datum to which each speculator clings, even if, we must suppose, the preponderance of evidence might suggest otherwise. Because each speculator's belief in a "critical level of interest" cannot be falsified, we must infer that no learning can take place. In light of this, it is not surprising that Keynes would conclude that financial markets generate inefficient and perverse outcomes.

23 This is not to say that these synthetic a priori categories tell us how the world "really is." Even the basic notion of the orderliness of nature may be "merely a result of the method by which we perceive it" (Hayek 1952, 176). For that which is truly without order could not induce the creation of a mental category for the perception of it.

24 Carl Menger also suggests that the expectations of economic actors are embodied in their habits, not their thoughts. In commercial societies, "almost every product comes into existence under the tacit, and as a rule quite unconscious, supposition of the producer that other persons, linked to him by trade, will provide the complementary goods at the right time" (Menger 1981, 63).

25 It might seem that we have exaggerated the differences between the pictures Keynes and Hayek paint of market action. Both thinkers rejected, though for different reasons, the model of rational maximizing. For Keynes, rationality must give way to "animal spirits." For Hayek, one might argue, the social environment shapes the actions of humans in roughly the way the biological environment shapes the actions of animals. Thus, it might seem, Keynes and Hayek had similar ideas about market action. The animal spirits of Keynes, however, are radically divorced from cognition, as the history of the term reveals (Koppl 1991). In Hayek, by contrast, evolution shapes thought and action to fit both one another and the environment external to the actor. Thus, in spite of the common repudiation of rational maximizing, there is no very close similarity between Keynes's ideas on animal spirits and Hayek's evolutionary perspective.

26 It may strike the reader that Hayek's mentor, Ludwig von Mises, had a theory of markets quite close to Hayek's even though, by Hayek's own account, Mises professed an "extreme rationalism" (Hayek 1981, xxiii). The example of Mises would seem to argue against seeing much connection between epistemology and the theory of markets. But important differences between the epistemologies of Mises and Keynes reduce or eliminate the force of this example.

In an essay originally published in 1933, Mises distinguished between "conception" and "understanding." Conception is "discursive reasoning" whereas "understanding seeks the meaning of action in empathic intuition of a whole." Mises thought these two ways of learning about the world operate under quite different epistemological principles. His rationalism applied only to conception. With conception, "strict logic rules"; where understanding enters, "subjectivity begins." For Mises, "conception is reasoning; understanding is beholding" (Mises 1981a, 133–34). This distinction allowed Mises to give the job of learning about the plans of others to "understanding." Thus we form our expectations about the actions of others through "understanding." Only "conception," which has no business inferring people's purposes, is subject to the strictures of rationalism (see Koppl 1996).

    It may even be appropriate to downplay Mises's rationalism. In Hayek's judgment, though he "never fully abandoned" the rationalist "starting point" from which "as a child of his time he could not escape," Mises "largely emancipated himself" over time from "rationalist-constructivist" thinking (1981b, xxiii–xxiv). Whatever the merits of these remarks by Hayek, we argue in the body of this chapter that Keynes achieved no similar emancipation.

27 Boehm's (1982) observation that subjectivism is an ambiguous notion reflects in our view the existence of varieties of subjectivism, just two of which have been discussed here. The differences among such varieties are substantive. Consider, for example, that the subjectivist Lachmann (1986, 32) rejected the notion of unintended consequences, a long-standing pillar of (subjectivist) Austrian economics. Sorting out the differences and intersections among subjectivisms seems a necessary step in the continued extension of the subjectivist research program. See, for example, O'Driscoll and Rizzo 1995, Koppl 1994, Lewin 1994, and Vaughn 1994.

28 Keynes's full employment model is made determinate by a fiscal and monetary agency. Allan Coddington (1982) raises the question of asymmetries in the knowledge Keynes assumes that private and public actors hold. An alternative viewpoint is that policymakers render private expectations benign by restructuring the system, especially along institutional lines. In this sense, Keynesian policymakers impose a Cartesian rationalist or constructivist vision upon the system.

29 Hayekian expectations are subjective, forward looking, and endogenous. But not all endogenous expectations theories are subjectivist. Thus, our discussion is not meant to apply to the rational expectations hypothesis. For a comparison of Hayek and rational expectations, see van Zijp 1993 and Butos 1997.

30 We think it fair to say that work on Hayekian ideas has become an identifiable and progressive research program. See, for example, the recent collection of essays in Birner and van Zijp 1994.

References

Agonito, Rosemary. 1975. Hayek Revisited: Mind as a Process of Classification. *Behaviorism* 3.2:162–71.

Bartley, William Warren, III. 1984. *The Retreat to Commitment.* 2d ed. La Salle, Ind.: Open Court.

Birner, Jack, and Rudy van Zijp, eds. 1994. *Hayek. Co-Ordination and Evolution.* New York: Routledge.

Boehm, Stephan. 1982. The Ambiguous Notion of Subjectivism: Comment on Lachmann. In *Method, Process, and Austrian Economics*, edited by Israel M. Kirzner, 41–52. Lexington, Va.: D.C. Heath.

———. 1989. Subjectivism and Post-Keynesianism: Toward a Better Understanding. In *New Directions in Post-Keynesian Economics*, edited by J. Pheby, 59–93. Aldershot: Edward Elgar.

Burczak, Theodore A. 1994. The Postmodern Moments of F. A. Hayek's Economics. *Economics and Philosophy* 10.2:31–58.

Butos, William N. 1994. The Keynes-Hayek Macro Debate. In *Elgar Companion to Austrian Economics*, edited by Peter J. Boettke, 471–77. Brookfield: Edward Elgar.

———. 1997. Hayek and Rational Expectations. In *Austrians in Debate*, edited by W. Keizer, B. Tieben, and R. van Zijp. London: Routledge.

Butos, William N., and Roger G. Koppl. 1993. Hayekian Expectations: Theory and Empirical Applications. *Constitutional Political Economy* 4.3:303–29.

Caldwell, Bruce J. 1994. Hayek's Scientific Subjectivism. *Economics and Philosophy* 10.2:305–14.

Caldwell, Bruce J., and Stephan Boehm, eds. 1992. *Austrian Economics: Tensions and New Directions*. Norwell: Kluwer.

Carabelli, A. M. 1988. *On Keynes's Method*. New York: St. Martin's.

Coddington, Allan. 1982. Deficient Foresight: A Troublesome Theme in Keynesian Economics. *American Economic Review* 72.3:480–87.

Davidson, Paul. 1980. Post Keynesian Economics: Solving the Crisis in Economic Theory. *The Public Interest* (special issue):151–73.

Davis, John B. 1994. *Keynes' Philosophical Development*. New York: Cambridge University Press.

de Vries, Robert P. 1994. The Place of Hayek's Theory of Mind and Perception in the History of Philosophy and Psychology. In Birner and van Zijp 1994.

Fletcher, G. A. 1987. *The Keynesian Revolution and Its Critics*. New York: St. Martin's.

Gilbert, J. C. 1982. *Keynes' Impact on Monetary Economics*. London: Butterworth Scientific.

Hayek, F. A. 1952. *The Sensory Order*. Chicago: University of Chicago Press.

———. 1967. *Studies in Philosophy, Politics and Economics*. Chicago: University of Chicago Press.

———. 1973. *Law, Legislation and Liberty*. Vol. 1, *Rules and Order*. Chicago: University of Chicago Press.

———. 1978. *New Studies in Philosophy, Politics. Economics and the History of Ideas*. Chicago: University of Chicago Press.

———. 1979. *Law, Legislation and Liberty*, Vol. 3, *The Political Order of a Free People*. Chicago: University of Chicago Press.

———. 1981. Foreword to Mises 1981b.

———. 1988. *The Fatal Conceit*. Chicago: University of Chicago Press.

Heiner, Ronald A. 1983. The Origin of Predictable Behavior. *American Economic Review* 73.4:560–95.

Hicks, John R. 1967. *Critical Essays in Monetary Theory*. Oxford: Clarendon.

———. 1969. Automatists, Hawtreyans and Keynesians. *Journal of Money, Credit and Banking* 1.3:307–17.

Hodgson, Geoffrey M. 1985. Persuasion, Expectations and the Limits to Keynes. In *Keynes' Economics: Methodological Issues*, edited by Tony Lawson and Hashem Pesaran, 10–45. Armonk, N.Y.: Sharpe.

Horwitz, Steven. 1994. From *The Sensory Order* to the Liberal Order: Mind, Economy, and State in the Thought of F. A. Hayek. Paper presented at the Mont Pelerin Society, Cannes, France.

Keynes, John Maynard. 1937. The General Theory of Employment. *Quarterly Journal of Economics* 51:209–23.

——. 1972. *Collected Writings of John Maynard Keynes*. Vol. 10. *Essays in Biography*. London: Macmillan.

——. 1973a. *Collected Writings of John Maynard Keynes*. Vol. 7. *The General Theory of Employment, Interest and Money*. London: Macmillan.

——. 1973b. *Collected Writings of John Maynard Keynes*. Vol. 8. *A Treatise on Probability*. London: Macmillan.

Kirzner, Israel M. 1973. *Competition and Entrepreneurship*. Chicago: University of Chicago Press.

Kluever, Heinrich. 1952. Introduction to Hayek 1952.

Koppl, Roger G. 1991. Retrospectives: Animal Spirits. *Journal of Economic Perspectives* 5.3:203–10.

——. 1992. Reply to Moggridge, Ozawa, and Visser. *Journal of Economic Perspectives* 6.3:211–12.

——. 1994. Lachmann on Schutz and Shackle. In *Advances in Austrian Economics*, vol. 1, edited by Peter J. Boettke and Mario J. Rizzo, 289–302. Greenwich. Conn.: JAI.

——. 1996. Mises and Schutz on Ideal Types. *Cultural Dynamics* 9.1:63–76.

Koppl, Roger G., and Leland B. Yeager. 1996. Big Players and Herding in Asset Markets: The Case of the Russian Ruble. *Explorations in Economic History* 38:367–83.

Kyburg, Henry E., Jr. 1995. Keynes as a Philosopher. In *New Perspectives on Keynes*, edited by Allin F. Cottrell and Michael S. Lawlor. Durham, N.C.: Duke University Press.

Lachmann, Ludwig M. 1986. *The Market as an Economic Process*. New York: Basil Blackwell.

Lawson, Tony. 1993. Keynes and Conventions. *Review of Social Economy* 51.2:174–200.

Lewin, Peter. 1994. Knowledge, Expectations, and Capital: The Economics of Ludwig M. Lachmann. In *Advances in Austrian Economics*, vol. 1, edited by Peter J. Boettke and Mario J. Rizzo. Greenwich, Conn.: JAI.

Mason, Will E. 1996. *Classical versus Neoclassical Monetary Theories*, edited by William N. Butos. Boston: Kluwer.

McCloskey, Donald N. 1985. *The Rhetoric of Economics*, Madison, Wis.: University of Wisconsin Press.

Menger, Carl. 1981. *The Principles of Economics*. New York: New York University Press.

Mises, Ludwig von. 1981a. *Epistemological Problems of Economics*, translated by George Reisman. New York: New York University Press.

——. 1981b. *Socialism: An Economics and Sociological Analysis*. Indianapolis, Ind.: Liberty Classics.

Nishiyama, Chiaki. 1984. Introduction. In *The Essence of Hayek*, edited by Chiaki Nishiyama and Kurt R. Leube, xxxvii–lxviii. Stanford: Hoover Institution Press.

O'Donnell, R. M. 1989. *Keynes: Philosophy, Economics and Politics*. New York: St. Martin's.

O'Driscoll, Gerald P. 1977. *Economics as a Coordination Problem*. Kansas City: Sheed Andrews and McMeel.

O'Driscoll, Gerald P., and Mario J. Rizzo. 1995. *The Economics of Time and Ignorance*. New York: Basil Blackwell.

Popper, Karl R. 1979. *Objective Knowledge: An Evolutionary Approach*. Oxford: Oxford University Press.

Rizzo, Mario J. 1992. Austrian Economics for the Twenty-First Century. In *Austrian Economics: Tensions and New Directions*, edited by B. Caldwell and S. Boehm, 245–56. Norwell: Kluwer.

Runde, Jochen. 1990. Keynesian Uncertainty and the Weight of Arguments. *Economics and Philosophy* 6.2:275–92.

Ryle, Gilbert. 1949. *The Concept of Mind*. London: Hutchison's Universal Library.

Shackle, G. L. S. 1972. *Epistemics and Economics*. London: Cambridge University Press.

Skidelsky, Robert. 1992. *John Maynard Keynes*. Vol. 2, *The Economist as Savior, 1929–1937*. New York: Penguin.

Smith, Barry. 1995. The Connectionist Mind: A Study of Hayekian Psychology. In *Hayek, the Economist and Social Philosopher*, edited by S. Frowen. New York: St. Martin's.

Streit, Manfred. 1993. Cognition, Competition, and Catallaxy: In Memory of F. A. v. Hayek. *Constitutional Political Economy* 4.2:223–62.

Vanberg, Viktor. 1986. Spontaneous Market Order and Social Rules: A Critical Examination of F. A. Hayek's Theory of Cultural Evolution. *Economics and Philosophy* 2.1:75–100.

Vaughn, Karen I. 1994. *Austrian Economics in America*. New York: Cambridge University Press.

Weimer, Walter B. 1979. *Notes on the Methodology of Scientific Research*. Hillsdale: Lawrence Erlbaum.

———. 1980. For and Against Method: Reflections on Feyerabend and the Foibles of Philosophy. *Pre/Text* 1–2:161–203.

———. 1982. Hayek's Approach to the Problems of Complex Phenomena: An Introduction to the Psychology of the Sensory Order. In vol. 2 of *Cognition and the Symbolic Processes*, edited by W. B. Weimer and D. Palermo. Hillsdale: Lawrence Erlbaum.

White, Lawrence H. 1992. Appraising Austrian Economics: Contentions and Misdirections. In *Austrian Economics: Tensions and New Directions*, edited by B. Caldwell and S. Boehm. Norwell: Kluwer.

Zijp, Rudy van. 1993. *Austrian and New Classical Business Cycle Theories*. Aldershot: Edward Elgar.

50

ECONOMIC CALCULATION

The Austrian contribution to political economy

Peter J. Boettke

Source: *Advances in Austrian Economics* 5 (1998): 131–158.

If social phenomena showed no order except insofar as they were consciously designed, there would indeed be no room for theoretical sciences of society ... It is only insofar as some sort of order arises as a result of individual action but without being designed by any individual that a problem is raised which demands a theoretical explanation.

F.A. Hayek (1952a: 69)

If we had deliberately built, or were consciously shaping, the structure of human action, we would merely have to ask individuals why they had interacted with any particular structure. Whereas, in fact, specialised students, even after generations of effort, find it exceedingly difficult to explain such matters, and cannot agree on what are the causes or what will be the effects of particular events. The curious task of economics is to demonstrate to men how little they really know about what they imagine they can design.

F.A. Hayek (1988: 76)

I. Introduction

F.A. Hayek is perhaps the most broad ranging scholar to address economic issues since Adam Smith. His work has spanned across technical economics (1928, 1933a, 1935, 1937, 1939, 1941, 1945), philosophy of the social sciences (1943, 1952a, 1967, 1978), theoretical psychology (1952b), legal philosophy (1960, 1973, 1976, 1979a), and most recently social anthropology (1979b, 1988). Despite the diverse nature of his research, it has a common theme: How do socially institutions work, through the filter of the human mind, to coordinate human affairs?

But Hayek's attempts to pursue this question come to us in scattered concentrations on various specific topics. This had led some scholars to miss the unity of his life-work. T.W. Hutchison, for example, argues that there is a fundamental dichotomy in Hayek's thought – a Hayek I, who is under the influence of Ludwig von Mises, and a Hayek II, who rejects Mises's praxeological method and embraces the methodological views of Karl Popper (Hutchison 1984: 176–232).

Bruce Caldwell (1988) counters Hutchinson's interpretation. It wasn't Hayek who became a Popperian but Popper who became Hayekian. But Caldwell also sees a major transformation in Hayek's work. Due to the interwar intellectual debate over socialist economic calculation, Hayek was transformed from primarily a technical economist concerned with equilibrium theorizing to a broad social theorist concerned with the coordination problem in society in general. His transformation, Caldwell argues, is a result of his growing disenchantment with equilibrium theorizing. While Caldwell's argument is convincing, as far as it goes, even Hayek's earliest work in technical economics can be seen as preparing the way for his later work in a non-equilibrium, process-oriented social theory. In his 1928 essay on "Intertemporal Price Equilibrium and Movements in the Value of Money," for example, Hayek points out, albeit in embryonic form, a theme which permeates his later economic and social theory writings, the role of prices as guides to economic coordination processes through time. As Hayek put it:

> prices ... fulfill a particularly significant role with respect to the distribution of the individual processes through time, as the guide and regulator of all economic activity in the exchange economy. It is precisely this function which hitherto has received only brief mention in economics.
>
> (1928: 71)

Early Hayek, as well as later Hayek, is concerned with the communicative function of social institutions in general, whether they are money prices within the economic system or the rules of behavior within social interaction. Exploring this communicative function is what motivates his research, the tools he employs (such as equilibrium theorizing in his early work or order analysis in his more recent writings) are judged by how well they aid our understanding of that function.

This unity is indicated by Hayek's continuing interest in certain fundamental questions about the nature of the mind. John Gray (1986) has argued that the unity in Hayek's research centers on his neo-Kantian epistemology. Gray relies on Hayek's *The Sensory Order*, which though published in 1952, was originally conceived during his student days. And as Hayek says,

> though my work has led me away from psychology, the basic idea then conceived has continued to occupy me; its outlines have gradually developed, and it has often proved helpful in dealing with the problems of the methods of the social sciences.
>
> (1952b: v)

The research project of exploring the nature of the mind and its relation to human society does not only cover all of Hayek's work, but is part of a larger unity of a whole social scientific tradition tracing from Adam Smith to the modern Austrian school. Hayek's contribution to economics and social thought should be understood as the extension of a research program laid down by Adam Smith, Carl Menger, and specifically, Ludwig von Mises.[1] In this manner we can see the way in which Hayek's epistemology is translated into the core foundation of a theory of society.

In particular, Mises, the system builder, provided Hayek with a program for the study of the economic system and the social world. Hayek is the dissector and analyzer of that Misesian system. His work can be best understood as the continued attempt to make explicit what Mises left implicit, to refine what Mises stated explicitly, and to answer questions Mises left unanswered. As Hayek has said of Mises:

> There is no single man to whom I owe more intellectually, even though he was never my teacher in the institutional sense of the word.... I am to the present moment pursuing the questions which he made me see, and that, I believe is the greatest benefit one scientist can confer on one of the next generation.
>
> (1983: 17; 18)

This influence is obvious in Hayek's work on knowledge and the analysis of socialism, but these insights on knowledge dispersion and conveyance are inseparable from the rest of Hayek's work, from business cycles to the common law.[2] This chapter will explore the unity in Hayek's project and its connection to his theoretical predecessors.

II. The spontaneous order approach

Hayek's social theory project is the advancement and refinement of a tradition of social analysis that dates back to the Scottish Enlightenment and thinkers such as David Hume and Adam Smith. Hayek develops that tradition, however, in his own unique way by interpreting it in light of the economic and social theory tradition handed down to him via his intellectual mentors in the Austrian school of economics, Carl Menger and Ludwig von Mises. It is his Austrian perspective toward economic analysis that leads him to question the ability of modernist economics to understand spontaneously grown, complex social orders. As Hayek states:

> Even two hundred years after Adam Smith's *Wealth of Nations*, it is not yet fully understood that it is the great achievement of the market to have made possible a far-ranging division of labour, that it brings about a continuous adaption of economic effect to millions of particular facts or events which in their totality are not known and cannot be know to anybody.... A system of market-determined prices is essentially a system which is indispensable in order to make us adapt our activities to events and circumstances of which we cannot know.... [N]eoclassical economics, never clearly brought out what I call the "guide" or "signal function" of prices. That was due to the survival of the simple causal explanation of values and prices, assuming that values and prices were determined by what had been before rather than as a signal of what people ought to do.
>
> (1983: 19; 35–36)

It is this understanding of the spontaneous emergence of a complex, and beneficial, social order that informed Adam Smith's arguments for economic liberty and against the restraints of trade. The voluntary action of thousands of individuals, each pursuing his own interests, generates and utilizes economic information that is not available to any one individual or group of individuals in its totality.[3] Economic coordination relies upon the utilization of "local" or contextual knowledge (or what Hayek later terms knowledge of particular time and place) and not abstract "data." It is this emphasis on the use of contextual knowledge that underlies the critical defense of the liberal order from Smith to Hayek.

Consider, for example, Smith's discussion in his *The Theory of Moral Sentiments* concerning spontaneous order processes.

> The man of system ... is apt to be very wise in his own conceit, and is often so enamored with the supposed beauty of his own ideal plan of government, that he cannot suffer the smallest deviation from any part of it. He goes on to establish it completely and in all its parts, without any regard either to the great interests or to the strong prejudices which may oppose it: he seems to imagine that he can arrange the different members of a great society with as much ease as the hand arranges the different pieces upon a chess-board; he does not consider that the pieces upon the chess-board have no other principle of motion besides that which the

hand impresses upon them; but that, in the great chess-board of human society, every single piece has a principle of motion of its own, altogether different from that which the legislature might choose to impress upon it. If those two principles coincide and act in the same direction, the game of human society will go on easily and harmoniously, and is very likely to be happy and successful. If they are opposite or different, the game will go on miserably, and the society must be at all times in the highest degree of disorder.

(1759: 380–381)

Smith's case for economic liberty amounts to an argument and demonstration that individuals pursuing their self-interest can, and will, produce a social order that is economically beneficial.[4] On the other hand, government restraint of trade not only cannot gain access to the knowledge necessary to do the job in a reasonably effective manner, but also grants too much power to the agent that interferes with the free economic process.[5]

"A real understanding of the process which brings this about was long blocked," Hayek has argued, "by post-Smithian classical economics which adopted a labour or cost theory of value" (1983: 19). In addition, with David Ricardo's reformulation of Smith, the emphasis came to be much more concentrated on the long-run, static equilibrium outcome of economic activity. This trend became all the more apparent after the marginalist revolution in the 1870s with the rise of Walrasian general equilibrium and Marshallian partial equilibrium. Among the founders of the marginalist revolution, however, Carl Menger was unique in his emphasis on the spontaneous ordering of economic activity.[6] Menger, for example, devotes all of Book 3 of his *Investigations* (1883) to examining social institutions that emerge spontaneously. "We can observe," he wrote, "in numerous social institutions a strikingly apparent functionality with respect to the whole. But with closer consideration they still do not prove to be the result of an intention aimed at this purpose, *i.e.*, the result of an agreement of members of society or of positive legislation. They, too, present themselves to us rather as 'natural' products (in a certain sense), as the unintended results of historical development" (1883: 130). The examples of money, law, language, markets and communities are presented to demonstrate the prevalence of "organically" grown social institutions.[7]

For the proper study of these institutions, Menger emphasized, the social analyst cannot borrow the methods of the natural sciences. Rather, social theory requires the development of its own methods. Social institutions "simply cannot be viewed and interpreted as the product of purely mechanical force effects. They are, rather, the result of human efforts, the efforts of thinking, feeling, acting human beings" (1883: 133). Social institutions arise either due to a "common will directed toward their establishment" or as

141

"the unintended result of human efforts aimed at essentially individual goals." In the second case, complex social phenomena "come about as the unintended result of individual human effort (pursuing individual interests) without a common will directed toward their establishment" (1883: 133).

While recognizing the importance of social institutions that emerge out of conscious design, Menger (1883: 146) did argue that it is in explaining institutions which arise spontaneously that social theory is dealing with the most noteworthy problem of the social sciences. Moreover, Menger went on to argue that:

> The solution of the most important problems of the theoretical sciences in general and of theoretical economics in particular is thus closely connected with the question of theoretically understanding the origin and change of 'organically' created social structures.
>
> (1883: 147)

In order to demonstrate the power of spontaneous order explanations, Menger utilizes the example of the origin of money. A common medium of exchange emerges not as a product of anyone's design but as a result of individuals striving to better their condition.

Ludwig von Mises, who remarked that it was upon reading Menger's *Principles* that he became an economist (1978: 33), argues that Carl Menger's theory of the origin of money represents "the elucidation of fundamental principles of praxeology and its method of research" (1966: 405). Mises's vast contributions to economic science derive from his consistent application of what he called subjectivism to all areas of economic theory. This perspective is perhaps most vivid in his work on economic calculation and the importance of the institutions of private property and freely fluctuating money prices.

In his first major work, *The Theory of Money and Credit* (1912), Mises already pointed out the connection between private property, monetary calculation and the dynamic market process. "The phenomena of money," Mises argued, "presupposes an economic order in which production is based on division of labor and in which private property consists not only in goods of the first order (consumption goods), but also in goods of the higher order (production goods)" (1912: 41). And, this active process of exchange and production, in which money serves the indispensable function of facilitating coordination, is best understood as an interactive process of human evaluations and perceptions. As Mises wrote, it is a process which is "anchored deep in the human mind" (1912: 153).

The active process of bidding money prices up when demand exceeds supply and down when supply exceeds demand produces both the economic knowledge and incentives for various and diverse individuals to orient their actions toward each other. The system of monetary calculation "guides" individuals in their plan making. The problem with socialism, Mises contended, was that in the absence of this seemingly chaotic rivalrous process there was no way that economic planners could obtain the economic knowledge necessary to decide which of the various technologically feasible projects were economically feasible. Without private property in the means of production, there would be no markets for these goods. And, without a market for the means of production, there could not be any money prices established to reflect the relative scarcities of these goods. In the absence of money prices reflecting the relative scarcities of higher order goods, there would be no way to know which projects are economically feasible and which ones were not (see Mises 1920 and 1922).

Economic calculation, despite its imperfections, provides knowledge to individuals so they may separate from among the multitude of technologically feasible projects those which are economic. Freely fluctuating prices, and the economic calculation it affords, work to solve the generalized knowledge problem that society confronts. It is the market process's ability to reveal error and motivate learning that underlies its claim of superiority in dealing with the problem of dispersed knowledge in society.[8] Hayek's research throughout his career has elaborated on this Misesian insight, both in its positive form of the ability of the market process to convey the necessary economic knowledge for successful plan coordination and negative form of socialism's impossibility and interventionism's ineffectiveness at doing so.

III. Human agency, meaning and social theory

The human sciences begin with:

> what men think and mean to do: from the fact that the individuals which compose society are guided in their actions by a classification of things or concepts which has a common structure and which we know because we, too, are men.
>
> (Hayek 1952a: 57)

The data of the human sciences, in fact, "are what the acting people think they are" (1952a: 44). Indeed, as Hayek puts it, the human sciences, and economics, in particular, could be described:

> as a metatheory, a theory about the theories people have developed to explain how most effectively to discover and use different means for diverse purposes.
>
> (1988: 98)

We interpret the meaning individuals place on events because we "interpret the phenomena in light of our own thinking" (1952a: 135). These interpretations are not perfect and may not even be correct in any particular case, Hayek points out, but it is:

> the only basis on which we ever understand what we call other people's intentions, or the meaning of their actions; and certainly the only basis of all our historical knowledge since this is all derived from the understanding of signs or documents.
>
> (1952a: 135)

Not only do we rely upon our understanding of others, that we derive from our self-understanding, to theorize, but also in order to orient our actions to those of others. The pre-theoretical understanding of others, that is conveyed to us through language, enables us to cooperate socially with those who confront us anonymously. As Hayek states:

> All people, whether primitive or civilised, organise what they perceive partly by means of attributes that language has taught them to attach to groups of sensory characteristics. Language enables us not only to label objects given to our senses as distinct entities, but also to classify an infinite variety of combinations of distinguishing marks according to what we expect from them and what we may do with them ... all usage of language is laden with interpretations or theories about our surroundings.
>
> (1988: 106)

Our common-sense understanding of 'the other,' which comes to us through language, provides an invaluable source of knowledge in social understanding, both at the theoretical level and in our day-to-day existence. "It would be impossible," Hayek says, "to explain or understand human action without making use of this knowledge" (1952a: 43–44). Try to imagine, Hayek argues, what the social world would look like:

> if we were really to dispense with our knowledge of what things mean to the acting man, and if we merely observed the actions of men as we observe an ant heap or a beehive. In the picture such a society study could produce there could not appear such things as means or tools, commodities or money, crimes or punishments, or words or sentences; it could contain only physical objects defined either in terms of the sense attributes they present to the observer or even in purely relational terms. And since the human behavior toward physical objects would show practically no regularities discernible to such an observer, since men would in a great many

instances not appear to react alike to things which would to the observer seem to be the same, nor differently to what appeared to him to be different, he could not hope to achieve an explanation of their actions unless he had first succeeded in reconstructing in full detail the way in which men's senses and men's minds pictured the external world to them. The famous observer from Mars, in other words, before he could understand even as much of human affairs as the ordinary man does, would have to reconstruct from our behavior those immediate data of our mind which to us form the starting point of any interpretation of human action.

(1952a: 105)

Interpretation and understanding is only possible because we possess a pretheoretical understanding of what it means to be human. In other words, it is only because we can attribute *meaning* to human action that we can understand the diverse patterns of actions that make up the social world.

The key question for the social theorist is how the various and diverse images of reality that individual minds develop could ever be coordinated to one another. The social institutions that arise through the voluntary association of thousands of individuals serve to guide individuals in the process of mutual accommodation. The voluntary interaction of individuals reveals the various subjective pattern of trade-offs that individuals possess and utilizes this knowledge to promote plan coordination.[9]

Market participants, for example, do not possess knowledge of the real underlying economic factors in the economy. On the basis of *understanding*, individuals interpret the meaning of changes on the economic scene and orient their behavior accordingly. They rely on the freely established exchange ratio in the market to inform them about (1) current market conditions, (2) the appropriateness of past decisions, and (3) the future possibilities of pure profit. The market system provides ex ante information in the form of money prices reflecting the relative scarcities of goods so that economic actors may plan their future actions. The market system also provides ex post information through the system of profit and loss to inform market participants about the appropriateness of their past actions. If they bought cheap and sold dear they are rewarded, whereas if they bought dear and sold cheap they suffer losses. The array of market prices, however, also possess information about the possibility of pure entrepreneurial profit. The discrepancy between the current array of prices and the possible future array generates the discovery of ever new and fresh ways to shuffle or reshuffle resources in a manner that satisfies the demands of consumers. The market system as a whole, in its ex ante, ex post and discovery capacity, generates and utilizes economic knowledge "so tens of thousands of people whose identity could not be ascertained by months of investigation, are made to use the material or its products ... in the right direction" (Hayek 1945: 87).[10]

Social life, however, is not restricted to the market but encompasses a vast array of complex structures which enable us to successfully plan our actions in reference to others. The same procedure by which we understand successful plan coordination on the economic scene is applicable to other areas of our social existence. As Hayek has pointed out:

> While at the world of nature we look from the outside, we look at the world of society from the inside; while, as far as nature is concerned, our concepts are about the facts and have to be adapted to the facts, in the world of society at least some of the most familiar concepts are the stuff from which the world is made. Just as the existence of a common structure of thought is the condition of the possibility of our communicating with one another, of your understanding what I say, so it is also the basis on which we all interpret such complicated social structures as those which we find in economic life or law, in language, and in customs.
>
> (1943: 76)

Though the complex structures of society are the composite of the purposive behavior of individuals, they are not the result of conscious human design. The intentional, *i.e.*, meaningful, behavior of individuals affirm or reaffirm the overall order in society. But social order is not the result of conscious design and control.[11] Perhaps the greatest source of misunderstanding in our social world is the failure to view society as an interpretive process which translates meaningful utterances of the human mind into socially useful knowledge, so that the various anonymous actors on the social scene may come into cooperation with one another, even though this order is not any part of their intention. As Hayek states:

> We still refuse to recognize that the spontaneous interplay of the actions of individuals may produce something which is not the deliberate object of their actions but an organism in which every part performs a necessary function for the continuance of the whole, without any human mind having devised it. In the words of an eminent Austrian economist [Mises], we refuse to recognize that society is an organism and not an organisation and that, in a sense, we are part of a 'higher' organised system which, without our knowledge, and long before we tried to understand it, solved problems the existence of which we did not even recognise, but which we should have had to solve in much the same way if we had tried to run it deliberately.
>
> (1933b: 130–131)[12]

Much of Hayek's work, including his work on the common law and his recent statements on the co-evolution of reason and tradition, follows directly from his exploration of Mises's discussion of the foundation of a social order based on the division of labor. The Hayekian research program extends the spontaneous order approach beyond the realm of economic explanation to all realms of social interaction, including science, law, and history. Hayek's economics has sought to articulate the discovery role of the competitive market process, his legal philosophy has sought to examine the discovery process of the common law, and his philosophical anthropology explores the discovery process of history.

IV. Hayek, rationalism and the Law of Association

Law and principles of just conduct, rather than being the products of pure reason, evolve over time and take on new meaning as they are applied in new circumstances to resolve social conflicts. The recognition of the spontaneous ordering of social cooperation does not demean reason – in fact, it upholds man's reason in ordering his own affairs. Much of Hayek's work should be seen as an attempt to defend reason against its abuse under the guise of *scientism* or Cartesian rationalism. Consider the following statements from Hayek's work on the liberal society:

> Complete rationality of action in the Cartesian sense demands complete knowledge of all relevant facts. A designer or engineer needs all the data and full power to control or manipulate them if he is to organize the material objects to produce the intended result. But the success of action in society depends on more particular facts than anyone can possibly know. And our whole civilization in consequence rests, and must rest, on our believing much that we cannot know to be true in the Cartesian sense.
>
> (1973: 12)

> What we have attempted is a defense of reason against its abuse by those who do not understand the conditions of its effective functioning and continuous growth. It is an appeal to men to see that we must use our reason intelligently and that, in order to do so, we must preserve the indispensable matrix of the uncontrolled and non-rational which is the only environment wherein reason can grow and operate effectively.
>
> (1960: 69)

What Hayek's work does deny is that the complex order of society is a result of rationalist construction and human design. The order that emerges under a system of division of labor and private property was not

147

the result of anyone's design or intention, but was the composite of all the separate striving of individuals to realize their purposes and plans.

The social order made possible by the division of labor, Mises argued, was a result of the recognition of the benefits of such an order. The greater productive capabilities of the division of labor alert men to the gains of social cooperation. In this manner Mises generalizes Ricardo's principle of comparative advantage into the principle of association (see 1922: 256ff., 1966: 143ff.).

Much controversy surrounds Hayek's recent attempts to reformulate this principle and his use of cultural evolution in the explanation of the principle.[13] For example, David Ramsey Steele (1987) has argued that Hayek has abandoned the social theory project of the Scottish Enlightenment and embraced a holistic approach to social analysis that is alien to both that tradition and Hayek's earlier work on methodological individualism. Hayek's theory of group selection and cultural evolution is at best incorrect, and quite possibly damaging to the classical liberal project.[14] Hayek is reduced, Steele argues, by the logic of his own argument, to a naive conservative.

Viktor Vanberg (1986) raises a very similar criticism of Hayek's theory of cultural evolution. "A closer examination of Hayek's writings on this topic," Vanberg (1986: 83) argues:

> reveals that, in actual fact, he neither systematically elaborates nor consistently pursues such an individualistic, evolutionary approach to the question of why it is that rules can be expected spontaneously to emerge that increase the efficiency of the group as a whole and that provide solutions to "problems of society."

There is, Vanberg concludes, a tacit shift in Hayek's work from his earlier methodological individualism, where behavioral regularities emerge from the rational assessment of trade-offs among social participants, to the quite different emphasis on social rules which are followed because of the benefits that accrue to the group. This shift, to Vanberg, is undesirable and unjustified, and undermines our attempt to grapple with the problem of rule formation in social processes.

James Buchanan (1977, 1986a) has also reiterated these criticisms. But Buchanan's criticism is more fundamental. He challenges the very idea of extending the spontaneous order paradigm beyond the realm of economics. While the discovery process of competitive markets tends to produce some optimality conditions (sub-optimalities are eliminated in the pursuit of pure profit), there is no guarantee that legal processes yield the same result and certainly the discovery process of history cannot be relied upon. Buchanan finds Hayek's arguments about diffuse knowledge and the discovery process of the market convincing, but the extension of the argument to other social institutions creates problems, he believes, for grappling with what he calls the constitutional level of political economy. Hayek's conservativism doesn't allow for the deliberate reform of the rules of society. "There is no room left," Buchanan argues, "for the political economist, or for anyone else who seeks to reform social structures, to change laws and rules, with an aim of securing increased efficiency in the large" (1986a: 76).

Even Israel Kirzner, perhaps the leading representative of the modern Austrian school, follows Buchanan's essentially equilibrium criticism of Hayek. Kirzner is concerned that Hayek's extension of the spontaneous order approach beyond economics may lead us astray and undermine the defense of economic liberty. "The extraordinary power of arguments rooted in market theory should not be compromised," Kirzner warns, "by well-meaning but unhelpful reference to other kinds of spontaneous order" (1987: 46).

Kirzner distinguishes between traditional spontaneous order explanations found the writings of Adam Smith, *etc.*, which assumed individuals acting with regard to their self-interest within a given institutional framework, and the more recent literature on spontaneous order which emphasizes the plausibility of social coordination emerging out of the self-interested behavior of individuals within an environment without any given institutional framework. While the earlier work was able to demonstrate, Kirzner argues, that within a certain institutional environment the decentralized decisions of economic actors could be coordinated in a manner which allocated resources in an "objectively" efficient manner, the later work does not possess such a logic – there are no equilibrium conditions in law, language and custom.

Both Buchanan and Kirzner explicitly rely on the neoclassical description of competitive markets as Pareto Optimal. Buchanan, for example, argues that there are three reasons to adopt spontaneous order explanations: political, aesthetic, and economic. Political, because of a proper understanding of the spontaneous ordering of economic activity in a competitive market will possess tremendous import for economic policy decisions. Aesthetic, because spontaneous order explanations are intellectually more satisfying than expectations from design. Economic, because an understanding of spontaneous order allows us to "say that the workings of the market generate Pareto-efficient results" (1977: 29). But this third reason for adopting spontaneous order explanations of social coordination also limits there normative application beyond technical economics. We simply cannot say that either the legal or historical process possesses any logic which generates Pareto-efficient results. While the competitive market harbors tendencies to equilibrate and thus eliminate socially undesirable states of affairs, "the forces of social evolution ... contain within their workings no guarantee that socially efficient results will emerge over time." The social institutions which emerge "need not be those which are the 'best' " (1977: 31). Or, as Kirzner has put it:

> There is no guarantee that the English language my children learn at their mother's knee will be a 'better' language for purposes of social intercourse than, say, French – or Esperanto. The demonstration that widely accepted social conventions can emerge without central authoritarian imposition does not necessarily point to any optimality in the resulting conventions.

What is demonstrated in the spontaneous order explanation of free market process, on the other hand, "is that there does exist a spontaneous tendency toward social optimality under the relevant conditions" (1987: 48).

The Achilles heel of these criticisms, however, is their continued reliance on the neoclassical notion of optimality. The Hayekian program has become increasingly disillusioned with any idea of optimality conditions and equilibrium states as these concepts proved to frustrate rather than enhance our understanding of social interaction, as Buchanan himself has recognized (1986b: 73–74). As Hayek has put it:

> I am afraid that I have become – with all aesthetic admiration for the achievement – more and more sceptical of the instructive value of the construction by which at one time I was greatly fascinated, that beautiful system of equations with which we can show in imagination what would happen if all these data were given to us. But we often forget that these data are purely fictitious, are not available to any single mind, and, therefore, do not really lead to an explanation of the process we observe.
>
> (1983: 36)

The modern Austrian school, following Hayek, has sought to consistently advance an alternative approach to the study of economic activity. The Austrian theory of the market process stands in stark contrast to the more traditional equilibrium analysis of mainstream neo-classical economics. A theoretical perspective has developed which is built around both a deep appreciation of the subjective nature of the economic world and a recognition of how social institutions work through the filter of the human mind to coordinate activity. This economic process is neither an evolutionary natural selection process that assures the survival of the "best" or "fittest" nor is this process a chaotic and random walk. The discovery process of the competitive market is a learning process – a process of trial and error and experimentation in which the key component is the ability to reveal error and motivate the discovery of new knowledge about economic opportunities.

As Kirzner and Buchanan have themselves demonstrated, the market process does not lead to any optimal state. The market process is misspecified if presented as an equilibrium system. Free market processes are characterized by continuous sub-optimalities – in fact, that is what generates the whole process of learning and discovery. The superiority of the market process, as pointed out above in the discussion of economic calculation, lies not in its ability to produce optimal results, but rather in its ability to mobilize and effectively use knowledge that is dispersed throughout the economic system.

The criticism of Hayek's project on the grounds of his abandonment of methodological individualism, moreover, are misplaced for two reasons.[15] First, Hayek is mainly talking about the co-evolution of reason and tradition in the epoch when man was first emerging from his pre-human condition. Hayek's thesis is that our reason developed because we followed certain rules, not that we followed certain rules because of our reason. As he writes, cultural evolution:

> took place not merely after the appearance of Homo sapiens, but also during the much longer earlier existence of the genus Homo and its hominid ancestors. To repeat: mind and culture developed concurrently and not successively.
>
> (1979: 156)

This leads to a position which challenges the sort of isolated and atomistic methodological individualism characteristic of much economics. Social inquiry must begin with a recognition of the social embededness of the mind. As Chris Sciabarra argues:

> For Hayek, the individual cannot stand by himself – he is invariably an actor in a specific historical and cultural context. Hayek's arguments have an epistemological dimension as well. For Hayek, there is a limit beyond which we are unable to articulate the rules, customs and habits which govern our lives. We are internal to these rules and cannot take an external, transcendental role. To this end, even our consciousness operates according to rules of which we are not conscious – since these rules are internal to the operation itself.
>
> (1987: 90–91)

Second, the best way to understand what Hayek is trying to do in *The Constitution of Liberty, Law, Legislation and Liberty* and *The Fatal Conceit* is to restate and elaborate from a consistently non-rationalist perspective, the Mises's argument concerning the Law of Association. "We have never designed our economic system," Hayek states. "We were not intelligent enough for that" (1979: 164). Hayek is offering, as John Gray (1986: 130) points out:

> a more humble, sceptical and modest form of liberalism than that found in the French philosophers, a liberalism that has rid itself of the incubus of an hubristic rationalism – and which has most in common with the social philosophy of the thinkers of the Scottish Enlightenment, and, above all, with the outlook of David Hume. Hayek is, in effect, refining and completing this non-rationalist tradition of classical liberalism.[16]

As Hayek writes in *The Fatal Conceit*:

> To understand our civilization, one must appreciate that the extended order resulted not from human design or intention but spontaneously: it arose from unintentionally conforming to certain traditional and largely moral practices, many of which men tend to dislike, whose significance they usually fail to understand, whose validity they cannot prove, and which have nonetheless fairly rapidly spread by means of an evolutionary selection – the comparative increase of population and wealth – of those groups that happened to follow them.
>
> (1988: 6)

The institution of private (or separated) property, which man stumbled into, according to Hayek, made possible the growth of civilization. By following certain rules, which he could not justify nor even state, man cultivated his social world.[17] "Such activities in which we are guided by a knowledge merely of the principle of a thing," Hayek states, "should perhaps better be described by the term *cultivation* than by the familiar term 'control' " (1955: 19, emphasis in original).

Hayek argues that the coincidence of opinion concerning just rules of conduct will emerge through the purposive and meaningful dialogue of human interaction. Implicit rules of conduct will be respected among the various individuals in the social world before agreement is reached on articulated rules. It is these implicit rules through which the Law of Association operates to bring about the liberal extended order.

"It is only as a result of individuals observing certain common rules," Hayek argues, "that a group of men can live together in those orderly relations which we call society" (1973: 95). Man does not need to consciously recognize the benefits of society as a whole, but merely the benefits to him of the division of labor and exchange. Out of a process by which individuals strive to improve their lot in life, the rules of the extended order come to be respected. Neither do we need to live in a world where every other man believes as we do about fundamental values in order to live in harmony. All we need are rules or social institutions (conventions, symbols, *etc.*) that produce mutually reinforcing sets of expectations to maintain a degree of social order, and these rules or institutions must serve as guides to individuals so they may orient their actions. The rules of social intercourse must be rigid enough so as to confirm our expectations, but flexible enough to allow for changing circumstances and creative human potential. As Hayek argues:

> Living as members of society and dependent for the satisfaction of most of our needs on various forms of cooperation with others, we depend for the effective pursuit of our aims clearly on the correspondence of the expectations concerning the actions of others on which our plans are based with what they really do.
>
> (1973: 36)

Civilization can be cultivated through the judicious use of reason, but its complexity lies beyond the ability of human reason to design or control it. As Hayek states in *The Counter-Revolution of Science*:

> We flatter ourselves undeservedly if we represent human civilization as entirely the product of conscious reason or as the product of human design, or when we assume that it is necessarily in our power deliberately to re-create or to maintain what we have built without knowing what we were doing. Though our civilization is the result of a cumulation of individual knowledge, it is not by the explicit or conscious combination of all this knowledge in any individual brain, but by its embodiment in symbols which we use without understanding them, in habits and institutions, tools and concepts, that man in society is constantly able to profit from a body of knowledge neither he nor any other man completely possesses. Many of the greatest things man has achieved are the result not of consciously directed thought, and still less the product of deliberately coordinated effort of many individuals, but of a process in which the individual plays a part which he can never fully understand. They are greater than any individual precisely because they result from the combination of knowledge more extensive than a single mind can master.
>
> (1952a: 149–150)

V. Conclusion

Hayek's social theory is carrying on and advancing the tradition of social analysis that dates back to the Scottish Enlightenment thinkers, such as

David Hume and Adam Smith. His work, and especially his scholarly example, serves as an inspiration to several younger scholars who are attempting to stand on his shoulders and push his insights on the social world even further.

Hayek has claimed, for example, that the coercive powers of the State have corrupted the social institutions of money and law. He has himself suggested a framework to study these problems, but it is in the work of several younger scholars that these problems are now being explored in detail.[18] For some time his followers will be, as Hayek said of Mises, "pursuing the questions which he made [them] see" and that is the greatest gift one scientist can give to another.

Acknowledgments

I would like to gratefully acknowledge financial support in the form of the 1989 Summer Research Fellowship, School of Business Administration, Oakland University, Rochester, MI 48309. In addition, I would like to thank Don Lavoie for his critical comments on an earlier draft. Responsibility for remaining errors is my own.

Notes

1 Gray has most recently come to interpret Hayek as a naive conservative who abandons methodological individualism in his later work on social anthropology. This, however, is a misreading of Hayek as well be argued later in the paper. In fact, to a large extent, Gray's most recent repudiation of much of the liberal tradition of social philosophy results, ironically, from a serious misreading on his part. See Gray (1988) for a discussion of the problems he sees in the liberal project.

2 See Hayek (1959a: 52, fn. 7) for a discussion of the importance of Mises's work for the advancement of economic understanding.

3 As Smith wrote in connection with the multitude of activities that must coordinated to produce a simple woollen coat: "Observe the accommodation of the most common artificer or day-labourer in a civilized and thriving country, and you will perceive that the number people of whose industry a part, through but a small part, has been employed in procuring him this accommodation, exceeds all computation" (1776: 15).

4 This, of course, requires certain well-specified rules under which individuals are pursuing their individual interests, for example, the right of property. In the absence of private property, Smith would not be surprised by the "tragedy of the commons" problem.

5 See Smith (1776: 478). This of course, conflates the two arguments – the use of knowledge and the abuse of power – and it is not until after Mises's and Hayek's work concerning the problem of socialist calculation that the focus shifts to concentrate more directly on the use of knowledge in society. Nevertheless the argument is presented in embryonic form in Smith, as Hayek (1988: 14, 86–87) points out.

6 See William Jaffe (1976: 518–519; 520) where he argues that: Carl Menger

clearly stands apart from the other two reputed founders of the modern marginal utility theory.... It is not that Menger was unaware of tendencies to eventual equilibrium in the real world, but he was too conscious of the ubiquitous obstacles that, even ceteris paribus, impede the attainment of market equilibrium within anything less than secular delays. With his attention unswervingly fixed on reality, Menger could not, and did not, abstract from the difficulties traders face in any attempt to obtain all the information required for anything like a pinpoint equilibrium determination of market prices to emerge, nor did his approach permit him to abstract from the uncertainties that veil the future, even the near future in the conscious anticipation of which most present transactions take place.

7 As Menger stated, though, "The organic view cannot be a universal means of consideration; the organic understanding of social phenomena cannot be the universal goal of theoretical research in the field of the latter. Rather, for the understanding of social phenomena in their entirety the pragmatic interpretation is, in any case just as indispensable as the 'organic' " (1883: 135). For a recent discussion of this line of argument see Witt (1989).

8 Much of Mises's work, and especially the work of his student Israel Kirzner, on the nature of the market system and the entrepreneurial process, is an attempt to demonstrate how the institutions of a free market overcome the generalized knowledge problem that faces society. That is, how do social institutions serve to coordinate the dispersed, and often conflicting, plans of various actors in society? As Kirzner (1984: 415) argues, "The truth is that the market does possess weapons to combat (if not wholly to conquer) the problem of dispersed knowledge. These weapons are embodied in the workings of the price system, but not in the workings of a hypothetical system of equilibrium prices. The importance of prices for coping with the Hayekian knowledge problem does not lie in the accuracy of the information which equilibrium prices convey concerning the actions of others who are similarly informed. Rather, its importance · lies in the ability of disequilibrium prices to offer pure profit opportunities that can attract the notice of alert, profit-seeking entrepreneurs. Where market participants have failed to coordinate their activities because of dispersed knowledge, this expresses itself in an array of prices that suggests to alert entrepreneurs where they may win pure profits."

9 As Thomas Sowell writes about the decentralized process of market exchange and production: "Prices convey the experience and subjective feelings of some as effective knowledge to others; it is implicit knowledge in the form of an explicit inducement. Price fluctuations convey knowledge of changing trade-offs among changing options as people weigh costs and benefits differently over time, with changes in tastes and technology. The totality of knowledge conveyed by the innumerable prices and their widely varying rates of change vastly exceeds what any individual can know or needs to know for his own purposes" (1980: 167).

10 The development of this process cultivates the operation of advanced technological developments that depend upon the system's ability to mobilize the dispersed knowledge of thousands of individuals. As Lavoie argues: "the evolution of markets has delivered us into a world too complex for any individual intelligence to comprehend in detail, thus necessitating our reliance on the greater social intelligence embodied in market processes. These market processes, if they are to generate and embody a high degree of social intelligence, require relatively free competition among (de facto) private owners of capital and other resources and the continuous (and nonegalitarian) ebb and flow of wealth caused by this competitive process" (1985b: 51).

11 See Hayek (1976: 107–132) for a discussion on how the economizing behavior of individuals gives rise to the catallactic order even though that was not part of their intention.

12 Hayek's reference on this point is quite important and challenges those who wish to differentiate Mises from Hayek on their view of spontaneous processes of mutual accommodation. As Mises wrote in the section Hayek alludes to in the quote, "Organization is an association based on authority, organism is mutuality.... In recognizing the nature of the organism and sweeping away the exclusiveness of the concept of organization, science made one of its great steps forward. With all deference to earlier thinkers one may say that in the domain of Social Science this was achieved mainly in the eighteenth century, and that Classical Political Economy and its immediate precursors played the chief part" (1922: 262–263).

13 See, for example, the criticism of Hayek's project in Gray (1986: 116ff.) and (1988), Buchanan (1977, 1986a), Vanberg (1986), Steele (1987) and Miller (1989).

14 While Steele bemoans this, Geoffrey Hodgson (1988, 1989) rejoices in the inconsistency of Hayek's liberal project. Hayek's abandonment of "abstract individualism," Hodgson argues, undermines the case for the liberal society even if Hayek fails to recognize it. The breakdown of the classical liberal bias in economic science is a major advance, Hodgson argues. I will suggest, however, that (1) we should not be concerned with whether Hayek's project defends or undermines a certain set of policies, but rather that it aids us in understanding the world and that, as it turns out, (2) Hayek's argument actually does enhance his argument for classical liberalism.

15 See Yeager (1989) for a defense of Hayek against those who misread him as undermining human reason. As Yeager argues, Hayek "recognizes that in the evolution of the Common Law, for example, judges decided individual cases by trying rationally to identify, articulate and apply practices and rules already in effect, though not yet explicitly recognized. And he certainly accepts Carl Menger's account of the spontaneous evolution of money, according to which individuals rationally adopted practices that facilitated their transactions" (1989: 327).

16 Also see Herzog (1986) for a discussion of the importance of the Hume-Smith project for social theory.

17 Those who argue that Hayek's emphasis on the population growth that is made possible through private property is a deviation from the classical liberal tradition should remember that Adam Smith argued that "The most decisive mark of the prosperity of any country is the increase of the number of its inhabitants" (1776: 79). And, moreover, Mises argued that the choice between capitalism and socialism was a choice between property and freedom versus starvation, death and barbarism. As Mises wrote: "Whether Society is good or bad may be a matter of individual judgment; but whoever prefers life to death, happiness to suffering, well-being to misery, must accept society. And whoever desires that society should exist and develop must also accept, without limitation or reserve, private ownership in the means of production" (1922: 469).

18 On money see White (1984) and Selgin (1988) and on law see Barnett (1985 and 1986) and Benson (1988) for some of the attempts to grapple with these problems.

References

Barnett, R.
1985   "Pursuing Justice in a Free Society: Part I," *Criminal Justice Ethics (Summer/Fall)*, 50–72.
1986   "Pursuing Justice in a Free Society: Part II," *Criminal Justice Ethics (Winter/Spring)*, 30–53.

Benson, B.
1988   "Spontaneous Emergence of Commercial Law," *Southern Economic Journal*, 55, no. 3 (January), 644–661.

Boettke, P.
1989   "Austrian Institutionalism," *Research in the History of Economic Thought and Methodology*, 6, 181–202.

Buchanan, J.
1977   *Freedom in Constitutional Contract*. College Station: Texas A&M University Press.
1986a   "Cultural Evolution and Institutional Reform," in Buchanan, J. *Liberty, Market and State*. New York: New York University Press, 75–85.
1986b   "Order Defined in the Process of Its Emergence," in Buchanan, J. *Liberty, Market and State*. New York: New York University Press, 73–74.

Caldwell, B.
1988   "Hayek's Transformation," *History of Political Economy*, 20, no. 4 (Winter), 513–542.

Gadamer, H.
1960[1985] *Truth and Method*. New York: Crossroads Publisher.
Gray, J.
1986   *Hayek on Liberty*, 2nd Ed. New York: Basil Blackwell.
1988   "Mill's and Other Liberalism," *Critical Review*, 2, no. 2 & 3 (Spring/Summer).

Herzog, D.
1986   *Without Foundations*. Ithaca: Comell University Press.
Hayek, F.A.
1928[1984] "Intertemporal Price Equilibrium and Movements in the Value of Money," in Roy McCloughry (ed.), *Money, Capital and Fluctuations: Early Essays*. Chicago: University of Chicago Press.
1933a[1966] *Monetary Theory and the Trade Cycle*. New York: Augustus M. Kelley.
1933b   "The Trend in Economic Thinking," *Economica*, May, 121–37.
1935[1967] *Prices and Production*, 2nd Ed. New York: Augustus M. Kelley.
1937[1980] "Economics and Knowledge," reprinted in Hayek 1948, 33–56.
1939[1975] *Profits, Interest and Investment*. New York: Augustus M. Kelley.
1941[1975] *The Pure Theory of Capital*. Chicago: University of Chicago Press.
1942[1980] "The Facts of the Social Sciences," reprinted in Hayek 1948, 57–76.
1944[1976] *The Road to Serfdom*. Chicago: University of Chicago Press.
1945[1980] "The Use of Knowledge in Society," reprinted in Hayek 1948, 77–91.

1948[1980]	*Individualism and Economic Order*. Chicago: University of Chicago Press.
1952a[1979]	*The Counter-Revolution of Science*. Indianapolis: Liberty Classics.
1952b[1976]	*The Sensory Order*. Chicago: University of Chicago Press.
1955[1980]	"Degrees of Explanation," reprinted in Hayek 1967, 3–1.
1960	*The Constitution of Liberty*. Chicago: University of Chicago Press.
1962[1980]	"Rules, Perception and Intelligibility," reprinted in Hayek 1967, 43–65.
1967[1980]	*Studies in Philosophy, Politics and Economics*. Chicago: University of Chicago Press.
1969[1978]	"The Primacy of the Abstract," reprinted in Hayek 1978, 35–49.
1973	*Law, Legislation and Liberty*, Vol. 1. Chicago: University of Chicago Press.
1976	*Law, Legislation and Liberty*, Vol. 2. Chicago: University of Chicago Press.
1978	*New Studies in Politics, Philosophy, Economics and the History of Ideas*. Chicago: University of Chicago Press.
1979a	*Law, Legislation and Liberty*, Vol. 3. Chicago: University of Chicago Press.
1979b	"Three Sources of Human Values," epilogue to Hayek 1979a, 153–176.
1983	*Knowledge, Evolution and Society*. London: Adam Smith Institute.
1988	*The Fatal Conceit*. Chicago: University of Chicago Press.

Hayek, F.A., ed.
| 1935[1975] | *Collectivist Economic Planning*. New York: Augustus M. Kelley. |

Hodgson, G.
| 1988 | *Economics and Institutions*. Philadelphia: University of Pennsylvania Press. |
| 1989 | "Institutional Economic Theory: The Old versus the New," *Review of Political Economy*, 1, no. 3, 249–269. |

Hutchison, T.W.
| 1984 | *The Politics and Philosophy of Economics*. New York: New York University Press. |

Jaffe, W.
| 1976 | "Menger, Jevons and Walras De-Homogenized," *Economic Inquiry*, 14 (December), 511–534. |

Kirzner, I.
| 1984 | "Economic Planning and the Knowledge Problem," *Cato Journal*, 4, no. 2 (Fall), 407–425. |
| 1987 | "Spontaneous Order and the Case for the Free Market," in *Ideas on Liberty: Essays in Honor of Paul L. Poirot* (Irvington on Hudson: The Foundation for Economic Education), 45–50. |

Lachmann, L.
| 1986 | *The Market as a Process*. New York: Basil Blackwell. |

Lavoie, D.
| 1985a | *Rivalry and Central Planning*. New York: Cambridge University Press. |
| 1985b | *National Economic Planning: What is Left?*. Cambridge: Ballinger Publishers. |

Madison, G.B.
1989   "Hayek and the Interpretive Turn," *Critical Review*, 3, no. 2
                (Spring), 169–185.
Menger, C.
1871[1981]   *Principles of Economics*. New York: New York University Press.
1883[1985]   *Investigations into the Methods of the Social Sciences with Special*
                Reference to Economics. New York: New York University Press.
1892   "On The Origin of Money," *Economic Journal*, Vol. 2, 239–55.
Miller, D.
1989   "The Fatalistic Conceit," *Critical Review*, 3, no. 2 (Spring), 310–23.
Mises, L.
1912[1980]   *The Theory of Money and Credit*. Indianapolis: Liberty Classics.
1920[1975]   "Economic Calculation in the Socialist Commonwealth," reprinted
                in Hayek, ed., 1935, 87–130.
1922[1981]   *Socialism: An Economic and Sociological Analysis*. Indianapolis:
                Liberty Classics.
1957[1985]   *Theory and History*. Auburn: Ludwig von Mises Institute.
1966   *Human Action: A Treatise on Economics*, 3rd Rev. Ed. Chicago:
                Henry Regnery.
1978   *Notes and Recollections*. New York: Arlington House.
Selgin, G.
1988   *The Theory of Free Banking*. Totowa: Rowman and Littlefield.
Sciabarra, C.
1987   "The Crisis of Libertarian Dualism," *Critical Review*, 1, no. 4 (Fall),
                86–99.
Smith, A.
1759[1976]   *The Theory of Moral Sentiments*. Indianapolis: Liberty Classics.
1776[1976]   *An Inquiry into the Nature and Cause of the Wealth of Nations*.
                Chicago: University of Chicago Press.
Sowell, T.
1980   *Knowledge and Decisions*. New York: Basic Books.
Steele, D.
1987   "Hayek's Theory of Cultural Group Selection," *Journal of Liber-*
                tarian Studies, 8, no. 2 (Summer), 171–195.
Vanberg, V.
1986   "Spontaneous Market Order and Social Rules," *Economics and*
                Philosophy, Vol. 2, 75–100.
White, L.
1984   *Free Banking in Britian*. New York: Cambridge University Press.
Witt, U.
1989   "The Evolution of Economic Institutions as a Propagation
                Process," *Public Choice*, 62, no. 2 (August), 155–172.
Yeager, L.
1989   "Reason and Cultural Evolution," *Critical Review*, 3, no. 2
                (Spring), 324–335.

51

HAYEK CONTRA PANGLOSS ON EVOLUTIONARY SYSTEMS

Douglas Glen Whitman[1]

Source: *Constitutional Political Economy* 9 (1998): 45–66.

1. Introduction

Nearly all of the political and economic doctrines of Friedrich Hayek have drawn heated criticism from one quarter or another, but few have attracted so much critique and rebuke, from authors of diverse persuasions, as his theory of cultural evolution. The idea that the morals, customs, habits, conventions, and even laws of modern civilization may owe their origin to a lengthy process of variation, competition, and selection has a long—and sometimes unsavory—history in intellectual thought, and Hayek was by no means its first exponent. He may, however, be credited with reviving the concept as a serious tool for social theory and normative judgment in the latter half of this century, and his most evolutionarily oriented works, *the Fatal Conceit* (1988) and *Law, Legislation and Liberty* (1973, 1976, 1979), have served as a lightning rod for renewed discussion of the merits and flaws of evolutionary theory in the social sciences.

Among the most frequently repeated charges lodged against Hayek's theory of cultural evolution is that Hayek, like the Social Darwinists, has committed the Panglossian fallacy: he has suggested or implied that social evolution must necessarily produce the best of all possible worlds, a world in which "whatever is, is desirable," or (to put the economists' spin on it) "whatever is, is efficient."[2] John Gray (1989: 98), for instance, claims that "Hayek frequently affirms that the sheer persistence of a tradition or a form of life suggests that it must possess some general utility." Martin De Vlieghere (1994: 293) characterizes Hayek as contending that "only those cultural attainments can survive and spread that are beneficial. So, the very longevity of an institution proves its value...." According to Stefan Voigt (1992: 465, n.20), Hayek commits the naturalistic fallacy in his support of evolved institutions: "The currently existing institutions (the

160

'is') have emerged because they have been more viable than other institutions, from which Hayek concludes that they ought to exist."

In the economists' camp, Joseph Stiglitz (1994: 275) argues that "those who appeal to the evolutionary process [e.g., Hayek and Armen Alchian] also claim too much: There is no reason to believe that evolutionary processes have any optimality properties ...," and he goes on to say, "It seems nonsensical to suggest that we should simply accept the natural outcome of the evolutionary process." James Buchanan, an author usually friendly to Hayekian themes, nonetheless perceives Hayek as being adamantly opposed to all reform of evolved institutions. "We may share much of Hayek's skepticism about social and institutional reform, however, without elevating the evolutionary process to an ideal role," says Buchanan (1975: 194, ch. 10, n.1). "Reform may, indeed, be difficult, but this is no argument that its alternative is ideal." Sociologist Bjorn Hallerod (1992: 34) is notably less sympathetic. He argues that "Hayek ends up in a situation where every existing form of society is a good society or otherwise it would not exist," which means that Hayek must find even Nazism acceptable.

The critiques have been severe and sometimes overstated, but they are in substance correct: evolutionary systems cannot be characterized as unambiguously efficient or desirable (however these terms might be defined) in their effects. Where Hayek's critics err is in directing these criticisms at Hayek. Hayek's theory can be faulted in a variety of ways, but Panglossianism is not one of them.

My intention in this chapter is two-fold: first, to restate for the record Hayek's rejection of the idea that cultural evolution necessarily produces optimal results; and second, to elaborate some of the reasons why his theory need not imply any such thing. I will conclude by explaining how a better understanding of suboptimality in evolutionary systems can illuminate some areas of controversy that have arisen with regard to Hayek's theory.

The second goal will be pursued via an extended analogy with biological evolution. This approach may require some justification. It is my impression that many opponents of cultural evolution theories assume Panglossian implications because of a conscious or unconscious analogy with biological evolution, which is widely—and incorrectly—perceived as a process that produces optimal fitness in organisms relative to their habitats. Gray (1989: 98), for example, states as an objection to Hayek's theory, "we have nothing in society akin to the mechanism of natural selection of genetic accidents in Darwinian theory which guarantees the survival of useful social practices," as though he believes biological natural selection does make such a guarantee. My response, then, proceeds by showing that, even if the analogy between biological and cultural evolution is close (and the analogy does seem closer to me than many analysts would like to admit), biological evolution does not and cannot produce optimal results in all cases. Insofar as cultural evolution shares common features with biological evolution, it, too, will be subject to inefficiency.

Although Hayek often tries to distance himself from the analogy with biological evolution, he apparently does so not mainly because he doubts the analogy's validity, but because he wishes to eschew the errors of the Social Darwinists. Hayek repeatedly emphasizes that Darwin's theory of biological evolution was inspired by the evolutionary thinking of the moral and social theorists who preceded him (particularly David Hume, Adam Smith, and the other Scottish moral philosophers).[3] After Darwin, Hayek (1979: 154) laments, "those 'social Darwinists' who had needed Darwin to learn what was an older tradition in their own subjects, had somewhat spoiled the case [for cultural evolution] by concentrating on the selection of congenitally more fit individuals," rather than on the selection of rules and practices adopted by groups. Hayek hastens to point out the differences between cultural and biological evolution that make it the case that rules and practices are far more significant than individuals in the process of cultural evolution. Specifically, he notes that "cultural evolution *simulates* Lamarckism"; that cultural traits can be acquired "from an indefinite number of 'ancestors,'" not merely from one's parents; that learning as a mode of transmission makes cultural evolution occur more quickly than biological evolution; and that cultural evolution is more likely to be subject to group selection (1988: 25). Nonetheless, Hayek recognizes that while their specific mechanisms differ, all forms of evolution share common features. Although the "literal use" of Darwinian theory leads to "grave distortions" when focused upon individuals rather than rules, "the basic conception of evolution is still the same in both fields," he says (1979: 23). Biological and cultural evolution "both rely on the same principle of selection: survival and reproductive advantage. Variation, adaptation and competition are essentially the same kind of process, however different their particular mechanisms, particularly those pertaining to propagation."[4] Again, to the extent that cultural and biological evolution are united by kindred processes, they can be expected to exhibit similar characteristics, including their capacity to produce efficient and less-than-efficient outcomes.

In much of this chapter, I will be purposely vague about the definition of efficiency. Even within economics, efficiency has been defined in a variety of ways, from strict Pareto efficiency to wealth maximization. The standards by which the efficiency of rules and institutions are judged sometimes differ from the standards employed to judge efficient activity within given rules and institutions; for example, when Hayek speaks of the efficiency of rules, he usually seems to have in mind the degree to which rules promote the utilization of knowledge and the coordination of plans. Biologists typically employ the concept of "reproductive fitness," by which

162

they mean the capacity of traits to increase the probability of an organism surviving long enough to reproduce as effectively as possible subject to environmental constraints. In general, all such concepts of efficiency are related to the idea, broadly conceived, of "doing the best you can given certain constraints," and fortunately, the point I wish to make does not require any greater specificity. I will contend that, whatever specific definition of efficiency may be adopted, an evolutionary system could not be expected to achieve it in all cases, although some brands of efficiency may be more easily approached than others.

2. F. A. Hayek: no Panglossian

By all indications, Hayek was fully aware of the "all's for the best" charges that might be leveled against his theory. He was particularly concerned with the tendency of some social theorists to reject all evolutionary theories of culture out of hand because of the errors of Social Darwinism. His disclaimer is therefore worth quoting at length:

> Bertrand Russell provides a good example in his claim that "if evolutionary ethics were sound, we ought to be entirely indifferent to what the course of evolution might be, since whatever it is is thereby proved to be the best".... This objection, which A. G. N. Flew ... regards as "decisive," rests on a simple misunderstanding. I have no intention to commit what is often called the genetic or naturalistic fallacy. I do not claim that the results of group selection of traditions are necessarily "good"—any more than I claim that other things that have long survived in the course of evolution, such as cockroaches, have moral value.
>
> (Hayek 1988: 27)

Nor does he claim that the products of cultural evolution should be immune to criticism or change; again, it is best to quote Hayek directly:

> It would be wrong to conclude, strictly from such evolutionary premises, that whatever rules have evolved are always or necessarily conducive to the survival and increase of the populations following them.... Recognizing that rules generally tend to be selected, via competition, on the basis of their human survival-value certainly does not protect those rules from critical scrutiny.
>
> (Ibid.: 20)

Notably, Hayek believes that the cultural selection process selects for survival and reproduction of groups (a questionable hypothesis that will be considered later), yet *even by that criterion of efficiency*, the resulting rules cannot be assumed to be efficient. It would be particularly odd, then, for those rules to be efficient according to some other standard, such as neo-classical economic efficiency or classical liberal value judgments.

The above quotations appear in Hayek's latest work, but they do not represent retrenchments in the face of criticism of Hayek's previous works; the same message appears repeatedly in his earlier works. In the *Constitution of Liberty*, for instance, we find Hayek admitting,

> These considerations, of course, do not prove that all sets of moral beliefs which have grown up in a society will be beneficial. Just as a group may owe its rise to the morals which its members obey, . . . so may a group or nation destroy itself by the moral beliefs to which it adheres.
>
> (Hayek 1960: 67)

Of course, this statement could be interpreted as merely a view of selec-tionism-in-progress, in that "bad" moral views are characterized as leading inevitably to their own demise. The point, however, is that Hayek does not perceive the process as finished: at any point in time, including the present day, we may find undesirable rules and customs that have not been weeded out by selective forces, at least not yet. Hayek never eschews the modification and reform of rules; he simply points out that any such revi-sion of particular rules must necessarily take place in the context of a complex of other rules that are taken as given for the time being: "This givenness of the value framework implies that, in our efforts to improve them, we must take for granted much that we do not understand" (Ibid.: 63).

In *Law, Legislation and Liberty*, Hayek again emphasizes the need for reform of established rules—this time in the context of a narrower evolu-tionary system, the common law.

> The fact that law that has evolved in this way has certain desirable properties does not prove that it will always be good law or even that some of its rules may not be very bad. It therefore does not mean that we can altogether dispense with legislation.
>
> (1973: 88)

Indeed, Hayek (Ibid.: 89) even admits the possibility that general prin-ciples of justice (embodied in the remainder of the body of law) may "require the revision not only of single rules but of whole sections of the established system of case law."

These are not the statements of a Panglossian. But neither do they suffice to shield Hayek's theory from the charge that it implies that what-ever exists is the best of all possible worlds; Hayek's objections notwithstanding, his theory may have implications beyond his words. The question is, does an evolutionary theory unavoidably lead to Panglossian conclusions? In answering this question, we can gain insights by taking a closer look at the well-developed evolutionary theory of another field: biology.

3. The flaws of the adaptationist paradigm

Evolutionary biologists have, unfortunately, contributed in part to the misconception that evolutionary systems must yield optimal results. Particularly in the early days of biological evolutionary theory, biologists could be found using Spencer's phrase "survival of the fittest" and that phrase has proved more than a little misleading. Biologists of the "pan-adaptationist" stripe have perpetuated the idea that all traits of all extant organisms may be construed as optimizing those organisms' fitness relative to the environment. Even modern biologists occasionally slip into this way of thinking; consider the following passage from biologist Ledyard Stebbins:

> ... all modern species and races of organisms have existed as successful populations, well adjusted to their environment, for thousands or millions of generations. We would expect, therefore, that all mutations that might improve the organism's reproductive fitness to its particular environment would have occurred at least once during this long period. If so, they would have been incorporated by natural selection in the gene pool.
>
> (Stebbins 1977: 58)

From statements like this one, it would be easy—but wrong—to draw Panglossian conclusions. Although extreme adaptationism reigned for a while in the biological literature, most biologists (including Stebbins) now reject pan-adaptationism (Vromen 1995: 95f.).

Two highly problematic assumptions are required to justify evolutionary theories of the pan-adaptationist variety. The first is the "t goes to infinity" assumption: evolutionary processes are presumed to have reached the ultimate result that would obtain if the processes continued for an infinite period of time. The paradigmatic example is the anecdote about 100 monkeys (actually, just one would do) pounding on typewriters for an unlimited amount of time: sooner or later, one of the monkeys will type out the entirety of *Gone With the Wind*. If the t-goes-to-infinity assumption is taken seriously, the logic is inexorable; every combination of letters (or gene/trait combinations, or cultural taboos) will eventually appear. Everything that *can* happen *will* happen, so an appropriate selection mechanism will presumably capture the best of all possible worlds. In real-world processes, however, infinite time is never the case, at least not from the perspective of an analyst observing the products of evolution at any given point in time. From our perspective, evolution is an ongoing process, and we should not be surprised to find incomplete—and suboptimal—adaptation. The assumption of infinite time bypasses considerations of process altogether,

Indeed, it is tempting to argue that, once infinite time is presumed, the optimal result is implicit in the initial conditions, in much the same way that the solution to a system of equations is implicit in the equations themselves. I will resist that temptation, however, because a second assumption is necessary for that conclusion: a stable, exogenous environment against which selection takes place. The environment is, of course, the standard on the basis of which adaptation (and optimality) is usually measured; in most theories, the environment is actually the selective mechanism. When the environment is stable and exogenous, the adaptive "target" remains fixed, and infinite time assures the process will eventually achieve it. But with a moving target, even infinite time cannot force a conclusion of optimal adaptation. As J. Maynard Smith (1994: 97) has pointed out, "Optimization is based on the assumption that the population is adapted to the contemporary environment, whereas evolution is a process of continuous change. Species lag behind a changing environment." In other words, one cannot assume perfect tracking of environmental changes by changes in the genome of resident species. Even if time were infinite, the protean nature of the environment would restrict the relevant adaptation time for any organism to the interval between changes in its environs.

The endogeneity of the environment complicates the matter even further, by raising the possibility that the definition of a "good" mutation may depend crucially upon prior mutations. The appearance of a new, desirable trait in a species causes changes in the environment, and those changes alter the selective pressures impinging on the species—possibly rendering other prevailing traits non-adaptive. One pazzling consequence of such a path-dependent process is that fitness may not be transitive: trait B might supersede trait A, and C supersede B, and then A supersede C (Wesson 1991: 141). If changes in the traits of an organism can shape the environment as well as be shaped by it, the very idea of optimal adaptation gets murky because it is unclear that a steady-state relationship between organism and environment will always occur.

The twin assumptions of infinite time and stable environment underpin the usual case for optimality in evolutionary systems. When they are relaxed, we can understand a variety of actual phenomena in such systems as being non-adaptive or mal-adaptive, rather than dream up ad hoc justifications of how such phenomena might be optimal (as modern biologists have unfortunately tried to do in many cases[5]). This is true even when "adaptiveness" or "efficiency" has been defined specifically in terms of the environment that acts as a selective mechanism upon traits and organisms. That is, even if we specifically tailor our definition of efficiency to fit the direction of the evolutionary forces at work, we still cannot realistically expect perfectly efficient outcomes. *A fortiori*, we should not expect an evolutionary system to yield efficient outcomes with respect to some other brand of efficiency defined independently of the selective forces at work (except, perhaps, purely by coincidence).[6]

In what follows, I will explain some of the most widely recognized types of less-than-perfect adaptation in biological evolution. In addition to mentioning specific cases of such suboptimalities in biology, I will also provide some examples of how similar suboptimalities might occur in cultural evolution. Where possible, I draw my examples from Hayek himself. These examples should, however, be taken with a grain of salt: they are intended as suggestive, not definitive. A convincing case for why any one of the examples given indeed constitutes an example of suboptimal adaptation would probably require an article of its own.

3.1. Errors of omission, errors of commission

Naturalists regularly encounter organisms with traits that defy attempts at explanation in terms of adaptation to prevailing environmental conditions. Often the best explanation for such traits comes from an examination of the organisms' phylogenetic histories (even though optimality would imply that current conditions alone should provide sufficient explanation). Apparently, selective forces are not always strong enough to remove all unnecessary or harmful traits from a genome in a finite period of time. The best examples are the so-called "vestigial structures" that appear in numerous species, including human beings. Vestigial structures in humans include the vermiform appendix (may have been a gizzard in our ancestors), ear muscles (needed for directional hearing), and caudal vertebrae (used to be a tail).[7] None of these features provides any apparent selective advantage any longer, and appendices often require removal when they pose a positive danger to human life; they are actually mal-adaptive. These traits constitute errors of omission: they are features that selective forces have failed to eliminate.

It is not terribly difficult to imagine possible analogs in cultural evolution. Although Hayek often fails in his works to explain *why* the processes he describes may not always yield optimal results, he seems to have recognized the persistence of no-longer-adaptive traits as one possible reason. In *Law, Legislation and Liberty*, Hayek notes that mankind maintains multiple layers of rules, "according as [sic] traditions have been preserved from the successive stages through which cultural evolution has passed. The consequence is that modern man is torn by conflicts which torment him and force him into ever-accelerating further changes" (1979: 159). Hayek harks back to the conflict between new and old rules in *the Fatal Conceit* (1988: 18f.) when he attributes the collectivist desire to implement altruism society-wide to a misapplication of the morals of the small group (which evolved very early in humanity's cultural history) to the extended order called civilization (whose rules developed later, and often in conflict with the prior set of rules).

Biology also provides various cases in which traits that would clearly be beneficial are conspicuously absent. Smith cites the *sula bassana* gannet, which lays only one egg at a time, even though it would be capable of raising (and the environment capable of sustaining) two young at a time. A related gannet in very similar conditions does, in fact, lay two eggs at a time (Smith 1994: 98). Why, then, doesn't the *sula bassana*? Two answers seem plausible: first, that the environment has changed recently in a more favorable direction and the gannet's genome has not caught up yet; or second, such a mutation may have appeared one or more times but been eliminated by accident (say, because the one chick with the mutation happened to fall out of the nest and die before reproducing). The second scenario would constitute an error of commission, a case of selective forces accidentally eliminating a desirable trait. In either scenario, the fact remains that evolution has not placed all adaptive traits in the current genome.

Again, it is not difficult to imagine analogs in cultural evolution. Of course, many suggestions of "beneficial traits we haven't adopted" may be nothing more than the wishful thinking of social reformers or cultural entrepreneurs, but this observation does not mean that truly beneficial but unused or untried cultural traits cannot exist. Hayek admits this possibility with a particular example: "The institutions of property, as they exist at present, are hardly perfect; indeed, we can hardly yet say in what such perfection might consist. Cultural and moral evolution do require further steps if the institution of property is in fact to be as beneficial as it can be" (1988: 35). Some might argue that property rules and other customs and conventions are perfect as they are, but a belief in the idea of cultural evolution certainly would not warrant such a conclusion. There is every reason to believe that cultural evolution can produce errors of omission and commission just as does biological evolution.

3.2. Linkages and pleiotropism

Students of biological evolution have long been familiar with the fact that traits often travel together in packs, even when there is no apparent adaptive advantage to the traits appearing together. This may occur, for instance, when two or more genes are located very close to each other on a chromosome so that it is unlikely that they will be separated during crossing-over (the process in sexual cell division whereby chromosomes exchange sections, thus creating a greater variety of gene combinations). It may also occur in organisms in which crossing-over does not take place, such as in male fruit flies and some bacteria; in cases like these, the entire chromosome is the smallest unit of selection. In such situations, it becomes possible for non-adaptive or mal-adaptive traits to tag along with traits of high adaptive value, a phenomenon P. W. Hendrick calls "genetic hitch-hiking" (Dodson and Dodson 1985: 212).

Linkages between traits may also occur when a single regulator gene (a gene that activates or otherwise regulates the activities of other genes) turns a number of genes "on" or "off" as a group. If some of those genes confer substantial advantages, the unfortunate effects of other genes in the group may be outweighed. Some biologists suspect that a small number of mutations in regulator genes may have yielded the vast phenotypic differences that separated human beings from their ape-like ancestors; as Robert G. Wesson (1991: 272) puts it, "Hairlessness, tender skin, and exceptional intelligence seem all to be parts of an evolutionary package, elements of which are evidently unadaptive." Similar linkages may occur because of a pleiotropic gene, a single gene that causes multiple effects. An example of a pleiotropic gene is the gene for sickle cell anemia, which, in addition to its well-known harmful effects, provides some degree of protection against malaria (Stebbins 1977: 126).

It might be argued that some linkages are unavoidable, and it is therefore optimal for an organism to have linked traits so long as the good outweighs the bad (since optimal means only the best of all *possible* worlds). This is probably true of pleiotropic genes, and possibly true for regulator-complexes. Linkage by proximity, on the other hand, is clearly a matter of historical accident. The relevant question is, do these traits need to be connected? Are there no other formations or combinations of genes that could separate good from bad effects? If the answer is no, then the existing situation must be considered suboptimal.

Cultural analogs leap to mind. It is clear enough that many ideas and practices travel in groups, even though they could theoretically be separated. Religions, for example, are complex structures that comprise multiple beliefs and mores. One might expect a religion to persist if it provided sufficient selective advantages to outweigh any disadvantages involved. On this subject, Hayek argues:

> Customs whose beneficial effects were unperceivable by those practising them were likely to be preserved long enough to increase their selective advantage only when supported by some other strong beliefs; and some powerful or magic faiths were readily available to perform this role.
>
> (1988: 138)

Fantastic beliefs about the nature of the world might, therefore, piggyback on beneficial religious practices. Such beliefs could be disadvantageous because they impede the acquisition of more accurate and scientific models of nature, yet survive because they facilitate useful modes of behavior. (What constitutes a selective advantage or disadvantage in cultural evolution is, of course, an open question—one that will be partially addressed later.)

Another case of linkage in cultural evolution might arise from the fact that the growth of government power could have both beneficial and harmful consequences. As Hayek observes,

> Those [governments] that gave greater independence and security to individuals engaged in trading benefited from the increased information and larger population that resulted. Yet, when governments became aware how dependent their people had become on the importation of certain essential foodstuffs and materials, they themselves endeavoured to secure these supplies in one way or another.
>
> (1988: 44)

Consequently, security of trade routes and abuse of power have tended to travel together, although whether they can ever be separated is an open question.

3.3. Evolution by chance and evolutionary trends

Evolutionary change can also take place simply by chance, particularly in small, isolated populations. In a small population, the death of a single individual can have large repercussions in terms of gene frequencies. Over several generations, these random effects can drive out genes and reduce the variability of the population's genome (Sober 1994: 486). Random genetic changes can also accumulate over time with almost no effect, until a marginal mutation, such as the emergence or disappearance of a regulator gene, causes substantial changes to take place all at once. Most importantly, chance selection explains why adaptive mutations could appear yet fail to spread. Stephen J. Gould and Richard Lewontin (1994: 82) observe that "new mutations have a small chance of being incorporated into a population, even when selectively favored. Genetic drift causes the immediate loss of most new mutations after their introduction." In short, chance can provide the basis for the activation of complexes of linked genes and magnify the incidence of errors of commission.

A well-known, though trivial, cultural example of this phenomenon is the shrinking of the pool of surnames within small villages in New England, Wales, and elsewhere (Stebbins 1977: 127f.). When a new settlement was established by a small number of founders, the chance death of a single person could substantially reduce the frequency of the victim's surname in the population, even though the surname itself had no selective impact. Whether there exist non-trivial examples of chance selection in cultural processes depends in part on the level at which selection takes place. If group selection (as opposed to individual selection) is an actual phenomenon—as Hayek believed it to be—then some form of cultural drift should become more likely as groups become larger in size and fewer in number. To the extent that the entire world may be considered a single community, the relevant population has only a single member, and drift could therefore be quite dramatic. (The debate about levels of selection is a live issue in biological evolution as well as in cultural evolution that will be discussed more fully later.)

Biologists have also observed that selective processes can sometimes lead to the persistence and enlargement of trends; that is, a kind of evolutionary multiplier effect may cause the same mutation to occur again and again. Suppose gene A creates cellular conditions under which mutation B is likely to occur. Then an organism with gene A will tend to have progeny that carry both gene A and mutation B. If B has a selective advantage, then the progeny will be likely to survive and create progeny of their own that carry gene A and mutation B *twice*. And the next generation may have gene A and mutation B *thrice*. The phenomenon occurs because the same forces that favor a trait (mutation B) must also favor the genetic conditions that make the trait likely to occur in the first place (gene A). Possible examples include the multiplication of legs on the millipede and the growth of the brain in humans (Wesson 1991: 194). A possible example of trend persistence in cultural evolution, which seems in keeping with Hayek's previously cited suggestions about the abuse of government power, is that the forces which favor groups that solve certain coordination or public good problems may also favor the growth of institutions or attitudes that allow for these social solutions to be reached. (The institutions or attitudes that allow the solutions to be reached are analogous to "gene A"; the solutions themselves are analogous to "mutation B".) Selective forces may therefore reinforce cultural attitudes that favor an increase in social control even though only specific forms of social control yield a selective advantage.

3.4. Multiple adaptive peaks

Finally, biologists have also recognized the possibility that an organism may follow multiple routes in its adaptation to an environment. It is by no means certain that all routes must lead to the same end point; there may be different end points that represent the highest adaptability of an organism along the different paths. Such end points are referred to as "multiple adaptive peaks" (Gould and Lewontin 1994: 84). Which path is "chosen" may depend crucially on the order in which mutations occur. A beneficial mutation may arise early on in the phylogenetic history of a species and be incorporated into its genome. Then, subsequent mutations' "fitness" will depend on how well they fit with the organism's new genome. Thus, an early mutation may place an organism on a path to one adaptive peak rather than another as a result of historical accident.

A number of economists have observed the evident connection between the idea of multiple adaptive peaks and the game-theoretic concept of a coordination game. (Many of these economists owe much to J. Maynard Smith, who pioneered the use of game-theoretic tools in biology.) Viktor Vanberg (1986: 93) has used game theory to offer a sharp critique of Hayek's theory of cultural evolution, noting that "once a coordination rule is established in a group, it cannot be assumed that a shift to a more beneficial rule can, in general, be brought about by a spontaneous, invisible-hand process." To put that in biological terms, switching from one adaptive peak to another is an extremely unlikely phenomenon, even if one peak is demonstrably superior to the other. If a species reaches an adaptive peak that is not sufficient to preserve the species in the relevant environment, it seems more likely that it will go extinct than switch to a different evolutionary path. If, on the other hand, a suboptimal peak is sufficient for species survival, then the species could persist indefinitely in a less than optimal state.

Despite Vanberg's criticism, Hayek seems to have been aware of the possibility of multiple adaptive peaks; indeed, Hayek's cultural relativism (which may seem inexplicable to those who interpret Hayek as a Social Darwinist) is intimately related to the concept. Hayek does not deny the fact that some cultures have developed in completely different directions from that of Western civilization and yet somehow managed to survive:

> There are, undoubtedly, many forms of tribal or closed societies which rest on very different systems of rules. All that we are here maintaining is that we know only of one kind of such systems of rules, undoubtedly still very imperfect and capable of much improvement, which makes the kind of open or "humanistic" society possible where each individual counts as an individual and not only as a member of a particular group, and where therefore universal rules of conduct can exist which are equally applicable to all responsible human beings.
>
> (1976: 27)

Hayek deliberately argues, therefore, from the context of the adaptive route taken by Western civilization, and he argues for internal improvement within that system.

Hayek also recognizes the possibility that, even within a given tradition, path dependency may result in suboptimal consequences for particular subsets of that tradition. In the common law, for example, he points out that "The development of case-law is in some respects a sort of one-way street: when it has already moved a considerable distance in one direction, it often cannot retrace its steps when some implications of earlier decisions are seen to be clearly undesirable" (1973: 88). In situations like these, we find Hayek once again arguing for the occasional corrective reform, which would be unnecessary in a perfectly self-correcting (or instantaneously optimal) evolutionary system.[8]

4. Broader implications for the theory of cultural evolution

Biological evolution does not provide any justification for the belief that evolutionary processes necessarily lead to optimal results. But neither does it support the opposite conclusion, that evolutionary systems exhibit no desirable or efficient qualities whatsoever. Outrageously mal-adaptive traits have a high likelihood of being weeded out of the gene pool, and the organisms we observe in the natural world have clearly inherited remarkably sophisticated and effective structures and behaviors that allow them to survive and reproduce. The adaptiveness of at least a large number of traits observed in existing organisms has never been in question; what is in question is whether such traits represent the best solutions possible in all cases, and whether every single trait must serve some adaptive purpose. As Wesson has observed, "It is only necessary, however, that any particular characteristic be sufficiently functional to permit the species to survive. If there is an optimal shape of leaf for certain conditions of light and humidity, or webs for snaring flies, and so forth, most species are far from it" (1991: 154). The challenge for biologists, then, is to discern which traits took hold for truly adaptive reasons, which traits emerged for other reasons, and how such emergence took place.

The challenge for the evolutionary social scientist, I claim, is much the same. If evolutionary theory told us that all existing laws, customs, conventions, and mores were optimal adaptations to the conditions of human life, there would be little left to do but look around and describe what is already known to be best. But since evolutionary theory does not justify that conclusion, the social scientist's task is more difficult: he must attempt to identify which cultural norms possess truly adaptive qualities, which cultural norms emerged and persisted for non-adaptive reasons (and which may even have mal-adaptive effects), and how these norms came into being.

Evolutionary theory can, therefore, provide a sound basis for both advocacy of reform (when structures appear mal-adaptive or detrimental in some way) and for the defense of tradition (when the traditions seem to produce desirable results on net, or when they may be indispensable to the

173

ongoing system as a whole). (Of course, to engage in such internal criticism, one would have to approve, normatively, of whatever standard of "efficiency" is implicit in the selective forces at work—which Hayek appears to do.) That we should keep "good" traditions and change "bad" ones might seem truistic, but some of Hayek's critics have accused him of inconsistency in so arguing. De Vlieghere (1994: 294), for instance, calls Hayek's advocacy of piecemeal reform "lip-service" because it is "in contradiction with his Darwinian theory" which devalues the contributions of reason. Similarly, Barbara M. Rowland (1987: 54) says that Hayek "inconsistently" draws the conclusion "that people can learn from studying the valuable role evolved institutions have played in advanced societies" so that reforms will fit smoothly into the evolved order. But as we have seen, Hayek's reformist and traditionalist tendencies present no contradiction; they are perfectly consistent if viewed from an appropriate evolutionary perspective.

These statements should not be taken to imply, however, that Hayek's theory of cultural evolution has no flaws or drawbacks. Indeed, the criticisms and doubts about Hayek's theory are too numerous to state here.[9] I will instead show how the biological metaphor and a recognition of the possibility of suboptimality in evolutionary systems can help us to address some unresolved issues associated with Hayek's approach.

4.1. Gradualism

One conclusion that Hayek has drawn from his evolutionary analysis is that gradual or piecemeal change ought to be preferred to radical or wholesale change. At first, this conclusion appears to fit in with the evolutionary paradigm nicely. In the biological sphere, Stebbins states, "If an organism is well adjusted to its environment, slight changes in its genetic makeup may alter it better to modifications of that environment, but drastic alterations of one or a few characteristics are almost certain to make it function more poorly under any environment" (1977: 60). In Hayek's view, ill-advised reformers who wish to jettison rules or conventions whose functions are not immediately clear or whose systemic implications are not understood may seriously threaten the stability of an interdependent system. Hayek therefore advises that all reforms be judged within the context of a complex of other rules taken for the time being as given.

While all these points are well taken, Hayek's plea for gradualism cannot be taken as a universal rule—at least, not on the basis of evolutionary arguments alone. The potential existence of multiple adaptive peaks indicates that a system very different in all respects from the status quo could, conceivably, have more desirable qualities. In order for such a peak to be reached, radical changes might be required. For Hayek to argue against such wholesale reform, he must (and does) muster other arguments that he has elaborated elsewhere. For instance, in his case against socialism, Hayek might like to say that evolutionary considerations alone should be sufficient to relegate socialism to the dustbin of bad ideas. And evolutionary arguments do carry him part of the way to that conclusion, inasmuch as they lead the analyst to consider the functional properties of institutions such as several property and security of contract. But it is not inconceivable, *prima facie*, that the status quo represents but one of many adaptive paths. In order to make the case against socialism, Hayek must also rely on a variety of other tools such as economic theory to demonstrate that socialism could not, in fact, achieve the results its proponents suggest.[10]

Hayek also grounds his argument for gradualism on a strong epistemological challenge: people whose civilization has evolved along one path may simply lack the knowledge necessary to identify viable alternatives that differ substantially from the status quo. That other adaptive paths are conceivable does not imply that ignorant human beings can see what they are and implement them. To theorize that evolution could have led to a different and possibly superior outcome is fine, but to say precisely what that outcome would have been is an act of the imagination, and trying to realize an imaginary outcome in the real world is to engage, not in evolutionary theory, but in rational constructivist design. When proposed changes differ only marginally from the status quo, the imagination can (perhaps) be relied upon for some valid judgments; but in the case of massive system-wide changes, the demands placed on human knowledge are far higher.[11] It was exactly that sort of hubristic endeavor to which Hayek applied the term, "the fatal conceit."

4.2. The dual selective mechanism of cultural evolution

There is a great deal of confusion, in both Hayek's work and the literature on cultural evolution in general, about the exact means by which selection takes place in cultural evolution. It is often unclear whether the emergence of cultural norms is a matter of individual and collective choice or purely a product of impersonal environmental factors. An understanding of how evolutionary systems may fail to yield optimality can shed light on this matter.

An evolutionary system consists of two fundamental features: units of selection, and a selective mechanism. The selective mechanism consists of those forces in the system which allow for the differential survival and reproduction of the units of selection. Units of selection are structures or entities that have the capacity to replicate themselves (that is, to reproduce) under certain conditions. In biology, the most fundamental units of selection are genes (out of which higher level structures such as organisms

175

and species are formed). But if genes are the most basic units of selection in biology, what are the corresponding units of selection in cultural evolution? The smallest units are, in fact, cultural traits or features with the capacity to be adopted, consciously or unconsciously, by human beings. Richard Dawkins dubbed these entities "memes." In his words.

> Examples of memes are tunes, ideas, catch phrases, clothes fashions, ways of making pots or of building arches. Just as genes propagate themselves in the gene pool by leaping from body to body via sperm and eggs, so memes propagate themselves in the meme pool by leaping from brain to brain via a process which, in the broad sense, can be called imitation.
>
> (Dawkins 1976: 206)

If memes are indeed the smallest such units, then the psychology and preferences of individuals may constitute significant selective forces, inasmuch as these factors determine which memes can successfully "infect" human minds. "We do not have to look for conventional biological survival values of traits like religion, music, and ritual dancing," Dawkins argues, "though these may also be present" (Ibid.: 214).

The simplest way to grasp this point is to conceive of cultural evolution as a massive hitchhiker trait. The mutations that created the ability of the human brain to imitate, learn, and evaluate obviously had substantial adaptive qualities for the human species, and for that reason they tended to be selected. But such a brain is capable of far more than enhancing an organism's survival and reproduction; this sort of brain can also desire, imagine, and create. The complex of mutations that created the human mind set in motion myriad effects, only a fraction of which necessarily possessed biologically adaptive qualities; the rest just came along for the ride. Biologist Philip Kitcher observes, "All that natural selection may have done is to equip us with the capacity for various social arrangements and the capacity to understand and to formulate ethical rules" (1994: 440). In so doing, natural selection created the conditions for another kind of evolution, cultural evolution, that is only peripherally related to biological factors. The entire process of cultural evolution may be accurately characterized as a playing out of the full implications of a particular genetic configuration—the human brain—that emerged from the process of biological evolution.

Consequently, human culture may be regarded as responding to a dual selective mechanism. On the one hand, the reproductive capacities of units of cultural transmission (memes) are subject to a selective process in terms of their plausibility, attractiveness, utility, and ease of imitation—as determined by the human minds that consciously or unconsciously adopt them. These standards may or may not have anything to do with the memes' capacity to help or hinder the survival and reproduction of human beings in their environments. On the other hand, which cultural traits human beings adopt will often have indirect impacts on human survival and reproduction, and natural selection of an environmental variety will necessarily come into play if the impacts are sufficiently positive or negative. I will refer to selection of the former variety as "psychological selection," and to selection of the latter variety as "environmental selection." I should note that what I am calling environmental selection is the sole selective mechanism at work in biological evolution, while both forms of selection are at work in cultural evolution.[12]

Like any evolutionary process, cultural evolution does not exhibit a strictly linear chain of causality. The feedback generated by selective forces (in this case, psychological and environmental selection) means that the reason a trait comes into being may differ from the reason a trait persists. Cultural traits come into being because humans are equipped with brains capable of imagining and conceiving of different rules, practices, and ideas. But of the many cultural traits that may come into being, only some will survive both psychological and environmental selection. (Similarly, in biological evolution many traits can come into being via mutation and recombination, but only some will survive the process of selection.)

The two selective mechanisms of cultural evolution need not always work in the same direction. Sometimes they will reinforce each other; other times they may conflict. It is even possible that some cultural traits may run contrary to the apparent demands of environmental selection, because of the overwhelming influence of psychological factors. Cavalli-Sforza and Feldman provide a fascinating example: the decline of birth rates among European women after the onset of industrialization. If child-bearing were a purely genetic disposition passed from mother to daughter, a disposition to limit one's child-bearing would tend to die out in an environment wherein raising more children were possible. Those mothers with a disposition to bear more children would pass that disposition to more future mothers, while those with a disposition to bear fewer children would pass that disposition to fewer future mothers. The fact that the European birth rate diminished indicates that some form of cultural transmission of dispositions had to have been at work; only then could horizontal (intra-generational) and oblique (from one generation to non-offspring members of the next) transmission of dispositions have taken place. That is, the ability of European women to learn a new disposition rather than inherit an old one made a drop in the birth rate possible.[13]

But how could this environmentally mal-adaptive meme have survived the process of environmental selection? The answer lies in recognizing the dual nature of cultural selection. Evidently, the disposition to limit one's pregnancies became psychologically (and financially) appealing to women after industrialization took place in Europe; as a result, the disposition to have more children suffered from a magnified "death" rate, since large numbers of women were abandoning it. Successful memes must survive at this psychological level of selection before the environmental level of selection can even become operative. On the environmental level, the disposition to restrict one's pregnancies might have been expected to lead to its own demise *if* its net effect had been to reduce the number of the disposition's adherents in each generation. But the European population was still, on the whole, rising because of improvements in sanitation, food provision, and other factors. As a result, a meme yielding lower birth rates was enabled to survive despite the selective advantage of higher birth rates in the context of environmental selection.[14]

Perceiving cultural evolution as responding to a dual selective mechanism allows the idea of spontaneous order, a concept to which Hayek devoted a considerable amount of attention, to be more fully integrated into the theory of cultural evolution. A spontaneous order such as a market-based economic system does not respond to or serve the specific, unitary ends of a society; rather, it serves the multiplicitous and largely unknown ends of all the individuals whose transactions create the order. This sort of order is an "abstract order of the whole which does not aim at the achievement of known particular results but is preserved as a means for assisting the pursuit of a great variety of individual purposes" (Hayek 1976: 5). It is not at all clear why an order that serves individuals' multifarious purposes should survive in an evolutionary system in which survival and reproduction of groups is the only criterion for natural selection (as Hayek sometimes implied). One of the advantages of a spontaneous order is its capacity to mobilize information that is dispersed among many individuals in the order. Among the pieces of information transmitted (or summarized) by this sort of order, in addition to information about technologies and resource supplies, are the subjective tastes and preferences of the participating individuals. The need for such information would be inexplicable if group survival and reproduction were the only selective forces at work; the tastes of individuals would be precisely irrelevant. It is only because there is another type of selection involved—the satisfaction of the psychological demands of human minds—that information about tastes and preferences might be relevant to an adaptive process.

4.3. Group selection and methodological individualism

In explaining his theory of cultural evolution, Hayek embraces the concept of group selection: the idea that cultural traits and behavioral features are naturally selected on the basis of advantages and disadvantages they create for the groups of people who practice them. A number of authors have found Hayek's group selectionism troubling, and Vanberg (1986) argues that group selection conflicts with Hayek's professed methodological individualism. Since the idea of group selection is "theoretically vague, inconsistent with the basic thrust of Hayek's individualistic approach, and faulty judged on its own grounds," Vanberg (1986: 97) contends that group selection ought to be jettisoned to save methodological individualism. Geoffrey Hodgson (1991) agrees with Vanberg that there is a conflict between the two doctrines, but recommends instead that methodological individualism should be abandoned (or at least modified) in order to keep group selection. Some of the insights from the foregoing discussion of the dual selective mechanism of cultural evolution may help to resolve the Vanberg-Hodgson debate.

Vanberg defines methodological individualism as "the guiding principle that aggregate social phenomena can be and should be explained in terms of individual actions, their inter-relations, and their—largely unintended—combined effects" (Vanberg 1986: 80). Group selection conflicts with methodological individualism, Vanberg argues, because it attempts to explain cultural norms in terms of the functional roles they play for groups rather than their emergence through individuals' behavior. He proceeds to argue that group selection is a troublesome and flawed concept even in biology, because it is unclear how "altruistic" behavior patterns that benefit groups could possibly survive in the presence of selective pressures that favor "selfish" behavior by individuals. Vanberg says that it seems to be the "dominant opinion among biologists" that the conditions necessary for true group selection "rarely exist in nature" (Ibid.: 69). Interestingly, Vanberg also maintains that methodological individualism was a factor in the development of the theory of biological evolution because it supported a shift "from the species as the theoretical unit to the individual organism as the central unit of analysis" (Ibid.: 80).

Hodgson argues cogently that Vanberg has misconstrued the biological literature on the debate over units of selection. The biological "reductionists" on whom Vanberg relies for support do not contend that the *individual organism* is the most basic unit of selection in the evolutionary process. Reductionists like Richard Dawkins contend, on the contrary, that selective forces ultimately operate on the smallest units of selection, *genes*. The misleadingly labeled group selectionists, on the other hand, argue that natural selection operates on higher level structures as well. Genes come in complex groups called individual organisms, organisms come in groups called populations, populations comes in groups called species, and so on; and all of these structures, the group selectionists believe, may be subject to weeding and culling by evolutionary forces. "In other words," Hodgson says, "selection operates simultaneously on different types of unit, depending on the time-scale and the type of selection process" (1991: 69). The real debate in biology, then, is not selection of individuals versus selection of groups, but selection of genes versus selection at multiple levels of a hierarchy. To the extent that Vanberg relies on the support of biological reductionism to support methodological individualism, his argument collapses because there is no particular reason to focus on individuals. "Simple reduction to the individual level is unacceptable because the same arguments concerning reduction from groups to individuals apply equally to reduction from individual to gene. To avoid this double standard, one must either accept multiple levels of selection, or reduce everything to the lowest level [i.e., genes] in the manner of Dawkins . . . and Williams" (Ibid.: 71).

Although Vanberg's use of reductionist argumentation is vulnerable to Hodgson's critique, the case for methodological individualism is stronger. In most of his analysis, Vanberg implicitly portrays individuals as units of selection in the evolutionary process. If this were the theoretical basis for methodological individualism, then methodological individualism would indeed be threatened by Hodgson's clarification of the levels-of-selection debate. But the earlier discussion of the dual selective *mechanism* of cultural evolution suggests that the individual human is not merely a unit of selection; the individual human is actually part of the selective mechanism that influences the survival and reproduction of cultural traits (or memes). And it is this fact, I will argue, that is crucial in the case for methodological individualism. In addition, it dissolves the alleged conflict between methodological individualism and group selection, allowing the concepts to co-exist in the same theory.

For the social scientist interested in the process of cultural evolution, the relevant explananda are the cultural norms (including beliefs, rules, behavioral regularities, and institutions) that emerge from that process. In order to understand why some memes have survived and prospered while others have grown rare or disappeared, he must direct his attention to the selective forces that have imposed differential death rates on various cultural practices and beliefs. That means asking, first and foremost, how and why some practices and beliefs were adopted in the first place by human beings and others were not. In other words, it is necessary to enquire into the effects of psychological selection, the first prong of the dual selective mechanism. Then, the analyst must explore the systemic effects that would result from the adoption of certain norms. Such effects might include changes in the constraints that influenced individuals' adoption of those norms in the first place, in which case another round of psychological selection could occur, and the same process could be iterated indefinitely. The systemic effects of norms might also include changes in the capacity of individuals and groups to serve their physiological needs, resulting in population growth or population loss; that is, the second, environmental, prong of the dual selective mechanism could come into play.

It might appear that allowing for two selective mechanisms, instead of just psychological selection, represents a break from methodological individualism. But there is no contradiction here: the tenets of methodological individualism do not require that social phenomena be explained without reference to the constraints that impinge on individuals' actions. If environmental constraints affect the survival of individuals (and the groups composed of them) in such a way that the norms they practice and the things they believe have a reduced probability of being absorbed by other individuals (either outsiders or subsequent generations), then the environmental prong of the dual selective mechanism is consistent with a methodological approach that explains social outcomes in terms of the actions, choices, and behaviors of individuals.

Notably, in this account individuals are not units of selection upon which selective forces operate, except insofar as an individual may be perceived as a conglomeration of multiple memes and genes. What is essential for a methodologically individualist account of the evolution of cultural outcomes is that individuals constitute a filter (i.e., a selective mechanism) through which memes must pass before they can begin to have systemic effects. Vanberg is correct to chastise Hayek for giving too little attention to this filtering process in his later work: Hayek regularly refers to the unexpected prosperity of groups that "happened to change them [cultural rules] in a way that rendered them increasingly adaptive" (Hayek 1988: 20) while giving little detail about how the individuals in those groups might "happen" to adopt such changes. Vanberg is also correct, therefore, to draw attention to the question of how, for instance, groups of individuals might happen upon appropriate rules for escaping Prisoners' Dilemma-type situations. It is also clear, however, that groups that did—somehow—find solutions to that kind of dilemma (e.g., tit-for-tat or "grudger" strategies) would create advantages for their members over the members of other groups that did not discover similar solutions. In other words, if a set of beneficial social rules can survive the gauntlet of psychological selection, then groups of individuals who adopt those rules will be favored by environmental selection. It is worth pointing out that the psychological gauntlet may not be as difficult to clear as Vanberg suggests, since individuals may be guided as much by an instinct to imitate as by rational optimization. (Hayek contends that that kind of rationality is a product, not a predecessor, of cultural evolution (Ibid., 21).) Of course, any strategy that survived psychological selection would still have to be capable of surviving environmental selection as well. (That is, it would have to be an "evolutionarily stable strategy," to borrow J. M. Smith's terminology.)

Finally, I should be explicit about how this discussion relates to the issue of group selection. Without necessarily agreeing with the group selectionist hypothesis, it is easy enough to see that group selection is at least not incompatible with methodological individualism, once it is recognized that methodological individualism does not depend upon individual organisms being the (sole) unit of selection. With the methodological issue out of the way, the debate between Vanberg and Hodgson largely disappears. Like the biologists from whom they draw support for their respective positions, Vanberg and Hodgson apparently agree that group selection is a conceivable phenomenon; they merely disagree about its empirical relevance in the world. Opinion on this matter seems to have converged on the position stated by Sober:

> Group selection acts on a set of groups if, and only if, there is a force impinging on those groups which makes it the case that for each group, there is some property of the group which determines one component of the fitness of every member of the group.[15]

There remains a debate as to how often these conditions hold, in both biological and cultural evolution. But Vanberg's coordination games and Prisoners' Dilemmas present fine examples of how these conditions could, at least in principle, apply to certain real-world situations faced by human beings. There seems to be some basis, therefore, for Hayek's focus on group selection in his evolutionary theory.

5. Concluding remarks

The critics of theories of cultural evolution have often chided cultural evolutionists for their alleged belief that "whatever is, is desirable." Although some theorists of cultural evolution (like the Social Darwinists) have in fact reached such conclusions, Friedrich Hayek was not one of them. Repeated statements by Hayek indicate that he did not regard cultural evolution as a perfect process.

Nor does an evolutionary approach justify or imply such a conclusion. The well-developed field of biological evolution provides innumerable examples of how an evolutionary process may fail to produce perfectly adapted organisms. The assumptions of infinite time and constant environments could sustain the idea of perfect adaptation, but these assumptions are untenable. In a real-world evolutionary system, whether of the biological or cultural variety, one should therefore not be surprised to find errors of omission and commission, "hitchhiker" traits, chance selection, trend persistence, and path dependence.

Indeed, such "suboptimal" phenomena in the phylogenetic history of mankind may be responsible for the very existence of cultural evolution. Trend persistence and chance, as well as adaptive selection, led to the formation of a powerful human brain capable of imitation, learning, and cognitive thought. That brain produced multiple effects, only some of which could be considered adaptive on a purely biological level. The other traits merely tagged along, and among those traits was the capacity for desires and preferences—often for things with no discernible adaptive value whatsoever, such as fine art and literature. The very persistence of cultural traits that are non-adaptive (or even mal-adaptive, in the sense of counteracting the demands of environmental selection) constitutes a fantastic error of omission; human beings are constantly engaged in a multitude of costly, energy-consuming activities that add nothing to the reproductive fitness of the species. The species can remain in existence because the biological advantages of having powerful brains—such as providing food, shelter, and clothing—are sufficient to justify the biological burdens of having those brains.

Those burdens include the vast majority of what we call "culture" (and few people would consider them burdens in a pejorative sense of the word). The process of cultural evolution may usefully be treated as responding to two masters. One is environmental selection, meaning the process by which certain cultural traits may lead to the demise or proliferation of those who hold them because they inhibit the production of food, cause the population to shrink, etc. The other is psychological selection, meaning the process by which some cultural traits dwindle and others spread because of their appeal, utility, plausibility, and capacity for imitation by human minds. Both sets of selective forces are, of course, highly imperfect; both are subject to all of the adaptive limitations imposed by finite time, trait linkage, path dependence, and so on.

When a two-fold selection criterion is fully and explicitly incorporated into Hayek's theory of cultural evolution, the theory can more easily be squared with Hayek's theory of spontaneous order. The idea of a dual selective mechanism also provides a ready defense against the charge that his theory conflicts with the principles of methodological individualism. Stripped of all Panglossian implications, real or imagined by critics, Hayek's theory of cultural evolution may provide a powerful tool for the analyst searching for a critical theory of social development and the growth of institutions.

Notes

1 The author wishes to thank Roger Koppl, Mario Rizzo, an anonymous referee, and participants at the Austrian Economics Colloquium at New York University for their useful comments and suggestions.
2 In Voltaire's novel *Candide*, the eminent Dr. Pangloss maintained that we live in the best of all possible worlds. "It is proved," he said, "that things cannot be other than they are, for since everything is made for a purpose, it follows that everything is made for the best purpose" (Voltaire 1947 [1759]: 20).
3 Hayek (1960: 59); Hayek (1973: 23); Hayek (1979: 154); Hayek (1988: 23f.).
4 Hayek (1988: 26). Indeed, Hayek argues that the same principles are applicable to the study of *all* complex orders: "We understand now that *all* enduring structures above the level of the simplest atoms, and up to the brain and society, are the results of, and can be explained only in terms of, processes of selective evolution ..." Hayek (1979: 158).

5 See Gould and Lewontin (1994: 78f.).

6 Examples of types of "efficiency" defined independently of the selective forces at work might include conformity to an aesthetic standard, or consistency with an ideological viewpoint such as classical liberalism.

7 Dodson and Dodson (1985: 213).

8 The fact that detrimental path dependence is possible in an evolutionary system does not necessarily mean it is common. Some of the most famous examples of detrimental path dependence in economics, such as the alleged inferiority of the QWERTY keyboard, have turned out to be unfounded. See Liebowitz and Margolis (1990).

9 See Kley (1994) for examples.

10 This does not mean that a socialist system could not be created in the first place, only that it could not work the way its proponents suggest it would. As noted earlier (in section 3.1), an evolutionary system is capable of a form of retrogression when no-longer-adaptive traits have been superseded but not weeded out. Hayek attributes the collectivist impulse behind socialist schemes to a misapplication of small group morals to the extended order that evolved later.

11 The Eastern European economies that are attempting to transform themselves into market economies after the socialist experiment may face similar problems of trying to implement a "jump" from one path to another. They have the advantage, however, of knowing from observation of existing market economies that a market economy is at least possible (an advantage not shared by the socialists early in this century, who tried to engineer a jump to a purely hypothetical socialist economy).

12 My distinction between psychological and environmental selection parallels Cvalli-Sforza and Feldman's distinction between "cultural" and "Darwinian" selection, which they define as follows: "...cultural selection refers to the acquisition of a cultural trait, while Darwinian selection refers to the actual test by survival and fertility of the advantages of having or not having the trait" (Cavalli-Sforza and Feldman 1981: 16). I have chosen not to adopt their terminology because their use of the word "cultural" might be misleading. I use the word "cultural" to refer to *all* traits that are not transmitted genetically, and I use "psychological" and "environmental" to refer to the selective forces that impinge on cultural traits.

13 See Sober (1994: 482–4).

14 It has been suggested to me that simple cost-benefit analysis would be sufficient to explain the drop in European birth rates. But this explanation begs the question: the whole issue is *which* costs and benefits may be considered. The environmental (i.e., strictly biological) costs and benefits clearly pointed toward *more* child-bearing (since better sanitation, food, etc., made children easier and cheaper to sustain). A lower birth rate could only have arisen from "cost-benefit analysis," then, if some psychological costs and benefits could also come into play.

15 Quoted in Hodgson (1991: 70).

References

Bradie, M. (1994) "Epistemology from an Evolutionary Point of View." In: Sober, E. (ed.) *Conceptual Issues in Evolutionary Biology*, 2nd ed., Cambridge, Mass.: The MIT Press.

Buchanan, J. M. (1975) *The Limits of Liberty: Between Anarchy and Leviathan.* Chicago, Ill.: University of Chicago Press.

Cavalli-Sforza, L., and Feldman, M. (1981) *Cultural Transmission and Evolution: A Quantitative Approach.* Princeton, N.J.: Princeton University Press.

Dawkins, R. (1976) *The Selfish Gene.* New York: Oxford University Press.

De Vlieghere, M. (1994) "A Reappraisal of Friedrich A. Hayek's Cultural Evolutionism." *Economics and Philosophy* 10(2): 285–304.

Dillon, L. S. (1978) *Evolution: Concepts and Consequences,* 2nd ed. St. Louis: The C.V. Mosby Company.

Dodson, E. O., and Dodson, P. (1985) *Evolution: Process and Product.* Boston: Prindle, Weber & Schmidt.

Eldredge, N. (1985) *Unfinished Synthesis: Biological Hierarchies and Modern Evolutionary Thought.* New York: Oxford University Press.

Gould, S. J., and Lewontin, R. C. (1994) "The Spandrels of San Marco and the Panglossian Paradigm: A Critique of the Adaptationist Programme." In: Sober, E. (ed.) *Conceptual Issues in Evolutionary Biology.*

Gray, J. (1989) *Liberalisms.* London: Routledge.

Hallerod, B. (1992) "Friedrich August von Hayek—Apostle for Freedom?" *Sociologisk Forskning* 29(3): 12–34.

Hayek, F. A. (1960) *The Constitution of Liberty.* Chicago, Ill.: University of Chicago Press.

Hayek, F. A. (1988) *The Fatal Conceit: The Errors of Socialism.* Chicago, Ill.: University of Chicago Press.

Hayek, F. A. (1973) *Law, Legislation and Liberty, vol. 1: Rules and Order.* Chicago, Ill.: University of Chicago Press.

Hayek, F. A. (1976) *Law, Legislation and Liberty, vol. 2: The Mirage of Social Justice.* Chicago, Ill.: University of Chicago Press.

Hayek, F. A. (1979) *Law, Legislation and Liberty, vol. 3: The Political Order of a Free People.* Chicago, Ill.: University of Chicago Press.

Heath, E. (1992) "Rules, Function, and the Invisible Hand: An Interpretation of Hayek's Social Theory." *Philosophy of the Social Sciences* 22(1): 28–45.

Hodgson, G. M. (1991) "Hayek's Theory of Cultural Evolution: An Evaluation in the Light of Vanberg's Critique." *Economics and Philosophy* 7: 67–82.

Kitcher, P. (1994) "Four Ways of 'Biologizing' Ethics." In: Sober, E. (ed.) *Conceptual Issues in Evolutionary Biology.*

Kley, R. (1994) *Hayek's Social and Political Thought.* Oxford: Clarendon Press.

Liebowitz, S. J., and Margolis, S. F. (1991) "The Fable of the Keys." *Journal of Law and Economics* 33 (April): 1–25.

Rowland, B. M. (1987) *Ordered Liberty and the Constitutional Framework: The Political Thought of Friedrich A. Hayek.* New York: Greenwood Press.

Smith, J. M. (1994) "Optimization Theory in Evolution." In: Sober, E. (ed.) *Conceptual Issues in Evolutionary Biology.*

Sober, E. (ed.) (1994) *Conceptual Issues in Evolutionary Biology,* 2nd ed. Cambridge, Mass.: The MIT Press.

Sober, E. (1994) "Models of Cultural Evolution." In: Sober, E. (ed.) *Conceptual Issues in Evolutionary Biology.*

Stebbins, G. L. (1977) *Processes of Organic Evolution.* Englewood Cliffs, N.J.: Prentice-Hall, Inc.

Stiglitz, J. (1991) *Whither Socialism?* Cambridge, Mass.: The MIT Press.

Tomlinson, J. (1990) *Hayek and the Market.* London: Pluto Press.

Vanberg, V. (1986) "Spontaneous Market Order and Social Rules: A Critical Examination of F. A. Hayek's Theory of Cultural Evolution." *Economics and Philosophy* 2: 75–100.

Voigt, S. "On the Internal Consistency of Hayek's Evolutionary Oriented Constitutional Economics—Some General Remarks." *Journal des Economistes et des Etudes Humaines* 3(4): 461–76.

Voltaire (F.-M. Arouet) [1947 (1759)] *Candide.* Translated by John Butt. Penguin Books.

Vromen, J. J. (1995) *Economic Evolution: An Enquiry into the Foundations of New Institutional Economics.* London: Routledge.

Wesson, R. G. (1991) *Beyond Natural Selection.* Cambridge, Mass.: The MIT Press.

52

HAYEK, SOCIAL JUSTICE, AND THE MARKET

Reply to Johnston

Edward Feser

Source: *Critical Review* 12(3) (Summer 1998): 269–281.

Friedrich A. Hayek was unusual among critics of political action in the name of social justice in that he questioned not just the wisdom or efficacy of schemes advocated to achieve it, but even the very *meaningfulness* of the idea of social justice—though he also argued that the attainment of social justice was a practical impossibility and that pursuit of it would lead inevitably to totalitarianism. In an earlier article in this chapter (Feser 1997), I spelled out in detail and offered a defense of Hayek's case against social justice—a defense David Johnston ("Is the Idea of Social Justice Meaningful? Rejoinder to Feser," *Critical Review* II, no. 4) finds wanting. What follows is a defense of my defense.

The meaninglessness of the idea of social justice

One of the complaints I made in the earlier piece was that Hayek's critics (including Johnston, in an earlier paper of his, 1997a) paid too little attention to the argument about meaninglessness, especially given that Hayek himself attached great importance to it. It is a merit of Johnston's reply that he there acknowledges this argument's centrality, and attempts directly to respond to it. But this attempt fails.

Hayek's argument, in a nutshell, was that talk about justice and injustice has application only where there is some agent or agents who can be said to have acted justly or unjustly, and that in the case of the distribution of wealth produced in the market order, there simply is no agency responsible for bringing about that distribution; therefore, there can be no meaning attached to the idea that a distribution of wealth in a market order can be just or unjust, and the notion of social or distributive justice is without content.[1]

Johnston challenges this argument by suggesting a putative counterexample to its main premise that talk about justice or injustice presupposes an agency responsible for the justice or injustice. A man might wrongfully be convicted of a murder, he says, even though all parties involved are acting in accordance with the law and in good faith, because exculpatory evidence fails to appear. In such a case, the man clearly suffers an injustice, even though "no one could reasonably be accused of a wrongful or unjust action" (1997b, 610). Although there are obviously agents involved who brought about the unjust result, the point, Johnston says, is that "they did not intentionally and with foresight wrongfully convict an innocent man, and those agents cannot be held responsible for committing an injustice, as they could be if they had deliberately convicted an innocent man, even though an injustice has occurred" (ibid.).

One problem with this example is that it is misleading to say that "no one could reasonably be accused of a wrongful or unjust action." The parties involved acted in good faith, and so we are loath morally to condemn them; but what they did was still clearly unjust. And thus it is perfectly appropriate to say that they performed an unjust action. They are, indeed, not morally *culpable* for the action under the circumstances, but that doesn't mean they didn't act unjustly. By the same token, though it would be correct to say that they are not *morally responsible* for the unjust act, it doesn't follow that they aren't "responsible" in another sense—obviously they are, in the sense that but for their deliberate actions, the conviction wouldn't have occurred.

This leads to the main problem with the illustration, in virtue of which it fails even as a prima facie counterexample, namely the fact that there *are* agents involved who are directly responsible for bringing about the injustice—it is irrelevant whether they *intended* the injustice or not. Hayek's point is not that in a market economy, there *are* agents who directly determine that a certain distribution results, only they don't do it intentionally; it is rather that there is no one who determines the distribution *at all* in the relevant sense, that is, the sense in which the jurors, lawyers, etc. determine the fate of the wrongfully convicted man: by directly putting him in the situation he's in (though doing so without intending an injustice). In the case of the wrongfully convicted man, if someone asked "Who did this to you?", the right answer would be "Those jurors and lawyers did!" even though the parties referred to acted in good faith. But in the case of a person who fails in the marketplace, not as a result of broken contracts, extortion, or the like, but simply because no one wanted what he had to offer, the right answer to the same question would be "No one." No one "sat at the controls" of the market, as it were, and determined (justly or unjustly, intentionally and with foresight or otherwise) that such a person would fail; the failure was rather the result of a blind, impersonal process.

It's true that in my earlier discussion of Hayek's argument, I spoke of there being no one who "intentionally and with foresight" brings about the market's results, but Johnston appears to misunderstand the point of this qualifier. There is obviously a *sense* in which the jurors, lawyers, etc. in his example *do* act intentionally and with foresight in committing the injustice against the accused: They know exactly what they're doing, after all: namely convicting a man; they just don't realize they're doing him an injustice (and thus in another sense they *don't* do what they do intentionally and with foresight). And it's in the sense of acting "intentionally and with foresight" in which the jurors, lawyers, et al., do indeed act that *no one* in the market acts: that is, intentionally and with foresight to bring about a given distribution.

Now of course there are people whose actions do have an effect on what happens in the market—pretty much everyone, in fact. But they don't in *any* sense act intentionally and with foresight *to bring about the resulting distribution*: It's not as if, collectively, they act intentionally and with foresight to bring about distribution X (the way the jurors and lawyers act to bring about the conviction), only without intending X to be unjust. My point in using the qualifier was precisely to make this clear. It was further made clear, I thought, by my example of the "distribution" of body hair in society: That this distribution has the character it has is determined by human behavior—mating and grooming habits and the like—but it is obviously in no sense the result of human action in the way the conviction in Johnston's example is. In his example, there are agents who intentionally and with foresight directly bring about the conviction, even if they don't intend that it be unjust; while the same can't be said of the distribution of body hair. In this respect, that distribution is much like all sorts of results of human action, such as the cumulative effect on the atmosphere and weather patterns billions of human beings no doubt have simply by virtue of breathing, or the effect they have (or fail to have) on Greenland by virtue of not deciding to live there, or the effect they have on sea levels by deciding (on summer weekends, say) in large numbers to frolic in the oceans. Results like these are remote enough from anything that could plausibly be regarded as intention, foresight, design, or planning that they are accurately described as results of impersonal processes. And Hayek's point is that the distribution of wealth that results from the market process is much more like these sorts of results than it is like the result arrived at in something like a criminal trial. It is a distribution, in short, that is produced by actions that are in *no* sense intended to bring it about.

Moreover, Johnston's wrongful conviction example, even if it were like the case of the market, would in fact undermine his overall position. For the parties involved in the example, given that they acted in accordance with legal procedures, etc., are not culpable for redressing the injustice done to the accused if it is later discovered that he was wrongfully convicted. That is, even though their actions produced the injustice, we would not suppose, given the circumstances, that they should be required to pay damages to the accused, say, for the time he spent in jail. If so, then, by the same token, even if the distribution that results from the market process could be described as unjust, so that those who do not succeed in the market can in some sense be described as having suffered an "injustice," it would not follow (as Johnston would presumably say it does) that anyone who succeeds in the market is thereby culpable for "paying damages" (as it were) to the unsuccessful, in the form of taxes used to fund welfare programs and the like. So long as the market's "successes" act in good faith and play by the rules—like the jurors, lawyers, and so on—then the former should, like the latter, be deemed to be free of any compensatory obligations to those unintentionally "hurt" by the process.[2]

Johnston also says, against Hayek's argument, that even if the detailed person-by-person results of market transactions can't be foreseen, the broad outlines of the resulting distribution can be foreseen and, insofar as public policy can alter the distribution, intentionally modified. But he thereby ignores the response I made to this sort of objection in the earlier paper (1997, 598–600). To reiterate only the most relevant point here: Just because we could, presumably, affect mating and grooming habits by legal means if we so desired, it doesn't follow that the current distribution of body hair is just or unjust. Neither does Johnston's point show that the distribution of wealth can meaningfully be described as just or unjust. (Nor should this be surprising: I never claimed, after all, that foreseeing and intending a distribution were *sufficient* conditions for that distribution's being just or unjust, only that they were *necessary* conditions.)

Moreover, the foreseeability of some future distribution, even if it *did* entail the justice or injustice of that distribution, tells us nothing about the justice or injustice of the *current* distribution. So suppose an advocate of social justice who wants, say, a more equal distribution than the current one, points out that such a distribution could be achieved if only we implemented policy P (so that, let us grant for the sake of argument, the future distribution could meaningfully be spoken of as just). It still wouldn't follow that the current distribution is just or unjust if this distribution (especially the parts of it the social justice advocate doesn't like) were itself not foreseen or intended. So, however else one could justify the implementation of P, he couldn't do so on grounds of social justice. And, of course, the whole point of appealing to social justice (usually) is to try to justify some redistributive or interventionist scheme. So even if Johnston's argument didn't have the problems it does have, it wouldn't help the social justice advocate in defending the sorts of policies he wants to defend. Even Hayek acknowledged that in some contexts particularly in a full-blown socialist economy—since in that case some agency *would* be directly responsible for the distribution of wealth—the phrase "social justice" *would* have meaning. But this is no comfort to the social justice advocate who finds himself in a market economy: So long as, and to the extent that, it remains a market economy, he can't justify a transition to some other sort of system by appealing to social justice.

Social justice, unfeasibility, and totalitarianism

Though the charge of meaninglessness was his primary objection against the ideal of social justice, Hayek did have other arguments against it as well, namely that it was impossible to achieve and that its pursuit would inevitably end in totalitarianism; and Johnston says something about my defense of these arguments.

Noting that it is the attempt "fully and consistently" to attain social justice that I represented Hayek as claiming would lead to totalitarianism, Johnston (1997b, 608–609) replies that the same objection can be made against the pursuit of all sorts of social goals: "Fully and consistently" to eliminate crime, for example, would no doubt require the institution of a police state. But that doesn't mean that, to avoid a police state, we ought not try to eliminate crime *at all*. Rather, we ought try to eliminate it to the degree consistent with the realization of other important values, such as liberty, personal privacy, and the like. Similarly, though the full and consistent pursuit of social justice might indeed lead to totalitarianism, all this entails is that we perhaps ought to settle for a partial realization of that goal, not that we should abandon it entirely.

This is fair enough, as far as it goes; but it doesn't go very far. In particular, Johnston does not seriously deal with the *reasons* Hayek thinks the pursuit of social justice must lead to totalitarianism, reasons that make it clear why the analogy with crime-fighting is not a strong one, and which I discussed at length in the earlier paper (1997, 587–89).

First of all, there is the fact that if Hayek's argument about meaninglessness is sound, the notion of social justice cannot even be made sense of except in a full-blown socialist economy, so that it is more or less a conceptual truth that the pursuit of social justice entails the institution of socialism. And it is obvious that there are serious problems involved in trying to avoid totalitarianism in *that* sort of system.[3]

But even apart from appeal to the meaninglessness argument, there are other reasons to doubt that the attempt to achieve social justice could fail to be a serious threat to freedom, such as the fact that there simply are no generally agreed-upon standards of desert, merit, need, and so forth. Thus, in trying to distribute or redistribute wealth in a "socially just" way, the state would simply have to impose a single standard on all. Johnston acknowledges this to be a problem to which most advocates of social justice are not sensitive enough, but he points out that the same problem afflicts all sorts of government activities, "from the most rudimentary goals of crime prevention and defense to the most exotic promotion of the arts" (1997b, 611).[4]

I find it surprising that Johnston would so blithely suggest this as an adequate response to the objection at hand, especially given that the objection was put forward by possibly the most influential twentieth-century proponent of classical liberalism. A classical liberal cannot fail to regard Johnston's response as question begging. If by "crime prevention" Johnston means simply the prevention of murder, theft, and the like, then it is implausible to suggest that very many (if any) who accept the legitimacy of at least some sort of state are going to object to the values underlying such governmental activity. But if, as seems more likely, Johnston has in mind such activities as enforcement of laws against drugs, prostitution, and the like, then at least many of the Hayekian persuasion are going to object to *these* laws just as much as (and for many of the same reasons as) they object to the pursuit of social justice. Enforcement of drug laws, for example, has, in the view of many (indeed, including many in the "social justice" camp) become objectionable because it poses a serious threat to property rights and personal privacy. Thus, it will hardly do for Johnston to appeal to such laws as though they were uncontroversial cases of the legitimate imposition of the values of some upon all. And though it might seem to social-justice advocates an exaggeration to view government funding of the arts as an imposition of values that is but the first step on the road to serfdom, it would do them well to remember their own often-hysterical reactions to suggestions made by those among the "religious Right" that if government is to fund art, it can legitimately have a say in determining which values can and cannot be expressed in it. In dealing with the problem that Johnston acknowledges plagues a great many state activities, then, consistency requires that the advocate of social justice, if he himself finds troubling the idea that others might impose on him values of which he disapproves, recognize the fact that opponents of his own values have just as legitimate an objection to his imposition of the ideal of social justice on them.

Of course, the classical liberal (and especially libertarian) response to this problem—which is more or less Hayek's own response[5]—is simply to avoid, to the greatest extent possible consistent with the existence of a state at all, involving the state in areas where the imposition of values might occur. So it will hardly count as an adequate response to Hayek's argument to appeal to other cases of governmental imposition of values as if Hayek accepted them, or would have to accept them, as legitimate. Perhaps one *can* distinguish, in a non-arbitrary way, legitimate impositions of values from illegitimate ones; I am not simply ruling out that possibility from the start. The point is just that the Hayekian position is skeptical of such impositions in general, for the same reason it is skeptical of the imposition of the ideal of social justice, so that the burden of proof is on Johnston to show that such a distinction can be made if his objection is to have any force.

Johnston also fails to address the other respects in which the pursuit of social justice, in Hayek's view, poses a threat to freedom; ways that further distinguish this case from such cases as crime prevention. Again, these are discussed at length in my earlier paper, and I won't restate here everything that was said there. Suffice it to say that social justice is in tension with the rule of law in a way other governmental goals are not. Given differences in ability and resulting differences in rewards, governments pursuing social justice will have to impose greater burdens on some citizens than on others. Given the increase in political power entailed by redistribution in the name of social justice, coupled with the inherent tendencies of bureau-cracies to act in their own self-interest rather than in the interest of the groups they were created to serve, governmental agencies cannot but fail to grow and increase in power indefinitely, to be increasingly less account-able, and to be increasingly subject to corruption. And given the moral attitudes associated with the demand for social justice, an entitlement mentality cannot fail increasingly to permeate society, leading to ever-greater demands for government to determine everyone's economic stand-ing in a "socially just" manner (and thus increasing state control over the economy—with disastrous economic results that tend to lead to even *more* control), and to the degeneration of politics into a spectacle of special interests warring over control of state power and resources. The very nature of the pursuit of social justice, Hayek argues, is such that it *cannot* be limited in the way Johnston suggests. For it unleashes dangerous forces, both political and psychological, which cannot be restrained, and which have a tendency inexorably to push society in a totalitarian direction.[6]

Johnston's failure to deal with these arguments also vitiates his sugges-tion (repeated from his earlier paper) that Hayek's argument has force only against the usual strategies used to achieve social justice rather than against the end of social justice itself, so that it might be possible to achieve social justice by means other than the institution of a full-blown socialist command economy (1997b, 609). We have just seen why *any* political attempts to achieve social justice are likely to have, to a very great extent, just the sorts of untoward results that a command economy would have. Still, though Johnston presumably had smaller-scale political meas-ures in mind, he isn't explicit about this; it is possible he meant that there might be private-sector strategies available for approximating the realiza-tion of social justice. But Hayek would not object to nonpolitical efforts along these lines (from the practical point of view, that is; there's still the conceptual problem about the very meaningfulness of the idea of "social justice"). Final evaluation of Johnston's suggestion must wait upon his provision of some hint at just what alternatives to the usual strategies for achieving social justice he has in mind. I had criticized his earlier article for being extremely vague on this score, and unfortunately this is one criticism he does not try to answer in his rejoinder. (Johnston says that the fact that

Hayek and I do not envisage such alternatives is "indicative of the poverty of [our] social imaginations" [1997b, 609]; apparently his own "social imagination" is no less impoverished.)

Hayek's ethical presuppositions

Johnston's final (and, he seems to think, most telling) response to my defense of Hayek is to note that Hayek himself acknowledged that we have to make a rational choice between possible social arrangements, and to suggest that Hayek's own defense of his choice of the market order is at least as arbitrary and problematic as standard appeals made to social justice in defense of welfarist or socialist policies, if not more so. Of course, Hayek argued against opting for the pursuit of social justice in part on the grounds that it would bring about results far worse than the conditions the advocate of social justice wants to alleviate. But "by what standard," Johnston asks, "would these results be 'far worse'? To this question neither Hayek nor Feser seems much inclined to offer an answer" (1997b, 612).

Johnston, however, doesn't seem much inclined to *look* for an answer; else he would have seen that one is provided in my earlier article, beginning with the sentence immediately following the one in which I say that Hayek thinks the results of pursuing social justice would be "far worse than the circumstances the advocate of social justice wants to alleviate" (Feser 1997, 586). For I there begin my exposition of Hayek's claims that social justice is unrealizable and leads to totalitarianism. Johnston appears to suppose that by "far worse," Hayek and I mean "far worse" by reference to some moral standard at least as contentious as the ethic of social justice; but the context of my remark shows quite clearly that this is not the case. Hayek's argument is that the results of pursuing social justice would be far worse than what its advocates want to alleviate, *even by reference to their own standards.* That is, since, presumably, the advocates of social justice—and pretty much everyone else, for that matter—would, as much as Hayek does, desire to avoid economic collapse and totalitarianism, they should—if Hayek's arguments are cogent—forsake their commitment to social justice.

Johnston makes much of the fact that Hayek makes a positive case for the market in terms of its ability to satisfy the wants of the greatest number of people to the greatest possible extent, and that this defense is a kind of "utilitarian" defense—something he says my remarks in the earlier article indicate I don't understand (1997b, 612–13). But the point I was making is that Hayek, contra some of his critics, is not, in giving this "utilitarian" defense, arguing that the market order is the most *just* order. I didn't deny that his defense is a utilitarian one; I denied only that it is a defense in terms of a *utilitarian theory of justice.* This is not "a verbal quibble," as Johnston alleges (1997b, 613). For two reasons, it is crucial that Hayek's defense of the market, even if it is a moral defense, is *not* a defense in terms of justice. First, if it had been a defense in terms of justice, Hayek would have been contradicting his claim that the market as a whole (as opposed to the individual transactions taking place within it) is neither just nor unjust; that is, that the concept of justice simply doesn't apply to it. Second, calling a social arrangement *just* has implications that other moral ascriptions do not, implications which are at odds with Hayek's position: If justice demands X, then it follows that people have a rightful claim (a *right*) to X, one that it is plausible to suppose government should enforce; while if it is only charity or benevolence or kindness or what have you that requires X, then even if it thereby follows that someone should provide me with X, it doesn't follow that I have a (government-enforceable) right to it. It might be that respect for benevolence requires that I give you my extra coat if it's cold outside; it doesn't follow that justice requires it, or that you have a right to my coat. In appealing to utilitarian considerations, Hayek is simply saying that if, out of benevolence, we'd like to maximize the satisfaction of the wants of as many people as possible, we should opt for the market; he isn't saying (and wouldn't and couldn't say, given his position on social justice) that a concern with *justice* should lead us to do this.

In any case, Johnston claims that Hayek's appeal to such moral considerations, since they are controversial and largely undefended, undermines the strength of his case against social justice: Maximizing the satisfaction of wants is one possible goal, but equalizing their satisfaction is another, and Hayek gives no reason to prefer the former to the latter (1997b, 613). But this is confused. Hayek's case against social justice is one thing; his case for the market is another. Even if the latter were to fail, this would, by itself, have no implications for the strength of the former. Suppose that Hayek is wrong in claiming that there are strong moral grounds for maximizing the satisfaction of desires, or wrong to suppose that the market would do so—how would this show that the notion of social justice does, after all, have meaning in the context of a market economy; or that it could be achieved; or that it would not, after all, lead to totalitarianism?

Moreover, unless Hayek's case against social justice is refuted, maximizing the satisfaction of desires would win by default over equalizing this satisfaction. For Hayek's critique of social justice undermines the standard case for trying to equalize the satisfaction of desires in the first place, in suggesting that the notion that such a distribution is what "justice" calls for is without meaning; and it provides a positive reason for rejecting the goal of equalization of desires in suggesting that the attempt to make a distribution come out according to any particular pattern has disastrous consequences.

In support of his claim that maximization and equalization are on a par, Johnston repeats the assertion made in his earlier paper that an "egalitarian distribution of wealth is as 'open' or 'purposeless' a goal ... as the goal of maximizing aggregate wealth" (1997b, 613) (the point being that if Hayekian spontaneous order is to be preferred, this by itself does not necessarily favor one possibility over the other). What Johnston has in mind, as we see in his earlier article, is that an equal distribution, like an unequal, market-generated one, "would not presuppose agreement on the *ends* to which that wealth [once generated] should be applied" (1997a, 592, emphasis mine). But this isn't the sort of "openness" or "purposelessness" Hayek has in mind in saying that a market distribution is open or purposeless. He has in mind rather the fact that no one needs to plan for it or engineer it in order for it to come about (even though we know, in broad outlines, what the resulting distribution will look like); whereas tinkering has to be done with the economy in order to guarantee an egalitarian distribution. Egalitarianism requires agreement on ends (unless these ends are simply to be imposed on all); everyone has to agree to submit to a system of rules that would redistribute wealth so as to realize an egalitarian distribution. So everything Hayek says about the advantages of spontaneous orders as against planned formations, if it is otherwise unobjectionable, does favor an unhampered market distribution over an egalitarian one.

Thus, even if we grant—as I acknowledge we should—that Hayek's own positive ethical presuppositions need greater articulation and defense than he gave them,[7] this has no bearing on the strength of his critique of social justice. Nor should this be surprising: As intellectual history shows us, one rarely needs an airtight positive vision of one's own in order to punch holes in, and even utterly destroy, the arguments of an opponent. Hume's project is only the best-known example of this phenomenon. In economics, Hayek and his teacher Mises are widely considered, even by many who reject their positive commitment to the unbridled free market, to have decisively refuted the view that central planning of the economy is possible. The most that Johnston has shown, then (though I do not grant that he has shown even this much), is that Hayek's achievement regarding the issue of the moral foundations of the market is, like these other examples, a purely negative one. It remains an achievement nonetheless.

Notes

1 The reader is referred to my earlier paper for a fuller elaboration and defense of this argument, an argument Hayek himself develops in *The Mirage of Social Justice* (1976), volume two of his trilogy on *Law, Legislation, and Liberty*.
2 It will not do to say, in reply to this, that among the rules successful economic actors would have to follow in order to act in good faith in the first place would be rules requiring payment of taxes to fund such programs. For it is precisely by an appeal to social justice that such taxes are typically justified so that such a response would beg the question.

3 Given this point, and the points that follow—which are largely restatements of arguments made in the earlier paper—it is mystifying why Johnston should say that Hayek's claim that social justice can be achieved only in a thorough-going totalitarian socialist economy is "unfounded" and "entirely undefended by Hayek and Feser" (1997b, 609).

4 Johnston also says that an argument to the effect that lack of agreement on such standards entails that the idea of social justice is meaningless would be misconceived (1997b, 611). Fair enough; but then, neither Hayek nor I ever gave such an argument.

5 I am aware that it is unclear to what extent Hayek would go along with the recommendations of his more thoroughgoing libertarian followers regarding the proper functions of government. My point is just that the considerations that led Hayek to be wary of the pursuit of social justice also led him to be wary of many other state activities, and have led many of his admirers to advocate, for Hayekian reasons, an even more minimal state than he did.

6 See Friedrich Nietzsche's "Of the Tarantulas" in his *Thus Spoke Zarathustra* for a vivid description of the poisonous, destructive attitudes that arguably underlie many demands made in the name of social justice.

7 Though the value of Hayek's positive contribution in this area, particularly his defense of traditional morals in terms of cultural evolution (in e.g. *The Fatal Conceit*), is, in my view, often underestimated.

References

Feser, Edward. 1997. "Hayek on Social Justice: Reply to Lukes and Johnston." *Critical Review* 11(4): 581–606.

Hayek, F. A. 1976. *Law, Legislation, and Liberty*, vol. 2. *The Mirage of Social Justice*. Chicago: University of Chicago Press.

Hayek, F. A. 1988. *The Fatal Conceit: The Errors of Socialism*, ed. W. W. Bartley, III. Chicago: University of Chicago Press.

Johnston, David. 1997a. "Hayek's Attack on Social Justice." *Critical Review* 11(1): 81–100.

Johnston, David. 1997b. "Is the Idea of Social Justice Meaningful? Rejoinder to Feser." *Critical Review* 11(4): 607–614.

Nietzsche, Friedrich. 1969. *Thus Spoke Zarathustra*. New York: Penguin Books.

53

KEYNES, HAYEK, AND "RELIGION" AS A NECESSARY SOCIAL INSTITUTION

John F. Henry

Source: *History of Economics Review* 28 (Summer 1998): 126–128.

Recent issues of this chapter have been given over to articles dealing with Keynes and with economists of the Austrian persuasion. In particular, two articles addressed similarities between Keynes and Hayek: Lawson brought forward certain methodological relationships (Lawson, 1996), while Shearmur analyzed various connections between Keynes and Hayek in their respective views on the State (Shearmur, 1997).

This chapter establishes and evaluates another such relationship that is certainly an aspect of these two most prominent theorists' views on the State but also speaks to a certain underlying understanding of the nature of capitalist organization that informs their respective methodological positions. Both Keynes and Hayek argued for the social necessity of "religion"—understood as an ideological force—as an institution that aided the maintenance of a capitalist economy, which tended to self-destruct if left to its own individualist tendencies.

In September 1925, shortly after their marriage, Keynes and Lydia Lopokova visited the fledgling Soviet Union. It is well known, of course, that Keynes registered marked disdain for that early socialist experiment, partly because it based its hopes on "the common man" or the "boorish proletariat" and partly because he believed socialism to be economically inefficient. Yet, Keynes observed something in that society that caused him to reflect on a failing of capitalism: communism as a "religion" had a great moral force that served as a unifying and galvanizing principle utterly lacking in capitalist society:

> The exaltation of the common man is a dogma which has caught the multitude before now. *Any* religion and the bond which unites

co-religionists have power against the egotistic atomism of the irreligious....

If irreligious capitalism is ultimately to defeat religious communism it is not enough that it should be economically more efficient—it must be many times as efficient.

(Keynes, [1925b] 1972, pp. 267–8)

Hayek entitled the concluding chapter of *The Fatal Conceit*, "Religion and the Guardians of Tradition." Here, in his culminating work, Hayek stressed the tension between the "primitive instincts" of solidarity and collectivism, represented by early communism, and the fragmentation and individualism of the "extended order" (capitalism). The latter may be most beneficial in terms of increasing output and permitting growth in population, but the competition and individualism it necessitates run counter to those primitive instincts that run deep in the human psyche. An irrational resistance to capitalism is generated, based on those primal instincts, and an irrational support for a socialist alternative develops. Religion, understood as religion proper, develops as an evolutionary response to the lost paradise (so it is believed) of primitive communism and serves as an ideological mechanism to maintain the community bonds that are severed by the march of individualism:

We owe it partly to mystical and religious beliefs ... that beneficial traditions have been preserved and transmitted at least long enough to enable those groups following them to grow....

As an order of human interaction became more extended, and still more threatening to instinctual claims, it might for a time become quite dependent on the continuing influence of some such religious beliefs—false reasons influencing men to do what was required to maintain the structure enabling them to nourish their enlarging numbers.

(Hayek, 1988, pp. 136, 138)

Both Keynes and Hayek noted the need for some socializing institutional force that prevented individualism from fracturing the society that lay at the foundation of the capitalist economy promoting that individualism. Granted, they approached this issue from different vantage points (though, as Lawson informs us, these differences are not as acute as usually perceived), and they promoted public policy recommendations that represented quite dissimilar points on the political spectrum. Keynes, in particular, argued that the competitive structure that once provided capitalism with its historic vitality had been gutted by the transformation to large-scale, oligopolistic firms (a transformation that he dated to the end of the nineteenth century [Keynes, (1919) 1971, pp. 9 ff.]) and proposed that something of a collectivist solution to the problems of capitalism must be developed in the modern period (including a socialized investment program [Keynes, (1926) 1972, pp. 287–9; (1936) 1973, p. 164]). Hayek, of course, saw significant state encroachment as anathema (though, as Shearmur demonstrates, this is not to be understood as *no* state intervention). Both, however, did understand that capitalism posed a danger to its own organization in its competitive, divisive structures and processes. And both saw a need for some force that overrode, in large measure, the resulting anti-social consequences of this economic order.

Further, where it is clear that Hayek saw religion (as normally understood) to be the social force that substitutes for the cohesion of the primitive tribe, Keynes was more expansive in his recommendation. For Keynes, "religion" was to be understood as an ideological force that may include religion proper but is not limited to religion. He didn't lay out a specific program in this respect, but one could argue that it could be inclusive of, say, patriotism, nationalism or similar ideologies supportive of capitalist property relations.

Indeed, a scanning of Keynes' writings finds a marked concern for institutional and ideological arrangements that he believed were necessary for modern capitalism to survive. For example, in his discussion on labor policy to be developed in the modern period, he recommended the reintroduction of the Saturnalia, a pre-class society celebration surrounding the winter solstice that had been subsequently used in propertied societies to allow a controlled, institutionalized venting of the anger and frustrations of the producing portions of the population in order to minimize potential revolutionary developments (Keynes, [1925a] 1972, p. 303). (This pre-Christian, pre-class festival, after many social and political gyrations, has devolved into Christmas. See Nissenbaum, 1996.)

Another illustration is Keynes' recommendation regarding policies promoting redistribution (Keynes, [1936] 1973, pp. 372–4). In part, to be sure, his proposals were directed at purely economic consequences for a redistribution of income would raise aggregate spending through the effect on the aggregate marginal propensity to consume. But he also (and perhaps more importantly) believed that the property relations of capitalism would be better safeguarded if the distribution of income were less unequal than that which results from the normal operations of the economy (Ibid., p. 380).

Both Keynes and Hayek, then, saw capitalism as not simply the sum of mechanical relationships among variables, producing results of a purely economic nature, where those relationships were devoid of social foundations or consequences. Rather, they saw the economy as based on a social order where the consequences of the workings of that economy could have serious deleterious effects on that order. Both sought to promote ideas and policies that would defend capitalism—against itself. Granted, they approached their respective examinations of capitalism from different vantage points, and they usually promoted different policy programs to maintain capitalism. But both Keynes and Hayek were in agreement that the individualizing effects of a capitalist economy needed to be tempered by some social and ideological force that preserved the underlying society. Both saw the social need for "religion."

Note

This chapter is based in part on a presentation at the Association for Institutionalist Thought annual meeting in Denver, Colorado, April 1998. I thank the Office of the Dean, School of Social Sciences and Interdisciplinary Studies, and the Office of Graduate Studies and Research, CSU Sacramento, for their support. For comments on this chapter, I thank Stephanie Bell. For technical assistance, I thank Charlene Heinen.

References

(All references to Keynes are from Donald Moggridge, ed., *The Collected Writings of John Maynard Keynes*. London: Macmillan and Cambridge University Press for the Royal Economic Society.)

Hayek, F.A. 1988. *The Fatal Conceit*. Chicago: University of Chicago Press.

Keynes, J.M. [1919] 1971. *The Economic Consequences of the Peace*. Vol. 2.

——[1925a] 1972. Am I a Liberal? Vol. 9. Pp. 295–306.

——[1925b] 1972. A Short View of Russia. Vol. 9. Pp. 253–71.

——[1926] 1972. The End of Laissez-Faire. Vol. 9. Pp. 272–94.

——[1936] 1973. *The General Theory of Employment, Interest, and Money*. Vol. 7.

Lawson, T. 1996. Hayek and Keynes: A Commonality. *History of Economics Review*. 25, Pp. 96–114.

Nissenbaum, S. 1996. *The Battle for Christmas*. New York: Vintage Books.

Shearmur, J. 1997. Hayek, Keynes, and the State. *History of Economics Review*. 26. Pp. 69–82.

54

BETWEEN WICKSELL AND HAYEK

Mises' theory of money and credit revisited

Riccardo Bellofiore

Source: *American Journal of Economics and Sociology* 57(4) (October 1998): 531–578.

I Introduction

Any rereading of von Mises' writings on monetary theory must take earlier interpretations into account. Outside the circle of his closest Austrian followers, the best-known, most authoritative, and representative interpretation is that offered by Schumpeter. In his History of Economic Analysis, the theory "sketched out by Professor von Mises" is described in the following terms:

> Suppose that banks emerge from a period of recovery or quiescence in a liquid state. Their interest will prompt them to expand their loans. In order to do so they will, in general, have to stimulate demand for loans by lowering their rates until these are below the Wicksellian real rate, which, as we know, is Bohm-Bawerk real rate. In consequence, firms will invest – especially in durable equipment with respect to which rate of interest counts heavily – beyond the point at which they would have to stop with the higher money rate that is equal to the real rate. Thus, on the one hand, a process of cumulative inflation sets in and, on the other hand, the time structure of production is distorted. This process cannot go on indefinitely, however there are several possible reasons for this, the simplest being that banks run up against the limits set to their lending by their reserves – and when it stops and the money rate catches up with the real rate, we have an untenable situation in which the investment undertaken on the stimulus of an 'artificially' low rate proves a source of losses: booms end in liquidation that spell depressions.
>
> (Schumpeter, 1954, p. 1120)

Schumpeter adds with some irony that Mises' theory was "further developed by Professor von Hayek into a much more elaborate structure of his own, which, on being presented to the Anglo-American community of economists, met with a sweeping success that has never been equaled by any strictly theoretical book ... A strong critical reaction followed that, at first, but served to underline the success, and then the profession turned away to other leaders and other interests. The social psychology of this is interesting matter for study" (Schumpeter, 1954, p. 1120).

Schumpeter had suggested much the same view in Business Cycles, where he picks on "only one aspect," "though a fundamental one" of the Mises-Hayek theory. In this work he addresses the influence of banks' policies in determining the motive force and the turning points of cycles, in order to contrast it with his own model, in which it is not the "initiative of the banks" offering cheap money that fuels the upward movement, just as it is not the rise in the interest rate that marks its end.[2]

We get a wholly different picture from a contemporary "Austrian," Roger Garrison. Wicksell's cumulative process is here understood as the mechanism that brings the system back into equilibrium after a monetary expansion has increased the agents' cash balances beyond the desired level. Mises' essential contribution should consist of breaking with the idyllic picture of a stable equilibrium, which is only disturbed temporarily by changes in the money supply. We are invited to notice how Mises' analysis gives center place to the disequilibrium dynamic of relative prices and to the consequent distortions in the structure of production:

> Most modern developments in monetary theory are based on the Swedish formulation, that is, they focus on the liquidity provided by holding money. Research typically takes the form of estimating the demand for money and investigating the stability of the demand function. But whatever the configuration of the supply and the demand for money, the operation of the real-cash-balance effect is the same in its essentials. ... By comparison, developments in monetary theory based on the Austrian formulation focus on the information provided by money prices. Attention is drawn to changes in relative prices and in particular to differential price changes in the various stages of production. This has directed research efforts toward the structure of capital rather than toward the demand for money.
>
> (Garrison, 1981, p. 100)

Although each has the merit of drawing attention to complementary aspects of Mises' thought, these interpretations are reductive.

The Schumpeterian interpretation stops short in referring to Mises' view of the turning point marking the end of the inflationary cumulative process, and the constraints that the supply of bank credit encounters because of the shrinking of reserves and consequent deterioration of bank liquidity over the cycle. As we have just seen, Schumpeter acknowledges this is "the simplest" among the "several possible reasons" that in Mises' view prevent the process from going on indefinitely. As we shall show in this chapter, a reading of this sort, in line also with Garrison, completely loses sight of the key point of the monetary analysis embodied in the Theory. Mises' first concern is to show that Wicksell's extreme case of a single bank and of a "pure credit system," in which there is no limit to the amount of credit the bank(s) can create, is anything but unrealistic; on the contrary, it is representative of the natural working of a modern monetary economy.

In Mises' view, money growth, leading to an inflationary spiral and an unjustified lengthening of the period of production, cannot go on undisturbed. There must be an "inevitable" reaction within the economic mechanism that produces a rise in interest rates and destroys the "false" prosperity. But this reaction does not arise from the constraints banks encounter in the creation of credit. Rather, it comes from the agents' spending decisions, which, in the final phase of the cycle, bring about a rise in the price of consumption goods relative to capital goods. The rise in this price shows the entrepreneurs that during the boom, the real structure of production moves against consumption and moves instead in favor of investment despite individual preferences. The clash between the structure of production and consumers' preferences enforces the liquidation of firms undertaken on the basis of the false signal given by excessively low rates of interest.

In the Theory, the process just outlined is an increase in the interest rate on capital. And, for Mises, sooner or later this rise will spread to the interest rates on the money market. If the banks try to resist this adjustment by keeping the loan rate below the real rate, and persist in injecting ever greater inflationary doses, the monetary system quickly undoes itself. If, on the other hand, the banks do not accelerate the growth of the money supply then, in the face of even heavier demand, the rise in the rate of money interest comes back to equilibrium with the real rate.

It is from this outlook that Mises made his biting criticisms of Wicksell's Interest and Prices, to which Wicksell replied point for point in his 1914 review of the Theory. Mises accuses Wicksell on two counts relative to the cycle. First, he referred to the end of the expansionary phase to the banks' liquidity problems when the more innovative part of the monetary analysis in Interest and Prices should have led him to see that there is, in theory, no such limit to the cumulative process. Mises' retort to Wicksell clearly shows that there must be something wrong in Schumpeter's reading; at the same time, this issue is almost completely neglected by Garrison, who wrongly attributes to Wicksell an automatic readjustment perspective.

Second, Mises criticizes Wicksell of having relied on a general price level, making it impossible to inquire about relative prices and denying himself the means to pick out the forces that determine the upper turning point even in a pure credit model. This is the point that Garrison stresses, although from a very partial perspective, and that Schumpeter's over-simple interpretation fails to catch.

Corresponding to these two criticisms of Wicksell, we follow two features of Mises' theoretical endeavor. One ultra-Wicksellian, taking to the extremes the Swede's claim that the capitalist process is unstable because of its monetary system. Here, the accent is on the fact that a "developed" banking system fosters disequilibrium and makes it unlimited theoretically. The other is strictly "Austrian" and came to form the heart of Hayek's elaborations; it underlines the perverse allocative effects of an increase in the amount of money through a shift in relative prices distorting the structure of production. The real changes in the structure of capital are seen as the locus where the cycle manifests itself and the painful reestablishment of equilibrium takes place.

II The money supply: the role of fiduciary media

Let us then look at Mises more closely. The growth of money in the broad sense,[3] what Mises thinks is the only apt theoretical meaning of the word inflation[4], is caused by an increase of fiduciary media, that is, of banknotes and of bank credit in excess of reserves of money proper.[5]

When the banks do not restrict themselves to the intermediary role of lending third parties' money, and therefore also release "circulation credit," newly created purchasing power does not correspond to any sacrifice neither by the bank nor by the depositors. The latter do not give up any purchasing power and can withdraw their deposits on demand; in any case, sure and readily exchangeable claims to money proper are a perfect substitute for it. Their functional equivalence to money in the narrower sense causes the money-substitutes to circulate more widely and allows more of them to be issued than there are reserves. Setting aside the very low technical costs of the issue of banknotes and of credit creation, the banker is able to give credit almost free. The only warning that it has to heed is that of ensuring "his ability to satisfy promptly that proportion of the claims that is actually enforced against him" (Mises, 1971, p. 267). Mises then asks: is there some upper limit to credit creation by the banking system?

Mises' claim, defended forcefully in the Theory and present also in his later writings, is exactly that, from the point of view of the strictly monetary mechanism, there is no force stopping the banking system as a whole from expanding its loans at will.[6] He starts his argument from the simplest case of the single bank, working out Wicksell's insights in great detail.[7]

Payments are supposed to be made only by bookkeeping transfers or by means of the issue of notes. Cash payments are considered too small to be of interest, and are disregarded. On these hypotheses, there are no constraints to the issue of money-substitutes. Given that there are, by definition, no leakages out of circulation, the single bank can never find itself in trouble. It, therefore, does not need to keep reserves of money in the narrower sense. The same holds true if there are a number of banks acting with the same intentions as to granting loans and issuing banknotes.[8]

Mises recognizes that no bank can put more money substitutes into circulation than are actually requested by its customers' business with each other, where the bank's clientele include everyone who accepts the money-substitutes.[9] Despite the difficulty of giving a practical definition of this ceiling,[10] if it were not respected, then outflows to the customers of other banks would exceed inflows, and the issuing bank would have to find some way of dealing with the debts toward them. In the two cases considered so far, this risk is absent. This is obvious for the case of a single bank. But it holds true when banks merge, given that no individual bank has to face a negative balance at the clearinghouse. It is in the banks' interest to extend their loans as far as they can because they earn interest on the free credit creation. In any case, an expansion that goes ahead pari-passu does not undermine either the reputation or the liquidity of the banks. On these grounds, the case of the banks' tandem movement is not merely of theoretical interest, but it approximates well to the behavior of the banks in the institutional context that Mises saw shaping up at the end of the nineteenth century.

To clarify how the clearing mechanism works, Mises refers to a monetary system with a pyramidal structure. At the apex, there is a monopolistic note-issuing bank, whose customers are mostly contained within the national (political) borders, and which normally has the State behind its privileges. At the base, there are competing banks whose liabilities circulate in a smaller area.[11] This, then, is an open economic system with a "mixed" money – that is, with a hierarchy among two types of money.[12] The commercial banks can find themselves having to make payments in the issuing bank's money, which they do not produce themselves. They will hold assets from the central bank in readiness for the redemption of money-substitutes according to a desired reserve ratio so as to be able, if need be, to obtain credit from it. The issuing bank, in turn, can be required to settle uncompensated foreign purchases; and this induces it to hold reserves of commodity money.[13] In a situation of this sort, the conclusions reached for the single bank and for banks expanding at the same rate in a closed economy, no longer hold.

Mises does not explicitly consider the case of a closed economy when analyzing the clearing mechanism. It is not, however, hard to see how his analysis implies that there can be constraints to credit creation by the commercial banks. The limits are set by reference to the decisions of the note-issuing bank, but they are less binding than they would be in the case of an open economy. The overall amount of credit extended by the commercial banks depends on the amount of legal tender chosen by the central bank. Yet there is nothing to stop the central bank from increasing the banking system's credit potential by issuing more banknotes. If the commercial banks do not work together, they need to hold reserves; but, in a closed economy, the central bank does not, and can expand its liabilities at will.

For open economies, Mises recognizes that the whole banking system in a given area must observe a boundary to the expansion of credit. He explains that the existence of such a limitation is due to the fact that a given nation's banking system is being considered side by side with those of other countries, subject to its various monetary policies. In a situation of this sort, which is not unlike that which occurred in the first half of the nineteenth century,[14] we do not find the conditions for an unlimited creation of fiduciary media irrespective of the note-issuing banks' reserve funds of precious metals. Even in an open economy, as long as the issuing banks are following uniform policies, allowing the commercial banks to follow their lead, there is nothing to hold back the expansion of credit, which is what Mises sees happening.[15]

Just as the potential supply of money in the broader sense has no preset upper limit, demand does not restrict effective supply. If the banks are to expand their credit, they must find a corresponding demand. However, they have the power to produce such a demand: "The quantity of fiduciary media flowing from the banks into circulation is admittedly limited by the number and extent of the requests for discounting that the banks receive. But the number and extent of these requests are not independent of the credit policy of the banks; by reducing the rate of interest charged on loans, it is possible for the banks indefinitely to increase the public demand for credit. And since the banks – as even the most orthodox disciples of Tooke and Fullarton cannot deny – can meet all these demands for credit, they can extend their issue of fiduciary media arbitrarily" (Mises, 1971, p. 354).

On the basis of this analysis of the money supply, Mises observes that Wicksell's account of an "organised credit economy" concentrated on the case of "pure credit" is far from illogical. Indeed, it is quite proper and applies also to less strict conditions than the Swede had presupposed. As long as nonconvertible paper money is the only sort in circulation and the banks increase their liabilities at the same pace, the supply of money substitutes is infinitely elastic. By definition, within a world economic system there cannot be any "external drain."[16] Nor is there any need for an adjustment mechanism to deal with "internal drain." For this would presuppose that inflation, the inflow of fresh fiduciary media, would give rise to an outflow of commodity money from circulation on account of an increase in demand for it as cash and for industrial purposes – something that is explicitly ruled out under these hypotheses. Furthermore, we know

> That all credit-issuing banks endeavor to extend their circulation of fiduciary media as much as possible, and that the only obstacles in their way nowadays are legal prescriptions and business customs concerning the covering of notes and deposits, not any resistance on the part of the public. If there were no artificial restriction of the credit system at all, and if the individual credit-issuing banks could agree to parallel procedure, then the complete cessation of the use of money [in the narrower sense] would only be a question of time. It is, therefore, entirely justifiable to base our discussion on the above assumption [of a situation akin to the "pure credit" system].
>
> (Mises, 1971, p. 358)

The tendency toward the pure credit system, the only one on which banking theory should start dealing with interest rate policy and relative prices in pure theory, is already written into the actual trend. If it has not been yet fully realized, that is because of legal and political obstacles, which hold on to the use of metallic money at the national and international level. Sticking to the assumption of pure credit and supposing that no commodity money circulates, Mises concludes that "there is no longer any limit, practically speaking, to the issue of fiduciary media" (Mises, 1971, pp. 358–359; emphasis added).

It is worth pointing out three features of Mises' monetary analysis. First, in the passages we have been discussing, we find a particularly lucid and consistent analysis of the creation of the money supply. In modern terms, the Theory highlights how, in a fiat money system, an individual bank's credit potential is constrained by the market share in deposits, whereas there is no such limit for the banking system taken as a whole or for banks growing in concert.[17] Moreover, whereas in a closed economy where the central bank is liquid by definition, it is not so in an open economy where payments are not regulated by the bank's liabilities and it is necessary for the bank to get hold of reserves of means of payment that are accepted abroad.

Second, there is the distinction between the banks as "cloakrooms" (and bankers as mere middlemen) among final borrowers and primary lenders, and as creators of (bank) credit ex nihilo. Mises sets off from the idea that, as long as they issue only monetary certificates (notes and deposits wholly covered by reserves), the banks put into circulation purchasing power that is already present in the system but whose origin he does not explain. We can thus understand those who want to attribute to Mises the traditional idea that the collecting of deposits is a necessary condition prior to the granting of loans. But there is room for a very different reading. For, Mises says very clearly that when the issue of banknotes or the extending of loans become a normal banks' business, they lend from a fund "that did not exist before the loans were granted" (Mises, 1971, p. 271). From here there is only one step to stating that in a modern banking system, loans always precede deposits.[18] With the passage of time, however, Mises is more insistent on the need to keep the closest possible correspondence between credit extended and reserves of money. To this end, he discusses a variety of possible means of monetary reform. Thus, the monetary economy is referred back to "commodity credit," the one ruling in a barter economy, and banks are forced to operate as simple intermediaries in transferring purchasing power from savers to entrepreneurs. But, when money substitutes serve the same functions as money in the narrower sense, and it becomes possible to issue more of them than there are money certificates, the banking system has the means for the creation of bank money.[19] The equality between loans and deposits of money proper must then be interpreted in Mises as an equilibrium condition, or better still, as a brake imposed on banks to hinder investments exceeding savings.[20]

Third, we saw at the outset that a very authoritative – and, maybe, the most widespread among non-Austrian authors – reading of Mises attributes to him the idea that the inflationary process comes to an end because the banks are compelled to raise the interest rate to deal with liquidity problems arising from an internal and/or external drain of metallic money. He does allow that a sequence of this sort can indeed come about, but he does not appeal to it in the abstract reconstruction of the business cycle. What stops him is his powerful reference to Wicksell's pure credit, even in a mixed-money economy. So powerful a reference that Mises takes Wicksell to task for the contradiction between that model (which is the Swede's underlying picture of the cumulative process) and the readjustment mechanism that Mises sees at work on the same pages of Interest and Prices. It is worth quoting Mises at length here:

> But if we start with the assumption, as Wicksell does, that only fiduciary media are in circulation and that the quantity of them is not legislatively restricted, so that the banks are entirely free to extend their issues of them, then it is impossible to see why rising prices and an increasing demand for loans should induce them to raise the rate of interest they charge for loans. Even Wicksell can think of no other reason for this than that since the requirements of business for gold coins and bank-notes becomes greater as the price level rises, the banks do not receive back the whole of the sums they have lent, part of them remaining in the hands of the public; and that the banks reserves are consequently depleted

while the total liabilities of the banks increase; and that this must naturally induce them to raise their rate of interest. But in this argument Wicksell contradicts the assumption that he takes as the starting-point of his investigation. Consideration of the level of its cash reserves and their relation to the liabilities arising from the issue of fiduciary media cannot concern the hypothetical bank that he describes. He seems suddenly to have forgotten his original assumption of a circulation consisting exclusively of fiduciary media, on which assumption, at first, he rightly laid great weight.

(Mises, 1971, p. 356; emphasis added)[21]

Even for the extreme but essential case of pure credit, Mises does not wish to deny that there is an automatic mechanism bringing the rate of money interest back into line with the rate of natural interest. The positive difference between these two rates gives rise to inflation, to the change in relative prices and to the deformation of the real structure of production. In his view, this process must have an ineluctable end. But that is produced not by factors working the monetary side, namely by the limits on the supply of money in the broader sense, but by factors affecting the real side of the model, namely by individuals' choices as between consumption and saving. We proceed to consider the latter.

III Banking policy and the business cycle: interest on capital and the adjustment process

In Part Three, chapter five of the Theory, there is a first version of the Austrian theory of the cycle that played so prominent a role in the debates of the 1930s. Mises refined it in 1928 and then Hayek significantly developed it. We shall here leave to one side Hayek's contributions and stick to Mises' own original exposition, pointing out its relation to the monetary questions previously discussed.

Mises starts with two premises. One is the temporal view of production proposed by Menget and Bohm-Bawerk. The other is Wicksell's distinction between the rate of natural interest and the rate of money interest. Mises adopts Menger's classification of goods in accordance with their distance from final consumption. Immediate consumption goods, which directly satisfy human needs are goods of the first-order, their value depends on the expected utility from consumption. The heterogeneous range of intermediate goods that are used in production contribute only indirectly to the satisfaction of human needs and make up the category of goods of a higher-order: their value is, so to speak, "reflected," and is established by a process of imputation back from the lower order goods in whose production they help, in accordance with the marginal contribution they make.[22] The more time that separates the higher order goods from

210

consumption, the higher their order. There is therefore a full-blown stratification, a vertical structure in the linear movement from production to
consumption. This reflects the fact that production takes time and is influenced by past decisions, which are fixed, and by forward-looking expectations.

From here it is only a short step to viewing interest as a compensation
for the individual's disutility in abstaining from consumption. Bohm-
Bawerk fills this lack by claiming that present goods have a technical superiority over future goods and moving from there to construct a theory of
capital and interest. Adding the intermediate goods and the consumption
goods gives the subsistence fund that, over time, can maintain and assist
workers in the production of future goods. With a given employment,
more indirect methods of production mean a longer average production
period. This is the average time lapse between the input of origin-specific
resources and the output of the consumption good. The greater capital-
intensity results in a postponement of consumption and then in a cost
increase. For Bohm-Bawerk, individuals undervalue future goods relative
to present goods for two psychological reasons. The first reason is the individual's expectation of enjoying a higher provision of consumption goods
in the future. The second is the underestimation of the future due as much
to uncertainty about life-expectancy as to myopia and weakness of will.
Bohm-Bawerk holds that these two motives – which are, according to him,
empirically ascertainable – lead to a positive time preference. Advances of
money, which correspond to the transfer of present goods into the future,
should be compensated by the payment of interest. But there is something
more about interest. Roundabout methods of production are, on Bohm-
Bawerk's account, more productive. They produce a greater quantity of
consumption goods from the same amount of factors of production, even if
the return is lower with every increase in capital intensity.[23] This is the
famous third reason that explains why interest is positive: according to
some readers, it picks out the nonsubjective, technical cause that permits
future repayment of interest over and above the capital borrowed to be
invested in longer and more efficient processes.

The Theory takes from Wicksell the distinction between the rate of
natural interest and the rate of money interest. The rate of money interest
is simply the rate of interest asked on loans of money in the broad sense.
Mises gives a detailed account of Wicksell's various definitions of the rate
of natural interest. As a first move, the natural rate of interest is characterized as "the rate of interest that would be determined by supply and
demand if actual capital goods were lent (in kind) without the mediation
of money" (Mises, 1971, p. 355).[24] This first definition, appropriate to a
barterlike economy, is immediately followed by another, which fits a monetary economy where money, and not real capital goods, is lent. The rate
of natural interest is a peculiar level of the rate of money interest, the one

211

"established by the free play of the forces operating in the market" and "determined by the whole economic situation" (Mises, 1971, pp. 360–361 and 355). This is the rate that would be set when no new fiduciary media are created. Wicksell refers to this as the normal rate, the rate at which, as Mises says, "the general level of commodity prices no longer has any tendency to move either upwards or downwards" (Mises, 1971, p. 355). It is the rate that would put voluntary savings and investments in equilibrium.[25] It is this second definition that is important if we are to follow Mises' reasoning in the Theory.

For Mises, as for Wicksell and Bohm-Bawerk, there is no fixed capital and no explicit account is given of the bond market. The capital market is included in, and confused with, the money market. Both reflect what happens to the relation between money demand and the real supply of goods. Although the demand for real capital goods necessarily translates itself into a demand for money in the broader sense, the loans' supply comes not only from banks but also from other parties who offer their savings. Unlike Wicksell, Mises supposes that changes in the demand for commodities that come about because of a variation in the amount of fiduciary media released into the system, not only affect the aggregate price level but also systematically cause changes in the price of production goods relative to consumption goods.[26] The price of production goods, in turn, foreshadows the price of the consumption goods that, in time, those production goods help to produce. The relative price of actual consumption goods against production goods is a proxy for the premium of present goods over future goods. Hence, a change in the ratio between the price of first-order goods and that of higher-order goods means a change in the interest on capital (the difference between the value of the prospective products of a capital good and the value of the capital good) that throws back on the loan market.[27,28] Like the rate of natural interest, interest on capital is a money magnitude. In macroeconomic equilibrium, they are identical; but they come apart when investments and voluntary savings are in disequilibrium.

Following Bohm-Bawerk, Mises adds that the interest rate defines the length of the average production period. More exactly, the interest rate to be paid on the unit of capital employed over a longer period should equal the marginal product of the longest process being considered. The rate of natural interest is that at which the subsistence fund is enough to pay the wages to the workers for the whole of the production period.[29] A reduction of the rate of money interest below the rate of natural interest makes it seem profitable to lengthen the average production period because the lower cost of money would offset the lower marginal productivity of the more capital-intensive process? A fall in the loan rate pushes up the present value of the expected return on capital goods, raising the price of intermediate goods relative to consumption goods (i.e., lowering the interest on capital) and at the same time invigorating the production of capital goods. But since, ex hypothesi, the subsistence fund is unchanged, longer production processes cannot be carried to term.

Here we have the specific and original claim of Mises' theory of the cycle. Banks have it in their power to influence the price of present goods relative to future goods and thus, to cause reductions in the interest on capital. Such changes will, however, turn out to be short-lived. Unless individuals' free choices about savings have changed in the meantime, that relative price will eventually have to rise. Thus, what happens in the money market, where banks rule the roost, temporarily affects real accumulation. But real accumulation is, in the end, determined by individuals' preferences over present and future consumption.

These four sentences summarize Mises' account of the business cycle in the Theory[31]:

> The increased productive activity that sets in when the banks start the policy of granting loans at less than the natural rate of interest at first causes the prices of production goods to rise while the prices of consumption goods, although they rise also, do so only in a moderate degree, viz., only in so far as they are raised by the rise in wages. Thus the tendency towards a fall in the rate of interest on loans that originates in the policy of banks is at first strengthened. But soon a counter-movement sets in: the prices of consumption goods rise, those of production goods fall. That is, the rate of interest on loans rises again, it again approaches the natural rate.
>
> (Mises, 1971, 362–63, emphasis added)

Mises' logical sequence can be reconstructed as follows. Let us begin by supposing for simplicity's sake a situation of general stationary equilibrium. By arbitrarily fixing the bank rate, the banks have the power to lower the rate of money interest below the rate of natural interest.[32] In the pure credit model that Mises takes as his reference point, the rate of money interest can be reduced almost to nil, given that there are no costs in the production of bank money and that automatic adjustment mechanisms due to bank liquidity problems are missing. On the other hand, the lowering of the rate of money interest is a false signal that induces entrepreneurs to lengthen the production processes. In this way, more capital goods are produced, with financing from the banks,[33] alongside the already-existing processes. Demand for production goods, including labor, increases. However, the pressure on the higher order goods is greater than that on the goods that wage earners purchase.[34] The ratio between the prices of production goods and the price of consumption goes up, that is, interest on capital falls. As we saw from the passage quoted, this reinforces the tendency of the rate of money interest to fall.[35] What emerges is a structure of vertically differentiated profits[36] according to how high one is up the scale of goods. Entrepreneurs' expectations about the distribution of consumption over time seem to be confirmed by the market,[37] and that encourages them to lengthen the average production period.

The more "capitalistic" (roundabout) production processes could be introduced only by taking labor and intermediate goods away from old production lines. These are now made on a reduced scale, which means a reduction of supply at the end of the period. The longer production processes will be able to produce more (or different) consumption goods only in the future. If we suppose with Mises that the wage earners consume the whole of their income, then, given that the available output at the beginning of any specified period is leftover from the previous one, the increase in money wages will for face an unchanged real supply of consumption goods. The price of consumption goods rises in proportion to the nominal wage and, hence, workers' wages remain constant.

Mises' argument supports the idea that expansion on the part of the banks generally leads directly to a fall in the relative price of consumption goods over production goods and the interest on capital.[38] At this point, forces on the real side of the model pull in the opposite direction. In the following period, the effects of the lengthening of the average production period are felt. Labor and intermediate goods are moved toward even earlier processes, now reducing the present supply at wage earners' disposal for consumption in this period. The increase in prices and wages in the preceding period raises the demand for finance, which the banks satisfy fully. The wage-bill rises again just when the available quantity of consumption goods is falling because the old, shorter, lines employ fewer production goods and the new, longer, ones have not yet come to completion. Thus, the prices of consumption goods go up further as the workers' real consumption shrinks. Here is a classic case of "forced saving," which can be made harsher if capitalists and entrepreneurs enlarge their consumption, that is, if they reduce their savings because of the lower interest rate.[39] Unless bank finance is again raised for the stages of production that are furthest from consumption, inflation in the price of consumption goods will rise faster than that in the price of production goods; consequently, interest on capital, which had fallen, will now turn around and move back to a higher level.[40]

In the Theory, Mises stops at this point, with the definition of the upper turning-point. The readjustment mechanism can be identified with the movement of the price of higher-order goods relative to the lower-order goods, which is in turn driven by changes in the production structure. The crisis is started by the issue of new fiduciary media, which causes a greater withdrawal of production goods (capital, labor) from the production of consumption goods than is justified by the propensity to save. Because

214

production takes time, excess investments relative to voluntary saving show up as misdirected investments.[41] Once there has been a reversal of the profitability accruing to the processes of production of the various orders of goods, it becomes worthwhile to shorten the production period again. The increase in the production of consumption goods takes resources away from the new, longer processes that had been started after banks' expansionary initiative. They cannot be brought to completion on the scale projected or turn out to be hopeless failures.[42] If the banks do not resist the upward pressure on loan interest rates, deriving from the individuals' preferences about the allocation of income between consumption and saving, then the system will tend to a new equilibrium, with no inflation but with a higher price level.[43,44]

The final equilibrium reached after the disequilibrium might not be the same as that from which the process began. Indeed, the Theory underlines some indirect effects of the lowering of the bank rate that can lower the rate of natural interest in the long term. Inflation opens up differential profits in the short term. The consequent displacement of income and property can give rise to long-term changes in time preference. Mises writes that it is the entrepreneurs who are the first to take advantage of inflation; belonging in the highest income brackets, they can better provide for the future and therefore have a lower time preference. The tendency to save increases voluntarily following the rise in the share of investments, which are encouraged by bank policy. The fall in interest on capital is permanent in this case because it mirrors a fall in the rate of natural interest.[45] The growing subsistence fund prevents the price of consumption goods from rising relative to the price of production goods, and allows the lengthening of the production period to run its course.[46] The involuntary squeeze on the purchasing power of those whose income has lagged behind inflation could also produce a permanent decrease in the rate of natural interest. If the unwanted withdrawal from consumption lasted long enough, some of the more roundabout production processes could be brought to completion before the rise in the ratio of present consumption price relative to future consumption forced them to be abandoned, which is what Wicksell postulated in Interest and Prices. Mises supposes these sequences to be unlikely and, in any case, unimportant. On one hand, far from growing, voluntary saving can decline as the result of the lower money interest rate. On the other hand, banks generally do not restrict their issue of fiduciary media to what is allowed by the forced saving that can be imposed on the system. In Mises' view, the eventual inversion of the ratio of the price of consumption goods to the price of production goods causes a destruction of capital much larger than any advantage accruing from forced saving.

Before going on, it is worth addressing two questions. First, can the banks stop the readjustment out of the disequilibrium and keep the economic system on a path of higher than spontaneous capital accumulation, driven by individuals' unhampered choices? Second, what is the most fundamental cause of the capitalist "crisis?"

The Theory's answer to the former must begin with what we showed in the previous section to be the heart of the book's monetary theory, that is, the recognition that the banking system can sustain unlimited growth of fiduciary media. The banks can, therefore, persist with a policy of repeated reductions of the bank rate. They delay the moment when the more roundabout processes, undertaken on the basis of the first lowering of the money interest rate, are dropped. Bank policy now must carry with it an accelerating inflow of new fiduciary media into the system. Indeed, this avalanche of money (in the broader sense) can support too high an investment rate only if it is to push up production goods prices more quickly than the rise in consumption goods prices. But this latter means an ever-faster fall in money's purchasing power. The continued increase in the price inflation rate brings about expectations of further intensification of the process. The demand for money balances, which had hitherto been fairly stable, collapses, worsening the inflationary spiral. The rise in prices is now more than proportional to the growth of money. A genuine flight from money begins that "must lead to a fall in the objective exchange-value of the money-and-credit unit to the panic-like course of which there can be no bounds. Then the rate of interest on loans must also rise in a similar degree and fashion" (Mises, 1971, p. 363). Once this point is reached, the forces of reequilibrium get the upper hand, by means of nothing other than the impending destruction of the monetary system itself. Having reached the edge of the abyss, the banks must retreat and accept a rise in the interest rate.

As to the second question, Mises thinks that the systemic cause of the business cycle is essentially political. He draws the reader's attention to a change of mind between the first edition and the second of the Theory. Whereas in 1912 he picks out the discretionary lowering of the rate of money interest by the banks as just one of the possible causes of expansion, in 1924, the initiative of the banks is presented as a complete and exhaustive starting point of the cycle. A perverse mix of inflationary ideology and etatism lie at the heart of the crisis. The former regards what is believed to be too high a money interest rate as the primary culprit for slow growth, which then presses for cheaper money supply. For the latter, money is a mere creation of the state and can, in its very nature, be manipulated. Etatism eliminated all the institutional barriers to the issue of fiduciary media by conferring the monopoly over the issue of banknotes on the central banks, which took on the role of lender of last resort. Solvency guaranteed in all circumstances leads to incautious policies by the banks, which could bring about a case of moral hazard.

As a class, the entrepreneurs are led astray by the distorting effects of arbitrary banking policy. The business cycle must be attributed to this "collective" error, which cannot be avoided in the present institutional and ideological conditions. In a monetary economy, firms can guess consumers' intertemporal choices only indirectly, through the interest rate on the loan market. They do not recognize their mistake at an early stage, first because the rate of money interest is rising in nominal terms, although it is falling relative to return on production, and subsequently because the shift in relative prices validates for a while the fall in interest. The fact that, in the rising phase of the cycle there is a spiral of distorted signals reinforcing each other and leading the capitalist economy into crisis is explained by the role that the relative price system plays in spreading knowledge through the system's short-term permeability, by the banks' discretional decisions, and by the opacity of the causes of changes in the rate of money interest in a world subject to change and uncertainty.[47]

IV Between Wicksell and Hayek

The foregoing reading of the closing part of the Theory, first edition,[48] turns on a central claim that can be articulated in two directions. On the one hand, Wicksell's pure credit model is not merely of theoretical utility but also has a practical value because it is sufficiently close to the actual working of a modern monetary economy. Thus, at the core of monetary analysis we should place the assumption that the banking system as a whole encounters no technical limits to credit creation. On the other hand, there is in fact a limit to the banks' issue of fiduciary media. This is the shortage of saving as a consequence of individuals' intertemporal choices. It is this real factor that eventually pushes up interest on capital and compels the banks to raise the rate of money interest to prevent the monetary system from tumbling. The former point brings us to the Mises-Wicksell encounter just before the Great War; the latter naturally leads on to Hayek's theoretical elaboration on the Misesian theme. To get a clearer picture of the nature and originality of his contribution to monetary theory, we must look, then, at Mises' connections with Wicksell and with his best-known disciple, Hayek.

Mises' criticisms of Wicksell in the Theory were not left unanswered. Indeed, in 1914, Wicksell published a review of the first edition of the book in Zeitschrift fur Volkswirtschaft, Sozialpolitik und Verwaltung. Mises never replied to the review, leaving his objections to Wicksell in subsequent editions of the Theory as they were in the first – we do not know, in fact, whether Mises ever saw it. Likewise, with few exceptions, the secondary literature on Mises shows no trace of Wicksell's review. This oversight may be one of the reasons why Mises' monetary analysis has often been given overhasty interpretation.[49] Hence, it is worth giving it close attention.

The review takes up each of Mises' main charges in sequence. Mises reproaches Wicksell's criticism of quantitative theory with the fact that the explanation of the changes in the state of price equilibrium variation does not establish that very equilibrium state. Second, according to Mises, the disequilibrium between the rate of money interest and the rate of natural interest could not continue undisturbed ad infinitum even in a fiat, unconvertible paper money system. A first case in point is the lengthening of the period of production; here, changes in production make the rate approach the money interest rate. The other instance is the one already reviewed in the previous section, that is, the ratio of the production goods price to the consumption goods price eventually goes up bringing the loan rate back into equilibrium with the rate of return.

In Wicksell's view, there is a clear separation between value theory and monetary analysis. In the former, the value of commodities is set by marginal utility. The latter is concerned with movements in the absolute price level. It hinges on the relation, which may be a disequilibrium, between demand and overall supply in the goods market. This relation is affected by the situation of the money market, while marginal value theory is of no use here. The base of Mises' discussion of changes in the objective exchange value of money is precisely the relation between money supply and demand for commodities, as in Wicksell. But he strenuously resists the suggestion that monetary theory should not be integrated with subjective value theory. In his reply, Wicksell does not directly address Mises' alternative theory of the value of money, nor the regression theorem that is its cornerstone. Rather, he observes that "exactly what he means remains obscure, in spite of his wordy explanations." To defend his own position, Wicksell denies that there is any problem here. In a pure cash economy, where only commodity money is in circulation, the requirement that there be cash balances sets a ceiling to the demand for money and indirectly limits the highest level that prices can rise to. In an organized credit economy, where there is a developed banking system, the working of the system is completely different. In the extreme case of pure credit, "we can readily see that equilibrium may be maintained at any height of prices ... the question becomes merely one of trying to explain the cause of variation, including stability, of the price level that has been reached and that is, in any case, purely conventional. In other words, at this point in the inquiry, 'the state of price equilibrium' can be constructed in the same way that in mechanics we can construct the state of stable or neutral equilibrium; it does not change on its own, but even if it does change, those changes do not call forth forces that would necessarily re-establish the original state."[50]

Wicksell, however, focuses his review on the two other criticisms because it is there that Mises "directly addresses the opinions I have put forward about the relation between money interest and the commodity prices." Wicksell's second answer concerns the alleged readjustment mechanism consisting of a falling natural interest rate as a consequence of the lengthening of the period of production, which had arisen from the initial positive gap between the natural interest rate and the money interest rate. This mechanism, like the one recalled earlier in Section III, operates on the real side of the model and is independent of the monetary regime in force. In this connection, Wicksell could have directed Mises' attention to those parts of Interest and Prices where he hints at the possible real consequences for accumulation. As one commentator has observed, the effects of relative price changes on income distribution and on saving, which make up the core of the Theory's discussion of the social consequences of inflation, follow in the footsteps of Wicksell's work, rather than contradict it; they complete and complement it.[51]

In the review, Wicksell takes another route. For him the lengthening of the period of production is not a necessary consequence of the positive differential between the two rates. The relative decrease of the rate of money interest, he observes, brings about a profit for the entrepreneur, even if the production period is unaltered. The entrepreneur may not, for the time being, increase capital intensity. At first, he can simply pocket and consume that "extra gain." He may subsequently invest it in widening the size of production, while keeping its structure unaltered. The consequent increase in bank finance will bring about a rise in nominal wages. If prices stayed steady, this would push up real wages and change the relative cost of the factors of production: this would effectively drive toward a deepening of capital structure. But prices do not stay fixed. As Mises himself stresses, because the subsistence fund does not increase, and could even shrink if a lower rate money interest discouraged savings, the wage increase gives way to a rise in commodity prices. Despite higher nominal wages, entrepreneurs find themselves in the same situation as before: they continue to enjoy an extra gain without there being any force driving them to lengthen the production period.

At first sight the second volume of the Lectures takes a more open attitude toward the argument that it is a reduction in the rate of natural interest that brings the two rates into equilibrium. Wicksell writes, "it cannot be completely ruled out that such a thing should happen." This has led to talk of there being concessions to his critics.[52] But Wicksell says only that the decrease in the yield is due to forced saving, assuming a supply of voluntary savings that is inelastic relative to the interest rate. By contrast, as we saw in Section III, Mises maintains the exact opposite. He takes forced saving to be an unlikely and, in any case, secondary event. And he holds that in the cumulative process, voluntary savings fall and that this fall accelerates as inflation deepens. However, Wicksell's objection is important because it focuses on a double difficulty at a sensitive point in the Austrian theory of the cycle. Although he does not come clean on the issue,

Mises seems to suppose, as Hayek would later, that the lengthening of the period of production is due to a fall in the ratio of the rate of money interest to wages paid to workers employed in different stages of production. If the distortion of the production structure is to be set in motion, the price of consumption goods should not rise with, or faster than, the price of intermediate goods. Indeed, it is exactly because the price of consumption goods rises more slowly than that of intermediate goods that the structural change gets going. Wicksell's criticism highlights how, within the marginalist outlook he shares with the Austrians, the replacement of labor by capital depends on relative factors' prices. It shows also that, in a model where the positive differential between the two rates stimulates bank finance of production, and therefore, is directly or indirectly taken up into the wage bill, there should be an almost instantaneous wage rise proportional to the decrease in the objective exchange value of money: if the higher wages are immediately spent, consumption goods prices will have to rise. As a result, the lowering of the rate of money interest will produce not a shift in relative prices, as Mises would have it, but on the contrary, as in Wicksell's model, a parallel increase in all prices. Hicks found same difficulty in Hayek; according to Hicks some delay (of consumption relative to wages, or in the wage rise) must be supposed for the latter's "story" to make sense.[53] As for Mises, the textual evidence is in favor of the idea that it is wages and not consumption that is lagging. But he gives no justification for this position, and it would be up to Hayek to come back to explore the matter.[54]

Wicksell does not directly face Mises' last and main criticism. Mises asserts that Wicksell was not faithful to the pure credit model he saw as the ideal touchstone for the working of a truly monetary economy. Wicksell returns it ad hominem to his critic. Mises, he writes, seems to accept the claim that credit demand is stimulated or restrained "by the difference between what one believes one can earn with money on hand, and the interest actually asked by banks." Under present circumstances, far from the extremes of a solely cash economy and a pure credit system, that margin is only one of the factors affecting the price level, whereas in a pure credit system, it is the "only regulator of commodity prices." Supposing that an "ideal banking setup" is in place, there is no limit to the issue of fiduciary media except the eruption of a crisis whereby hyperinflation degenerates into a flight from money. It is only where commodity money is actually used in transactions that a price rise poses a danger to bank reserves because it increases the requests for metallic money – a danger that banks avert only by raising the loan rate. Wicksell concludes that "to be sure, (it) is precisely the position I have taken." Given that, "at the close of these rambling and, unfortunately, not very clear remarks, Mises comes astonishingly to exactly the same position as I," Wicksell claims not to understand "why then do we argue."

Gustavo Del Vecchio quickly perceived the agreement between the two economists on the point at issue. He published a long article on the fundamental questions of the value of money in the Giornale degli economisti for 1917, in which he gave over a section to the controversy between Mises and Wicksell starting from the "crucial point" of their unanimity over the "hypothesis of gratuitous and unlimited credit."[55] Del Vecchio first recalls that, for Mises, "deplenishment of the reserves and the industrial use of metal, which are the two limits to bank circulation, have no meaning on Wicksell's underlying hypothesis that only credit issued by a single bank is in circulation." He goes on to observe that in his reply to Mises, "in effect, Wicksell goes no further than to reaffirm the principle of the unlimited capacity of the banks to give credit, since he accepts the consequences of the principle: the aforementioned limitations are secondary under the present arrangements of monetary circulation, and they could be altogether absent in an ideal circulation regime." We may add that Mises' criticism of Wicksell does not seem to take account of the fact that the passages of Interest and Prices he quotes as evidence of Wicksell's having abandoned his own earlier assumption of the theoretical priority of pure credit, are quite clearly presented by Wicksell as special cases due to the presence of institutional bonds of "the monetary system of actual fact."[56]

Nevertheless, for more than one reason, Mises' position is significant. Wicksell's monetary theory has often been accused of being ambiguous over the meaning to be given to the hypothesis of pure credit.[57] Patinkin's orthodox and still authoritative reading is based on the claim that the central case of Wicksell's analysis is that of an open economy under gold standard.[58] When a country has a trade surplus, the inflow of gold increases banks' reserves and allows them to increase the money supply by lowering the rate of money interest. With a steady rate of natural interest, prices rise and thus eliminate the banks' excess reserves. This is a variation on the theme of automatic readjustment, based on internal and external drains of metallic money, which is what Mises attributes to Wicksell. But there is the important difference. Whereas Patinkin sees in this instance the core of Wicksell's most important contribution, namely the discussion of the dynamic stability of a monetary economy as guaranteed by the real balance effect, Mises takes it to be an apostasy from Wicksell's customary rigor, which had led him "rightly" to privilege the case of pure credit. This difference of opinion is all the more noteworthy given the many points of contact between Patinkin and Mises. Although, like Mises, Patinkin takes the disequilibrium at the cycle's starting point to be set off by a lowering in the rate of money interest and not by a rise in the natural rate, as in Wicksell, it is alien to the Theory to see the fall in rate of money interest as following from an exogenous rise in the reserves, as in Patinkin's argument. Moreover, so far as the intention of analysis is concerned, like Mises, Patinkin aims to individuate "(the) forces which bring the cumulative process to an end."[59] But Patinkin identifies those forces with the limitations on the banks' issue of credit money (fiduciary media) due to "the effect of higher prices on the reserves of the banks," while Mises clearly separates the two questions of the limits that restrict the credit potential of the banks and of the readjustment mechanism. On the one hand, Mises follows Wicksell in denying that there are any restraints on the issue of fiduciary media by the banking system as a whole. On the other, he goes further than (and, as we have seen, partially against) Wicksell in emphasizing the relative price of consumption goods against production goods over the cycle, as the force that pushes the two rates into equilibrium. Whatever judgment we entertain about the readjustment mechanism, what Mises has on his side is a more solid and convincing reconstruction of the way a monetary economy works in the presence of a developed banking system.

Another reason to be interested in Mises' position over the unlimited capacity of the banking system to expand credit is that it allows us to clarify one point in Hayek's evolution that has caused considerable controversy. At first sight, the usual interpretation of the Austrian theory of the cycle, as referring to the upper turning point to banks' liquidity constraints, is confirmed in the pages of Monetary Theory and the Trade Cycle[60] and of Prices and Production.[61] Indeed, we might trace the beginning of that interpretation to those passages, which Hayek, then at the center of the theoretical debate, published in English before the translation of the Theory. Hayek's reasoning is as follows.

In a closed monetary economy with a central bank that issues banknotes on the basis on the basis of legal money convertible into gold, the amount of deposits created by the banks can grow without requiring that the issuing institution adopt an expansionary policy or (against what Mises supposes, seeing in this arbitrary active bank intervention "the" cause of the cycle) even without a lowering of the loan rate. Here Hayek follows Wicksell in thinking the positive gap between the two rates comes from the side of the rate of natural interest. Demand for finance will grow.[62] As not to lose clients, individual banks will be induced to hold steady the loan rate, thereby reducing the coefficient of free reserves. This choice is also influenced by the fact that at the given risk-level, the choice not to satisfy demand implies a greater opportunity cost for the bank. Moreover, in the rising tide, borrowers' riskiness is lower. At the same time, other banks will see their position at the clearing improve, with base money increasingly flowing into their vaults; they too will be motivated to increase their loans. Because growth is general, assets and liabilities at the clearing house will more or less balance at the end of the period for each bank, and the absolute amount of bank reserves will not be touched. In this way, there is an "elastic" deposit multiplier, there is a progressive reduction in the ratio between reserves and the deposits created by the banking system as a whole. According to Hayek there is, in general, no limit to a process of this kind, which does not require any action on the part of central or commercial bankers, and which is simply the result of competition on the credit market by self-seeking banks. In consequence, it is a process that could take place in just the same way even in a free banking system. But Hayek adds a condition: that the ratio between cash payments and payments by check remain unchanged. This condition is breached as the expansionary phase proceeds, when the price of consumption goods begins to rise more quickly than the price of production goods. At this stage, there is a relative rise in cash payments, and an absolute and rising loss in banks' reserves, which demands that they raise the loan rate as a precaution. This way of seeing things can be clearly detected behind Hayek's statement of 1931 that "for obvious reasons, the banks cannot continue indefinitely to extend credits" (Hayek, 1935, p. 90).

The disagreement with Mises seems plain. The opposition between the two is explicit over the banks' active or passive role in determining the cycle. Although it is implicit, and we do not know how conscious, there is no less clear a difference over the possibility of an inflationary drift in a free banking system. Here, Hayek is closer to Neisser than to Mises.[63] Most relevant to our concerns is that Hayek gives the impression of being a believer in a bound, but flexible deposits multiplier. In this, he takes a step back from the radical position of Mises' (and, before him, Wicksell's) monetary analysis. But this is not the right way to put the matter.[64]

In Prices and Production, Hayek says that the fact that the banks have to stop credit expansion is independent of whether or not there are regulations about reserves.[65] In Capital and Industrial Fluctuations, he is even clearer. Hayek now specifies that the conclusion of Prices and Production, that the rate of credit expansion could not be maintained indefinitely over time, should be explained by "institutional reasons, such as traditional banking policies or the operation of the gold standard." And he adds: "But I think it can be shown without great difficulty that even if these obstacles to credit expansion were absent, such a policy would, sooner or later, inevitably lead to a rapid and progressive rise in prices which, in addition to its other undesirable effects, would set up movements which would soon counteract, and finally more than offset, the 'forced saving.' "[66] In a system free of technical or institutional restraints producing a credit squeeze, the contraction will inevitably come about because to make the price of intermediate goods rise more quickly than the price of consumption goods, and hence to prevent the outbreak of a crisis, banks must allow prices to increase quickly. In Hayek's reasoning, this result depends crucially on the fact that the supply of consumption goods does not grow at the same speed as monetary demand, that nominal wages accelerates, and that the expectation spreads of further rises in prices, making inflation go into a spiral. In two contributions on the "Ricardo effect," Hayek returns to the problem. In the first, of 1942, he presupposes, following Wicksell, a perfectly elastic bank money supply at the ruling rate of money interest and he makes no reference to any reserve binding constraint. In the second, of 1969, he admits that the limit to the money supply is not automatic and then observes that "this inevitable check only comes when inflation becomes so rampant – as the progressively higher rate of inflation required to maintain a given volume of investment must make it sooner or later – that money ceases to be an adequate accounting basis" (Hayek, 1969, p. 471; Hayek, 1978, p. 174).

When he abandons the idea of an automatic monetary brake due to the drain of reserves, the analytic scheme within which Hayek develops his arguments is clearly none other than Mises' original model. In this, the banks are forced to interrupt expansion by the avalanche of fiduciary media, by the acceleration of inflation, by the expectations of further price rises and, finally, by the flight from money.

V Concluding reflections

From what we have seen, Mises' reasoning is as follows: The banking system provides the entrepreneurs the finance they need for production. It does not act as a pure intermediary – a "cloakroom" – as traditional theory tells us. In the institutional conditions of the modern system of payments that Mises saw arising at the beginning of the twentieth century, the banking system creates its own liabilities ex nihilo. Therefore, loans precede deposits. From a normative point of view, the equality between deposits and reserves should, however, be regarded as the necessary condition for the monetary economy not to degenerate into inflation and into the distortion of the structure of production. If bank loans do not correspond to an equal amount of voluntary saving, there would be an increase in the amount of money (in the broader sense). In a system with fiat paper money and banks expanding credit in concert, bank money supply becomes infinitely elastic. It is thus freed from the constraint to maintain any relation with some basic money, if there is one. The banking system is not restrained on the demand side either. For simply by lowering the bank rate, it can bring about an increase in entrepreneurs' demand for credit. In this way it creates a positive gap between the rate of money interest and the rate of natural interest.

We might be tempted to find an heterodox element in this reasoning – an endogenous money supply view. But Mises obtains the endogeneity of the money supply at the cost of making the initial lowering of the rate of money interest exogenous. He thus reaches an objective that is at once theoretical and political. For he can counterpose to the Marxian claim that there is in capitalism an internal tendency to collapse, the idea that capitalism is put into crisis from the outside by the thoughtless initiative of the central and commerical banks, which is the poisoned fruit of the ideology of interventionism.[67] On the other hand, it cannot be denied that Mises was the first to see clearly how Wicksell's hypothesis of a single bank in a pure credit system has a paradigmatic role in and a radical impact on monetary analysis. This is the idea, which he picked up and developed, that the banking system can, if it wants, allow an unlimited amount of credit.

Having once recognized the explosive potential instability of a monetary economy, Mises' ultimate objective was to render its consequences impotent. The analytic solution he offers involves a readjustment mechanism working mainly on the real side of the model. The upper turning point is reached when the price of consumption goods rises relative to the price of production goods. Mises identifies this relative price with a rise in the loan rate. The lengthening of production processes is reversed and deflation gets under way. If, on the other hand, the banks resist the reequilibrium of the money rate of interest with the rate of natural interest, they have to bring down the bank rate again. Fiduciary media are issued in greater and accelerating amounts, bringing about ever faster price inflation, a flight from money, and the collapse of the monetary system. But Mises' sequence is not very convincing. As Hawtrey pointed out in his Economic Journal review of the translation of the Theory, there is nothing compelling in the identification of the loan rate and the relative price of consumption goods against production goods, nor in the idea that the increase in that relative price gives way to a consequent increase in the rate of (money) interest.[68] There is no reason why banks could not just keep the new, lower, level of the bank rate the same even when that relative price rises. There is no need to think that banks have to decide a further fall in the bank rate to check the readjustment mechanism. And there is nothing in the economic situation Mises envisaged that will make them to turn back, or that will convince them that they have taken the wrong path. Nor, as Albert Hahn pointed out, is there reason to expect hyperinflation with the consequent flight from money. If, after the original gap between the two rates has been set up, the lower rate of money interest only rises in nominal terms, following price inflation, the quantity of money will continue to grow at the same pace, without accelerating, and the rate of price increase will stabilize.

Of course, the inflation caused by bank policy will, in the meantime, have produced a displacement of income and wealth. Whether this should be regarded as temporary and harmful for capital accumulation is subject to dispute. Mises and Hayek assert that the degeneration of credit inflation into hyperinflation in a very short span of time cannot be avoided. But money inflation, with its consequent forced savings, could usher in a future increase in output. This can be because (a) the fresh credit has gone to finance innovations, (b) there might have been unemployed resources in the system at the beginning of the cycle, or (c) demand-side pressure on the labor market pushes in favor of the further introduction of new and better production techniques. In Schumpeter's words, a possible reply to Mises is that, "whether temporary or not," the essential role of the banking system in allowing novelty in, and expansion of, production, "is nevertheless very important." So much so, that it is the differentia specifica of capitalism. Far from being illegitimate, as Mises and Hayek suppose, the breaking of the equilibrium caused by banks' role in credit creation is a constitutive element in the accumulation process.[70] But this alternative story would be a million miles from the one Mises was interested in telling.

Notes

1 This chapter was presented in 1996 and 1997 at international conferences in Lisbon, Antwerp, and Washington. I wish to thank Richard Arena, Lapo Berti, Marina Colonna, Nicole) De Vecchi, Pierre Garrouste, Augusto Graziani, Hataid Hagemann, David Laidler, Cristina Marcuzzo, Marcello Messori, Laurence Moss, Riccardo Realfonzo, Mario Seccareccia, George Selgin, Hans-Michael Trautwein, Lawrence White, and Carlo Zappia for their comments. Financial support from MURST 40% and 60% grants is gratefully acknowledged.

2 Schumpeter (1939, pp. 634–8). A similar account of the upper turning point can be found in, among others, Kuznets (1930, pp. 149–50); Barry (1981, p. 23); Pribram (1983, p. 350); and, referring more to reality than to theoretical issues, Desai (1987).

3 Mises distinguishes between money in the broader sense and money in the narrower sense. The former encloses commodity money, credit money, and fiat money. This is not the place to go further into the distinction between the second and the third. We may note, however, that Mises frequently expresses doubts about whether fiat money in his sense, the coin or paper that government has declared to be money and given legal tender, has ever had any historical reality as such, without previously existing as credit money. Mises labels as credit money noncommodity money made up of noninterest bearing claims that can no longer be redeemed on demand at face value, although they continue to circulate as media of exchange. Credit money should not be included under the heading of fiat money because in the former, the original obligation has not been canceled and the claims have been subject to independent valuation. Money in the broader sense includes also money substitutes. These are banknotes and bank deposits that serve the same purpose as money in the narrower sense. Because they are convertible and secure claims to payment, they have the same value as money in the narrower sense, which they replace. If the issuer holds reserves of money in the narrower sense equivalent to the money-substitutes, we have here what Mises calls money-certificates, which leave the overall amount of money unaffected. But if money substitutes are not wholly covered by money in the narrower sense, then we have fiduciary media, which add to the total of money in the narrower sense to the extent that they exceed the amount of cash reserves.

4 On this definition, it is possible to have inflation even though prices are stable or even falling.

5 The mere renewal of the fiduciary media does not constitute credit expansion.

6 See, for example, a crystal-clear statement like the following: "The circulation

of fiduciary media ... is only elastic in the sense that it allows of any sort of extension of the circulation, even completely unlimited extension, just as it allows of any sort of restriction. The quantity of fiduciary media in circulation has no natural limits" (Mises, 1971, p. 312; emphasis added). See also the quotations carried below.

7 Cf. Wicksell, 1936 (orig. ed. 1898), pp. 65–75. Wicksell begins by imagining "a state of affairs in which money does not circulate at all, neither in the form of coin (except perhaps as small change), nor in the form of notes, but where all domestic payments are effected by means of the Giro payment and bookkeeping transfers" and "that the whole monetary system of a country is in the hands of a single credit institution, provided with an adequate number of branches, at which each independent economic individual keeps an account on which he can draw cheques" [pp. 70–71]. The Theory refers rather to a situation in which commodity money is absent (apart from bank reserves) and only fiduciary media circulate. Unlike Wicksell, he envisages also the use of banknotes, and not only of bank deposits, as means of payment. In such a system paper money is inconvertible, like fiat money. In modern terms, it is possible to have, in addition to bank money, also a "base money" of legal tender. As far as the credit potential of the banking system as a whole is concerned, however, Mises arrives at the same conclusions as Wicksell had reached for a pure credit situation. What Mises discusses can be regarded as a case of "broadened" pure credit. Indeed, when he speaks of a pure credit system in the Theory, it is this reformulation of his own that he has in mind. For a critical analysis of Wicksell's monetary theory, see Bellofiore (1992); Chiodi (1983).

8 "If there is only a single bank issuing money-substitutes, and if these money-substitutes have an unlimited capacity of circulation, then there are no limits to the extension of the issue of fiduciary media. The case would be the same if all the banks had a common understanding as to the issue of their money-substitutes and extended the circulation of them according to uniform principles" (Mises, 1971, pp. 325–326; emphasis added). And again:

For obvious reasons an individual bank is not in a position to do this [i.e. to extend its issue of fiduciary media arbitrarily] so long as its competitors act otherwise; but there seems to be no reason why all the credit-issuing banks in an isolated community, or in the whole world, taken together could not do this by uniform procedure. If we imagine an isolated community in which there is only a single credit-issuing bank in business, and if we further assume (what indeed is obvious) that the fiduciary media issued by it enjoy general confidence and are freely employed in business as money-substitutes, then the weakness of the assertions of the orthodox theory of banking is most clear. In such a situation there are no other limits to the bank's issue of fiduciary media than those which it sets itself' (Mises, 1971, p. 354, emphasis added).

9 In Mises (1949), the idea of a bank's clientele is more clearly defined: "A bank can never issue more money-substitutes than its clients can keep in their cash holdings" (p. 438), "the number of people who assign to the demand-claims against this bank the character of money-substitutes" (p. 444). Thus, the customers are those who accept the notes and deposits of the bank as substitutes for money proper, and who are, therefore, ready to hold them among their liquid assets. "Since the overissuance of fiduciary media on the part of one bank ... increases the amount to be paid by the expanding bank's clients to other people, it increases concomitantly the demand for redemption of its money-substitutes. It thus forces the expanding bank back to restraint" [ivi]. In this way a limit is set to the issue of fiduciary media.

10 See Mises (1971, p. 326).

11 See Mises (1971, pp. 326–27).

12 According to Leijonhufvud (1987, p. 271), the "Austrian" theory of the business cycle would be empirically confirmed when credit is expanding within a small open economy based on the gold standard. These were roughly the conditions prevailing in Austria in Mises' and Hayek's day. Nevertheless, Mises' thought is of the widest application. First, we have to define how the monetary economy works in Mises' framework – similar to, but less extreme than, Wicksell's pure credit system. (It is less extreme because, as we say in the text, Mises' is a system with mixed money; but it is similar because in both we find an infinite elasticity of the credit-money supply.) We should then take note of the qualifications to be made to the analysis when the banks, either by regulation or out of prudence, are required to take account of the possible conversion of the fiduciary media into money in the narrower sense. That is, limits to credit creation arise when the banks do not move in step or when there is a circulation of commodity money.

13 Mises takes the circulation of unconvertible paper money to be a phenomenon restricted within each country. Obstacles of a primarily political nature make him think that it is not very likely that any supernational world banking system could be set up.

14 This is for Mises the historical background behind the analytical work of the Currency School "merely concerned to examine the consequences of an inflation of fiduciary media in the case of the co-existence of several independent groups of banks in the world, starting from the assumption that these groups of banks did not all follow a uniform and parallel credit policy" (Mises, 1978, p. 354). See also Mises (1928, p. 123), where he stresses how a single country cannot sustain a rise in prices because of the so-called external drain. The worsening trade balance would lead to a flight of commodity money, followed by a decline in reserves and, hence to a tightening of credit from the banks, which would have to rebuild their liquidity. But, if we stop the inquiry here, Mises holds that we overlook the more fundamental case of the generalized increase of fiduciary media, which takes place at the same time in all countries. We therefore fail to perceive the core of the problem that is of growing practical significance, "of special importance in our age of attempted cooperation among the banks of issue, in which all countries expanded equally" (Mises, 1933, in Mises, 1990, p. 213). See also Mises (1990, p. 77).

15 "If we imagine the whole credit system of the world concentrated in a single bank, it will follow that there is no longer any presentation of notes or withdrawal of deposits; in fact the whole demand for money in the narrower sense may disappear. These suppositions are not at all arbitrary." (Mises, 1971, p. 358). Commodity money would disappear from circulation, and might even disappear from commercial and central banks' vaults. The elasticity of bank money would become infinite.

16 See note 13.

17 Cf. Graziani (1994, pp. 87–99), Schneider (1962, pp. 21–82) is an exemplary treatment always worth consulting; see, more recently, Chaineau (1990, pp. 34–140). Closer to Mises' intentions are Allais, 1987 and Salin, 1990. Humphrey, 1987 reviews the contributions of Pennington, Torrens, Joplin, Marshall, and Davenport as forerunners of the classic distinction, made by Phillips, 1921, between the credit potential of banking system and that of the single bank; he assumes, in the traditional way, however, an increase in reserves as the prime mover, for which no cogent reason is given; hence, he

ignores the dissenting and much more convincing line offered by Wicksell and Mises.

18 The idea of "phases" in the institutional development of the banking system, as suggested by Chick, 1986 (see also Desai, 1989), could perhaps be used to throw light on Mises' views. At first, there are many small banks, which are geographically semi-isolated. The circulation of their liabilities as means of payment is limited. They function mainly as cloakrooms for money savings and their capacity to offer credit is closely constrained by their reserves, which in turn depend on deposits. Deposits therefore precede loans. In the next phase, there are fewer banks but each is bigger. Deposits are used as means of payment. Clearing mechanisms develop. Bank money is now a multiple of reserves, while deposits begin depending on loans. In the third phase, the deposit multiplier increases as a consequence of interbank lending. Simultaneous with the third, the fourth phase sees the central bank take on the role of lender of last resort. At this point, "If a policy of stable interest rates is in place ... reserves virtually disappear as a constraint on bank behaviour" (Chick, 1986, p. 197). Demand for credit dominates the scene, determining actual supply, the deposits and, hence, reserves. In the fifth and, so far, last phase, banks develop "liability management" and the credit supply "leads" the process of money creation. On this story, the Theory accounts for the move from the second phase to the two successive phases, with some aspects of the fifth (the stress on the banks' active role), but queries what the laws will be that regulate the money supply when the move is completed. It is worth adding that, whatever its historical value, the sequence proposed by Chick cannot be seen as an argument supporting the logical priority of the collecting of deposits over loans. The reason is the same as that which explains why Mises' regression theorem is unconvincing as a ground for the value of money: what comes first historically does not necessarily get at the essence of a phenomenon, which, if anything, in the case of money and banking, becomes clearer only when its is fully developed. On this issue, we rather side with Schumpeter. Among the many possible references, the most relevant is Schumpeter, 1970, ch. 2.

19 See Mises, 1971, pp. 267–268.

20 Some interpretation of this sort is further confirmed by the similarity that Mises notes between his views and the near-contemporary views of Hahn, 1920, Schlesinger, 1914, and Schumpeter, 1934. See Mises, 1928, p. 121.

21 Obviously, there must be some explanation for the legend that has Mises supporting the idea that it is banks' liquidity problems that return the system to equilibrium. The explanation may be that readers have been led astray by the rhetorical slide that we find in the post-Theory writings. Some examples may help. In Monetary Stabilization and Cyclical Policy (Mises, 1928, pp. 158–159), he is repeating the arguments that we have reported about the absence of a ceiling to the expansion of circulation credit in a pure paper money system. But he adds, without elaboration, that the banks cannot keep the rate of monetary interest below the rate of natural interest in the long term. Mises seems here to be referring to the relations that we shall discuss in the following paragraph. In The Cause of Economic Crises (Mises, 1931, pp. 183–184), he claims that, even if the banks wanted to, they could not carry forward the policy of credit expansion indefinitely. What follows explains that what Mises has in mind here is the panic caused by the inflow of fresh fiduciary media and the consequent flight from money into foreign currencies (if we are in an open economy) and into real assets. This reaction has nothing to do with a shortage of bank liquidity.

He says that this critical point – the crash of the monetary system – might not be reached either because the economy is open or as a result of legal restraints on the creation of money. "In any event, the policy of expanding credit must come to an end, if not sooner due to a turnabout by the banks, then later in a catastrophic breakdown." We find the same in "La theorie dite autrichienne du cycle economique" (Mises, 1936, pp. 3–4). And again, in Human Action, there is the same claim but with the accent moved on to the impossibility of maintaining the expansionary phase of the business cycle even if bank credit were indefinitely increased. The banks are usually scared by the growth in nominal magnitudes, but even if they insist on increasing loans, the return to equilibrium would be forced by the oncoming disintegration of the monetary system (Mises, 1949, pp. 555, 562). Unlike in the Theory, we can see that in the later works unlimited increase in the amount of money is presented more as an extreme and unlikely occurrence than as the true starting point of a satisfactory monetary analysis. This may have led readers to pay less attention than it is due to the argument of the earlier book. Its theoretical importance, however, is undiminished.

22 Following Mises' terminological convention (Mises, 1949, pp. 93–4, 503, 636; but see also Mises, 1971, p. 29), we should speak of original, nature-given, factors of production for labor and land, of intermediate goods for the produced means of production (instrumental goods and goods in process), and production (or producers') goods or factors of production for the sum of intermediate goods and unproduced means of production (raw materials, land, labor). Particularly in the Theory, Mises tends to ignore the role of land and raw materials. Intermediate goods and production goods are distinguished by the fact that the former excludes while the latter includes labor. However, Mises often, especially in discussing the business cycle, uses the two terms indifferently. They are then equivalent to capital goods, given that his analysis only takes circulating capital into account. For an explicit reference to the Theory showing the identity of production and intermediate goods see below, note 26; for an example from a later work, see Mises, 1949 p. 553, where a distinction is made between a rise in the price of producers' goods and a rise in wages. For a similar, but not identical, classification of goods, see Hayek, 1935, pp. 36–37.

23 In Bohm-Bawerk's original writings only circulating capital is contemplated. The process is of the kind continuous input point output. Because it ignores fixed capital, and thus a situation in which the services of the latter give rise to a continuous flow of output at various dates, the argument is not of general validity.

24 See also Mises, 1928, p. 122. Cf. Wicksell, 1936, p. xxv: "This natural rate is roughly the same thing as the real interest of actual business. A more accurate, though rather abstract, criterion is obtained by thinking of it as the rate which would be determined by supply and demand if real capital were lent in kind without the intervention of money." Subsequent debates have shown that there is a crippling difficulty in the fact that there are as many own rates of interest as there are commodities. Although we cannot discuss this criticism here, see Sraffa, 1932a, 1932b and, for further comment, Chiodi, 1983, pp. 40–44.

25 Cf. Wicksell, 1935, II, p. 193, where he speaks more exactly of the "rate of interest at which the demand and supply of savings exactly agree" and he adds that this rate roughly corresponds to the expected yield on new capital goods. The uniqueness of this rate is guaranteed by the fact that both Mises and Wicksell presuppose here full employment.

26 Given that production goods include also labor, and that a wage inflation entails a rise in the price of consumption goods, Mises is supposing tacitly that an increase in the relative price of production goods against consumption goods carries with it an increase in the price of intermediate goods. This is one place in which he seems to be identifying production goods with intermediate goods. See note 22.

27 "[T]he oft-repeated question of the precise connexion between variations in the objective exchange-value of money [e.g., the inverse of the price-level of the consumption goods] and variations in the rate of interest betrays an unfortunate confusion of ideas. The variations in the relative valuations of present goods and future goods are not different phenomena from the variations in the objective exchange-value of money" (Mises, 1971, p. 349). With given demand, an increase in the supply of money in the broader sense (or a reduction in the demand for money, given the supply), brings out excess cash balances, which implies a market pressure towards higher goods' prices. But money does not flow into the economic circuit uniformly, going in the first place toward intermediate goods. Hence, the rise in the price of consumption goods and, which is the same thing, the fall in the value of money, is at first all of a piece with the rise in the relative price of production goods over consumption goods. That is, there is a fall in interest on capital. Nevertheless, according to Mises, money's influence on time preferences is short-lived and eventually the flows of fresh money onto the commodity market will be consumed in the proportions fixed by agents' choices regardless of banking policy.

28 The translation in the English edition of Kapitalzins generically as "interest" and not as "interest on capital" may have helped conceal the complex relation, which we find in the Theory and are trying to bring to light, among the reduction of the rate of money interest, changes in relative prices and the consequent variations in the real rate of interest.

29 See Mises (1971, p. 360).

30 See Mises (1971, p. 361).

31 Not by accident, they are quoted by Hayek as the heading of Lecture III ("The working of the price mechanism in the course of the credit cycle") of Prices and Production from the first edition of the Theory (Hayek, 1935, 2nd ed., p. 69).

32 A lower bank rate on the market establishes through competition among lenders a lower rate of money interest and brings about an increase in fiduciary media (Mises, 1971, pp. 351–52; see also Mises, 1928, p. 122). Some confusion has been caused here by the fact that Mises sometimes discusses the sequence just outlined (from a lower rate of money interest to an increase in the amount of money [in the broader sense]), and sometimes its reverse (from increased issue of fiduciary media to a lower interest rate). The former sequence refers to the fact that banks' readiness to expand loans at a lower interest rate increases entrepreneurs' demand for credit and so increases the actual amount of money (Greaves, 1978, pp. xl–xli). At other times, it seems that Mises is thinking about a larger influx of commodity money into bank reserves that depresses the interest rate on the loan market. We may have a similar movement from the money supply to the interest rate even with an unconvertible paper money system. This can happen if, through open-market operations, central banks increase the high-powered money, allowing banks to lend at a lower rate (Skousen, 1990, p. 327). In Human Action, Mises explicitly examines a variety of ways this can happen. In addition to that in which the central banks lower the discount rate, he also considers a budget deficit financed through the

issuing bank's money creation that ends up indirectly increasing the reserves of the commercial banks (Mises, 1949, p. 570). He claims, however, that in the latter case, the distorting effects on production will be smaller or even lacking (see note 38). In any case, on the "widened" pure credit model embraced in the Theory, reserves play no role.

33 Given what we said in the last section, the banks, whose autonomous initiative is at the root of the increase in credit demand and that have unlimited elasticity of supply, have no difficulty satisfying firms' fresh requests for money capital. New fiduciary media are added to the money (in the broader sense) that was circulating. Also in Human Action Mises supposes that everyone who wants to borrow at the ruling interest rate, adjusted to take account of the various categories of risk, can do so; compare with Mises (1949, p. 552).

34 Although it is central to setting the business cycle going in the Austrian model, this relative price effect cannot be taken for granted, given that the financing of increased production of capital goods involves an increase in the payroll and therefore, a corresponding increase in demand for consumption goods. We shall return to this question later on.

35 Mises (1928, p. 122), discusses how an immediate and direct decrease in the interest rate on loans arises out of bank action and how it is followed by a further reduction "distinct in character and degree."

36 Inflation favors the firms whose receipts grow more quickly than their costs in proportion to the increase in the commodity's price: "If the objective-exchange value of money falls, the entrepreneur gains; for he will still be able to meet part of his expenses of production at prices that do not correspond to the higher price-level while, on the other hand, he will be able to dispose of his product at a price in accordance with variation that has meanwhile occurred" (Mises, 1971, p. 348). The creation of new fiduciary media impinges on a situation in which there is no inflation and price expectations are static.

37 The entrepreneurs are also reassured by the rise in the prices of consumption goods, which assures them that in the future they will be able to sell off consumption goods at rising prices despite the fact that at the moment their costs have begun to rise. Compare with Mises (1949, p. 553).

38 Mises claims that this effect is not present when the new money entering the system goes not to finance production, but directly into spending, as happens, for instance, when a budget deficit is financed by the central bank (see also note fn. 32). In such a case, the price of consumption goods relative to the price of production goods may immediately rise, and the tendency to a lowering of the interest rate be soon more than canceled by its tendency to rise.

39 Mises observes that no one in the system has to give up purchasing power because of the inflow of new fiduciary media, no sacrifice accompanies the issue of new money. Credit creation ex nihilo speeds up the accumulation of capital by imposing forced saving: "The cost of creating capital for borrowers of loans granted in fiduciary media is borne by those who are injured by the consequent variation in the objective-exchange value of money" (Mises, 1971, p. 314). Schumpeter (1912) and Hahn (1926, p. 951) attribute to Mises the first use of the notion of forced saving (erzwungenes Sparen), as does Hansson (1992). F. Hayek (1932) brilliantly surveys the long history of the concept. To be precise, the term was already employed by Wicksell (1936, pp. 303–4): "The real saving which is necessary for the period of investment to be increased is in fact enforced – at exactly the right moment – on consumers as a whole" (emphasis original). In Monetary Stabilization and Cyclical Policy (Mises, 1928, p. 121), Mises admits that he had described the phenomenon in the first

1912 edition of the Theory, but he also says that he "do[es] not believe that the expression was actually used there"; Kuznets (1930, p. 148) concurs. Moreover, Mises minimizes the importance of the phenomenon as all in all inessential to describing the process of inflation. It is here worth noting Mises' idiosyncratic use of the term. It is more complex than the simple squeeze on the purchasing power of people whose money income does not keep up with inflation, which causes an absolute and involuntary reduction in real consumption. For Mises, there is forced saving if the reduction in real consumption by wage workers tallies with an increase in voluntary saving by those who have benefited from the redistribution of income and wealth (Mises, 1928, pp. 121, 126; Mises, 1949, p. 548). In other words, there is forced saving when money growth lowers the rate of natural interest, which is Mises' analyses in the second section of the chapter in the Theory we are discussing. As Machlup notes (Machlup, 1943, pp. 31–33), what we have here is a secondary increase in saving voluntary but not spontaneous as a result of the greater loans due to the banks' artificial expansionary policies. For Mises, however, it is unlikely that the principal beneficiaries of inflation, mainly entrepreneurs, should not decrease the share of their income given to saving when the money interest rate decreases. Insofar, however, as that increase happens not only temporarily but permanently, Mises' forced saving gives way to a new equilibrium characterized by a higher capital (and subsistence) subsistence fund and so limits the harm that the banks inflict on the economy through their action. This point was at the heart of the apparently bizarre Wien-Claudi (1934) reading of Mises as in favor of inflation.

40 The same process is analyzed in similar terms in Human Action (Mises, 1949, p. 558, emphasis added):

The ensuing boom in the prices of producers' goods may at the beginning outrun the rise in the prices of consumers' goods. It may thus bring about a tendency toward a fall in the originary rate of interest. But with further progress of the expansionist movement the rise in the prices of the consumers' goods will outstrip the rise in the prices of producers' goods. The rise in wages and salaries and the additional gains of the capitalists, entrepreneurs, and farmers, although a great part of them is merely apparent, intensify the demand for consumers' goods. There is no need to enter into a scrutiny of the assertion of the advocates of credit expansion that the boom can, by means of forced saving, really increase the total supply of consumers' goods. At any rate, it is certain that the intensified demand for consumers' goods affects the market at a time when the additional investments are not yet in a position to turn out their products. The gulf between the prices of present goods and those of future goods widens again. A tendency toward a rise in the rate of originary interest is substituted for the tendency toward the opposite which may have come into operation at the earlier stages of the expansion.

Gootzeit (1994) rightly draws attention to the cyclical movement of the relative price of consumption goods against consumption goods in Mises' account of the accumulation process. But his account of the Theory is far from convincing. In Gootzeit's view, in that book we find only a picture of the expansionary phase of the cycle where the prices of consumption goods are continuously rising. Their increase would happen suddenly whereas the prices of production goods would be stable. No upper turning point of this relative price is clearly sketched out: the realignment of the two interest rates would be due to the pressure of demand for loans on the rate of money interest, and not on the dynamic of the relative prices. Gootzeit holds that it is only in Human Action that Mises clearly says that the credit expansion at first pushes up the relative price of production goods against consumption goods (i.e., lower the originary interest, which portrays the positive time preference), and later on decrease it (i.e., raise the originary interest). As we have seen in the text, the Theory already contains an explicit, albeit rudimentary, description of the relative price mechanism and of the effects of bank policy on the interest on capital. Moreover, the pure credit hypothesis means that the banks are not compelled to raise the loan rate when firms increase their demand for finance. If there is a difference between Human Action and the Theory it is rather in the analysis of deflation. See Mises, 1949, pp. 566–570, where the author describes what happens when due to a restrictive open-market operation, an increase in the free banks' reserve coefficient, or the bankruptcy of some banks, the total of fiduciary media falls, producing a rise in the interest rate on the loan market. Therefore, it is not in the Theory, as Gootzeit believes, but in Human Action that the disequilibrium between the two rates may be eliminated by the rise in the money rate – but here we are definitely outside the pure credit model with its almost horizontal credit supply. Nevertheless, the difference between the two books is more apparent than real; it is mainly due, as we noted earlier, to the fact that Mises came to put less rhetorical (as opposed to substantive) weight on the hypothesis of pure credit in setting out his ideas in the later writings.

41 Taking issue with Haberler (Haberler, 1941, pp. 29–72), Mises firmly remarks in Human Action that what we have here is malinvestment and not overinvestment (Mises, 1949, p. 559). He says that the more capital-intensive production lines are set up without a simultaneous adequate inflow of greater voluntary saving. This situation conspires with the contemporary increase in the demand for consumption goods in pushing up their relative price, shifting entrepreneurs' evaluations, and hence, leading the new projects to be terminated. For Mises during inflation there is almost no increase in capital goods. The same amount is only redistributed throughout the cycle toward production lines further up the line in a way that does not conform to consumer preferences. However, his distinction between overinvestments and malinvestments is not quite so clear cut as he seems to think. Given that, in the cycle, the supply of consumption goods falls and that of intermediate goods increases, what is happening here is indeed an increase in the share of investment that does not correspond to any increase in the tendency to save.

42 These points are not treated in the Theory, but they can easily be deduced from it; for a full-fledged account cf. Mises (1949, pp. 563–564).

43 "That ratio between the prices of goods of the first order and of goods of higher orders, which is determined by the state of the capital market and has been disturbed merely by the intervention of the banks will be approximately re-established, and the only remaining trace of the disturbance will be a general increase in the objective exchange-value of money due to factors emanating from the monetary side" (Mises, 1971, p. 364). The new equilibrium reached after the inflationary interval re-establishes the previous one only approximately either (a) because there are shifts in agents' choices due to the emergence of new data during disequilibrium (Mises, thinks such an event is likely, but he gives no theoretically cogent reason for it, and thus these shifts must be qualified as exogenous changes) or (b) because the indirect effects of the lowering of the bank rate on the rate of natural interest can reduce it permanently, of which more in a moment.

44 Once inflation is under way, the rate of money interest comes to be indexed to

price increases in dealings on the loan market. Mises does not think this brings the two rates back into equilibrium, but only that it will stop the gap between the two interest rates from widening. The Theory takes fully into account the so-called Fisher effect. Under inflation, the entrepreneurs see their nominal profits rising and are therefore willing (and compelled by the competition) to pay a higher interest rate following the increase in prices (Mises, 1971, p. 349). Hence, the rate of money interest chases the rate of natural interest without ever catching it up (cf. also Mises, 1923, p. 10). As we have already seen, Mises supposes static expectations for almost the whole of the cycle, and he measures the rate of money interest and the rate of natural interest in nominal terms. The rise in the rate of money interest merely offsets the increase in real yield due to price inflation. In Mises (1928), where the term "price premium" is introduced for the first time to refer to the expected price increase, it is noted that "[e]ven if the banks do not lower the actual interest rate any more, the gap widens between the 'money interest rate' and the 'natural interest rate' which would prevail in the absence of their intervention" (p. 123). In the initial equilibrium, no price increase is expected; hence, the fall of the rate of money interest is both nominal and real. With prosperity, when the money interest rate begins to rise following inflation, it still "continues to lag behind the rate which would conform to the market, i.e., the 'natural interest rate' augmented by the positive price premium" (ibid.; cf. also Mises, 1936, p. 4). The same claim is repeatedly made in Human Action (see Mises, 1949, pp. 548, 551, 558). It is only in hyperinflation that things change: expectations now do not merely reflect previous inflation rate but anticipate the future state of the market (cf. Mises, 1923, pp. 8–9). This leads to a drastic fall in the demand for money, which loses its role as the temporary abode of purchasing power. Prices rise quickly and more than proportionally relative to the growth of money. It is only at this point, Mises says, that the loan rate of interest can then rise without bounds (Mises, 1971, p. 363).

45 At least according to Machlup (Machlup, 1940, p. 189) within these limits, we would have a case of healthy inflation.

46 See Mises, 1971, pp. 347–348. Cf. also Mises, 1928, p. 121.

47 Hoover, 1988, p. 236 and Van Zijp, 1993, pp. 28–29 rightly stress this point. In the Theory, the role of prices as information-bearers in a monetary economy is not made explicit; but it is at the core of the writings on the impossibility of rational calculation in a socialist economy (Mises, 1920, 1922), which were published between the two editions of the book on money.

48 In later writings, Mises will manifest doubts over Bohm-Bawerk's theories of the rate of interest [as Mises already reveals in a note to the second edition of the Theory: compare with Mises (1971, p. 339); see also Mises (1940, pp. 439–44) and Mises (1949, p. 488), and, for his new interest rate theory, pp. 524–537] and of the average period of production [which he labels as "an empty concept," Mises 1949, p. 489]. We cannot pursue this stream in this chapter.

49 Apart from Gustavo del Vecchio's timely reference to the debate between Mises and Wicksell (of which more is said later in the text), Wicksell's review resurfaced in the literature when Wicksell's biographer Uhr published two works (Uhr, 1960, pp. 255–265; 1985). In both of these, however, the focus is almost wholly on the indeterminacy of the price equilibrium level in Wicksell's theory and on the lengthening of the production period in Mises'. Although he makes no reference to Wicksell's review Laidler (Laidler, 1991a, p. 299) rightly connects Mises' first moves toward the Austrian theory of the cycle with the

fact that "Mises, not[ed] the crucial role played by a commodity money in restoring equilibrium between Wicksell's money and natural interest rates, and not[ed] that this particular institution, though highly desirable, did not seem essential to the economic system." We find little else in Laidler other than this brief, and above all implicit, reference. In a work published in the same year (Laidler, 1991b, p. 152), this author asserts that the first edition of the Theory did not contain that specific combination of Wicksell plus forced saving that is the prototype of the Austrian theory of the cycle (cf. also Caldwell, 1995, p. 14). In the same strain, Laidler in yet another paper (Laidler, 1994, pp. 21–22), also says that Cassell, 1923 was the first to put forward the role of the differential between the two interest rates in fostering a lengthening of the period of production (p. 6). Claims of this sort are clearly textually ungrounded, as we can see not only from Wicksell's review, but also from the changes he made to the second Swedish edition of the Lectures (1935) at the prompting of Mises' and Davidson's criticisms (on which, in addition to Uhr's writings cit., see the classic contributions of Thomas, 1935, 1936). All of these were a reaction to the skeleton of the prototype of Austrian business cycle theory already contained in the first edition of the Theory. Hawtrey, 1935 (p. 515) notices how the abandonment of the hypothesis of convertibility into commodity money was crucial for Mises' demonstration of the inevitability of crisis; he accurately summarizes the issue Mises is addressing: "Of course convertibility into commodity money may impose a limit. But how does the position work out when there is no prescribed limit to the creation of fiduciary media?" Some writers of the Austrian school correctly set out Mises' theory of the cycle by reference only to fiat paper money: for all, see Moss (1976, pp. 36–37). Dempsey (1943), a little gem, in pp. 42–49 offers by far the best and clearest examination both of Mises' criticisms of Wicksell and of the relations between the two writers – but he seems to be unaware of Wicksell's review of the Theory. Wicksell's review is now available in English in Bien-Greaves and McGee (1993), in a translation that is unfortunately made useless by a number of mistakes in rendering the cruces of the argument.

50 We find the comparison between a genuinely monetary economy and the physicist's notion of a stable or neutral equilibrium already in Interest and Prices (cf. Wicksell, 1936, pp. 100–101; but see also Wicksell, 1935), where prices in money terms are compared to "an easily moveable object, such as a cylinder, which rests on an horizontal plane," which can be set in motion using "a certain force" here, the gap between the two rates. Deviation from equilibrium is progressive and accelerated until some time after the moving force ceases to act. Wicksell concludes "once the cylinder has come to rest, there is no tendency for it to be restored to its original position. It simply remains where it is so long as no opposite forces come into operation to push it back." Compare this, and our translation in the text, with what is offered by Bien Greaves and McGee, 1993, p. 198, which suggests the exact opposite: "the question becomes merely one of trying to explain the cause of relative price shifts in an otherwise entirely normal configuration of prices. In other words, the state of price equilibrium may be compared with the so-called neutral equilibrium in mechanics: it does not change automatically, but forces are gradually set in motion by various changes which necessarily tend once more to restore the previously existing balance." Bien Greaves and McGee must however be thanked because their annotated bibliography and the update, Bien Greaves (1995) greatly help Mises' scholars.

51 Dempsey (1943, p. 48).

52 See Uhr (1960, pp. 257–258).

53 Compare with Hicks (1935). See Scheide (1986, p. 586) for one among the
many possible examples of the interpretation that calls in aid a delay in consumption. We rather agree with Ellis (1934, p. 336) and Balogh (1956, p. 657),
who support the claim that Mises supposed the delay to be in wages. For confirmation, see the passage of the Theory where he says "[t]he increased productive activity that sets in when the banks start the policy." It must be
admitted that Mises' position on this issue is far from clear. At first, in Monetary Stabilisation and Cyclical policy, he says that wages rise immediately,
because of the livelier productive activity, but that they are not spent immediately (Mises, 1928, p. 120), but then he asserts, more convincingly, that the
prices of consumption goods rise "only to the extent that wages and profits
rise" (ibid., p. 125). As Colonna notes, Hayek would resolve the question by
appeal to two hypotheses. The first is that "when longer processes are set
going, though old lines are not renewed, the ones under way are still pursued
until intermediate goods pass through all the stages in the production process
and reach the final consumption." The second is that "the artificial lowering of
the money interest rate, affecting the relative utility of the factors of production also for old firms, requires a partial substitution of capital for labor also in
the processes under way so as to free some of the originary means of production (labor) already employed. As a consequence old firms may continue to
operate without any change in the total of their resources." If the former is
more or less clearly present in Mises, the second is not; with them, the consequence is that at first wages do not rise in proportion to the rise in the price
of intermediate goods and there is no shrinking in the production of consumption goods.

54 Wicksell's argument is not unproblematic either. Apart from needing the postulate that entrepreneurs consume the whole of the extra profit, he ends up
giving the impression that real phenomena depend only on real factors and
that the monetary variables act only on the price level (on this see Donzelli,
1988, p. 71). In this connection, we should recall that Wicksell is, in a sense,
gaily inconsistent, sometimes stressing the real consequences of inflationary
disequilibria.

55 The article has now been collected in Del Vecchio, 1967, the passages quoted
are on pp. 138 and 144. This contribution is important in being the only record
by a contemporary of Wicksell's review. Although we shall see how crucial the
question was for his own theoretical work, not even Hayek took note of it.

56 Wicksell (1936, p. 101); see also p. 252. In the same sense, see Dempsey (1943,
p. 42).

57 Trautwein (1995).

58 See note E in Patinkin (1965). For a detailed presentation and criticism of
Patinkin's reading, see Chiodi (1983, pp. 89–113).

59 Patinkin (1965, p. 591).

60 See the whole of chapter IV, which accounts for the fundamental cause of
cyclical fluctuations, Hayek (1933, pp. 139–192).

61 See Hayek (1935, p. 90).

62 Mises did not put into the first edition of the Theory this hypothesis about the
ultimate precipitating cause of inflation, at least in this extreme form. But he
holds to it fiercely in the second edition, which followed the great inflations of
Germany and Austria. In Hayek's view, it is a weak point and wholly inessential to the monetary theory of the cycle in the Wicksell-Mises form. Hayek
himself refers favorably to the criticisms of Mises on just this matter made by

Lowe, 1928 and Neisser, 1930; and he takes his master to task for an approach on which the inflationary tendency of the contemporary credit system is not endogenous in the full sense of the term (Hayek, 1933, pp. 144–50). Machlup (1940, pp. 247–248) and Haberler (1939, pp. 64–67) are supporters of the Austrian theory on Hayek's side. Phillips et al. (1937, p. 139) favor Mises and are skeptical of Hayek's alternative.

63 We are referring to Neisser's review of Mises (1928; Neisser, 1930). In that review, Neisser challenges the espousal of free banking as an institutional arrangement where banks' issue of fiduciary media would be checked. Neisser writes that "Only in an economically oriented non-private bank can one expect to find concern for cyclical changes and the indispensable policy for maintaining reserves." On the contrary, in a free banking system the prudent bank will be forced to follow the footsteps of the incautious bank: "in the event of a sudden strong demand for credit and cash money the prudent bank would have no fewer demands [of redemption in the legal media of exchange, eventually gold] made on it than the incautious bank; and since no cash reserves yield 100% if the emission business continues to be economically profitable privately, the cautious bank would have to suffer to about the same extent the consequences of its competitors' lack of caution, while the advantages of higher interest returns to the banking business had not been similarly advantageous to it." We may note a change of tone in Hayek's later writings (for them all see Hayek, 1976a, 1976b; for comment, see Colonna, 1990, pp. xxi–xxiii) where the abolition of the central bank's legal monopoly on the issue of the national currency would permit a more efficient and automatic control of the money supply. Here we have a rapprochement with Mises' claim (in this direction see Van Zijp-Visser (1994) pp. 85–86).

64 As is demonstrated by Colonna's elegant reading (1990, pp. xxviii and xlii–xliv), which recalls the many passages in which also Hayek, like Mises before him, refers, more or less plainly, to a system not dissimilar from Wicksell's pure credit. Colonna rightly concludes: "We must, therefore, give up the hypothesis that, on Hayek's theory, the specific behaviour of the banks is the cause that brings about the return to less capital-intensive production methods." See also Colonna (1994, pp. 41–44). Followed by a host of other writers, Hansen-Tout (1933, pp. 133–135; as quoted in Cunningham Wood, 1991) criticized the claim that the upper turning point of the cycle depends essentially on some alleged technical impossibility of indefinite growth in the volume of bank credit. For extended bibliography, see Colonna; we only note here some recent commentaries that raise the issue of how legitimate it is to assume, in the Hayekian framework, some restraint on the reserve side: Ruhl (1994, pp. 191–192) and Trautwein (1994, p. 80). As we explain in the text, Hayek replied to his critics' attacks by reverting to what was effectively Mises' original position on the final limit that in any institutional setting, including the pure credit system, hyperinflation ends up setting. This is a position that Hayek probably took for granted in his early writings, not feeling the need to set it out explicitly. Among other things, this is confirmed by a note in Monetary Theory and the Trade Cycle where he says "we need not stay to examine the case of a continuous increase in circulating media, which can only occur under a free paper standard" (Hayek, 1933, p. 176), and again by the continuation of the passage from Prices and Production quoted in the text, "and even if [banks] could [extend credits indefinitely], the other effects of a rapid and continuous rise of prices would, after a while, make it necessary to stop this process of inflation" (Hayek, 1935, p. 90). The conclusions of the last part of the Theory

hold well for a fiat-paper standard; it is there that we find the first description of the "other effects of a rapid and continuous rise of prices" to which the last quotation alludes.

65 See Hayek (1935, p. 71).

66 Compare with Hayek (1934, p. 192; p. 156 in Cunningham Wood, 1991, p. 156).

67 Heimann (1945, pp. 223–224) rightly stresses how Mises' theory of the business cycle offers an argumentative structure that turns socialist conclusions on their head. Whereas the socialists held that capitalism was an unstable mode of production destined to collapse for internal reasons, he attributes the crisis to the banks' unjustified, but persistent, interference with the market mechanism.

68 Hawtrey (1935, p. 515), writes: "A relative rise in the prices of consumption goods can perfectly well coexist with a low rate of interest. The result will be an extra profit to the dealers in consumption goods, which might make them willing to pay a higher rate of interest. But if the banks choose to go on lending at a lower rate, that merely means that the extra profit persists" (emphasis original).

69 In his 1924 review of the Theory, Hahn is generally favorable to the Theory. Like Hawtrey and Wicksell before him, Hahn points out that the banks can, without sliding into hyperinflation, keep steady their interest rate below Wicksell's natural rate. If the banks lower the rate on loans by means of credits that cause inflation, can this interest rate remain at the lower level, "if later banks continue to extend the same amount of loans, or are banks compelled to extend supplementary new loans because – if they only keep the same outstanding amount of credit – there would be a fast increase of the rate of interest?" (Hahn, 1924). Hahn's reply is clear: "it is very likely that the first and only credit expansion will be necessary and sufficient to lower the rate of interest; we can thus assume that there is no need to extend larger loans to keep a low interest rate." Of course, once inflation has increased in the economy, starting from a situation of stable prices and the inflow of new bank money, this will give rise to an increase in the nominal rate because "the oncoming price rise is included in the expectations of those who supply and demand interests" – even though Hahn appends "this does not necessarily always happen; and when it happens, it happens very late." If it did not happen, there would be a fall in the real rate (the nominal rate deflated by inflation). This latter rate would soon become negative and the credit demand would then become virtually unlimited. In this way we would have the continuous and accelerated growth in the money supply that Mises described. But if the nominal rate grows in line with prices, it will be possible, simply by maintaining, period on period, the same real rate (in the sense just defined) at the lower level, to satisfy entrepreneurs' demand with the issue of new fiduciary media at a given pace.

70 Schumpeter (1956, p. 114).

References

Aliais, M. (1987). "The Credit Mechanism and its Implications." In Arrow and the Foundations of the Theory of Economic Policy, G. R. Feiwel (Ed.). London: Macmillan. 491–561.

Balogh, T. (1956). "Fluttuazioni Economiche." Dizionario di Economia Politica. C. Napoleoni (Ed.). Milano: Comunita. 654–682.

Barry, N. P. (1981). "Austrian Economists on Money and Society." National Westminster Bank Quarterly Review (May): 20–31.

Bellofiore, R. (1992). "Monetary Macroeconomics before the General Theory. The circuit Theory of Money in Wicksell, Schumpeter and Keynes." Social Concept VI (June): 47–89.

Bien Greaves, B. (Ed.). (1995). Mises: An Annotated Bibliography. 1982–1993 Update. Irvington-on-Hudson, NY: The Foundation for Economic Education.

Bien Greaves, B. and McGee, R. (Eds.). (1993). Mises: An Annotated Bibliography. A Comprehensive Listing of Books and Articles by and about Ludwig von Mises. Irvington-on-Hudson, NY: The Foundation for Economic Education.

Caldwell, B. (1995). "Introduction." In F. A. Hayek (Ed.), Contra Keynes and Cambridge (pp. 1–48). London: Routledge.

Cassel, G. (1923). The Theory of Social Economy. London: Jonathan Cape.

Chaineau, A. (1990). Mecanismes et Politiques Monetaires. Paris: Presses Universitaires de France.

Chick, V. (1986). "The Evolution of the Banking System and the Theory of Saving, Investment and Interest." Economies et Societes, Serie MP, ni 3 XX (8–9), 111–127.

Chick, V. (1992). On Money, Method and Keynes. Aldershot: Edward Elgar.

Chiodi, G. (1983). La Teoria Monetaria di Wicksell. Firenze: La Nuova Italia Scientifica.

Colonna, M. (1990). "Introduzione." In F. A. Hayek (Ed.), Prezzi e Produzione. Il Dibattito Sulla Moneta (pp. xvii–lxxvi). Napoli: Edizioni Scientifiche Italiane.

Del Vecchio, G. (1967). "Le questioni Fondamentali Sul Valore Della Moneta." In Ricerche Sopra la Teoria Generale Della Moneta, Padova: Cedam.

Dempsey, B. (1943). Interest and usury. London: Dennis Dobson.

Desai, M. (1987). "Endogenous and Exogenous Money." In J. Eatwell, M. Milgate, and P. Newman (Eds.), The New Palgrave. A Dictionary of Economics. Vol. II (pp. 136–137). London: Macmillan.

Desai, M. (1989). "The Scourge of the Monetarists: Kaldor on Monetarism and on Money." Cambridge Journal of Economics XIII (March): 171–182.

Desai, M. (1995). Macroeconomics and Monetary Theory. Aldershot: Edward Elgar.

Donzelli, Franco. (1988). "Introduzione," in F. A. von Hayek, Conoscenza mercato e pianificazione. Bologna: Il Mulino.

Ebeling, R. J. (Ed.). (1983). The Austrian Theory of the Trade Cycle and Other Essays. Auburn: Ludwig von Mises Institute.

Ellis, H. S. (1934). German Monetary Theory 1905–1933. Cambridge, MA: Harvard University Press.

Garrison, R. W. (1981). The Austrian-Neoclassical Relation. A Study in Monetary Dynamics. Doctoral Thesis. Virginia.

Gootzeit, M. J. (1994). "Mises on Cyclic Relative Price Changes During the Cumulative Process." Economies et Societes, Serie (Economia, Histoire de la pensee economique XIX (4), 93–109.

Graziani, A. (1994). La Teoria Monetaria Della Produzione. Arezzo: Banca Popolare dell'Etruria e del Lazio/Studi e Ricerche.

Greaves, P. L., Jr. (1978). "Introduction" to Ludwig von Mises, On the Manipulation of Money and Credit (L24).

von Haberler, G. (1939). "Money and the Business Cycle." In R. Ebeling (Ed.), The Austrian Theory of the Trade Cycle and Other Essays. New York: Center for Libertarian Studies.

von Haberler, G. (1941). Prosperity and Depression. Geneva: League of Nations.

Hahn, L. A. (1920). Volkswirschaftliche Theorie des Bankkredits. Tubingen: Verlag J. C. B. Mohr.

Hahn, L. A. (1924). "Review" to the Theory of Money and Credit, 1st German edition. Archiv fur Sozialwissenschaft und Sozialpolitik LIII, 509–516.

Hahn, L. A. (1926). "Kredit." Handwosrterbuch des Staatswissenschaften V: 944–953.

Hansen, A. H. and Tout, H. (1933). "Annual Survey of Business Cycle Theory: Investment and Saving in Business Cycle Theory." Econometrica I (April): 119–147.

Hansson, B. A. (1992). "Forced Saving." In J. Eatwell, M. Milgate, and P. Newman (Eds.), Palgrave Dictionary of Money and Finance a cura di Vol. II. (pp. 140–142). London: Macmillan.

Hawtrey, R. G. (1935). "The Theory of Money and Credit by Professor Ludwig von Mises." Economic Journal XLV (September) 509–518.

von Hayek, F. A. (1932). "A Note on the Development of the Doctrine of 'Forced Saving.' " Quarterly Journal of Economics XLVII (November), 123–133.

von Hayek, F. A. (1933). Monetary Theory and the Trade Cycle. London: Jonathan Cape.

von Hayek, F. A. (1934). "Capital and Industrial Fluctuation." Journal of Political Economy LXXVII (March/April), 274–285.

von Hayek, F. A. (1935). Prices and Production. London: Routledge (1st ed. 1931).

von Hayek, F. A. (1942). "The Ricardo Effect." Economica n.s. IX (May), 127–152.

von Hayek, F. A. (1969). "Three Elucidations of the Ricardo Effect." Journal of Political Economy LXXVII (March/April), 274–285.

von Hayek, F. A. (1976a). Choice in Currency: A Way to Stop Inflation. London: Institute of Economic Affairs.

von Hayek, F. A. (1976b). Denationalisation of Money: An Analysis of the Theory and Practice of Concurrent Currencies. London: Institute of Economic Affairs.

von Hayek, F. A. (1978). New Studies in Philosophy, Politics, and the History of Ideas. London: Routledge.

Heimann, E. (1945). History of Economic Doctrines. An Introduction to Economic Theory. London: Oxford University Press.

Hicks, J. M. (1935). "A Suggestion for Simplifying the Theory of Money." Economica n.s. II (February), 1–19.

Hoover, K. (1988). The New Classical Macroeconomics. A Skeptical Inquiry. Oxford: Blackwell.

Humphrey, T. (1987). "The Theory of the Multiple Expansion of Deposits: What It Is and Whence It Came." Federal Reserve Bank of Richmond Economic Review LXXIII (March/April): 3–11.

Kuznets, S. (1930). "Monetary Business Cycle Theory in Germany." Journal of Political Economy XXXVIII (April): 125–163.

Laidler, D. (1991a). "The Austrians and the Stockholm School: Two failures in the development of modern macroeconomics?" L. Jonung (Ed.), The Stockholm School of Economics Revisited (pp. 295–327). Cambridge, England: Cambridge University Press.

Laidler, D. (1991b). The Golden Age of the Quantity Theory. Hertfordshire: Philip Allan.

Laidler, D. (1994). "Hayek on Neutral Money and the Cycle." M. Colonna and H. Hagemann (Eds.), The economics of F. A. Hayek, volume I, Money and Business Cycle (p. 326). Aldershot: Edward Elgar.

Leijonhufvud, A. (1987). "Natural Rate and Market Rate." J. Eatwell, M. Milgate, and P. Newman (Eds.), The New Palgrave: A Dictionary of Economics. Vol. III (pp. 609–610). London: Macmillan.

Lowe, A. (1928). "Uber den Einflu monetarer Faktoren auf den Konjunkturzyklus." Beitrage zur Wirschaftstheorie, Zweiter Teil, Konjunkturforschung und Konjunkturtheorie. Schriften des Vereins fur Sozialpolitik 173/II, K. Diehl (Ed.). Munich and Leipzig: Duncker & Humblot.

Machlup, F. (1940). The Stock Market, Credit and Capital-Formation. London: Macmillan.

Machlup, F. (1943). "Forced or Induced Saving: An Exploration into its Synonyms and Homonyms." Review of Economic Statistics XXV (1), 26–39.

von Mises, L. (1920). "Die Wirtschaftsrechnung im Sozialistischen Gemeinwesen" [Economic Calculation in the Socialist Commonwealth]. In F. A. Hayek (Ed.), Collectivist Economic Planning: Critical Studies of the Possibilities of Socialism (pp. 87–130). London: Routledge & Kegan.

von Mises, L. (1922). Die Gemeinwirtschaft: Untersuchungen uber den Sozialismus [Socialism: An Economic and Sociological Analysis]. London: Jonathan Cape.

von Mises, L. (1923). Die geldtheoretische Seite des Stabilisierungsproblems [Stabilization of the Monetary Unit – From the Viewpoint of Theory]. Munich and Leipzig: Duncker & Humblot.

von Mises, L. (1928). Geldwertstabilisierung und Konjunkturpolitik [Monetary stabilization and cyclical policy]. Jena: Gustav Fischer.

von Mises, L. (1931). Die Ursachen der Wirtschaftskrise: Ein Vortrag [The Causes of Economic Crises]. Tobingen: J.C.B. Mohr.

von Mises, L. (1936). "La Theorie dite Autrichienne du cycle economique." Bulletin Periodique. Societe Belge d'Etudes et d'Expansion, XXXV, vol. 103.

von Mises, L. (1940). Nationalokonomie: Theorie des Handelns und Wirtschaftens. Geneve editions Union.

von Mises, L. (1949). Human Action: A Treatise on Economics. New Haven, CT: Yale University Press.

von Mises, L. (1971) The Theory of Money and Credit. New Haven, CT: Yale University Press.

von Mises, L. (1978). On the Manipulation of Money and Credit. Percy L. Greaves Jr. (Ed.). Dobbs Ferry, NY: Free Market Books.

von Mises, L. (1990). Money, Method, and the Market Process: Essays by Ludwig von Mises. Richard M. Ebeling (Ed.). Auburn, AL and Norwell, MA: Praxeology Press of the Ludwig von Mises Institute and Kluwer Academic Press.

Moss, L. S. (1976). "The Monetary Economics of Ludwig von Mises." In The Economics of Ludwig von Mises. Toward a Critical Reappraisal, L. Moss (Ed.), (pp. 13–49). Kansas City: Sheed & Ward.

Neisser, H. (1930). "Notenbankfreiheit?" Weltwirschaftliches Archiv XXXII (2),447–461.

Patinkin, D. (1965). Money, Interest and Prices. New York: Harper & Row.

Phillips, C. A. (1921). Bank Credit. New York: Macmillan.

Phillips, C. A., McManus, T. F., et al. (1937). Banking and the Business Cycle: A Study of the Great Depression in the United States. New York: Macmillan.

Pribram, K. (1983). A History of Economic Reasoning. Baltimore: John Hopkins University Press.

Ruhl, C. (1994). "The transformation of business cycle theory: Hayek, Lucas and a change in the Notion of Equilibrium." M. Colonna and H. Hagemann (Eds.), The Economics of F. A. Hayek, volume I, Money and Business Cycle (pp. 168–202). Aldershot: Edward Elgar.

Salin, P. (1990). La Verite Sur La Monnaie. Paris: Editions Odile Jacob.

Scheide, J. (1986). "New Classical and Austrian Business Cycle Theory: Is There a Difference?" Weltwirschaftliches Archiv CXXII (3), 575–598.

Schlesinger, K. (1914). Theorie der Geld-und Kreditwirschaft. Munchen and Leipzig: Duncker & Humblot.

Schneider, E. (1962). Money, Income and Employment. London: Allen & Unwin.

Schumpeter, J. A. (1934). The Theory of Economic Development. An Inquiry into Profits, Capital, Credit, Interest, and the Business Cycle. Cambridge, MA: Harvard University Press.

Schumpeter, J. A. (1939). Business Cycles. Philadelphia: Porcupine Press.

Schumpeter, J. A. (1954). History of Economic Analysis. London: Allen & Unwin.

Schumpeter, J. A. (1956). "Money and the Social Product." International Economic Papers VI: 148–211.

Schumpeter, J. A. (1970). Das Wesen des Geldes. Gottingen: Vandenhoeck & Ruprecht.

Skousen, M. (1990). The Structure of Production. New York: New York University Press.

Sraffa, P. (1932a). "Dr. Hayek on Money and Capital." Economic Journal XLII (March), 42–53.

Sraffa, P. (1932b). "A Rejoinder." Economic Journal XLII (June), 249–251.

Thomas, B. (1935). "The Monetary Doctrines of Professor Davidson." Economic Journal XLV (March), 36–50.

Thomas, B. (1936). Monetary Policy and Crises. A Study of Swedish Experience. London: Routledge.

Trautwein, H.-M. (1994). "Hayek's Double Failure in Business Cycle Theory: A note." M. Colonna and H. Hagemann (Eds.), The Economics of F. A. Hayek, Volume I, Money and Business Cycle (pp. 74–81). Aldershot: Edward Elgar.

Trautwein, H.-M. (1995). Pure Credit Economies in Monetary Theory. Conference on Money, Financial Institutions and Macroeconomics, York University, Toronto, Canada. Mimeo.

Uhr, C. G. (1960). Economic Doctrines of Knut Wicksell. Berkeley: University of California Press.

Uhr, C. G. (1985). "Wicksell and the Austrians." Research in the History of Economic Thought and Methodology III: 199–224.

Wicksell, K. (1914). "Review" to Ludwig von Mises, Theory of Money and Credit. Zeitschrift fur Volkswirschaft, Sozialpolitik and Verwaltung XXIII (1–2), 144–149.

Wicksell, K. (1934). Lectures on Political Economy. Vol. I. London: Macmillan.

Wicksell, K. (1935). Lectures on Political Economy. Vol. II. London: Macmillan.

Wicksell, K. (1936). Interest and Prices. London: Macmillan.

Wien-Claudi, Franz. (1936). Austrian Theories of Capital, Interest, and the Trade Cycle. London: S. Nott, 1936.

van Zijp, R. (1993). Austrian and New Classical Business Cycle Theories: A Comparative Study Through the Method of Rational Reconstruction. Aldershot, Hants: Edward Elgar.

van Zijp, Rudy, and Hans Visser. (1994). "Mathematical Formalization and the Domain of Economics," in J. Birner and R. van Zijp (Eds.), Hayek, Coordination and Evolution: His Legacy in Philosophy, Politics, Economics and the History of Ideas. London: Routledge, 1994, pp. 67–93.

55

MONETARY CAUSES OF THE BUSINESS CYCLES AND TECHNOLOGICAL CHANGE

Hicks vs. Hayek[1]

Harald Hagemann

Source: *Indian Journal of Applied Economics* 7(4) (1998): 61–77.

1. Introduction

The economics of Keynes and Hayek were a lifelong challenge for Hicks in developing his own theory. Whereas the first is well known to a wider public, and can be expressed in four letters, IS-LM,[2] Hayek's influence on Hicks is of a more critical nature and still only known to a small group of academic economists. After Hicks's dramatic *Hayek Story* (1967), which caused Hayek (1969) to write his late "elucidations" of the Ricardo effect which had come to occupy a central place in the theory of industrial fluctuations when emphasis shifted from money and interest to capital and profit (see Hayek, 1939: 3 ff.), it has become commonplace to state that Hayek's business-cycle theory largely failed to gain general acceptance because of the quick success of Keynes's *General Theory* after 1936. Apart from the inconsistencies in Hayek's combination of Cantillon and Ricardo effects (see Hagemann and Trautwein, 1998), that, 'what Hayek was saying appeared to have little relevance' compared 'to the opportunities that had been opened up by the *General Theory*' (Hicks, 1967: 205). As Hayek had next to nothing to say about the later stages of the cumulative process of deflation and the lower turning point of the cycle, his theory seemed utterly out of step with the reality of the Great Depression.

Hicks always had been sceptical about Hayek's claim that the economy would be in equilibrium if there were no monetary disturbances. This is already manifest in his early essay on equilibrium and the trade cycle which essentially is the result of Hicks's grappling with Hayek's *Prices and Production* and Hayek's 1928 concept of intertemporal equilibrium. Here we find Hicks arguing against Hayek's statement 'that a change in the

245

effective volume of monetary circulation is to be regarded as an independent cause of disequilibrium. I cannot accept this in its literal sense, though I am prepared to agree that in a world of imperfect foresight monetary changes are very likely to lead to acute disequilibrium' (Hicks, 1982 [1933]: 32). Hicks realized that to analyze money one must consider uncertainty and expectations. He had a long struggle to present an inherently dynamic version of the economy in which agents' present decisions represent attempts to cope with an uncertain future in view of monetary and real constraints imposed upon them by past actions. But although Hicks made important contributions to monetary theory over a period of almost six decades,[3] he did not become too tired to emphasize 'the *real* (non-monetary) character of the cyclical process' (Hicks, 1950: 136). Indeed it had been one of the main objectives of his *Contribution to the Theory of the Trade Cycle* 'to show that the main features of the cycle can be adequately explained in real terms' (ibid).

2. From Hayek's LSE seminar in the early 1930s to the neo-Austrian theory in capital and time

It was one of Hayek's major contributions to have shown the importance of the temporal structure of production processes for cyclical fluctuations. Hicks repeatedly pointed out how much he had been influenced by Hayek in whose seminar at the London School of Economics he participated between 1931 and 1935. In particular Hayek had introduced him to the work of Wicksell, who had linked Böhm-Bawerk with Walras, and had made Hicks think of the productive process as a process in time. However, there is a remarkable difference. For Hayek cyclical adjustment problems arise because of monetary factors, like changes in savings behaviour and in particular credit expansion which distorts the system of relative prices. Hicks, on the other hand, always had been sceptical about Hayek's claim that the economy would be in equilibrium if there were no monetary disturbances. Although he took over from Hayek the idea that the impact of an impulse on the real structure of production is most important, it is very clear for Hicks that, unlike in Hayek, the divergence from a steady-state path and the dynamic adjustment process are not caused by monetary but by real factors like technological change.

> Where ... I do not go along with him [Hayek] is in the view that the disturbances in question have a monetary origin. He had not emencipated himself from the delusion ... that with money removed 'in a state of barter' everything would somehow fit. One of my objects in writing this book has been to kill that delusion. It could only arise because the theory of the barter economy had been insufficiently worked out. There has been no money in my

model; yet it had plenty of adjustment difficulties. It is not true that by getting rid of money, one is automatically in 'equilibrium' – whether that equilibrium is conceived of as a stationary state (Wicksell), a perfect foresight economy (Hayek) or any kind of steady state. Monetary disorders may indeed be superimposed upon other disorders; but the other disorders are more fundamental.

(Hicks 1973: 133–4)

Thus it becomes clear that Hicks's neo-Austrian model is designed as a barter-type economy in which money is at best the medium of exchange. It therefore cannot be granted 'that some anti-Say's law prevails, as in Keynes's *General Theory* model' (Morishima, 1989: 185). Since Hicks's own neo-Austrian theory has nothing to say about the problems of a monetary economy, it cannot take account of Keynesian unemployment but it can allow for the employment consequences of a physical restructuring of capital due to increased mechanization, i.e. technological unemployment. Hence Hicks's finding that the introduction of improved machinery may lead to a temporary contraction in output, and in employment, in the early phase of the traverse does not, in itself, contradict Say's law of markets. It is manifest that this type of 'neo-Austrian' theory is as much inspired by Ricardo as by Böhm-Bawerk and Hayek, a fact openly admitted by Hicks (1985: 156): 'So where we have come to on this Austrian route, is close to Ricardo ... to his latest insights, which he did not live to follow up. The Austrian method is indeed a Classical method'.

By the late 1960s Hicks had clearly become fascinated by the *Ricardo machinery effect*, i.e. the employment consequences of the introduction of a different, more 'mechanized' method of production. Hicks came to the defence of what he regarded as the central message of Ricardo's analysis of the machinery question: there are important cases in which the introduction of a new type of machinery might reduce both real output and employment in the short run, the harmful effect might persist for quite a time, but the increased investment caused by higher profits due to the increased efficiency of a new production process should eventually lead to a path of output and employment which is above that one which could have been achieved with the old production process.[4]

Hicks has not been the last of many great economists who have been attracted by Ricardo's chapter on machinery. In his *Path of Economic Growth*, Lowe (1976) characteristically starts his investigation of the macroeconomic consequences of technological change and of the necessary conditions for bringing an economy back to an equilibrium growth path from Ricardo's analysis of the machinery problem. Recently Samuelson (1988, 1989) has set out to vindicate Ricardo's propositions that machinery can hurt wages and reduce output and employment. Samuelson's exposition contains numerical examples that lead to a new long-run equilibrium position with unemployed labour, i.e. to *permanent* techno-logical unemployment. In Ricardo's numerical example, the economy takes off from a stationary state equilibrium and the evolution of the gross and net produce is calculated for three successive periods, depicting the effects of the construction and utilization of machinery on aggregate output (Ricardo, 1951: 388–90). There is, however, no indication that the economy will arrive at another uniquely determined equilibrium, i.e. the subsequent development of profits, investment, output and employment is largely left in the dark. For that reason Ricardo's example can be regarded as an 'early and rude type of traverse analysis' (see Kurz, 1984) which con-tains a capital shortage theory of *temporary* technological unemployment. According to Ricardo's view capital accumulation and output expansion will in the long run act as a compensating factor to the initial displacement effect of machinery. This has been fully grasped by Hicks who in the late 1960s set out to accomplish Ricardo's traverse analysis.

The employment consequences of technological change had been in the centre of the life-long research interest of Adolph Lowe whose writings on business cycle theory, particularly on the methodological requirements a theory of the business cycle has to fulfil, were the major challenge for the young Hayek.[5]

3. The problem of the business cycle: methodological reflections

In his 1926 article 'How is business cycle theory possible at all?' Lowe (1997) emphasized not only the relevance of the departmental scheme to the analysis of the business cycle but also that the concept of equilibrium that has been central in all systems of economics since the Physiocrats is logically bound up with a closed interdependent, and therefore a static, system. Lowe's critical analysis of the existing literature on business cycle theories led him to the following conclusion:

> The business cycle problem is no reproach *for*, but a reproach *against* a static system, because in it it is an *antinomic* problem. It is solvable only in a system in which the polarity of upswing and crisis arises analytically from the conditions of the system just as the undisturbed adjustment derives from the conditions of the static system. Those who wish to solve the business cycle problem must sacrifice the static system. Those who adhere to the static system must abandon the business cycle problem. J. B. Say, who consciously took this step, came with regard to reality in the logical neighbourhood of Palmström, who deduces with razor-like sharpness, '*dass nicht sein kann, was nicht sein darf*'.
>
> (Lowe, 1997: 267)

Lowe stated the problem clearly: if economic theory is satisfactorily to explain the business cycle, it cannot do so simply by outlining the consequences of a disturbing factor exogenously imposed upon an otherwise static economy. Rather, it must seek for some causal factor endogenous to the system itself which can distort the rigid interrelations implied in the system of static equilibrium.

How did Hayek react to Lowe's claim for a fundamental revision of the methodological foundations of business cycle theory? First, there are important elements common to both Hayek's and Lowe's positions. Hayek (1933: 28) explicitly agreed with Lowe's view on the relation between *empirical* observation and *theoretical* explanation:

> Our insight into the *theoretical* interconnections of economic cycles and into the structural laws of circulation has not been enriched at all by all these phase descriptions and calculations of correlations.... Now it would of course mean to misunderstand the logical relationship between theory and empirical research to expect an immediate furtherance of the *theoretical* system from an increase in *empirical* insight.
>
> (Lowe, 1997: 246)

Furthermore, Hayek accepted Lowe's seminal argument that all existing theories of the business cycle suffer from the fundamental weakness that they rely on *exogenous* shocks or disturbances and adjustments to such shocks in an equilibrium framework. Such a procedure could hardly result in a satisfactory theory to explain economic fluctuations which occur in a somewhat regular fashion. The logic of equilibrium theory

> properly followed through, can do no more than demonstrate that such disturbances of equilibrium can come only from outside i.e. that they represent a change in the economic data and that the economic system always reacts to such changes by its well-known methods of adaptation, i.e. by the formation of a new equilibrium.
>
> (Hayek, 1933: 42–3)

Trade cycle theory, like any other economic theory, must fulfil two criteria of correctness to avoid the pitfalls of creating cyclical fluctuations via the introduction of exogenous shocks into an otherwise static system.

> Firstly, it must be deduced with unexceptionable logic from the fundamental notions of the theoretical system; and secondly, it must explain by a purely deductive method those phenomena with all their peculiarities which we observe in the actual cycles. Such a theory could only be 'false' either through an inadequacy in its

logic or because the phenomena which it explains do not correspond with the observed facts.

(Hayek, 1933: 32–3)

Hayek explicitly points to the parallels of his argument with the views
expressed by Lowe (1928). Most important, however, is his making
common cause with Lowe in identifying the incorporation of cyclical phenomena into equilibrium theory as the crucial problem of business cycle
theory and in the demand for an endogenous factor causing the cycle.

Nevertheless, the two authors differ fundamentally in the conclusions
drawn from their methodological reflections. This holds in particular for
the role of the concept of equilibrium. While Lowe claims that the traditional concept of a static equilibrium has to be replaced by a new concept
of a dynamic system in which the polarity of upswing and crisis takes the
same position as the equilibrium in a static system (see, e.g., Lowe, 1926:
267–8), Hayek adheres to the concept of equilibrium as an indispensable
tool for economic theory in general and the understanding of intertemporal price relationships in particular. To start from the assumption of
equilibrium therefore is essential for Hayek's explanation of cyclical fluctuations. *Prices and Production* is characterized by Hayek's 'conviction
that if we want to explain economic phenomena at all, we have no means
available but to build on the foundations given by the concept of a tendency towards an equilibrium' (Hayek, 1935: 34). For the analysis of
dynamic questions it is essential to incorporate the element of time into
the notion of equilibrium and to take into consideration differences in the
prices of the same goods at different points in time.

Hayek's adherence to the concept of equilibrium in his business cycle
analysis has theoretical as well as empirical reasons. While he regards the
free market economy as inherently stable so that all movements can essentially be regarded as equilibrating adjustment processes, Lowe is convinced of disorderly tendencies in uncontrolled industrial markets in which
profit maximization has lost its classical determinacy. Hence his later plea
for interventionism in order to combine political and economic freedom
with the goal of collective rationality (see Lowe, 1965).

Hayek's business cycle theory rests on the idea that prices determine
the direction of production. The function of prices as an intertemporal coordination mechanism is to give entrepreneurs the required information
for their investment and allocation decisions. If in an equilibrium framework supply and demand are equilibrated via the price mechanism, how is
it possible that cyclical fluctuations are a regular phenomenon, since no
change *within* the system can give rise to it?

The obvious, and the only possible way out of this dilemma, is to
explain the difference between the course of events described by

static theory ... and the actual course of events, by the fact that, with the introduction of money ..., a new determining cause is introduced. Money being a commodity which, unlike all others, is incapable of finally satisfying demand, its introduction does away with the rigid interdependence and self-sufficiency of the 'closed' system of equilibrium, and makes possible movements which would be excluded from the latter. Here we have a starting point which fulfils the essential conditions for any satisfactory theory of the Trade Cycle.

(Hayek, 1933: 44–5)

4. Identifying the endogenous factor: money and credit versus technological change

It was Lowe's closest collaborator, Fritz Burchardt, who in his outstanding 1928 paper on the history of monetary trade cycle theory, which even his main opponent Hayek (1929a: 57) praised as 'very valuable in its historical part', showed how structural changes in economic history alter the character of theory. During the nineteenth century crisis theory evolved into trade cycle theory. Credit expansion and interest-rate movements became more important as symptoms of the cycle. Recognizing monetary influences in particular manifesting themselves through changes in the price level, Burchardt concluded that monetary factors alone cannot explain cyclical phenomena. In his view non-monetary factors have to play an important role. This holds especially for technical progress which is recognised as the central determinant of the cycle. With reference to Wicksell's influential theory, for example, Burchardt emphasized that, although changes in the market rate of interest are important for movements of the price level, the real impulse for the disturbance of equilibrium of an economy is given by technical progress which leads to an increase of the natural rate (see Burchardt, 1928: 119).

Hayek, on the other hand, pointed out that any theory of business cycles must take the influences arising from money (and credit) as its starting point. A theory of the monetary economy therefore could explain processes like cyclical fluctuations characterized by disproportionate developments that are unthinkable in the equilibrium system of a barter economy. The starting-point for the explanation of crises has to be a change in the money supply automatically occurring in the normal course of events, and not evoked by any forcible interventions (see Hayek, 1928b: 285–6).

Hayek not only regarded his trade cycle theory most decisively as a monetary one but also emphasized that a theory of cyclical fluctuations other than a monetary one is hardly conceivable. Accordingly, he saw the main division in trade cycle theory to be that between monetary and non-monetary theories. However, in a new footnote to the English translation of *Geldtheorie und Konjunkturtheorie*, Hayek made an important qualification:

> Since the publication of the German edition of the book, I have become less convinced that the difference between monetary and non-monetary explanations is *the most important* point of disagreement between the various Trade Cycle theories. On the one hand, it seems to me that within the monetary group of explanations the difference between those theorists who regard the superficial phenomena of changes in the value of money as decisive factors in determining cyclical fluctuations, and those who lay emphasis on the real changes in the structure of production brought about by monetary causes, is much greater than the difference between the latter group and such so-called non-monetary theorists as Prof. Spiethoff and Prof. Cassel. On the other hand, it seems to me that the difference between these explanations, which seek the cause of the crisis in the scarcity of capital, and the so-called 'underconsumption' theories, is theoretically as well as practically of much more far-reaching importance than the difference between monetary and non-monetary theories.
>
> (Hayek, 1933: 41)

This change of emphasis is not surprising since Hayek from the beginning stressed two arguments:

1. His trade cycle theory essentially is a monetary one. But while *monetary* factors *cause* the cycle, *real* phenomena *constitute* it. Although cyclical fluctuations caused by monetary factors, in particular credit expansion, are unavoidable in modern industrial economies, it is the impact on the real structure of production which is most important.

2. Monetary theory has by no means accomplished its task when it has explained the absolute level of prices. Thus he argued against simplified quantity theories which focus exclusively on the relationship between the quantity of money and the general level of prices. The classical dichotomy has to be seen as a cardinal error of economic theory. A far more important task of monetary theory is to explain changes in the structure of relative prices caused by monetary 'injections' and the consequential disproportionalities in the structure of production which arise because the price system communicates false information about consumer preferences and resource availabilities. Misallocation of resources due to credit expansion may even occur despite price level stability, i.e. constant prices cannot automatically be regarded as a sign of monetary stability, as Hayek (1925) has pointed out with reference to US monetary policy during the prosperous 1920s.

These arguments also form the basis for Hayek's reaction against the criticism which has been raised by Burchardt and Lowe against monetary theories of the trade cycle. On the one hand, Hayek explicitly agrees to several points of criticism. In particular he views Lowe's most important argument against contemporary monetary theories of the cycle as unquestionably valid, even with reference to the theory as it has been developed earlier by his admired tutor Mises. The argument concerns the *exogenous* character of the theory as it comes in by taking arbitrary interferences on the part of the banks as the starting point. Hayek thus dedicates the whole Chapter IV of *Monetary Theory and the Trade Cycle to* the issue raised by Lowe and to show that he neither has to rely on arbitrary interferences on the part of the banks nor on the general tendency of central banks to depress the money rate of interest below the natural rate but that the fundamental cause of cyclical fluctuations is of an *endogenous* nature.

> The situation in which the money rate of interest is below the natural rate need not by any means originate in a *deliberate lowering* of the rate of interest by the banks. The same effect can be obviously produced by an improvement in the expectations of profit or by a diminution in the rate of saving which may drive the 'natural rate' (at which the demand for and the supply of savings are equal) above its previous level; while the banks refrain from raising their rate of interest to a proportionate extent but continue to lend at the previous rate, and thus enable a greater demand for loans to be satisfied than would be possible by the exclusive use of the available supply of savings. The decisive significance of the case quoted is not in my view due to the fact that it is probably the commonest in practice, but to the fact that it *must inevitably recur* under the existing credit organisation.
>
> (Hayek 1933: 147–8)

The most important reason for an improvement in the expectations of profit which leads to an increase of the natural rate is the occurrence of technical progress, an argument which exactly had been made before by Wicksell and was repeated by Burchardt. However, when Hayek maintains that a discrepancy between the natural and the money rate of interest does not presuppose any deliberate action by the monetary authorities, and that technical progress may cause an increase in the natural rate which is not matched by an immediate adjustment of the money rate, the important question then is whether this discrepancy, and hence money and credit, is or is not *essential* for the emergence of cyclical fluctuations. Lowe would argue that it is not, i.e. that, although the fluctuations may be intensified if excessive credit is given to innovators, the latter would also occur in the absence of additional credit money. Hayek, on the other hand, insists that a satisfactory model of business cycles must be a monetary one. Whereas he recognizes the importance of non-monetary factors, such as technical progress, as a propagation mechanism for cyclical fluctuations, he nevertheless views monetary factors as the ultimate cause.

We can identify here Hayek's most innovative achievement. While Wicksell in his cumulative process analysis concentrated on changes in the purchasing power of money and never developed his monetary theory into a business cycle theory, Hayek accomplished precisely that task. He combined Wicksell's analysis of the cumulative process with the classical concept of forced saving to produce a monetary theory of cyclical fluctuations (especially in the production of capital goods) in which the expansion of bank credit leads to disturbances in the system of relative prices and distortions in the time structure of production via discrepancies between the natural (equilibrium) rate and the market rate of interest.

The main point of criticism levelled by Hayek against Burchardt and Lowe is that they follow Wicksell supposing

> that only general price changes can be recognized as monetary effects. But general price changes are no essential factor of a monetary theory of the Trade Cycle; *they are not only unessential, but they would be completely irrelevant if only they were completely 'general' – that is, if they affected all prices at the same time and in the same proportion.*
>
> (Hayek, 1933: 123, original italics)

With regard to the role of technical progress we find a significant change in Hayek's writings over time. In *Monetary Theory and the Trade Cycle*, Hayek supported Wicksell's argument that monetary expansion is frequently induced by changes in the 'capital rate', i.e. from improvements in profit expectations. Hayek (1933: 191–2) mentioned technical progress as a major factor behind such changes. Thus he recognized the importance of technical progress as part of the impulses and implicitly also of the propagation mechanism for cyclical fluctuations. In later writings he payed little attention, if any, to technical progress. Apparently he did not want to modify his insistence on the inevitability of crisis and the return to the original equilibrium position. However, reducing the Ricardo effect to a choice-of-technique problem required a switch in the assumptions about the cause of monetary expansion, from technological change to an autonomous lowering of interest rates (see Hagemann and Trautwein, 1998).

In contrast to economists like Hayek who regarded the cycle as caused by monetary factors, Lowe emphasized the role of *technical progress*. Indeed, technical progress was seen by him as the central determinant of both the cycle and the long-run growth trend, i.e. he denied the possibility of separating these two aspects from each other. The research programme of the Kiel school consisted in the attempt to develop a theory of accumulation, technical progress and structural change. Against the background of the microelectronics revolution it turns out that the programme as well as the methods used are pronouncedly up-to-date in many respects. The main research interest of the group was on the construction of a theoretical model of cyclical growth with the basic working hypothesis that a satisfactory explanation of industrial fluctuations must fit into the general framework of an economic theory of the circular flow as it was developed by Quesnay and Marx. The first step consisted in the construction of a model that incorporated both the physical and the value dimensions and that could be made amenable to dynamic transformation. For Lowe and the other members of the Kiel school the physical and technical aspects represent a fundamental determinant of an economic system, especially as important constraints on structural change and behaviour during transition processes. This structural dimension could only be neglected if the production factors were perfectly flexible, mobile and adaptable in the face of change. In order to develop a frame of reference for a sectoral study of economic growth the attention of the Kiel group was directed back to classical analysis, since neither the Lausanne nor the Cambridge school, with their emphasis on price variables and the far-reaching exclusion of the physiotechnical structures, offered a fruitful starting-point. Lowe's attempt to develop a theory of accumulation, technical progress and structural change culminated more than 40 years later in *The Path of Economic Growth* (1976). It shows Lowe as the second pioneer, after John Hicks, in the field of traverse analysis, i.e. in studying the conditions that have to be fulfilled in order to bring the economy back to an equilibrium growth path after a change in one of the determinants of growth, such as the supply of labour or technical progress.

5. Conclusions

By the late 1960s, when Hicks came to the defence of the Ricardo machinery effect he based his traverse analysis on a *neo-Austrian* representation of production structures in which time as the essence of capital enters production in a twofold way: as the duration of the process by which labour inputs are converted into consumption goods, and in the sense of intertemporal joint production of final output at different dates, a sequence generated by the fixed capital goods. Capital is thus an expression of sequential production. By dealing explicitly with fixed capital goods, Hicks's theory differs from that of Böhm-Bawerk and the Hayek of *Prices and Production*, who confined their models to working capital and, therefore, could only work with production processes of the flow input – *point* output type. Since Hicks regarded capital goods to be the source of a whole stream of final consumption goods at different dates, i.e. he considered productive processes to be of the *flow* output type, he explicitly abandoned typically Austrian concepts such as Böhm-Bawerk's construction of the average period of production or the notion of the degree of roundaboutness. Thus Hicks saw the decisive advantage of his neo-Austrian approach over that of the 'old' Austrians in the incorporation of fixed capital, the lack of which had been the Achilles' heel of the Austrian model, first pointed out by Burchardt (1931/32).

Hayek responded to Burchardt's critique by conceding that the stages model or vertical approach, which he had used in *Prices and Production* "gives the impression of a simple linearity of the dependency of the various stages of production which does not apply in a world where durable goods are the most important form of capital" (1939: 21–2). However, in his business cycle theory he stuck to the Austrian model and thus continued to neglect circular flows.

The analysis of the impact of process innovations on industrial structures is the strength of the horizontal or sectoral model whereas it has some difficultes in coping adequately with product innovations and in defining the time profile of the interindustry adjustments in the system. Hicks saw the decisive advantage of the Austrian method in its ability to cope with the important fact that process innovations nearly always involve the introduction of *new* capital goods which cannot *a priori* be physically specified. It is exactly this argument which had caused Hicks to move away from the horizontal model of *Capital and Growth* (1965) to the vertical model of *Capital and Time* (1973), since in process innovations

> the only relation that can be established [between the capital goods that are required in the one technique and those that are required in the other] runs in terms of costs, and of capacity to produce final output; and this is precisely what is preserved in an Austrian theory.
>
> (Hicks 1977: 193)

Thus Hicks, the life-long critic and modifier of Hayek's original construction in business-cycle theory, returned not only to Austrian capital theory. He also reappraised the message of Ricardo's machinery chapter in a passage that seems to reproduce the broad message of the Ricardo effect in Hayek's business-cycle theory:

> To industrialize, without the savings to support your industrialization, is to ask for trouble. That is a principle which practical economists have learned from experience. It deserves a place, a regular place, in academic economics also.
>
> (Hicks 1973: 99)

But there is one decisive point which Hicks had in common with Wicksell whose ideas provided the starting point for Austrian trade cycle theory as it was developed by Mises and Hayek. Hicks always treated the cycle as fundamentally a real phenomenon reflecting technological change and the fluctuations in investment that accompanied them. Monetary disorders may be superimposed upon the real disorders but they are only of secondary importance. Wicksell also essentially held a real theory of the business cycle.[6] Wicksell's business-cycle analysis remained a fragment. Nevertheless his two articles 'The Enigma of Business Cycles' (1953) and 'A New Crisis Theory' (1998), both written in 1907 and influenced by the writings of Tugan-Baranowsky and Spiethoff make clear the importance he attributed to the cycle phenomenon as well as the identification of the unsteady stream of innovations as the 'deepest' cause of fluctuations. With regard to the central role of technical progress Wicksell is "far closer to the Marx-Schumpeter tradition in cycle theory than to any monetary tradition" (Laidler 1991: 145). This marks a decisive difference to Hayek for whom the cycle essentially is caused by monetary factors although real phenomena constitute it. Wicksell emphasizes technology shocks and perceives in real factors which lead to a change in the natural rate of interest the essential reason for business cycles. Nevertheless he does not suit for being identified as a forerunner of modern equilibrium business cycle theories since he is not only miles away from making the market-clearing hypothesis as a methodological principle but also accentuates intertemporal coordination problems as the essence of his economic thinking. Hicks, who in his late writings on monetary theory[7] came very close to a neo-Wicksellian approach, shared with Wicksell also the view that the business cycle is basically a real phenomenon. This is a fundamental disagreement with Hayek for whom monetary disorders were of first and not of secondary importance.

Notes

1 Paper presented at the *Journées d'Étude "Hicks"*, Sorbonne, Paris, October 23–25, 1997 and at the second Annual Conference of the *European Society for the History of Economic thought*, Bologna, February 27–March 1, 1998.
2 For greater details see Hamouda (1993, chpt. 8).
3 This dates from his 1935 'Suggestion for Simplifying the Theory of Money', a landmark in the evolution of the theory of liquidity preference with which Hicks became a very influential monetary economist, via his 1967 *Critical Essays in Monetary Theory* to his last book *A Market Theory of Money* (1989).
4 For a detailed analysis of Hicks's discussion of the employment consequences of the introduction of new machinery see Hagemann (1994b).
5 The following two sections are based on Hagemann (1994a).
6 See, for example, Boianovsky (1995) and Leijonhufvud (1997).
7 See, for example, Hicks's last book *A Market Theory of Money* (1989).

References

Boianovsky, M. (1995), Wicksell's business cycle, *The European Journal of the History of Economic Thought* 2: 375–411.

Burchardt, F.A. (1928), Entwicklungsgeschichte der monetären Konjunkturtheorie. *Weltwirtschaftliches Archiv* 28: 78–143.

Burchardt, F.A. (1931–2), Die Schemata des stationären Kreislaufs bei Böhm-Bawerk und Marx. *Weltwirtschaftliches Archiv* 34: 525–64; 35: 116–76.

Colonna, M. (1990), Hayek on Money and Equilibrium. *Contributions to Political Economy* 9: 43–68.

Colonna, M. and Hagemann H. (eds) (1994), *Money and Business Cycles. The Economics of F.A. Hayek*, Vol. I, Aldershot: Edward Elgar.

Cottrell, A. (1994), Hayek's Early Cycle Theory Re-Examined. *Cambridge Journal of Economics* 18: 197–212.

Hagemann, H. (1994a), Hayek and the Kiel School: Some Reflections on the German Debate on Business Cycles in the Late 1920s and Early 1930s. In Colonna and Hagemann (1994: 101–21).

Hagemann, H. (1994b), Employment and Machinery. In H. Hagemann, O.F. Hamouda (eds.), *The Legacy of Hicks*, London: Routledge, 200–224.

Hagemann, H. and Trautwein, H.-M. (1998), Cantillon and Ricardo Effects – Hayek's Contributions to Business Cycle Theory. *European Journal of the History of Economic Thought* 5, 292–316.

Hamouda, O.F. (1993), *John R. Hicks. The Economist's Economist*, Oxford: Basil Blackwell.

Hayek, F.A. (1925), The Monetary Policy of the United States after the Recovery from the 1920 Crisis, in F.A. von Hayek (1984), 5–32.

Hayek, F.A. (1984 [1928a]), Intertemporal Price Equilibrium and Movements in the Value of Money. In R. McCloughry (ed.), *Money, Capital and Flactuations. Early Essays of F.A. Hayek*, London: Routledge, 71–117.

Hayek, F.A. (1928b), Einige Bemerkungen über das Verhältnis der Geldtheorie zur Konjunkturtheorie, in K. Diehl (ed.), *Betträge zur Wirtschaftstheorie. Zweiter Teil: Konjunkturforschung und Konjunkturtheorie*, Schriften des Vereins für Sozialpolitik, 173/II, Munich and Leipzig: Duncker & Humblot.

Hayek, F.A. (1933 [1929]), *Monetary Theory and the Trade Cycle*, New York: Kelley (Reprint, 1966).

Hayek, F.A. (1935), *Prices and Production* (2nd ed.), New York: Kelley (Reprint, 1967).

Hayek, F.A. (1939), *Profits, Interest and Investment and Other Essays on the Theory of Industrial Fluctuations*, London: Routledge.

Hayek, F.A. (1942), The Ricardo Effect. *Economica* 9: 127–52.

Hayek, F.A. (1969), Three Elucidations of the Ricardo Effect. *Journal of Political Economy* 77: 274–85.

Hicks, J. (1982a [1933]), Equilibrium and the Cycle. In *Money, Interest and Wages. Collected Essays on Economic Theory*, Vol. II, Oxford: Clarendon Press, 28–41.

Hicks, J. (1935), A Suggestion for Simplifying the Theory of Money. *Economica* 2: 1–19.

Hicks, J. (1950), *A Contribution to the Theory of the Trade Cycle*, Oxford: Clarendon Press.

Hicks, J. (1965), *Capital and Growth*, Oxford: Clarendon Press.

Hicks, J. (1967), The Hayek Story. In *Critical Essays in Monetary Theory*, Oxford: Clarendon Press, 203–15.

Hicks, J. (1973), *Capital and Time. A Neo-Austrian Theory*, Oxford: Clarendon Press.

Hicks, J. (1977), *Economic Perspectives. Further Essays on Money and Growth*, Oxford: Clarendon Press.

Hicks, J. (1985), *Methods of Dynamic Economics*, Oxford: Clarendon Press.

Hicks, J. (1989), *A Market Theory of Money*, Oxford: Clarendon Press.

Kurz, H.D. (1984), Ricardo and Lowe on machinery, *Eastern Economic Journal* 10: 211–29.

Laidler, D. (1991), *The Golden Age of the Quantity Theory*, London: Philip Allan.

Laidler, D. (1994), Hayek on Neutral Money and the Cycle. In Colonna and Hagemann (1994: 3–26).

Leijonhufvud, A. (1997), The Wicksellian Heritage, *Economic Notes* 26: 1–10.

Löwe, A. (1997) [1926], 'How is Business-Cycle Theory Possible at all?' *Structural Change and Economic Dynamics* 8: 245–270.

Lowe, A. (1928), Über den Einfluß monetärer Faktoren auf den Konjunkturzyklus, in K. Diehl (ed.), *Beiträge zur Wirtschaftstheorie. Zwelter Teil: Konjunkturforschung und Konjunkturtheorie*, Schriften des Vereins für Sozialpolltik, 173/11, Munich and Leipzig: Duncker & Humblot.

Lowe, A. (1965), *On Economic Knowledge. Toward a Science of Political Economics*. New York: Harper & Row.

Lowe, A. (1976), *The Path of Economic Growth*, Cambridge: Cambridge University Press.

Morishima, M. (1989), *Ricardo's Economics, A General Equilibrium Theory of Distribution and Growth*. Cambridge: Cambridge University Press.

Neisser, H. (1990) [1932], The Wage Rate and Employment in Market Equilibrium. *Structural Change and Economic Dynamics* 1: 141–163.

Neisser, H. (1934), Monetary Expansion and the Structure of Production. *Social Research* 1: 434–457.

Ricardo, D. (1951 [1821]), *Principles of Political Economy, and Taxation* (3rd ed.), ed. by P. Sraffa, *Works and Correspondence of David Ricardo*, Vol. I, Cambridge: Cambridge University Press.

Samuelson, P.A. (1988), Mathematical vindication of Ricardo on machinery. *Journal of Political Economy* 96: 274–82.

Samuelson, P.A. (1989), Ricardo was right! *Scandinavian Journal of Economics* 91: 47–62.

Trautwein, H. -M. (1996), Money, Equilibrium and the Cycle: Hayek's Wicksellian Dichotomy. *History of Political Economy* 28: 27–55.

Wicksell, K. (1953) [1907a], The Enigma of Business Cycles, *International Economic Papers* 3: 58–74.

Wicksell, K. (1998) [1907b], Eine neue Krisentheorie, in: E. Streissler (ed.), *Studien zur Entstehung der ökonomischen Theorie*. Vol. 18, Berlin: Duncker & Humblot.

Wicksell, K. (1934 [1913]), *Lectures on Political Economy*, Vol. I. London: Routledge.

56

WHY DIDN'T HAYEK REVIEW KEYNES'S *GENERAL THEORY*?

Bruce Caldwell

Source: *History of Political Economy* 30(4) (1998): 545–569.

Two problems of historiography are highlighted in this chapter about F. A. Hayek, John Maynard Keynes, and *The General Theory*: the sorts of questions historians typically ask and the reliability of self-reports from major historical figures.

Historians, of course, usually try to explain why something happened, but not always. Occasionally the more interesting question is, why did something that apparently should have happened, not happen? This question has captured the attention of many historians of economic thought who typically have asked it in the hope of solving some riddle in the past.

We know, for example, that while lying on his deathbed Adam Smith instructed two of his close friends to burn sixteen volumes of his letters, lecture notes, and manuscripts, a practice that was, alas, not unusual in his time. What is curious is that Smith chose to hold back from the fire a small collection of incomplete essays. Vernard Foley (1976) asks, Why didn't he burn these papers, too? Are they, rather than his other more famous works, the key to his thought?

Carl Menger, a founder of the marginalist revolution, was also for a time the economics tutor for Crown Prince Rudolf of Austria. In his introduction to a book in which the Crown Prince's lecture notes are reproduced, Erich Streissler (1994) questions why Menger didn't use this golden opportunity to promote his own marginalist views. Why did he teach his young charge classical economics à la Adam Smith instead?

In his book *Stabilizing Dynamics*, Roy Weintraub (1991) follows the same pattern when he asks why Paul Samuelson, in his work on stability analysis, chose not to make use of the readily available Liapunov method, a step that would have solved certain problems that took much longer to address without it. Weintraub (54) likens his query to the problem of "the dog that did not bark" in the Sherlock Holmes story "Silver Blaze." Indeed, such investigations seem invariably to result in historical reconstructions that read a lot like mystery stories.[1]

Despite their intrigue, "nonbarking dog" stories are not particularly common, for they pose a number of problems for historians. First, there is the simple fact that for every event that actually occurs, there is virtually an infinite number of events that might have occurred. The historian's first job is to convince the reader that only one event (out of all the possible events) that didn't happen, should have. Once that is accomplished a second problem emerges: now the historian must reverse gears to show why that which should have happened in fact did not. A historian pursuing a nonbarking dog story shoulders a double burden of proof: The more convincing he or she is in advancing one argument, the harder the second argument is to establish. These problems are particularly nettlesome when, as in the examples above, what is at issue are a person's motivations and when there is no written record (letters, diary entries, and so forth) explaining or rationalizing whatever did take place.

Another nonbarking dog question in the history of economic thought is the subject of this chapter: Why didn't Hayek write a review of Keynes's *General Theory of Employment, Interest and Money* ([1936] 1973)? After providing some background information on the protagonists, I will show that Hayek might reasonably have been expected to have written a review. I will then examine some reasons why it did not happen. This particular instance is unlike the examples above, however, in a remarkable way, for it turns out that Hayek himself wrote frequently about why he never wrote a review! As such our explanatory task is simplified considerably, or so one might at first surmise. But even with Hayek's assistance, a new (though ancient) problem emerges: that of the reliability of self-reports. Although in the end I will proffer an explanation of why no review was written, we will see that the problem of self-reporting appears in this case to be a real one. The "riddle of the review" may well remain an unsolved mystery in the history of economic thought.

1. Some background on Keynes and Hayek

Friedrich A. Hayek received degrees from the University of Vienna in 1921 and 1923, then spent about sixteen months in the United States. While there he studied the workings of the Federal Reserve system and learned some basic statistical smoothing techniques. In 1927 the Austrian Institute for the Study of Business Cycles was created, and Hayek was appointed its first director. In this capacity he traveled to London to attend a meeting of European institutes that were gathering statistics and doing research on the trade cycle. It was there that he first met Keynes, an encounter he would recall in a paper published in 1966:

I first met him in 1928 in London at some meetings of institutes of business cycle research, and though we had at once our first strong disagreement on some point of interest theory, we remained thereafter friends who had many interests in common, although we rarely could agree on economics. He had a somewhat intimidating manner in which he would try to ride roughshod over the objections of a younger man, but if someone stood up to him he would respect him forever afterwards even if he disagreed.

(Hayek [1966] 1995, 240)[2]

Keynes by then had achieved international fame for *The Economic Consequences of the Peace* ([1919] 1971), in which he offered an economic and moral appraisal of the terms of the treaty as well as a devastating account of the political maneuverings he had observed at the Paris Peace Conference. In Britain he was best known as a commentator on current economic issues. More important for our purposes, Keynes in the late 1920s was working on a book on theoretical economics, one that he hoped would establish his reputation as a monetary theorist. After much delay, *A Treatise on Money* was finally published on 31 October 1930.

Hayek, sixteen years Keynes's junior, was working in the same area. He had begun his own volume on the history of monetary theory and policy of which four chapters, covering roughly from 1650 to 1850, had been completed. In 1929 he published another work, *Geldtheorie und Konjunkturtheorie* (see Hayek [1933] 1966). The book contained Hayek's version of the Austrian (or "Mises–Wicksell") theory of the origins of the trade cycle. In the same year Hayek's critique of the underconsumptionist theories of the American writers Waddill Catchings and William Trufant Foster appeared in a German economics journal.[3]

Hayek's writings caught the eye of Lionel Robbins, the recently appointed head of the economics department at the London School of Economics and at age thirty the youngest professor of economics in England. In the spring of 1931 Robbins invited Hayek to the LSE to give four lectures. Published later that year as *Prices and Production*, the lectures were a big hit. Hayek was offered a visiting position for the following academic year and, soon thereafter, the Tooke Chair of Economic Science and Statistics.

In short order Hayek's battle with Keynes began. In the August 1931 issue of the journal *Economica*, Hayek published the first half of a lengthy critical review of Keynes's *Treatise* (Hayek [1931] 1995, chap. 3). One of his biographers tells us that "Keynes was obviously very unhappy with the August part of the review, for his copy of that issue of *Economica* is among the most heavily annotated of the surviving copies of his journals, with no less than 34 pencilled marks or comments on the 26-page review" (Moggridge in Keynes 1973, 243). Keynes's "Reply" was published in the

November issue, before the second half of Hayek's review appeared in February 1932 (Hayek 1995, chaps. 4 and 6). Keynes used about as much space in his reply attacking Hayek's book as he did defending his own. As the following passage indicates, Keynes's low opinion of *Prices and Production* comes across very clearly:

> The book, as it stands, seems to me to be one of the most frightful muddles I have ever read, with scarcely a sound proposition in it beginning with page 45 [Hayek provided historical background up to page 45; after that came his theoretical model], and yet it remains a book of some interest, which is likely to leave its mark on the mind of the reader. It is an extraordinary example of how, starting with a mistake, a remorseless logician can end up in bedlam.
>
> (Hayek [1931] 1995, 27–28)

The dispute on the pages of *Economica* generated a correspondence between Hayek and Keynes: they ultimately exchanged twelve letters between 10 December 1931 and 29 March 1932. Piero Sraffa's harsh review of *Prices and Production* in the March 1932 issue of the *Economic Journal*, and the comment and reply that followed in June, must also be considered as part of this ongoing contest between rival theories of the workings of a monetary economy.[4]

Beginning probably sometime in the spring of 1932 Keynes began to revise his theory. One historian argues that although by his Easter term lectures (in April and May 1932) Keynes was still using the analytical tools of the *Treatise*, the voice of *The General Theory* had finally begun to emerge (Patinkin 1976, 72). The process whose ultimate conclusion was the publication of Keynes's masterwork in February 1936 has become one of the most studied episodes in the history of economics, partly because of its intrinsic interest, and partly because of the abundance of materials that has survived, including Keynes's own notes, draft tables of contents, correspondence, the notes of students, and related publications. As a biographer has noted, "Although scholars will always hope for more, it is probably the case that with the *General Theory* they have the most voluminous record surrounding the creation of any classic work in economics" (Moggridge 1992, 557).

Hayek was also busy. But he did not prepare a review of *The General Theory*. Why not?

2. Is it reasonable to expect that Hayek would have reviewed *The General Theory*?

There are a number of reasons why it is reasonable to expect that Hayek would have reviewed *The General Theory*. First, one of the principal reasons that Hayek initially came to England from Austria was, as one commentator has put it, "to provide a counter-attraction to Keynes" (J. Robinson 1978, 2). Lionel Robbins was the person behind the scenes in this matter. Robbins probably first began thinking of Hayek as a candidate for "counter-attraction" when he read the German version of "The 'Paradox of Savings,'" published in 1929. In the late summer of 1930, Keynes invited Robbins to join the Committee of Economists, a small group of specialists that had been charged with writing a report on policies to combat the Depression. Keynes hoped to use the group to disseminate his own views, and Robbins soon found himself disagreeing with the others, both about the origins of the downturn and about appropriate remedies. Robbins ultimately wrote a dissenting report.[5] He also tried, unsuccessfully, to get the committee to hear evidence from economists whose views were closer to his own. Hayek was among the names he had submitted. Very soon thereafter came the invitation for Hayek to lecture at the LSE.

In an interview a half century later Hayek recounted the event and how serendipitous it had all seemed. (Recall that he had just completed four chapters of a history of monetary theory, which is why he could produce such an original lecture.)

> When I gave in Vienna my initial lectures as Privatdozent, I chose for my subject this kind of underconsumption theory which had then become acute in England. And Robbins could read German. That's an almost unique feature, an English professor who could read German literature—that's good luck, that he pounced on my subject: This is the thing we need at the moment, to fight Keynes. So I was called in for this purpose, produced of course a lecture which was original, which suggested more knowledge of the history of English theory than anybody else. Was sympathetically received by Robbins, who had been influenced by the Austrian school. We at once understood each other. This combination of accidents led to my appointment in London. It was luck from beginning to end.
>
> (Hayek 1994, 77)

It is also significant that Hayek had successfully challenged Keynes. As previously noted, the rivalry between the two was established early on. It is arguable that Hayek had the better part of the initial encounter. Both of their theories built on a framework that had been created by the Swedish economist Knut Wicksell. Wicksell's work was well known within the Austrian tradition. His first book, published in 1893, was an attempt to integrate the Austrian theory of capital with marginal productivity theory, all within a general equilibrium framework. Only after having tried to provide such "microfoundations" did Wicksell turn to a discussion of a monetary economy in *Interest and Prices* ([1898] 1965). In the *Treatise* Keynes completely ignored Wicksell's earlier contribution, borrowing only from *Interest and Prices*. Not surprisingly, Hayek in his review targeted the absence of a capital-theoretic foundation in Keynes's book.[6] In his reply Keynes more or less granted Hayek's point. This was probably why he felt it necessary to take the extraordinary step of hatcheting Hayek's *Prices and Production* in his reply. It was as if Keynes were saying, "Well, yes, my theory has its problems, but they are nothing compared to those in Hayek's work."

This is not to say that Hayek won their rencontre outright. Because it had capital-theoretic foundations, Hayek's theory *appeared* the more well developed and consistent of the two. But his framework was unfamiliar to his English readers, and many observers still found it hard to judge between them. All that was clear was that a contentious dispute had started. John Hicks, writing during the heyday of the Keynesian revolution, recalled it this way: "It is hardly remembered that there was a time when the new theories of Hayek were the principal rival of the new theories of Keynes. Which was right, Keynes or Hayek?" (Hicks 1967, 203).

Despite Hayek's early successes, for a variety of reasons the tide had begun to turn in Keynes's favor by the middle of the decade. Hayek himself became engaged on a number of new fronts. The exchange between Hayek and Sraffa that began with Sraffa's review of *Prices and Production* was, if anything, even more obscure than the earlier one between Hayek and Keynes, but few could mistake Sraffa's scathing tone. In 1933 Frank Knight began his assault on Austrian capital theory which Hayek was to answer in 1936. The year before he had been busy editing two essays to be contributed to *Collectivist Economic Planning*, a volume that set off the British version of the socialist calculation debate.[7] These new battles not only dissipated Hayek's strength, they suggested to the neutral observer that very few economists outside of the LSE (and indeed, not even all of those who were within it) agreed with Hayek's ideas.

Meanwhile, Keynes's star continued to rise. He was frequently in the public eye, offering policy advice, delivering speeches, and writing articles. Keynes also made it clear that he was developing (with the help of a bevy of brilliant disciples at Cambridge) a new theory of aggregate income, one that would correct the deficiencies in his earlier work. All of this created a general anticipation for *The General Theory*. And it wasn't just Keynes's own self-promotion; members of the Cambridge Circus were doing their able best to change the minds of any recalcitrant Hayekian devotees. Abba Lerner, Nicholas Kaldor, and G. L. S. Shackle were among the more prominent of their new recruits.

All of this suggests that the stakes had increased by 1936. Hayek had experienced an early victory, but, having been challenged simultaneously from a number of directions, he was losing ground fast. A critical review of his chief rival's new theory never could have been more important. Instead, no response came; at least, not until much later, in 1963, when Hayek first publicly stated his regret at not having reviewed Keynes's book: "I have to the present day not quite got over a feeling that I had then shirked what should have been a plain duty" (1995, 60).

Hayek not only shirked a duty, he missed a golden opportunity. Why?

3. Hayek's explanation(s) of why there was no review

I have identified five different places where Hayek reflects on why he did not review *The General Theory*.[8] The first is an essay that was part of a series of lectures delivered in October 1963 at the University of Chicago, but was not published until 1995. The second is an article that appeared in 1966 (Hayek 1995, chaps. 1 and 12). The third rather brief reference to the episode occurred in a series of interviews that Hayek gave in the late 1970s and published in 1983. He returned to the topic twice in the 1980s, first in an article in *The Economist* (Hayek 1995, chap. 13), and second in an interview with the philosopher and, at the time, his prospective biographer, W. W. Bartley III (Hayek 1994, 88–98).[9]

In the essays from the 1960s, Hayek offers two reasons for not having written a review, and hints at two others. The first reason involved his experience with Keynes following his extensive review of the *Treatise*:

> The somewhat disappointing upshot of all the pains I had taken with the *Treatise* was that not long after I had published the second part of my review it became known that Keynes had himself fundamentally altered his theoretical framework and was preparing a new and very different version. I must confess that it was partly due to this experience that when *The General Theory* appeared I did not return to the attack—out of a feeling that before one could complete a systematic examination, Keynes would probably again have changed his views.
>
> (Hayek [1963] 1995, 60)

This reason, that Keynes would probably soon change his mind again, appears in all five of Hayek's retrospective accounts.

The second reason was that, after reading *The General Theory*, Hayek got a vague but persistent feeling that he was opposed not so much to Keynes's theory, but to his whole approach and, in particular, to Keynes's use of aggregates, which hid from view changes in relative prices:

> I did feel from the beginning, though I did not see it then as clearly as I do now, that the difference did no longer concern

particular points of analysis but rather the whole method of approach.... As I saw it, an examination of the validity of *The General Theory* would have made it necessary to take issue with the whole macrodynamic approach, the treatment of the economic process in terms of aggregates and statistical totals, a theory which was concerned only with price levels and total income streams and in effect took the whole structure of relative prices for granted and provided no tools to explain changes in relative prices or their effects.

(Ibid.)

Hayek offers this explanation in both the 1963 and the 1966 accounts, but in the latter he adds that it "in retrospect appears to me the decisive one" ([1966] 1995, 241).

There are some differences between the 1963 and 1966 accounts. In 1963, after elaborating the "Keynes would change his mind" thesis, Hayek says: "But there was another reason than mere tiredness of controversy which made me hesitate" ([1963] 1995, 60). Now, "tiredness of controversy" is evidently not the same thing as thinking that Keynes would change his mind: one might wish to avoid wasting one's time, and yet not be tired. Therefore, this constitutes another possible reason. In the same transition place in the 1966 paper Hayek says, "Though he had called it a 'general' theory, it was to me too obviously another tract for the times, conditioned by what he thought were the momentary needs of policy" ([1966] 1995, 241). This suggests that Hayek thought that the theoretical edifice in *The General Theory* was designed to promote a specific set of policy views. As such, this might be viewed as an *additional reason* for why he thought Keynes would change his mind: it was suggested not only by Keynes's past behavior, but also by the type of book that was *The General Theory*.

Hayek never mentions "tiredness of controversy" again. His allusion to *The General Theory* as a "tract for the times" is a repetition of a charge that he had made in a brief piece in a symposium on the work of Keynes published in 1959 in *The Christian Science Monitor* (Hayek 1995, 237–39), but it is not repeated in subsequent accounts.

In the fall of 1978 Hayek was interviewed as part of the Oral History Program at the University of California at Los Angeles. Interviewers included, among others, Armen Alchian, Robert Bork, James Buchanan, Axel Leijonhufvud, and Leo Rosten. The question of the review comes up twice: in his discussion with Alchian on 11 November and again in the interview with Rosten on 15 November. In both instances the reason Hayek gives is that soon after he had completed his review of the *Treatise* Keynes had told him. "Well, never mind, I no longer believe that" (Hayek 1983, 408; compare to 114–16).

Hayek discusses the review twice in the 1980s and tells essentially the same story in both instances. Interestingly, however, he modifies his earlier account:

> It was not merely (as I have occasionally claimed) the inevitable disappointment of a young man when told by the famous author that his objections did not matter since Keynes no longer believed in his own arguments. Nor was it really that I became aware that an effective refutation of Keynes's conclusions would have to deal with the whole macroeconomic approach. It was rather that his disregard of what seemed to me the crucial problems made me recognize that a proper critique would have to deal more with what Keynes had not gone into than with what he had discussed, and that in consequence an elaboration of the still inadequately developed theory of capital was a prerequisite for a thorough disposal of Keynes's argument.
>
> ([1983] 1995, 251–52)

The meaning of Hayek's somewhat opaque final sentence is clarified in his interview with Bartley:

> I had been criticized for the fact that in *Prices and Production* I had a very inadequate theory of capital; that in this crude Böhm-Bawerkian form of an average period of production, it was inadequate. So I had started writing a great book on capital and money, which ultimately dealt with the money phenomenon. It took me very much longer than I thought; I worked seven years on the thing. I was dead tired of the subject before I got to the monetary aspects.
>
> (Hayek 1994, 90–91)

The book to which Hayek refers is *The Pure Theory of Capital*, which was published in 1941. As Hayek points out, the book did not contain a well-worked-out alternative to Keynes's theory of a monetary economy. Of course, Hayek could still have launched a separate (if belated) attack on Keynes. But he goes on to note that in 1940 he had joined forces with Keynes in an attempt to avoid policies that would create either rationing or inflation during the wartime mobilization. Because they were then on the same side, Hayek decided to postpone his attack:

> The main cause for this postponement was that I soon found myself supporting Keynes in his struggle against wartime inflation, and at that time wished nothing less than to weaken his authority. Although I regard Keynes's theories as chiefly responsible for the

inflation of the past quarter of a century, I am convinced that this was a development which he did not intend and which he would have endeavored with all his strength to prevent.

([1983] 1995, 252)

It should also be noted that Keynes and Hayek became personally closer during the war. At the beginning of the war the LSE was evacuated to Cambridge, and Keynes helped Hayek get rooms at Kings College.

What about after the war? Hayek apparently was biding his time in the hope that Keynes, who had revealed his anti-inflationist tendencies, would oppose the policies being promoted by some of his followers. Again fate intervened. In 1952 Hayek recalled their last conversation, in which he asked Keynes

> whether he was not concerned about what some of his disciples were making of his theories. After a not very complimentary remark about the persons concerned, he proceeded to reassure me by explaining that those ideas had been badly needed at the time he had launched them. He continued by indicating that I need not be alarmed; if they should ever become dangerous I could rely on him again quickly to swing around public opinion— and he indicated by a quick movement of his hand how rapidly that would be done. But three months later he was dead.
>
> (Hayek [1952] 1995, 232; see also Hayek 1994, 92)

To summarize, Hayek did not write a review of *The General Theory* for the following reasons:

1 He thought, based on his experience with the review of the *Treatise*, that Keynes would change his mind again. (Mentioned five times, but de-emphasized in the last two accounts.)

2 He thought, because *The General Theory* was "a tract for the times," that Keynes would change his mind again. (Mentioned once, in 1966.)

3 He had the vague feeling that a proper critique would require him to challenge Keynes's entire macroeconomic approach. (Mentioned four times; cited as the "decisive" reason in 1966, but de-emphasized in the last two accounts.)

4 He was "tired of controversy." (Mentioned once, in 1963.)

5 He was then engaged in preparing a model, one with its own improved capital-theoretic foundations, which he hoped would soon be available as an alternative to Keynes's model. (Emphasized in the last two accounts.)

6 The alternative model never was put forward. By the time *The Pure Theory of Capital* came out Hayek and Keynes were fighting on the

same side against wartime inflation, so Hayek didn't want to weaken his influence. (Emphasized in the last two accounts.)

7   Finally, Hayek held back criticism at war's end because he had hopes that Keynes would come out against the policies of his followers. But Keynes died before this happened. (Their final conversation; first mentioned in 1952, repeated in the 1980s.)

Note that the last two reasons explain why Hayek did not attack Keynes during the war years. If we restrict ourselves to the reasons why no review was written in the 1930s, only statements 1 through 5 are germane.

4. Some problems with Hayek's explanation(s)

Hayek's explanations are not unambiguous, and indeed, there are good reasons to treat his stories with some skepticism. Hayek didn't start writing about the question of the review until the halcyon days of the Keynesian movement. Given this timing, and the fact that he was completely opposed to the Keynesian approach, his statements about it must be considered with caution.[10]

Next, Hayek's story changes rather substantially through time. He emphasizes two reasons in 1966 and calls the second of these (his vague feeling of unease about macroeconomics) "decisive." This seems clear enough, but in the 1980s both major reasons are downgraded, the two that were mentioned in passing (Hayek's "tiredness of controversy" and Keynes's book being a "tract for the times") are wholly ignored, and two new reasons are offered as most important. Which accounts are we to believe?

Perhaps most damning is the tendency of Hayek's stories to leave the reader with the feeling that his memories are just a bit too consistent. Look, for example, at three of Hayek's descriptions of his first meeting with Keynes in London (these descriptions may be compared to a pertinent quotation at the start of this chapter):

> We at once had our first theoretical clash—on some issue of the effectiveness of changes in the rate of interest. Though in such debates Keynes would at first try ruthlessly to steamroller an objection in a manner somewhat intimidating to a younger man, if one stood up to him on such occasions he would develop a most friendly interest even if he strongly disagreed with one's views.
>
> ([1963] 1995, 59)

> There we had our first difference on economics—on the rate of interest, characteristically—and he had a habit of going like a

steamroller over a young man who opposed him. But if you stood up against him, he respected you for the rest of your life.

(1983, 114)

We at once had a conflict, very friendly, about rate of interest. Inevitably. He did, in his usual manner, try to go like a steamroller over the young man. But the moment—I must grant him this—the moment I stood up with serious arguments, he took me seriously and ever since respected me.

(1994, 89)

These remarkably similar accounts span three decades. Anyone who has viewed the requisite number of television courtroom dramas can immediately see the problem: rather than providing a spontaneous recollection of what actually happened, the suspect seems to have memorized a carefully constructed script. Is this what happened? At a minimum it would seem that, doubtless due to its frequent repetition, Hayek's account had taken on a life of its own.

5. A proposed interpretation

Some might want to throw out all the information Hayek provided and just leave the riddle of the review unsolved. I will nevertheless propose here an interpretation. Under the circumstances, it would be disingenuous to say anything more than that I think that this account makes sense of the evidence. My approach will be to try to assess the veracity of the various reasons which Hayek has offered.

Before doing so, however, we will first examine a simple, even obvious, explanation, one that Hayek himself never offered, but which occurred to several early readers of this chapter: maybe no one asked him to do a review![11] There is no evidence that Hayek was asked by any of the major journals to do a review. We do know that Keynes sent him an advance copy of the book. Hayek sent back a letter of thanks in early February, noting that he was puzzled by some parts and troubled by others, and concluding, "If my present doubts remain I shall probably ask for your hospitality for some notes on particular points in the E.J." (Keynes 1979, 208).[12] This indicates that Hayek may initially have intended to do a review. Perhaps by the time he got around to asking for space, the *Economic Journal* had already promised the review to John Hicks, and Hayek simply decided not to pursue the matter further.

Though it is possible to reconstruct plausible scenarios along these lines, my inclination is to discount this as an explanation. Were this really the reason Hayek didn't write a review, why didn't he simply say so? And the answer is clear: Even if no one had asked him to write a review, Hayek

271

could have done one if he *had* wanted to. As Donald Moggridge has noted, "The book was reviewed everywhere—in the daily press, the quality weeklies and monthlies, the professional journals" (1992, 592). There were many outlets for reviews, and economists (Hayek among them) frequently made use of them.[13] Hayek was not *prevented* from doing a review; he *decided* not to do one. It is his decision that must be explained. Let's turn to the reasons he provided.

A.

Intringuingly, the part of Hayek's story that is the hardest to evaluate is that which he repeated the most often: the "Keynes would just change his mind again" thesis. It is certainly a plausible reason. Keynes's quick-silver variability was well known. The public perception was not based on his switching of theoretical frameworks when he moved from the *Treatise* to *The General Theory*. Rather, it was due to his pragmatic (and hence often inconsistent, given the British economic turmoil of the interwar years) approach to policy. The most famous of his apparent flip-flops occurred in the spring of 1931. Hoping to forestall Britain's abandonment of the gold standard, Keynes came out in support of a revenue tariff, a move that reversed his longstanding and vocal support of free trade. When England left gold that summer, Keynes dropped his support for the tariff. This earned him the sobriquet of "the boneless man" in the press and led to the following wonderful twist on the old joke about how economists never seem able to agree: "Where five economists are gathered together there will be six conflicting opinions, and two of them will be held by Keynes."[14]

It is easy to imagine Hayek simply latching on to this widely held image of his rival as his excuse for not writing a review. If Hayek had simply said, "It was Keynes, after all, who authored *The General Theory*; why should anyone expect him to believe what he had written six months hence? No one would have contradicted him." What complicates things is that Hayek did not say this.

A careful reading of Hayek's accounts reveals that he does not play on the popular image of Keynes's variability. Rather, he keeps referring back to his personal experience in reviewing the *Treatise*. And what he may well have had in mind was the last of the twelve letters that he and Keynes exchanged during their controversy. Recall the sequence of events: the first half of Hayek's review appeared in August 1931. Keynes's aggressive reply (as well as a reply to the reply from Hayek) followed in November. Then began a lengthy correspondence that did not conclude until March 1932, the month after the second half of Hayek's review appeared in *Economica*. Keynes ended his final letter, dated 29 March, with these words:

Having been much occupied in other directions, I have not yet studied your *Economica* article as closely as I shall. But, unless it be on one or two points which can perhaps be dealt with in isolation from the main issue, I doubt if I shall return to the charge in *Economica*. I am trying to reshape and improve my central position, and that is probably a better way to spend one's time than in controversy.

(Hayek [1932] 1995, 172–73)

The last sentence seems a likely source of Hayek's claim that Keynes had changed his mind.

This, then, is the dilemma. Hayek really had experienced firsthand, and in a not particularly pleasant episode, Keynes's propensity to change his mind. But at the same time, to simply say that Keynes would probably just change his mind again has the ring of a handy excuse; a reason that would be immediately understood if given to a contemporary. Which was it; reason or excuse? Neither can be ruled out, and indeed, it may ultimately have been both: Hayek may have convinced even himself that Keynes's theoretical inconstancy was reason enough not to bother with writing a review.

We will never know, I suspect, how important this reason was in Hayek's failure to act. My own inclination is to take Hayek at his word in his later accounts: though it may have played a role, Keynes's variability was not the principal factor behind Hayek's decision. My justification for reaching this conclusion is pretty weak: it just seems to me that *other* reasons seem *more* important.

B.

Hayek's second claim was that *The General Theory* was merely "a tract for the times" that would surely soon be revised and hence not something to be taken seriously. This claim might seem plausible to a reader in the 1930s, for whom Keynes was known principally as a witty, caustic, and often brilliant commentator on the current economic and political scene, the author of both *The Economic Consequences of the Peace* and "The Economic Consequences of Mr. Churchill." Such a reader might well think of *The General Theory* as "Keynes's latest book," rather than as a major theoretical work.

But there are reasons to question this explanation, too. Keynes thought he was writing, and claimed to others to be writing, a seminal work in economic theory.[15] In his obituary on Keynes, Paul Samuelson assessed the effort as follows:

Herein lies the secret of *The General Theory*. It is a badly written book, poorly organized. . . . It is not well-suited for classroom use.

It is arrogant, bad-tempered, polemical, and not overly generous in its acknowledgements. . . . Flashes of insight and intuition intersperse tedious algebra. And awkward definition suddenly gives way to an unforgettable cadenza. When finally mastered, its analysis is found to be obvious and at the same time new. In short, it is a work of genius.

(Samuelson [1946] 1950, 148–49)

The General Theory was many things, but it can hardly be mistaken for a policy pamphlet. If one compares it to Keynes's other writings, it is best considered the heir of *A Treatise on Money*; it certainly has little in common with any of his writings on policy. Hayek's claim might resonate with certain readers in the 1960s, but only because at that time the "neoclassical synthesis" view that Keynesian analysis was nothing more than "a special case" (albeit a highly relevant one for policy) was popular.

The claim that *The General Theory* was "a tract for the times" is best viewed as an *accusation* by Hayek rather than as a reason for his failing to write a review. Hayek is retrospectively faulting Keynes for calling what (in Hayek's opinion) was no more than a tract a *general* theory and chiding a later generation for lionizing the perpetrator. Indeed, had Hayek actually thought this about the book in 1936, it would have provided a perfect *entrée* for a critique. One can imagine the opening sentence: "Mr. J. M. Keynes has written a tract for the times which he, for reason known only to God and himself, has chosen to call a *general* theory. . . ."

C.

Hayek's third reason is his vague but persistent feeling that in order to write an adequate review he would have had to oppose the whole macroeconomic approach. This reason was mentioned twice by Hayek in the 1960s, and the second time he called it "decisive." On the other hand, in the 1980s he downplayed it.

This explanation, too, should probably be discounted. What is least believable about it is Hayek's claim that he had had a *vague* feeling of unease about macroeconomic approaches. There should have been nothing vague about Hayek's reaction to an approach that employed aggregates. Opposition to the use of aggregates is a long-standing methodological principle among Austrians. In a work published in the 1920s on the U.S. economy, Hayek himself explicitly criticized the notion of a general price level (Hayek [1925] 1984).

The source of the Austrian opposition is that aggregates mask the movement of relative prices, and relative price movements are an essential component of all Austrian theory. Changing relative prices play a key role in the Austrian theory of the cycle, they underpin the Austrian critique of central planning, and they are central in Hayek's own (just then developing) vision of the informational function of market prices. Even more, in one of the few places that Hayek does offer a criticism of Keynes's *General Theory* during this period, he points out that Keynes's "economics of abundance" ignores relative price movements (Hayek [1941] 1975, 373–76).

In the 1960s Hayek had developed a deep interest in methodological work. Furthermore, Keynesian macroeconomics was at its apex. It is understandable that when reminiscing during this period he might link his failure to write a review to a methodological criticism of macroeconomics. But it seems unlikely that a "vague feeling of unease" about aggregates was a causal factor in his decision in the 1930s.

D.

We can now address together the two reasons that in my opinion make the most sense; Hayek's own "tiredness of controversy" and the fact that he was working on his own model. The two explanations go hand in hand.

There were at least two senses in which Hayek could have been tired. He was doubtless both physically and mentally tired after having fought a running battle with the likes of Keynes, Sraffa, Knight, and a disparate group of socialist planners. But in addition, Hayek may well have been tired of what surely must have struck him as *pointless* controversy. Hayek was reserved, even a bit austere, and always the perfect gentleman; Joseph Schumpeter once chided him for his habit of giving his opponents the benefit of the doubt (Schumpeter 1946, 269). Hayek must have been disconcerted by the debating club antics, the offhand but razor-sharp insouciance of Keynes and his well-bred Cambridge clique.

In the last of his letters to Hayek regarding the *Treatise*, Keynes hinted that he, too, might be growing weary. His last sentence read, "I am trying to re-shape and improve my central position, and *that is probably a better way to spend one's time than in controversy*" (Hayek [1932] 1995, 173; emphasis added). It is interesting that Hayek chose the word "controversy," the same one used by Keynes in his letter, in describing his reticence to do a review.

But Hayek was not just tired of controversy. Soon after he had concluded his initial confrontation with Keynes he came to the stark realization that his own model had some severe problems. The problems lay with the Böhm-Bawerkian notion of an "average period of production"; that is, with the capital-theoretic foundations of his model. This was bad news indeed. Hayek had scored most of his points against Keynes precisely because of the absence of such foundations in the *Treatise*. This had also been the one place that Keynes had expressly admitted that Hayek was right. Were Hayek to give Keynes another chance to reply to one of his critical reviews, it is not difficult to imagine how Keynes might use the opportunity: "The reader will recall that Professor Hayek earlier faulted my *Treatise* for its lack of capital-theoretic foundations, but what is now clear is that my book lacked, unlike his, the *pretense* of a foundation...."

Now this is not to say that Hayek accepted the criticisms of the likes of Keynes and Knight.[16] But he did recognize that problems existed, and he was in the middle of an attempt to solve them. Rather than interrupt his effort in order to spar with Keynes, he decided to continue working on his own model. He thought (wrongly, it turned out) that he was near enough to completion that the profession would soon have before it two models of a monetary economy, and that his would be judged to be superior. This, in my opinion, was Hayek's reasoning, and is the principal reason why he decided not to review *The General Theory*.

Before concluding, let us return to one of Hayek's earlier reasons, his stated "vague sense of unease" about macroeconomics. Though we have raised questions about this explanation, there were other reasons that Hayek may have experienced some vague uneasiness in the 1930s. As I have argued elsewhere (Caldwell 1988), in the mid-1930s Hayek began questioning the ability of static equilibrium theory to accurately portray how markets worked. The equilibrium theory of his day assumed that agents possess full and objectively correct information, that is, that all the necessary data is already given to them. For Hayek, this approach ignores a fundamental question: How, in a world of dispersed and subjectively held information, do the plans of agents ever become coordinated? Hayek eventually favored replacing the equilibrium story of the workings of the market mechanism with what Austrians now call a market process story. In the latter, free markets are one of a number of institutions that can assist the process of social coordination. In good Austrian style, a central informational role in this story is assigned to freely adjusting relative prices.

This market process view provided the foundation for Hayek's critique of central planning. But it also had consequences for his own work. In a market process world, it might be possible to predict broad patterns of behavior, but not the sort of precise sequence of changes in relative prices that Hayek had outlined in *Prices and Production*. Hayek may have begun to recognize that the line of thinking he was developing in the 1930s posed problems for virtually any theoretical approach to social phenomena, including his own earlier efforts. If so, his vague but persistent feeling of unease may have been over this, rather than over the fact that Keynes was doing aggregate analysis.

6. Conclusion

Historical reconstructions are always provisional. Stories change as more evidence is discovered. In constructing our narrative we have been forced to put our trust in a famously unreliable source: the self-reports of one of the principals.[17] What are the chances that new, more trustworthy materials might surface in this case?

The chances are probably slight. Not much correspondence from the 1930s remains in the Hayek archives at Stanford. In this regard, Keynes is a much more attractive figure for historians than is Hayek. Keynes was continuously on the move between Cambridge, London, and his vacation home at Tilton, and was an excellent correspondent; he was always writing to whomever was left behind at the other two places. The resulting documentary trail is massive. Hayek, on the other hand, spent most of his nineteen years in England (with the exception of the war period) in only one place: London. He would talk to people like Robbins (who was both a colleague at the LSE and a close neighbor in the Hampstead Garden suburb), rather than send letters. Throughout his life Keynes never left the Cambridge-London-Tilton axis for long, so there were fewer chances that materials might be lost. Hayek made a number of large-scale moves—Vienna to London in 1931; London to Cambridge and back in wartime; London to Chicago in 1950—during which materials might easily have been lost or discarded.[18] Finally, few individuals could match Keynes's penchant for squirreling items away; even as a youth he kept meticulous records.[19]

It would be wonderful if some new stockpile of contemporaneous materials were suddenly discovered, as happened in 1976 when a large cache of Keynes's lecture notes and letters was found at Tilton. But even contemporaneous correspondence is not an infallible guide to an author's motives. Obviously, one can write with future generations in mind; or embarrassing entries can be discreetly removed, either by the figure in question, or by his heirs, or by others seeking to protect him; or, most fundamentally, intentions can be misread. When one speculates on motivation, there are many slips 'twixt cup and lip. Additional evidence simply provides more material that must somehow be fit into the historian's story. At best, it may help to eliminate certain reconstructions as implausible.

There is a final twist to our story. In the end Hayek did, in a manner of speaking, write a review, not of *The General Theory* per se, but of the whole Keynesian approach. For it turns out that in most of his accounts of why he did not review *The General Theory*, Hayek manages to slip in an assessment of Keynes's contribution. One of these even contained an inside joke that Keynes, would have appreciated, even as it smarted. At one point in criticizing Keynes, Hayek quotes the opinion of the "eminent" Victorian, Leslie Stephen (Hayek 1995, 249). Keynes famously despised the Victorian era, of course, but much worse, Stephen was the straight-laced father of two of his compatriots in the Bloomsbury group, Vanessa Bell and Virginia Woolf!

F. A. Hayek's formal and reserved exterior was like the skin of an

onion, hiding many layers beneath. This is a final reason why we will probably never really know why he failed to review Keynes's *General Theory*.

Notes

1 Interest in "nonbarking dog" questions is not limited to economists. For
  example, the "Silver Blaze" metaphor is used by the social historian Kevin
  McAleer (1994, 197) in reference to the *Sonderweg* (separate path) question of
  German history: Why didn't the development of the German Empire mirror
  those of other European nations? Why was its path so different?
2 In this and subsequent Hayek 1995 references, the date in brackets represents
  the year in which the cited material first appeared.
3 Hayek's previously unpublished chapters on English monetary theory comprise chapters 9 through 12 of Hayek 1991. The English translation of his book
  is *Monetary Theory and the Trade Cycle* ([1933] 1966). The journal article,
  translated as "The 'Paradox of Savings,'" is reprinted as chapter 2 of Hayek
  1995.
4 The correspondence is reprinted as an addendum to chapter 5 in Hayek 1995,
  and the exchange between Sraffa and Hayek appears there as chapters 7
  through 9.
5 This episode is recounted in Howson and Winch 1977 (46–72).
6 The relevant books are Wicksell [1893] 1970 and [1898] 1965. Both of Wicksell's
  books were translated from German into English only *after* Keynes had finished
  the *Treatise*. Indeed, in a footnote in the *Treatise*, Keynes admitted that "in
  German I can only clearly understand what I know already!" (Keynes [1930]
  1971, 5: 178 n. 2), so Hayek had a distinct advantage over Keynes in this area.
7 Hayek's papers on socialism are reprinted in Hayek 1997, and Hayek 1936 is
  his response to Frank Knight (1933, 1934, 1935).
8 Others exist. Hayek gave interviews to newspaper reporters, was interviewed
  for articles in journals, and replied to queries from scholars. His relationship
  with Keynes was a popular topic on such occasions. None that I have seen,
  however, adds anything of substance to the accounts listed here.
9 Bartley was also to have been Karl Popper's biographer, but he predeceased
  both of them.
10 Thus Hayek's constant reiteration of Keynes's propensity to change his mind
  might simply have been designed to discredit Keynes and to remind a later and
  more worshipful generation of one of their hero's most obvious foibles.
11 Martin Bronfenbrenner, Ross Emmett, and Maria Marcuzzo all came up with
  slightly different variants of this reason. Among those who reviewed *The
  General Theory* for the professional journals were: A. C. Pigou (*Economica*),
  John Hicks (*Economic Journal*), Brian Reddaway (*Economic Record*), Jacob
  Viner, with additional "Comments" by Frank Taussig, Dennis Robertson, and
  Wassily Leontief (*Quarterly Journal of Economics*), Alvin Hansen (*Journal of
  Political Economy*), C. O. Hardy (*American Economic Review*), and Abba
  Lerner (*International Labour Review*).
12 Keynes was the editor of the *Economic Journal*, and Austin Robinson the
  review editor. The latter tells the following story: "I was responsible for the
  review section of the *Journal*. I was given a ration of pages. We settled anything that needed to be settled on a Sunday morning, myself seated among the
  Sunday papers and the proofs of the *Journal* at the foot of Keynes's bed in his
  room at King's.... I remember telling him that I proposed to ask John Hicks to

review the *General Theory*. I thought he was sufficiently detached from its genesis, though he was by then in Cambridge. He thought it a good idea" (A. Robinson 1990, 166).

13 The reviews reprinted in Hayek 1997, for example, are taken from professional journals, but also from the *Spectator* (a weekly magazine) and the *London Times*.

14 See Johnson and Johnson 1978 (17) on "the boneless man" and Jones 1954 (19) on the joke. See Moggridge 1992 (640–41) for another example of Keynes's versatility.

15 Note this from Keynes's letter to G. B. Shaw on New Year's Day 1935: "To understand my state of mind, however, you have to know that I believe myself to be writing a book on economic theory, which will revolutionize—not, I suppose, at once but in the course of the next ten years—the way the world thinks about economic problems" (Keynes 1982, 42).

16 Keynes quotes Henrik Ibsen in attacking Hayek in *The General Theory*. The passage is at once lyrical and nasty; that is to say, vintage Keynes: Hayek is likened to a "wild duck" who "has dived down to the bottom—as deep as she can get—and bitten fast hold of the weed and tangle and all the rubbish that is down there" (Keynes [1936] 1973, 183).

17 We are fortunate in this case to have a number of self-reports by Hayek. Because the story was retold many times, its inconsistencies became clear. Oral historians who get a story only once should be particularly careful about the inferences they draw.

18 In a letter (1975) Hayek once explained the poor state of his correspondence as follows: "I have to confess that as a result of my repeated moves what older correspondence I have is in considerable disorder. But these moves also have been the occasion of recurrent ruthless destructions of accumulated letters."

19 See, for example, item number 13 in the "Personal Papers" file in the Keynes Archives at King's College, Cambridge, where a complete listing of all of Keynes's golf scores for the period 1898–1905 are recorded. At least there was something at which he was bad; in the first round he ever played (aged 13) he shot a 256.

References

Caldwell, Bruce. 1988. Hayek's Transformation. *HOPE* 20.4:513–41.

Foley, Vernard. 1976. *The Social Physics of Adam Smith*. West Lafayette, Ind.: Purdue University Press.

Hayek, F. A. [1925] 1984. The Monetary Policy of the United States after the Recovery from the 1920 Crisis. In *Money, Capital, and Fluctuations: Early Essays*, edited by Roy McCloughry. Chicago: University of Chicago Press.

——. 1931. *Prices and Production*. London: Routledge.

——. [1933] 1966. *Monetary Theory and the Trade Cycle*. Translated by N. Kaldor and H. M. Croome. New York: Kelley reprints. Originally published as *Geldtheorie und Konjunkturtheorie* (Vienna: Hölder-Pichler-Tempsky, 1929).

——. 1936. The Mythology of Capital. *Quarterly Journal of Economics* 50.2:199–228.

——. [1941] 1975. *The Pure Theory of Capital*. Chicago: Midway Reprint.

——. 1975. Letter to Helmut Wagner, 8 January. Box 56, number 42, Hayek Archives, Hoover Institution, Stanford, Calif.

——. 1983. Nobel Prize-Winning Economist. Transcript of an interview conducted in 1978 under the auspices of the Oral History Program, University Library, University of California at Los Angeles. Los Angeles: Regents of the University of California.

——. 1991. *The Trend of Economic Thinking*. Edited by W. W. Bartley III and Stephen Kresge. Vol. 3 of *The Collected Works of F. A. Hayek*. Chicago: University of Chicago Press; London: Routledge.

——. 1994. *Hayek on Hayek*. Edited by Stephen Kresge and Leif Wenar. Chicago: University of Chicago Press; London: Routledge.

——. 1995. *Contra Keynes and Cambridge: Essays and Correspondence*. Edited by Bruce Caldwell. Vol. 9 of *The Collected Works of F. A. Hayek*. Chicago: University of Chicago Press; London: Routledge.

——. 1997. *Socialism and War*. Edited by Bruce Caldwell. Vol. 10 of *The Collected Works of F. A. Hayek*. Chicago: University of Chicago Press; London: Routledge.

Hicks, John. 1967. The Hayek Story. In *Critical Essays in Monetary Theory*, edited by John Hicks. Oxford: Clarendon Press.

Howson, Susan, and Donald Winch. 1977. *The Economic Advisory Council, 1930–1939: A Study in Economic Advice during Depression and Recovery*. Cambridge: Cambridge University Press.

Johnson, Elizabeth, and Harry Johnson, eds. 1978. *The Shadow of Keynes: Understanding Keynes, Cambridge, and Keynesian Economics*. Chicago: University of Chicago Press.

Jones, Thomas. 1954. *A Diary with Letters, 1931–1950*. London: Oxford University Press.

Keynes, J. M. [1919] 1971. *The Economic Consequences of the Peace*. Vol. 2 of *The Collected Writings of John Maynard Keynes*. London: Macmillan.

——. [1930] 1971. *A Treatise on Money*. Vols. 5 and 6 of *The Collected Writings of John Maynard Keynes*. London: Macmillan.

——. [1936] 1973. *The General Theory of Employment, Interest and Money*. Vol. 7 of *The Collected Writings of John Maynard Keynes*. London: Macmillan.

——. 1973. *The General Theory and After: Part 1, Preparation*. Edited by Donald Moggridge. Vol. 13 of *The Collected Writings of John Maynard Keynes*. London: Macmillan.

——. 1979. *The General Theory and After: A Supplement*. Edited by Donald Moggridge. Vol. 29 of *The Collected Writings of John Maynard Keynes*. London: Macmillan.

——. 1982. *Social, Political and Literary Writings*. Edited by Donald Moggridge. Vol. 28 of *The Collected Writings of John Maynard Keynes*. London: Macmillan.

——. Personal Papers. The Keynes Archives, King's College, Cambridge.

Knight, Frank. 1933. Capitalist Production, Time and the Rate of Return. In *Economic Essays in Honour of Gustav Cassel*. London: Allen and Unwin.

——. 1934. Capital, Time and the Interest Rate. *Economica*, n.s., 1.3:257–86.

——. 1935. Professor Hayek and the Theory of Investment. *Economic Journal* 45.177:77–94.

McAleer, Kevin. 1994. *Dueling: The Cult of Honor in Fin-de-Siècle Germany*. Princeton, N.J.: Princeton University Press.

Moggridge, Donald E. 1992. *Maynard Keynes: An Economist's Biography*. London and New York: Routledge.

Patinkin, Don. 1976. Keynes' Monetary Thought: A Study of its Development. *HOPE* 8.1:1–150.

Robinson, Austin. 1990. Fifty-five Years on the Royal Economic Society Council. In *A Century of Economics: 100 years of the Royal Economic Society and the Economic Journal*, edited by John Hey and Donald Winch. Oxford: Basil Blackwell.

Robinson, Joan. 1978. The Second Crisis in Economic Theory. In *Contributions to Modern Economics*. New York: Academic Press.

Samuelson, Paul. [1946] 1950. Lord Keynes and the *General Theory*. In *The New Economics*, edited by Seymour Harris. New York: Knopf.

Schumpeter, Joseph. 1946. Review of *The Road to Serfdom*. *Journal of Political Economy* 54.3:269–70.

Streissler, Erich. 1994. Menger's Treatment of Economics in the Rudolf Lectures. In *Carl Menger's Lectures to Crown Prince Rudolf of Austria*, edited by Erich Streissler and Monika Streissler. Aldershot, England: Elgar.

Weintraub, E. Roy. 1991. *Stabilizing Dynamics: Constructing Economic Knowledge*. Cambridge: Cambridge University Press.

Wicksell, Knut. [1893] 1970. *Value, Capital and Rent*. Translated by S. H. Frowein. Reprint, New York: Kelley.

———. [1898] 1965. *Interest and Prices*. Translated by R. F. Kahn. Reprint, New York: Kelley.

57

TOWARD DEVELOPING A TWENTY-FIRST CENTURY ECONOMIC PARADIGM

Lessons from Myrdal, Schumpeter, and Hayek

James Angresano

Source: W. E. Halah and K. B. Taylor (eds), *Twenty First Century Economics: Perspectives of Socioeconomics for a Changing World*, London: St Martin's Press, 1999, pp. 27–250.

Introduction

A useful economic perspective is one that offers normative propositions and a conception of the socioeconomic reality that are shared by a growing number of social scientists.[1] If formal methods of analysis and coherent theories also are provided and accepted by a number of practitioners, the perspective can be considered a paradigm.[2] In order for a new perspective to establish itself as a serious, viable alternative to the neoclassical perspective, and thereby become part of *the* paradigm for social science practitioners in the academic community, it must provide a more realistic conceptualized reality than the neoclassical perspective currently provides. Doing so would enable its proponents to offer colleagues, students, and laypersons an alternative understanding of an economy's principal institutions and working rules than that which is currently provided by neoclassical economics as well as a basis for developing public policies for achieving its normative propositions. The objective of this chapter is not to set forth a new paradigm but to provide a starting point toward its development.

Our heritage of economic thought can serve as a guide toward developing a new economic perspective. A useful place to begin is to draw from three prominent economic philosophers: Gunnar Myrdal, Joseph Schumpeter, and Friedrich Hayek. While it is true that some of their normative propositions were diametrically opposed and they held significantly different positions regarding the efficacy of economic planning, they had much in common. Studying and articulating principal aspects of their conceptualizations of reality, criticisms of neoclassical economics, methods of analysis, and conclusions can serve as a solid foundation from which to begin building a new economic paradigm.

What did Myrdal, Schumpeter, and Hayek share?

While the early part of their respective careers was devoted entirely to technical aspects of economics, especially monetary and trade theory, all three devoted most of their professional lives to analyzing the dynamic process of change within an economy, accounting for social, philosophical, political as well as psychological aspects of societal growth and development.[3] Despite their having provided pathbreaking analysis of many pressing economic issues, their contributions have become tangential to mainstream economic analysis, primarily because they deemphasized pure economic theory while providing their own political philosophy. However, each has been considered among the greatest social science analysts of this century due to the striking breadth and depth of their theories and analyses and the innovative nature of their significant contributions to methodology, economic theory, history of economic thought, and economic history.

All three relied heavily on history in their analysis, and each was influenced by (and sought to account for) the economic, political, and social conditions of the era in which he was writing.[4] Each looked at particular economies over different time periods, and retrospective analysis indicates that each of them was "right" regarding his analysis, conclusions drawn, and policy proposals offered for the particular economies he analyzed. History also demonstrates that none of them offered policy proposals and predictions that would be correct for all economies over a long period. This should not be surprising, for no one is always right regarding the predictions of the path economies will follow. Viewed from an evolutionary-institutional perspective, over time economic institutions have a different impact on the performance of an economy, and the change in performance results in new attitudes which, in turn, lead to new institutions and new types of economy.[5] For example, prior to 1932 Sweden was not flourishing under laissez-faire policies. The nation grew and developed rapidly thereafter under a democratically controlled social economy with considerable contributions from both social insurance and welfare programs as well as entrepreneurs whose multinational corporations stimulated an export boom. However, the same government policies designed to alleviate poverty and create a more egalitarian society also contributed to the demise of the economy in the late 1980s and to partial abandonment of those policies. Similar paths of prosperity followed by recession under one set of institutions and policies can be identified for nearly all economies.

Other common features can be identified for two of these masters. As did Myrdal, Hayek received a law degree and doctorate in economics. Both published general works that included methodology of social science, and they shared the 1974 Nobel Prize in Economics. Schumpeter and Hayek were Austrians who placed the entrepreneurial personality and function at the center of their analysis. For those interested in predicting the path economies will follow in the early twenty-first century, it is noteworthy that Schumpeter and Hayek appear correct concerning their predictions that an economy with relatively little government interference in which entrepreneurial activity is permitted to flourish will prosper.[6] This is evident by the recent rapid economic growth of the East Asian economies, as well as growth in Poland and the Czech Republic compared to the rest of Europe.

Gunnar Myrdal

Despite being imbued with the neoclassical paradigm during his graduate education and macroeconomic policy development work during the early 1930s, Gunnar Myrdal (1898–1987) realized this paradigm was inadequate for analyzing broad social problems. He began to develop his own normative propositions, conception of the socioeconomic reality, critique of neoclassical economics, and method of analysis. In doing so he conceived an alternative approach to social science analysis that is consistent with such heterodox approaches to economics as institutional economics and social economics.[7] With his approach Myrdal was instrumental not only in promoting macroeconomic stabilization policy for Sweden during the early 1930s depression but also in laying the foundation for the social insurance and welfare programs that the nation gradually implemented thereafter. He also applied his interdisciplinary method of analysis (which incorporates history, politics, social psychology, and sociology with economic principles) to his landmark examination of race relations in the United States, implementation of economic recovery measures in Europe after World War II, and investigation of the causes of poverty in underdeveloped nations.

Normative propositions

Myrdal's goals are similar to those established for society during the optimistic era of Enlightenment. He believed economics should not be simply a discipline used to promote economic growth, efficiency, or macroeconomic stability. Instead, his interest in reforming society led him to believe that economics also should be an instrument for social and economic reform. The ideal Myrdalian society would be experiencing development, which to Myrdal meant the movement upward of the entire "social system." This system is comprised of attitudes and institutions whose condition or performance consists of both economic indicators (production, income, work conditions, consumption levels) and noneconomic indicators (attitudes toward life and work, levels of education and health, distribution of power throughout society). Myrdal advocated state intervention to correct outcomes where unregulated market mechanisms foster results that are undesirable. Each family would be guaranteed at least a simple and decent standard of living—with the ultimate goal being equalization of living and working conditions. Myrdal was not content with implementing policies that would establish a "welfare state" in Sweden but extended his vision to the establishment of a "welfare world" founded on social insurance and welfare schemes policies similar to those he proposed for Sweden.[8]

Conceptualized reality

Myrdal's conceived socioeconomic order consists of a wide set of social relations. There are a number of relevant, interrelated economic and noneconomic conditions that constantly interact to generate social change. Among the relevant economic conditions are the level and methods of production, productivity of labor, distribution of income, and level of consumption. Important noneconomic conditions he accounted for in his analysis include the nature of educational and health facilities and attitudes toward life and work—especially as influenced by religion. Other conditions were social mores and principal economic, social, and political institutions, particularly those that influence the stratification of power in society, and the working rules established by authorities for these institutions.[9] Consequently, Myrdal believed "economic" problems could not be studied in isolation but only in their demographic, social, and political setting.

Myrdal believed other forces besides self-interest (including emotion and interpersonal relationships such as trust) influence economic decisions of societal members. Further, he did not view inequality as a prerequisite for economic efficiency and growth. Instead, he believed that greater equality can stimulate efficiency and growth, as was the case for Sweden from the early 1930s to late 1980s. A commitment to shared values such as equality is felt to foster cooperation, rather than competition, among nonmarket institutions by achieving a consensus among decision makers. He would agree that institutions and processes such as Japan's Ministry of International Trade and Industry and France's indicative planning illustrate that nonmarket allocation and distribution schemes have been capable of promoting efficiency, growth, and greater equality.[10]

Unlike recent advisors to Central and East Europe, Myrdal did not believe that a large number of profit-oriented entrepreneurs offering supplyside innovations can be expected to emerge quickly in every nation—particularly in a nation whose economy is performing poorly and that suddenly seeks to stimulate investment while transforming its principal economic, political, and social institutions. Citing differences in conditions such as availability of raw materials, climate, population growth, government honesty and stability, and social motives and mechanisms between Western industrialized nations and the rest of the world, he argued against expecting the existence of some latent entrepreneurial class that will respond spontaneously and rationally to investment opportunities in all nations.

In Myrdal's conception of reality there existed a causal interrelatedness among technological, attitudinal, and institutional factors during the process of societal change. Unlike most economists, he argued that the original stimulus for initiating cumulative change within a complex social mechanism will stem from changes in attitudes and institutions rather than from technology or economic variables, such as prices or interest rates. Those seeking to direct the transformation of an economy, he argued, must recognize that attitudinal and institutional change have to precede changes in economic variables. He was adamant that there are no "economic problems" but rather that social systems have mixed and complex problems with economic, political, social, and cultural components—all aspects of which are highly interrelated and which needed to be studied in their cultural context. It is necessary for the analyst to identify causal relationships among these variables and propose policies consistent with a society's attitudes and institutions. He cited the "Green Revolution" (introduction of hybrid wheat and rice seeds that, under ideal conditions, would boost land productivity by about two to four times) as an example where his conception was ignored. Technological change preceded attitudinal and institutional change, with unfavorable results for decades in terms of a majority of poor farmers realizing few benefits from introduction of the new seeds without complementary changes (e.g., better access to water, fertilizer, or credit) being provided as well.

Myrdal recognized significant attitudinal and institutional differences among societies and therefore argued that no single set of policies would provide a panacea for any nation. Current advisors to Central and Eastern Europe, nearly all of whom do not share Myrdal's conceptualized reality, purport that their sweeping macroeconomic stabilization and privatization policies are, in fact, a panacea for all nations throughout the region. Myrdal would soundly criticize such policies, based on narrow, closed economic models that emphasize easily quantifiable variables to the neglect of noneconomic factors such as attitudes, health, and education as inappropriate and misguided, for they ignore the primary impediments to societal transformation and development. In the case of Central and Eastern Europe, these impediments include absence of achievement-oriented individualistic competitiveness, lack of a civic culture by which people willingly adhere to laws concerning commerce, absence of a business culture wherein people would be consumer oriented, and corrupt political authorities.

Criticism of neoclassical economics

Myrdal's criticism of neoclassical economics was extensive.[11] He recognized the inadequacy of its static equilibrium approach for analyzing societal problems, especially its assertion that the process by which changes in one basic, endogenous economic factor generates subsequent adjustments in other economic factors is typical of social change.[12] In particular, he was critical of the narrow neoclassical notion of economic determinism that holds that there is one "basic factor" that predominates to the extent that significant economic and social transformations are expected to ensue following a change in one factor, such as a change in relative prices or privatization of previously state-owned enterprises. As a result Myrdal chides most economists (including those holding a Marxist ideology or laissez-faire advocates) for failing to account adequately for noneconomic factors while placing emphasis on some basic factor to which all other economic and noneconomic variables are expected to adjust once the basic economic factor has been altered. The experiences of underdeveloped countries and post-1989 Central and Eastern European nations where favorable adjustments to promote growth were expected following high levels of investment or wide-scale privatization have both demonstrated the fallacy of the economic determinist view and its belief in a fatalistic tendency for society to adjust in a predictable manner to changes in economic variables without prior introduction of necessary changes in pertinent noneconomic conditions.

Myrdal also criticized neoclassical economics for being ahistorical, with proponents advancing their theories as universal propositions valid for every time, place, and culture. He was openly opposed to neoclassical economists' strong technical bent (to the neglect of the noneconomic factors he argued were important), especially its overemphasizing mathematics in analyzing and explaining societal behavior, and policy prescriptions that had their roots in traditional neoclassical theory—both of which were inappropriate for nearly all nations not belonging to the Organization for Economic Cooperation and Development (OECD). In particular, he chided neoclassical policymakers for reducing all problems to a matter of optimum allocation of resources and for assuming that efficiency and favorable economic growth would ensue following the establishment of competitive markets.

Method of analysis

Myrdal's method of analysis contains three distinctive aspects, each of which stands in sharp contrast to methods practiced by neoclassical economists: his positions regarding objectivity in the social sciences, interdisciplinary approach to analyzing issues, and theory of social change. Taken together, they comprise an analytical method that contains a useful theory that can serve as a basis for understanding the nature of a society's economy.

Myrdal argued that a social scientist was not able to hide his ideological persuasion. Rather, he believed the particular criteria chosen as the basis for evaluation by an analyst, the method of measuring these criteria, and the relative importance attached to each would be influenced by the analyst's viewpoint. Myrdal was fond of stating that "every view [conception of the socioeconomic reality and conclusions] has a viewpoint [normative propositions]." By this he meant that results of analysis are influenced by the normative propositions held by the analyst. Analysts may purport to be engaging in value-free, positive analysis, but all have "hidden values" that influence their conclusions and policy prescriptions. This, he argued, is particularly true of neoclassical economists, who seem to have a preference for free trade and laissez-faire domestic policy. Failing to state one's normative propositions explicitly leads to analysis and conclusions that Myrdal believed to be "biased"—systematically twisted in an opportunistic direction. For example, Myrdal would argue that the goals and policy prescriptions of Western advisors to Central and Eastern Europe have been riddled with the ideology inherent in neoclassical theory.

To reduce such bias in what generally is presented as "objective" analysis, Myrdal proposed that analysts accept that economics is a moral science and thereby identify explicitly their viewpoint, or normative propositions, so as to purge the analysis (to the extent possible) of distorting biases. He refuted the positivist claim of neoclassical economists that economic theory can prove certain norms exist. Instead he argued social scientists should accept that these normative propositions are extrascientific and do not emerge from the analysis itself, and that social laws do not exist as do physical laws of the universe. His method of analysis began with the specification of his explicit normative propositions, which he believed were relevant to the problems he analyzed.[13] Doing so, he argued, enabled him "(1) to purge as far as possible the scientific investigation of distorting biases which are usually the result of hidden biases; (2) to determine in a rational way the statement of problems and the definitions of terms for the theoretical analysis; (3) to lay a logical basis for practical and political conclusions."[14]

Myrdal's interdisciplinary approach to analyzing issues integrated history, politics, social psychology, and sociology with economics.[15] It was a departure from the traditionally rigid boundaries between separate social science disciplines as they had developed pragmatically to accommodate pedagogical purposes and the desire for research specialization. Such an approach made for a wider range of empirical observations and required common sense, rather than adherence to a strict theoretical framework, to choose or develop an appropriate theoretical framework for analysis of the issue in question. Although Myrdal relied on his theory of social change to structure his thinking, his approach featured a reduced emphasis on precision and formal analysis than that which characterizes of economic theory in the neoclassical tradition.

Myrdal applied his interdisciplinary approach to analyze and propose policies for Sweden, the United States, post-World War II Europe, and underdeveloped nations.[16] He began each analysis with an in-depth review of the history, attitudes, and institutions of the nation or region in question, seeking to identify the causal relations between social facts—particularly the impact of noneconomic variables on development. In analyzing Sweden's low population growth and poverty problems during the early 1930s, Myrdal sought to determine factors causing the secular trend in migration, cyclical fluctuations of migration, and how business cycles were reflected in migration.[17] His objective was to determine not only the interrelations between the movements of the factors affecting migration but also the relations between these factors and all other changes of an economic, social, or political character that influenced the low level of living then experienced by many Swedish families. In doing so Myrdal recognized that it was not possible to analyze migration as an isolated phenomenon but that it had to be studied in connection with all other factors determining the population size and composition. He viewed population as an interdependent mechanism influenced by cultural, economic, social, and political factors. Among his conclusions was that the roots of the poverty problem were the prevalent Swedish attitudes and institutions, particularly the tendency to blame the poor for their own plight and faith in the "do-nothing" laissez-faire policies. These findings served as the basis for his advocating planned, egalitarian reforms that became the basis for the Swedish democratically controlled social economy. Not only did these reforms succeed in alleviating poverty, but Sweden became one of the world's wealthiest nations by the late 1980s (albeit while encountering significant economic problems since then).

Recognizing that a theory of societal change was necessary before an analyst could observe the facts, and finding neoclassical theories lacking as a means for analyzing the problems he chose to study, Myrdal developed his own theory. To him theory was a broad vision of what essential facts are (conceptualized reality) and the causal relations between the facts (theory of social change). His theory of social change identified the principle of circular and cumulative causation. It is a dynamic causation process in which he recognized both the interrelationship among all relevant economic and noneconomic factors involved in the process of social change as well as the interlocking nature of the circular and cumulative aspects of change. In the Myrdalian methodology, the process of social change stems from changes in all relevant factors necessary to induce circular causation such that a social process would tend to become cumulative and often to gather speed at an accelerating rate. First, a change in one endogenous condition will include a response in secondary endogenous conditions. These changes, in turn, are likely over the long run to generate further changes as the interrelationships among conditions and changes create a cumulative causation process with the social system continuously moving away from any equilibrium position. Myrdal argued that changes which occur stimulate social change in one direction (positive or "spread effects," negative or "backwash effects") and that the ultimate resting place of the system is not easily predicted. This is because "coefficients of interrelation between all conditions in the social system ... and time lags ... usually are unknown ... [therefore] our knowledge of them is utterly imprecise."[18] Tendencies can be identified for the purpose of policymaking, but precision in forecasts cannot be expected.

Whether a policy's impact initiates a positive or negative movement depends if its initial impact has a favorable or unfavorable effect on any of Myrdal's six key variables to development: production and income, conditions of production, levels of consumption, attitudes toward life and work, institutions, and public policy. To each variable he assigned an equal value so any change upward or down in one necessarily pulls the other in the same direction. Positive changes in one condition (e.g., increased level of consumption) would result in secondary changes, thereby improving another condition (worker productivity), which, in turn, would promote greater output and income, which would complete the circle by reinforcing further increased consumption, the initial condition affected.

Myrdal was adamant that his theory of circular causation justified active state involvement to promote development; he argued that a tendency toward inequality was the outcome of the interplay of unfettered market forces—particularly so when the level of economic development was low so that a segment of the population could be characterized as in poverty.[19] He was particularly in favor of educational and institutional reforms, arguing that such reforms not only would prevent further poverty, but also would stimulate productivity of the needy so that development would ensue in a positive direction. Rather than suggesting a cookbook recipe of reforms for all societies, Myrdal's method relied on developing policies in an ongoing, instrumental manner (much as one plays chess) based on findings from an in-depth, interdisciplinary analysis of the society or region in question.

Joseph Schumpeter

Joseph Schumpeter (1883–1950) spent the formative and middle part of his professional life in Austrian academic and business circles. In 1932 he received an appointment to Harvard, where he remained for the rest of his career. Among his many major contributions, he is best known for his comprehensive, insightful analysis of economic growth and the dynamic properties of capitalist development and concurrent societal transformation, especially during the period 1870 to 1930 in the United States.

Normative propositions

Although his normative propositions were not as extensive and explicit as those proposed by either Myrdal or Hayek, Schumpeter was not a "value-free" economist. He held that society's interests were best served through rule by an elite entrepreneurial class. This position was based on his "explicit belief in the 'supernormal quality' of the bourgeoisie," especially the daring entrepreneurs and capitalists who provided the necessary financing.[20] His conceptualized reality contains further support for this view.

Conceptualized reality

Schumpeter's conception of capitalism's socioeconomic reality is embodied in his long-run view of capitalism's development. He views capitalism and competition "as a dynamic process, not a set of structural conditions or a static, equilibrium end-state."[21] He argued that "without ... development the capitalistic society cannot exist, ... without innovation there are no entrepreneurs, without entrepreneurship there are no capitalist profits and no capitalist momentum ... The atmosphere of industrial revolution— of progress—is the only atmosphere in which capitalism can survive."[22]

Schumpeter recognized the evolutionary nature of economies with industries in various stages of rise and fall. He believed economic development comes from "within the economic system ... it occurs discontinuously ... it brings qualitative changes or 'revolutions,' which fundamentally displace old equilibria and create radically new conditions. Economic development is accompanied by growth ... But mere quantitative growth does not constitute development."[23] To illustrate this, Schumpeter pointed out that an economy could grow by adding many horse-drawn carriages, but such growth would not lead to the development of an automobile industry.

Rather, the forces that stimulate development are new technologies in the form of innovations of new or previously existing inventions, that are deemed successful by market participants, when applied to the market place by an entrepreneur. The key factor is innovation—"the commercial or industrial application of something new—a new product, process, or method of production; a new market or source of supply; a new form of commercial, business, or financial organization."[24] The process of innovation, initiated by the entrepreneur, revolutionizes the economy from within, thereby destroying parts of the old structure while creating new structures. If this occurs on a broad scale, the process will generate a "perennial gale of creative destruction." Schumpeter's creative destruction manifests capitalism's achievements, for the new goods and services typically are not only of higher quality but also are available at a much lower cost. The primary beneficiary are members of the working classes who could afford items such as silk stockings or automobiles that, prior to the innovation that ultimately led to their being massed-produced, were affordable only to the wealthy class.

Schumpeter argued that capitalism would be characterized by overlapping business cycles that were irregular in length and varied in direction. Each business cycle would be influenced by some initial entrepreneurial innovations, then followed by "swarms" of subsequent innovations as the economy adapted to the original innovation. The reason other entrepreneurs are likely to copy or adapt to the initial innovation is their being stimulated by "animal spirits." Schumpeter, who coined this term before John Maynard Keynes made it famous, argued that these spirits consisted "of inexplicable impulses which inspire entrepreneurs to give free rein to their willfulness and which in this way enable the whole economy to develop and change."[25] As a result, prices fall, and eventually the competitive process will lead to establishment of a new equilibrium state where the typical firm receives low profits. At this point what had been an upswing may turn into a recession or depression due to overoptimistic or overpessimistic judgments that, given the "animal spirits" of entrepreneurs, tend to occur in swarms that coincide with the upswing and downswing cycle. That a recession inevitably follows the surge in economic growth and development, however, did not indicate to Schumpeter that "capitalism" is weak. Rather, he viewed the cycle of economic surges and recessions as part of the capitalist development process—a price paid for economic freedoms and for receiving greater choices of higher-quality goods and services.[26]

Schumpeter's conception of development places the entrepreneur in the heroic role of bearing the mechanism, innovation, that is the generator of the evolutionary process of development. Schumpeter shared Friedrich Nietzsche's view concerning the extraordinary powers of certain individuals to shape society. Nietzsche distinguished between the "overmen" and the "mass" or "herd," with the "overmen symboliz[ing] the rejection of any kind of conformism: they are a rare breed striving toward 'higher ends' and personifying the antithesis to mediocrity and stagnation."[27]

Schumpeter held a similar view, describing entrepreneurs as "the leaders who emerge vigorously from the mass."[28] The Schumpeterian entrepreneur not only must possess vision and daring but also must be driven to become a captain of industry. This special individual needs to be willing to move forward and innovate based on intitution. Only a few gifted persons can be successful entrepreneurs, for in addition to the aforementioned character traits, they also must be able to overcome difficulties faced, such as imperfect information about future demand and resource availability and costs, institutional resistance to any form of change, and the "antagonism of non innovators to the pioneer—in the form of legal and political obstacles, social mores, customs, and the like."[29]

Schumpeter recognized that an unequal income distribution would ensue from the capitalist development process but acknowledged this condition as the price of innovation and economic development. The price of not permitting such a condition was a static economy without either growth or development. The lures of high profits and status are required to attract entrepreneurial talent, without which capitalism could not survive and prosper. While development following entrepreneurial innovations creates extraordinary incomes for a few, Schumpeter argued that in the long run, capitalism tends to reduce income inequalities. It does so

first, by increasing equality of opportunity relative to earlier, more class-bound societies; second, by the creation of mass-produced products that benefit working masses more than they do any other sector of the economy; third, by philanthropy and social legislation underwritten by the process of capitalist economic growth; and fourth, because although inequality is necessary for the sustenance of capitalism, "absolute poverty" falls as capitalist development proceeds.[30]

In the Schumpeterian conception of development capitalist are also vital, for it is they who finance many entrepreneurs' innovations in return for a portion of the expected profits. A well-developed financial system therefore is a prerequisite for capitalist development. Schumpeter was among the first to recognize this imperative, and argued that capitalists acting as "financial intermediaries are essential for technological innovation and economic development."[31] Contemporary analysis supports his view.[32]

Criticism of neoclassical economics

Neoclassical economics was too static, according to Schumpeter, overly concerned with "the derivation of theorems from given technological, institutional, and motivational assumptions."[33] His challenge to economic orthodoxy therefore was quite fundamental. "Because capitalism is a dynamic system ... [he argued] it cannot be understood with the same theoretical apparatus used for examining the stationary economy. There are, in short, two domains—the stationary and the evolutionary—requiring two different organizing principles. ". . . the weakness of orthodox neoclassical economics exposed by Schumpeter's analysis lay, not in its incompleteness, but in its attempt to force dynamic elements into the static mold."[34] In opposition to the neoclassical view in which change within an economy is gradual, on the margin, not very disruptive, and heading toward some equilibrium via a process that is not painful, Schumpeter viewed societal transformation as being "rapid, large scale, disruptive, disequilibrating, and at times heroic but painful socioeconomic change."[35] In response, he synthesized a method analysis that focused on institutional change using his theory of capitalist development.

Method of analysis

As an analyst Schumpeter was "a special blend of eclectic and innovator" demonstrating both "methodological independence and creative insight."[36] He was among the first economists to recognize that "reality is always and everywhere an ideologically and normatively tinted phenomenon in the literature of innovative economics."[37] That is, he argued that his own conception of reality, or what he called "vision," was the basis for his analysis.[38] Ideology thereby entered Schumpeter's analysis "on the very ground floor, into the preanalytic cognitive act."[39]

Schumpeter's conception of a theory included "the actual sequence of the economic process as it goes on under its own steam, in historic time, producing at every instant that state which will of itself determine the next one."[40] From his early works it was clear "that his vision of the economic system was one where static equilibrating forces (explainable in terms of the general equilibrium theory) are confronted by dynamic forces of disequilibrium. These latter he sought to explain by constructing an original [dynamic] theory of development."[41] Schumpeter believed that "the pulsating processes of real-world economic life are better explained from an explicitly dynamic and evolutionary perspective."[42]

Schumpeter's method of describing the dynamic process of capitalist development is similar to Myrdal's circular and cumulative causation approach. Another method in common with Myrdal was the emphasis Schumpeter placed on economic sociology, which he considered to be "the interpretive description of economically relevant institutions, including habits and all forms of behavior in general, such as government, property, private enterprise, customary or 'rational' behavior."[43] In *Capitalism, Socialism and Democracy*, his "major work on economic sociology," Schumpeter argues "that capitalism will decline because its economic success will prepare social circumstances unfavorable to it should not be interpreted as historical determinism. It has nothing to do with a historical hypothesis or prediction. It is a theoretical hypothesis derived from certain assumptions about the interaction between economic and social factors, and its validity rests on instrumentalist methodology."[44]

Friedrich Hayek

The contemporary influence of Friedrich Hayek (1899–1992) could be considered more widespread than that of Myrdal or Schumpeter because two recognized schools of thought continue to embrace and refine his theories and normative propositions: the Austrian School (of which Hayek was an integral contributor while in Vienna, having developed and articulated some of its basic tenets) and monetarism at the University of Chicago, where Hayek was a faculty member late in his career. He believed his influence would increase after his death, once informing a student that "he was writing for the next century."[45] Perhaps he believed this because he devoted the mature phase of his career designing a system of rules to protect individual liberty. In the process he "sketched out a sweeping theory of social change that was broadly evolutionary in its structure."[46]

Normative propositions

Hayek was avowedly in favor of individual freedom, exercised within a laissez-faire market economy, while adamantly opposed to any form of government intervention in economic matters—particularly economic planning. He was convinced that "[t]he guiding principle that a policy of freedom for the individual is the only truly progressive policy remains as true today as it was in the nineteenth century."[47] In his ideal economy individuals would have the right to pursue their own ends, especially in regard to producing and selling what they wish if they violated no one else's property rights. Therefore, an important imperative for the Hayekian society was protection of property rights and recognizing the need to remove impediments to entrepreneurial action so as to permit spontaneous human reason and the pursuit of individual gain to flourish.

Strong preference for a laissez-faire market economy was logical and necessary for societal development, according to Hayek. In defense of this belief he wrote his greatest work, *The Road to Serfdom*, "a political book ... [in which] all I shall have to say is derived from certain ultimate values [and that] the beliefs set out in it are not determined by my personal interests."[48] Expressing a deep concern "with fundamental questions and ultimate values,"[49] Hayek warned free societies that there was a slippery slope from introducing some government intervention policies to the development of a totalitarian state. While recognizing that temporary monopolies are created due to the creativity of entrepreneurial innovations, he argues that in the absence of free competition, only government intervention can sustain a real monopoly (by inhibiting entry). Therefore, he held that only a laissez-faire market environment was conducive to the emergence of entrepreneurs and that it is the only economy capable of preserving individual freedom.

He was adamantly opposed to the large-scale, planned reordering of any society's social and economic institutions by the state. Naturally, he offered strong criticism of democratically controlled social economies, such as Sweden. Over 50 years ago he lamented about "[t]hat hodgepodge of ill-assembled and often inconsistent ideals which under the name of the Welfare State has largely replaced socialism as the goal of the reformers needs very careful sorting-out if its results are not to be very similar to those of full-fledged socialism."[50]

Conceptualized reality

Hayek's conception of reality are contained in his "presuppositions," which he believed were a priori true.[51] The two most important were his conception of competition and the entrepreneur and of government intervention and planning. Together they formed the building blocks of his dynamic theories and policy prescriptions.

Hayek believed competition was "first and foremost a discovery procedure. The economy is never in perfect equilibrium: there are always gaps to be filled by alert, profit-seeking entrepreneurs. Economic progress can ... never become wholly automatic: invention can never become a routine."[52] Entrepreneurs who "outperform the masses in mental power and energy"[53] were the primary agents involved in this process of discovering new and better ways to organize resources, a process that, while fraught with errors, was being improved constantly. Entrepreneurs would be alert to profit opportunities, see a discrepancy between existing production costs and future selling prices, then act to take advantage of that discrepancy. Using their knowledge and foresight, and exhibiting a willingness to take risks while pursuing their own self-interest, entrepreneurs would behave as arbitrageurs of profit opportunities they had discovered. In the process the Hayekian entrepreneur was a "long-distance rational planner" who manifested "the success of human reason in human action."[54]

The political ideals of a people and its attitude toward authority were affected by their political institutions, according to Hayek. Therefore, extension of government authority gradually would undermine and destroy any spirit of freedom. He believed that "discretionary [government] power is dangerous and is bound to be abused sooner or later," arguing that what such "control produces is a psychological change, an alteration in the character of the people."[55] To further emphasize this point, he argued that extensive government intervention that constantly restrained people from acting, in the name of preserving state control, "compresses, enervates, extinguishes, and stupefies a people, till each nation is reduced to be nothing better than a flock of timid and industrial animals of which government is the shepherd."[56]

Hayek believed individuals could possess only a limited range of knowledge, particularly as it pertained to prices of goods and services and resource costs as well as consumer tastes and that there are very high information costs to obtaining such knowledge. While entrepreneurs could be informed about relative scarcities and profit opportunities solely by market prices, any planning authority would lack such information since prices were not market determined and therefore are not what they "ought to be."[57] He lamented the tendency for a "fatal conceit" to prevail in society—"the idea that the ability to acquire skills stems solely from reason ... that humankind can shape the world according to wish ... or that evolutionary products can always be improved by human ingenuity."[58] He was quick to respond that given the limitations of human knowledge about the future and the impossibility of making many decisions concerning prices that would equate the desired behavior patterns of producers and consumers, "[a]ttempts to replace a spontaneous order with a conscious, comprehensive plan for society simply cannot work according to the planners' expectations."[59]

Criticism of neoclassical economics

By not relying on mathematical models of the economy or suggesting ways that government policies can improve an economy's performance, Hayek purported to be more realistic and more socially scientific than practitioners of neoclassical economics. He did not attempt to create abstract models of a macroeconomy that include the view that capital is homogeneous, that competition is a static end-state, that in the long run normal profits are earned and equilibrium achieved, that an economist can identify some grand welfare function that measures society's welfare, and that these assumptions and models can be used for public policy. Along with other members of the Austrian School, Hayek believed that such unrealistic models were the hallmark of conventional economic methods.

Method of analysis

Hayek's analysis became increasingly interdisciplinary as he sought to integrate his views of economic history, theory, and philosophy. In doing so he chose not to rely on mathematical models, holding that an economist cannot collapse the complexity of market arrangements into enormous aggregates. Instead he relied on verbal logic as his primary methodological tool. Further, while predicting the course societies would follow if government intervention were permitted unabated, Hayek believed that the future is so uncertain that the job of precise forecasting was not that of the economist but that of entrepreneurs. The latter need only predict specific price and cost changes arising from disequilibrium, enabling them to take advantage of profit opportunities.

Lessons

Social scientists seeking a new paradigm for analysis of twenty-first century economic problems should be encouraged by the contributions of Myrdal, Schumpeter, and Hayek.[60] Studying their major works, particularly *An American Dilemma* and *Asian Drama, Capitalism, Socialism and Democracy*, and *The Road to Serfdom* will demonstrate there can be an alternative to the reductionist neoclassical economic perspective—an alternative that yields more accurate predictions of the path and extent of societal development. These three scholars demonstrate a more realistic understanding of economies, and their respective methods of analysis are capable of providing a sound basis for policy formulation.[61]

What particular lessons can students and practitioners who seek a new economic perspective for the twenty-first century learn from Myrdal, Schumpeter, and Hayek? First, their conceptualized realities, criticisms of neoclassical economics, and methods of analysis indicate that there is an important place for dynamic, long-run analysis that is interdisciplinary—accounting for historical, political, and social aspects of the society being studied. Next, Schumpeter's and Hayek's normative propositions and conceptualized realities are consistent with recent evidence that indicates inefficient economic performance coincides with extensive government intervention. Therefore, Myrdal notwithstanding, there is the imperative of maintaining an economic environment conducive to entrepreneurial innovations, especially through establishing low income tax rates.[62] Certainly Schumpeter and Hayek would agree that

> "[e]ntrepreneurship may be, in large measure, a function of an institutional sociopolitical structure which permits protection ... to the innovator and the generation of pure economic profits through the manipulation of price, quantity, and quality variables via techniques which in the short run appear restrictive and monopolistic. Thus, the possibility of retention, at least temporarily, of above-normal profits from innovations may well stimulate a higher rate of innovation and technological improvement."[63]

Finally, the normative propositions and methods of analysis of these three economists demonstrate that analysts can avoid hidden biases and subjective value judgments (and therefore ideologically loaded analysis) by openly stating their value premises. Each man dealt explicitly with the "political element" inherent in his research, thereby enabling readers to evaluate the consistency of his conclusions without facing hidden biases. By not purporting to be "objective" and value free, Myrdal, Schumpeter, and Hayek provide analysis and conclusions that are more intellectually honest, and useful, than those offered by many practitioners of the neoclassical perspective. Those seeking to overcome this and other deficiencies of the neoclassical perspective by developing an alternative paradigm for analyzing twenty-first century economic problems would do well to use Myrdal, Schumpeter, and Hayek, among other heterodox contributors to economics, as their foundation.

Notes

1 The term "conceptualized reality" is used to represent the idealized image of the socioeconomic order as perceived by the analyst, an image conditioned by the cultural patterns of the society within which the analyst lives. It consists of two interrelated views: one involving a perceived relationship between social and economic forces within a society; the other pertaining to an interpretation of human behavior. A conceptualized reality gives direction to the analyst's work by influencing both the problems chosen for investigation as well as the conceived interrelationships between economic and noneconomic factors.

2 A paradigm is a universally recognized scientific achievement that provides model problems and methods of analysis for a community of practitioners.

3 Myrdal and Schumpeter sought to articulate the methodological foundation of neoclassical economics early in their careers with pathbreaking analysis of monetary theory. Yuichi Shionoya, "Schumpeter on Schmoller and Weber: A Methodology of Economic Sociology," *History of Political Economy* 23, no. 2 (1991): 193–219.

4 For example, Enrico Santarelli and Enzo Pesciarelli argue that Schumpeter was influenced by the "particular cultural climate of the early 20th C, especially the importance then of the great entrepreneurs." See "The Emergence of a Vision: The Development of Schumpeter's Theory of Entrepreneurship," *History of Political Economy* 22, no. 4 (1990): 677–696.

5 James Angresano, *Comparative Economics* (Englewood Cliffs, N.J.: Prentice-Hall, 1996).

6 This assumes that in evaluating and comparing the performance of economies, emphasis is placed on criteria such as economic growth, low unemployment, low inflation, and economic freedoms.

7 See James Angresano, "Gunnar Myrdal as a Social Economist," *Review of Social Economy* 44, no. 2 (1986): 146–148; and Gunnar Myrdal, "Institutional Economics," *Journal of Economic Issues* 12, no. 4 (1978): 771–783.

8 Gunnar Myrdal, *Against the Stream: Critical Essays on Economics* (New York: Vintage, 1975), 50.

9 For a presentation of a model of these interrelated factors as they comprise an economy, see Angresano, *Comparative Economics*.

10 For a detailed presentation of these institutions and their impact on the economy's performance, see ibid., chaps. 9–13.

11 For detailed criticisms of neoclassical economics, see the following works by Myrdal: *Rich Lands and Poor* (New York: Harper, 1957); *Value in Social Theory: A Selection of Essays on Methodology*, ed. Paul Streeten (London: Routledge & Kegan Paul, 1958); *Asian Drama: An Inquiry into the Poverty of Nations*, 3 vols. (New York: Pantheon, 1968); *The Political Element in the Development of Economic Theory* (Cambridge, Mass.: Harvard University Press, 1969); *An American Dilemma: The Negro Problem and Modern Democracy* (New York: Pantheon, 1975); *Against the Stream*; and "Institutional Economics."

12 Myrdal viewed the neoclassical perspective as too simplistic in its formulation of policies and representative of a monolithic, deterministic vision of the behavior of an economy. This vision viewed development as occurring in a linear, mechanical, simplified manner by which neoclassical economists assumed that once certain economic conditions had been established (i.e., privatization of previously state-owned enterprises or liberalizing rules pertaining to free trade), the market mechanism would emerge and prosperity would inevitably ensue.

13 For example, for the study of race relations and poverty in the United States, he selected the "American Creed." See Myrdal, *An American Dilemma*, 3–25. For poverty in underdeveloped nations, he identified his "modernization ideals." See his *Asian Drama*, 49–69.

14 Myrdal, *An American Dilemma*, lxxviii.

15 One Swedish social scientist paid tribute to Myrdal, arguing that "[a]t one time or another ... [Gunnar Myrdal] has worked seriously at history, politics, and sociology.... It is hard to think of any other economist of our generation who would have had the courage, competence, and energy to carry through such studies of such sweeping scope, in which the purely economic component is kept always in proper perspective." Erik Lundberg, "Gunnar Myrdal's Contribution to Economic Theory: A Short Survey," *Swedish Journal of Economics* 74, no. 4 (1974): 472–478; quoted on 480.

16 For a classic presentation of his method, see Myrdal, *Asian Drama* and *An American Dilemma*, particularly the appendixes.

17 This study was carried out with his wife, Alva. See Myrdal with Myrdal, *Kris I befolkningsfragan* (Crisis in the population question) (Stockholm: Bonnier, 1934).

18 Gunnar Myrdal, "What is Economic Development?" *Journal of Economic Issues* vol. 8 (1974): 729–736.

19 Gunnar Myrdal, *Rich Lands and Poor* (New York: Harper & Brothers), 1957.

20 Robert Heilbroner, "Was Schumpeter Right After All?" *Journal of Economic Perspectives* 7, no. 3 (1993): 87–96; quoted on 94.

21 John E. Elliott, "Joseph A. Schumpeter at 100 and the Theory of Economic Development at 72," Paper presented at the meeting of the Southwestern Economic Association, Houston, TX, 1983, 27.

22 E. Ray Canterbery, *The Literate Economist* (New York: HarperCollins, 1995), 269.

23 Elliott, "Schumpeter at 100," 10.

24 Ibid.

25 Santarelli and Pesciarelli, "Emergence of a Vision," 688.

26 Some analysts argue that "Schumpeter hypothesizes a Walrasian-type adjustment mechanism [in which] ... innovations first spread within a certain sector,

and then through the entire system.... Thus once these innovations have spread to all production sectors, the economic system returns to equilibrium. The cyclical pattern of development is due to the irregular pattern of occurrence of innovations in certain markets, where equilibrim is restored by means of an endogenous adjustment mechanism." Ibid., 688–689.

27 Ibid., 689.

28 Ibid.

29 Elliott, "Schumpeter at 100," 12.

30 Ibid., 26.

31 Robert G. King and Ross Levine, "Finance and Growth: Schumpeter Might Be Right," *Quarterly Journal of Economics* 108, no. 3 (1993): 717–738; quoted on 716.

32 Ibid, King and Levine's analysis presents cross-country evidence that supports the Schumpeterian view "that the financial system can promote economic growth." They conclude that there is a strong empirical link between a range of indicators of financial development and economic growth—and that "The data are consistent with the view that financial services stimulate economic growth by increasing the rate of capital accumulation and by improving the efficiency with which economies use that capital." Further, they cite their empirical findings to "conclude that Schumpeter might have been right about the importance of finance for economic development." They argue that he was right not only regarding the role of the entrepreneur as innovator of new technology, but also his emphasis on the key roles for financial intermediaries "as entrepreneurial selection and the financing of tangible and intangible investments that lead to innovation.

33 Elliott, "Schumpeter at 100," 20.

34 Ibid., 40–41.

35 Ibid., 42.

36 Ibid., 5.

37 Hans A. Jensen, "J. A. Schumpeter as a Forerunner of T. S. Kuhn," Paper presented at the meeting of the Eastern Economic Association, April 1978, Washington, D.C., 16.

38 Heilbroner, "Was Schumpeter Right?" 88. Schumpeter argued that "In every scientific venture ... the thing that comes first is Vision. That is to say, before embarking upon analytic work of any kind we must first single out the set of phenomena we wish to investigate, and acquire 'intuitively' a preliminary notion of how they hang together or, in other words, of what appear from our standpoint to be their fundamental properties."

39 Jensen, "Schumpeter as a Forerunner," 10.

40 Everett Johnson Burtt, Jr., *Social Perspectives in the History of Economic Theory* (New York: St. Martin's Press, 1972), 162.

41 Santarelli and Pesciarelli, "Emergence of a Vision," 678.

42 Elliott, "Schumpeter at 100," 10.

43 Ibid., 21.

44 Shionoya, "Schumpeter on Schmoller and Weber," 217. Schumpeter did not believe mid-twentieth-century capitalist economies would continue to repeat the pattern of development of the late nineteenth and early twentieth century. Instead he argued that capitalism would be weakened by the bureaucratization of economic life, especially rent-seeking behavior by mature, gigantic monopolies and the emergence of an intellectual elite—both of which would generate political and social attitudes that sought capitalism's destruction. He predicted that in the absence of innovations, economic development of the

capitalist economy would settle into the "routine of the circular flow in stationary general equilibrium." Elliott, "Schumpeter at 100," 6. It is noteworthy that following the growth and development of what would become United States Steel under the guidance of the quintessential entrepreneur of the nineteenth century, Andrew Carnegie, subsequent bureaucratized management and labor unions brought it down in absolute and relative economic strength as the firmed failed continually to introduce innovative cost-cutting measures—a practice Carnegie had championed. Meanwhile, foreign producers that emulated Carnegie's entrepreneurial practices were successful in capturing a large share of the world's steel market from their American competitors.

45 Norman Barry et al., Hayek's "Serfdom" Revisited (West Sussex, UK: Institute of Economic Affairs, 1984), lx.

46 Ibid., 123.

47 Friedrich A. Hayek, The Road to Serfdom (Chicago: University of Chicago Press, 1944), 240.

48 Ibid., xvii.

49 Barry et al., Hayek's "Serfdom" Revisited, xi.

50 Hayek, Road to Serfdom, viii.

51 Chiaki Nishiyama and Kurt R. Leube, eds., The Essence of Hayek (Stanford, Calif.: Hoover Institution Press, 1984), xlviii.

52 Barry et al., Hayek's "Serfdom" Revisited, 11.

53 Canterbery, Literate Economist, 262.

54 Ibid., 263.

55 Hayek, Road to Serfdom, xi, xii.

56 Ibid., xiii.

57 Hayek was highly critical of Oscar Lange's belief that "market socialism" in which planners could set prices in an efficient manner, arguing that "Lange appears to have been so confused between the knowledge possessed in day-to-day economic life by the individuals whose actions economics attempts to explain and the knowledge which the economist must pretend to possess in order to be able to do so, that he represents the latter as if it were something obviously perceivable to any observer of the economy." Nishiyama and Leube, Essence of Hayek, 57.

58 Frederic L. Pryor, "Review of The Collected Works of F.A. Hayek," Journal of Economic History 49, no. 4 (December 1989): 1072–1073; quoted on 1072.

59 Barry et al., Hayek's "Serfdom" Revisited, 122. Hayek believed that planners' minds cannot replace the knowledge and signals generated by the market, partly because millions of pricing decisions would be necessary and beyond the capability of any bureaucratic scheme with top-down authority. Therefore, Hayek concluded that "on the whole, societies which rely for this purpose on competition have achieved their aims more successfully than others. This is a conclusion which the history of civilisation seems eminently to have confirmed." Nishiyama and Leube, Essence of Hayek, 255. Schumpeter would agree.

60 Studying Myrdal's intellectual development would demonstrate the possibility for an economist trained in the neoclassical tradition to shift successfully toward the socioeconomic approach. Students and practitioners of economics seeking a paradigm that includes a multidisciplinary approach to broad social problems are likelier to avoid offering inadequate, inappropriate policies—not only for the United States but for foreign nations. Myrdal also serves as an example for those teaching economics—particularly if they are interested in reforming their programs to offer an alternative to the dominant neoclassical paradigm.

61 One scholar argues that "Schumpeter's conceptualization of economic leadership and internally-generated process of revolutionary, qualitative change are pregnant with implications transcending his own particular historical setting and social perspective." Elliott, "Schumpeter at 100," 42. Others would offer the same conclusion for both Myrdal and Hayek.

62 The recent economic problems encountered by two of Europe's most advanced "welfare states," France and Sweden, demonstrate that Hayek may have been correct when he argued that "the idea of a stable 'middle way' must be judged a mirage. It could happen only by a sheer (and continuously recurring!) fluke. Far more plausible is that such a system, given the fundamental processes involved, will become either a road to serfdom or a form of loophole capitalism with no guarantee of providing a secure basis for large-scale capitalist enterprise. The source of these ganders is the presumption that an elected government in a majoritarian democracy has an unlimited right to intervene in the voluntary arrangements of citizens. All such interventions are, of course, always labeled as being in the interests of 'social justice,' 'the public good,' 'compassion,' and so on. In practice, however, government intervention always creates losers as well as gainers, and it is to attract the support of the latter that the measures are undertaken." Barry et al., *Hayek's "Serfdom" Revisited*, 115.

63 Elliott, "Schumpeter at 100," 28.

58

TIME, COORDINATION AND IGNORANCE

A comparison between Hayek and Lachmann

Thierry Aimar

Source: *History of Economic Ideas* 7(1–2) (1999): 139–165.

Introduction

Hayek and Lachmann are the two leading representatives of the Austrian economics of ignorance defined in its relation to time[1]. Taking into account the implications of historical time, the analyses of Hayek (1937 onwards) and Lachmann are both dominated by the theme of the coordination of expectations and of the success of plans. The literature has never compared the respective contributions of these two authors regarding both their content and implications. This relative indifference seems surprising in the sense that they are both contemporary and that the doctrinal implications of their analyses are dissimilar. A confrontation of their work indeed raises the question of whether or not liberalism is capable of ensuring the coordination of individual plans.

Hayek (1937) and Lachmann (1971b; 1976b) both agree on the limits of the vision of Mises regarding the problem of coordination. Both authors claim to originate from the subjective tradition, inherited from Menger, but at the same time drawing wider conclusions than those of Mises. The latter made a perfect analysis of certain implications brought out by subjectivist phenomenon. He underlined the fragmented nature of knowledge between individuals, knowledge necessary for them to succeed in what they undertake. At the same time the role of market prices as vectors of the transmission of knowledge between players is highlighted. However, Mises failed to sufficiently account for the implications of subjectivism regarding expectations. Despite having contemplated the temporal and irreversible nature of action as early as 1933 (*Epistemological Problems of Economics*), he considered that the existence and freedom of the price system guaranteed the success of individual action. However, ignorance of the future however, praxeologically established, shows that market prices represent a necessary but not a sufficient condition for coordinating individual plans.

In *Economics and Knowledge* (1937), Hayek was the first to identify the limits of Mises' approach. In this work he laid out the need to complete the principle of the success of individual plans by a theory of the formation and coordination of actors' expectations. Lachmann, by developing the notion of 'radical subjectivism' elaborated a genuine taxonomy of the temporal implications of subjectivism.

By underlining the partial nature of Mises' explanation of coordination, Hayek and Lachmann both recognised the dynamic dimension of subjectivism. However, opposite views were to emerge following an analogous theoretical formulation. Hayek developed the notion of emerging 'spontaneous orders' which, as 'pattern prediction', should enable individuals to carry out their plans in an increasingly satisfying manner (1st section). Lachmann's approach is less optimistic. He questions the beneficial nature of institutions and considers that the likelihood of a forecast within the socio-economic environment is extremely low. The result of individual action is therefore undetermined (2nd section).

These different views obviously bring out major doctrinal implications. Two antagonistic principles are to be associated respectively with two dissimilar liberal commitments: an optimistic liberalism (Hayek), defender of the Rule of Law, and responsible for the functioning of spontaneous orders; a sceptical liberalism (Lachmann) which, whilst being opposed to the idea of the notion of the State as a regulator, does not recognise the ability of spontaneous institutions to coordinate plans (3rd section).

1. Hayek's 'pattern prediction'

As early as 1937, Hayek approached the topic of ignorance produced by time (1) and in answer to this latter produced the theory of spontaneous orders, enabling 'degrees of prediction' (2).

1.1 Economics and Knowledge: *the theme of coordinating plans*

For a long time Hayek's research was an extension of the work of Mises, be it regarding a theory of cycles (1931; 1935c, 1939) or the controversy between Austrians and Marxists (1935a; 1935b; 1940) over the possibility of an economic calculation in a collectivist regime. But with *Economics and Knowledge* (1937) Hayek took up a line of thought which led him to shed light on the epistemological and analytical limitations of Mises' work. He was led to search for a satisfactory answer to the problem of coordinating individual plans. Writing on the theoretical conditions of the similarity of 'subjective factors' and 'objective data', Hayek particularly highlighted the problem of forecasting the future, wondering how expectations came into existence and how they succeeded.

The temporal dimension of action demands that the idea of formation and success of expectations be integrated into the question of coordination through the notion of plan. Even beyond Hayek's writing, the meaning of the notion of coordination of individual plans should be pointed out.

On a social level, the success of individual forecasts requires two conditions to be fulfilled: firstly, that the expectations of various individuals concerning the future correctly match real events which will take place; secondly, that these expectations be heterogeneous. 'Successful' expectations must not be seen as identical or uniform but merely complementary. This point is essential as it conditions the existence of profit. Indeed, even if an expectation is confirmed by future events, entrepreneurs who identically forecast the same events will not make profit. They would take the same opportunities into account, and, while attempting to exploit them at the same time, would de facto cancel out profit. To exist, then, entrepreneurial profit needs the double hypothesis of confirmation and complementarity of individual expectations.

Mises had clearly understood that each player can only obtain information on the preferences of the other individuals in the economic community through the price system. But the network of relative prices reveals nothing other than the *present* evaluations and information about the players. However, as Mises himself was later to admit in *Human Action* (1966), the necessary knowledge for success is not only fragmented amongst individuals but also between the knowable present and the *unknowable* future. Beginning from here, upon what basis can players form their expectations and how can they prove to be right? Mises' theory offers no answer to this question.

We should distinguish between the idea of coordination by prices and coordinating by plans. The absence of any principle for coordinating individual plans leads to the logical conclusion that the destiny of each individual act is necessarily undetermined. The result of social processes should thus be considered as fundamentally uncertain. But for Hayek this conclusion, which obviously lessens the persuasive effect of the liberal argumentation, is in conflict with the existence of a society and an economy which he seems in *Economics and Knowledge*, to implicitly to consider as a structure for intemporal exchanges and whose reproduction is supposed to testify to the action of a principle for coordination of individual expectations.

As the latter may not be apprehended through praxeology one is therefore confronted with a problem in the Popperian sense, which justifies the questioning of Misesian problematic and the need to construct a more inclusive theory. It is upon this basis that Hayek will claim a new epistemological foundation for economic analysis[2]. However, in *Economics and Knowledge*, Hayek did not go further than a rather timid assertion of the necessity for an epistemological reconstruction of market theory. Indeed, he admits to being unable to give a theoretical answer to this problem of formulating correct expectations. A research avenue was thus visibly opened, but it was not exploited immediately. In answer to the theoretical question from *Economics and Knowledge*, Hayek gave that of 'patterns prediction' and 'spontaneous orders', spread out in a series of articles over a period of thirty years.

1.2 Rules as a complement of prices

The Austrian analysis of self-generated processes must be distinguished from Hayek's theory of spontaneous order as this is the true originality of Hayek within the Austrian tradition. Indeed, Hayek adds a predictive function to the summarising nature of certain spontaneous phenomenon enabling a process based upon the coordination of individual plans to be explained[3]. In *Economics and Knowledge*, Hayek introduces the reference to a learning process into his argumentation by which the actors manage, little by little, to match their expectations to reality. Expressed in this context, the coordination of expectations thus requires that the 'objective data' be relatively constant or of a foreseeable nature[4].

The main object of the theory of spontaneous orders is to explain this phenomenon. By constituting patterns of abstract regularities, spontaneous structures represent *patterns prediction* in Hayek's view. They reduce ignorance about the future and as such, enable the vast majority of expectations to turn out correct.

The Hayek argumentation is based on the notion of rules of just conduct. These rules represent a set of norms, traditions, conventions and institutions which condition individual behaviour[5]. One well known aspect of the literature (O'Driscoll 1977; Butler 1983; Steele 1993; Shand 1980) concerns the nature of information saving that this set of rules enables, to the extent that the fabulous amount of knowledge it regroups is not expressed in a concrete but in an abstract manner. This synthesis of knowledge is, in the final analysis, a transformation process of a number of individual and concrete facts into a statement of general rules incorporating the whole of the cognitive contents of these facts and giving them a general meaning[6].

However, the literature points less frequently to two other aspects of the rules of just conduct which are fundamental for Hayek: firstly, these rules are an answer to the problem of ignorance about the future. Because of the abstract nature of knowledge they express, they offer a range of tools which enable actors to adapt and reply to various situations likely to happen in the future. The individuals are thus given a further opportunity to see their plans come to fruition. Secondly, respecting these rules should lower ignorance as they also express the idea of a constancy in actors' behaviour regarding their reaction to the environment. Indeed, an absolute variability of data prevents any predictions being made as no regularity will be detectable in practical situations. Consequently the possibility of formulating predictions is proportionate to the transformation of these variables into constants[7]. The originality of Hayek is to deliver, via the rules of conduct, a theoretical formulation with the existence of these constants. 'Patterns predictions' are thus transformed into *patterns of predictions*.

It is clear that the predictions which these rules allow do not concern any particular facts and are often expressed much more by asserting the impossibility of certain situations than by the faculty of anticipating determined events. The constants, in a wide sense, are associated with a large number of variables which may be combined in extremely diverse ways. As such, there is no way one can arrive at both perfect and quantified predictions but merely at 'degrees of prediction' which will be expressed by the presence of partial regularities, of classes of situations within social structures[8]. Respecting the rules does not therefore come to terms with market uncertainty. Nevertheless, the prediction capacities they express attain a practical dimension. Faced with various situations or classes of situation, these rules show a set of attitudes or answers which will be widespread throughout groups of individuals[9]. These environmental modifications can thus be minimised or their effects on activity neutralised by setting individual behaviour within relatively constant or predictable structures. Beyond changes in circumstances, individuals reproduce the same type of acts thus creating relative stability. Indeed, these situation types enable a regularity to be created in social practice, thereby offering a wide scope for prediction. Although uncertainty does not disappear regarding particular situations, the rules of conduct enable most entrepreneurs to adjust their activities accordingly and to count on successful expectations.

As an answer to ignorance, rules of just conduct are able to reduce ignorance by forming a method of standardisation of individuals' reactions to an environment which is perceived and experienced subjectively[10]. Spontaneous orders represented by a set of rules of conduct are both the condition and consequence of man's recurrent acts and of the socio-economic conditions to which they give rise.[11]

2. Lachmann and the 'kaleidic worlds'

By underlining the heterogeneous nature of the notion of subjectivism, Lachmann's analysis echoes Hayek's line of thought regarding the temporal dimension of coordination (1). However, Lachmann is opposed to the idea of the stabilizing character of rules of just conduct being a theoretical principle (2).

2.1 'Radical subjectivism'

Lachmann shares the same notion of the dynamic implications of subjectivism as Hayek. In the history of the Austrian tradition, Lachmann became well known for having wished to develop all the implications of Menger's subjectivism of thought as it appeared to him in the 1920s when a student in Germany. Hidden by the symbolic figure of Hayek for many years, Lachmann always thought of himself as a 'radical subjectivist', and this issue had important consequences on his conception of economic problem[12]. In parallel to Hayek's view, Lachmann's conception contributed to the passage from the Austrian tradition of reflecting on available information transmission procedures to an analysis of the economic implications of ignorance of the future. Implicitly picking up on the research program laid down by Hayek in *Economics and Knowledge* (1937), Lachmann, in quite an original way, studied in *The role of Expectations in Economics as a Social Science* in (1943) the nature of the relation between time and knowledge, by dehomogenising the notion of subjectivism and approaching it from a temporal angle[13].

As action always takes place within a plan, we are logically led to consider economic phenomena from a temporal angle and to view the market, which expresses individual action, as a process. This temporal dimension is expressed by a change in information, itself having repercussions on individual strategies. The passage of time brings a flow of knowledge which requires the actors' constant re-appraisal of their plans, i.e. of the relationship structure between means and objectives: 'The time cannot elapse without the state of knowledge changing. The successive stages of market processes do not reflect the effect of a sequence of events on successive individual actions, but that of a sequence of interpretations of past and future upon them' (Lachmann 1986, p. 4).

It is within this framework that Lachmann brought to light the existence of an evolving subjectivism using a second level of analysis and by calling upon a logic of endogeneous change in preferences. Living within a universe where information is imperfect, every individual, *because of his action*, benefits from additional knowledge which should necessarily alter his perception of the environment and of the opportunities for satisfaction open to him. The consumer's subjective judgement is thus modified by the choice made. As players all have different knowledge processes at their disposal at the outset concerning their nature, quantity and also their structure, this further information brought by time is unlikely to be interpreted in the same way by each individual[14]. Quite the contrary, as their interpretations will most probably give rise to fundamentally divergent expectations. 'Experience shows that in the real world of desequilibrium different persons will typically hold different expectations about the same future event. If so, at best one person's expectation can be confirmed and all other expectations will be disappointed. Hence the assumption that all other expectations are confirmed cannot possibly hold' (Lachmann 1975, p. 204). The idea of a subjectivism of perception, dealing with both an interpretable past and present, thereby finds consequences in a subjectivism of expectations. It is as a constantly transformed answer to a flow of ever changing knowledge that subjectivism presents real implications regarding individual plans: 'Successive stages of market processes thus reflect nothing so much as successive modes of re-orientation as the mind of the actor fits means to ends in ever new forms prompted by new forms of knowledge and imagination. Old knowledge becomes obsolete as new knowledge is acquired, and there can be no question of the simple and precise form of relationship between independent and dependent variables in an otherwise constant environment. It is of course the continuously changing environment that compels periodic re-orientation' (Lachmann 1986, p. 5).

As ignorance about the future is produced by the individual act itself, this phenomenon has major consequences on the inter-subjective coherence of plans. On the basis of praxeological laws on human action, Lachmann defends the idea of a fundamentally indeterminate conception of the result of social phenomena. Now, this movement cannot be countered by Hayek's 'patterns prediction'.

2.2 Flexibility versus coherence: a structural conception of institutions

Lachmann took a great interest in the theme of institutions[15]. In the same way as Hayek, his study goes beyond the scope of formal institutions with the aim of enforcing the respect of property and contract rights. Indeed it is necessary 'to distinguish between the external institutions which constitute, as it were, the outer framework of society, the legal order, and the internal institutions which gradually evolve as a result of market processes and others forms of spontaneous individual action (...)'. These 'undesigned institutions can be regarded as successful plans which have crystallized into institutions through widespread imitation' (Lachmann 1971a, p. 81, 89). The Hayekian rules of just conduct belong to this last category. It may be deduced from the nature of Lachmann's reasoning that he adheres to the notion that rules of conduct reduce the scope for subjectivism. One the one hand, these rules represent an intermediary factor between evaluation and information[16]. The rule defines how aspects of the environment are selected. It determines the way in which events are perceived and which elements should be either retained or rejected by the mind. Information is thus received or otherwise by individuals according to the mode imposed by the norms of conduct. Indeed, time can only create additional and unforeseeable information if the mental structures of perception and abstraction are both personalised and open to additional changes in information. On the other hand, institutions take part in the definition of behavioural criteria acceptable to the community, defining the scope of profitable opportunities for the actors ('Institutions prescribe certain forms of conduct and discourage others', Lachmann 1991, p. 139). Taken overall, norms constitute both the condition and expression of a socialisation of perception and behavioural modes.

In fact, Lachmann is remarkably aware of this economic function of institutions: 'An institution provides means of orientation to a large number of actors. It enables them to co-ordinate their actions by means of orientation to a common signpost' (Lachmann 1971a, pp. 49–50). However, he does not believe that institutions are capable of supplying an adequate theoretical reply to the problem of future adaptation, thereby ensuring the compatibility of individual plans. Indeed, 'empirical general-isations' originating from past experience are not necessarily of much use when probing the future: 'The question arises whether information about a large number of similar circumstances could ever permit us to draw a general rule from them in such a fashion that we could use this rule, like a recipe, in an as yet undefined number of future cases' (Lachmann 1986, p. 52).

Above all, Lachmann questions the efficiency of institutions in the name of a structural concept of rules. In fact Hayek's reasoning forgets the complementary nature of rules. He accepts the fact that a part of the rules can no longer be tools for adaptation or prediction and as such become obsolete. Preserved as such, they are more an element of 'discoordination' than coordination, and should be replaced by other rules in an evolution-ary perspective. But the replacement of rules follows a marginal curve and the whole of the stock takes on the role of a cushion for change, imposed when certain rules are abandoned in favour of new ones. However, with regard to a structural concept of knowledge, it is not possible to adopt this view as the rules are interdependent and organically linked[17]. As part of an individual's knowledge is made up of knowledge about the behaviour of others, it indeed becomes impossible to envisage the change of an indi-vidual's stock of knowledge without it creates an evolutive or restructural effect on that of other individuals. The alteration of a single rule of this set demands transformations in the other rules so that the overall set should remain coherent. Logic thus requires that Hayek's set of rules on conduct should be in constant upheaval: 'It seems therefore that the need for coherence and permanence on the one hand and for flexibility on the other hand cannot be easily reconciled' (Lachmann 1971, p. 89). The existence of an order of general rules in no way guarantees that individual plans will be in agreement. Quite the contrary, the structural nature of these rules may well bring about considerable damage by prompting ignorance rather than elements for prediction[18].

The question of this ignorance emanating from a subjective and temporal universe led Lachmann to defend the notion of 'kaleidic' universes elaborated by Shackle (1972). The idea of a kaleidic economy or society evokes a vision of social structures subject to perpetual and unforeseeable changes. 'The world of the market economy is thus a kaleidic world, a world of flux in which the ceaseless flow of news daily impinges on human choice and the making of decisions' (Lachmann 1976b, p. 56). Convergence of individual plans thus becomes a constantly evolving venture. The permanent restructuration of the supply of information inevitably gives rise to a dynamic universe which, through a series of successive imbalances, renders the intertemporal coordination of activities undetermined. Hayek's theoretical issue of structures of prediction enabled by rules of conduct thus becomes undefendable.

3. Optimistic liberalism and sceptical liberalism

Reflexion on the predictive dimension of spontaneous orders naturally led Hayek to political recommendations centred on an optimistic defense of the advantages of liberalism (1). In contrast, the scepticism of Lachmann regarding the virtues of spontaneous order led him to a resigned defense of liberalism based upon the awareness of the inefficiency of interventionist solutions and not upon belief in the ability of institutions to enable the coordination of plans (2).

3.1 The doctrinal dimension of spontaneous order

The major line of Hayek's doctrinal thought consists in his refusal to link the economic rationality to a constructivist conception of the sphere of use of individual reason. On the informational ground, Hayek (1973) opposes constructed orders (*taxis*) and complex orders (*kosmos*). The former represent structures having a small number of elements, whose main feature is extreme regularity. The latter denote structures comprising a considerable amount of information but whose relations are far less strict due to their very multiplicity and the abstract nature of the knowledge transmitted. The level of events likely to be considered by a constructed order, due to the small number of elements explained, enables a high prediction. Conversely, spontaneous orders involve a greater number of facts on the quantitative level. Due to this very fact, this knowledge will not however be certain in the sense of fabricated orders.

This contrast finds its logical conclusion in Hayek's harnessing of Popper's distinction between an *open* and *closed society* (1945). From the angle we are studying here, a 'closed society' is distinguished by such a low degree of complexity that the data necessary for the coherence of individual plans are only accessible to particular minds. As such, social organisation may be controlled by a lucid leadership. Contrary to this, 'open society' (*Great Society* in Hayek's terms) is 'the product of man's increasing ability to communicate abstract thought'. An ongoing process of experimentation, imitation and generalisation enables the most adapted norms to be selected.

The beneficial nature of social institutions can not thus be evaluated using the powers of individual reason. Hayek denounced the 'constructivist' conception of institutions and norms. Constructivists are victims of a 'synoptical illusion' i.e. all facts to be taken into consideration are present in the mind of a given individual. As rules of conduct include a cognitive content which is infinitely greater than that which individual minds are capable of forming and mastering, the area of human interaction should thus be left to the interaction of impersonal forces and not be the object of a conscious production and regulation.

Hayek's conception of social justice is a logical conclusion to his analysis of spontaneous orders. Social (distributive) justice in contrast to procedural (commutative) justice emphasises results and not modes of social interaction. Implementing social justice presents a practical difficulty, that of determining a scale of repartition[19]. At the same time, it works to the detriment of the economic sphere by distorting the system of communication constituted by market prices. The truly important point however, is that the disruptions created subsequently give rise to increasing State intervention on the path to more powerful regulation[20]. The network of spontaneous rules governing activities is progressively replaced by an ever vaster set of finalised directives. Spontaneous order, disrupted by conscious and explicit rules, becomes increasingly less effective and its inherent patterns of prediction lose their efficiency. Instability increases and leads to new State intervention. In the long term, society as a whole is governed in the same way as fabricated orders.

As a reaction to this view, Hayek emphasises the procedural nature of rules governing political organisation. Butler (1983) underlines this notion: 'The object of policy in a free society, according to Hayek, should not be to redistribute incomes on some rather arbitrary notion of 'social justice' therefore, but to help the total product to grow as large and as rapidly as possible, so that the size of the share of any individual, taken at random, is maximised' (Butler 1983, p. 97). The political superstructure of spontaneous order is represented by the Rule of Law. The role of governments is to define a general framework within which norms can form and develop, guaranteeing, in the widest possible sense, the non-regulatory nature of the process of coordination of individual activities. The sole aim of the Rule of Law is to allow the rules of just conduct sufficient scope to form and develop.

However, for the last 100 years the democratic system has been suffering from a drift away from its original vocation i.e. to fight against the arbitrary, even if it be that of the majority. Coercion is used, not to force citizens to respect general rules, but to offer privileges to certain categories of individual, thus denying or ignoring the Rule of Law. The origin of this loss of control stems from a fault in the manner in which our institutions are constructed: the non-separation of executive and legislative powers. This produces arbitrary politics, the extension of State power and the destruction of the system of spontaneous order. In *Law, Legislation and Liberty* (1979), Hayek offers a new vision of political institutions which is a logical conclusion to the completion of his theoretical work[21]. He advocates a two-chamber system ('demarchy'), notable for its strict division between executive and legislative powers and thereby meeting the deficiences of modern western institutions[22].

One may wonder about Hayek's diagnosis of the increase of interventionism and about the ability of his solutions to provide an answer to the problem. Indeed it is far from certain that the institutional outline Hayek proposes will in fact provide an answer to his ambitions. But from our standpoint, the important thing is that, in his view, the Rule of Law is supposed to defend spontaneous order. Using the theme of 'demarchy', Hayek defends the idea that the State basically guarantees the functioning and efficiency of this order. It is solely in virtue of this faculty that the State should retain the monopoly of coercive violence. Hayek's liberalism is somewhat different to that of Mises, despite a formal identity being postulated by the notion of the Rule of Law. The only purpose of the doctrine of Mises was to enable free interaction and the cognitive function of the price system. Hayek's political thought, as expressed from the 1960s onwards, will provide an answer to his concern of maintaining and keeping spontaneous orders efficient as predictive structures. His aim was more to reduce ignorance about the future than to contribute to the circulation of existing information.

3.2 Sceptical liberalism

From Lachmann's point of view, it is impossible to predict the future choices of individuals. Indeed, from the moment the future is defined as unknown, nothing can guarantee the success of any expectation. Therefore there is no principle for the success of individual plans. Lachmann's stance regarding this observation is to establish that any prediction concerning the coordinating dimension of spontaneous economic and social structures is impossible[23]. Supported by the work of Shackle (*see bibliography*), he stresses that economic science, as any social science, is incapable of detecting future evolution: 'Our conclusion that economists must confine their generalizations to the knowledge past will be deplored by all those who see the main task of economics in the making and testing of predictions. Our answer has to be that the social world, unlike the solar system, is impelled by forces as mutable as thoughts and that no Newtonian model fits it' (Lachmann 1986, p. 32) and, quoting Shackle, Lachmann concludes: 'Predicted man is less than human, predicting man is more than human. I conclude, in an expression of mere personal convictions, that man in his pure humanity can neither predict nor be predicted' (Shackle 1958, p. 105, *cité par* Lachmann 1986, p. 32). Lachmann's problematic presents the underlying idea of a fundamental indeterminism within our social structures.

This view naturally leads him to question the relevance of the idea of tending toward equilibrium. As time creates unexpected change and restructuration of the rules, we cannot hope to see expectations converge. Therefore, it is not legitimate to assert that the market necessarily expresses a form of convergence: 'According to Lachmann, the strength of the forces of convergence depends almost entirely on the activities of entrepreneurs. If entrepreneurs take advantage of the price-cost discrepancies attending changing circumstances, the entrepreneurial function of using resources in search of profit (the process of innovation and imitation) will, as most Austrian economists agree, lead to a convergence of the plans of individuals in markets. However, because change is ever present and unpredictable, individuals have different expectations about the character and extent of change'. It is in this that 'the forces for the divergence of plans are likely to be stronger than those for their convergence' (Grinder 1977a, pp. 19–20).

It is possible to consider the problem from another angle. Any attempt to have individual plans converge necessarily provokes a break in the configuration of any plans of the moment. The idea of a tendency toward equilibrium thus loses much of its appeal. 'To be to speak at all of "the system having an inherent tendency towards equilibrium" we should therefore have to assume that the velocity with which the other elements adjust themselves to changes in tastes is always so high that no new change will occur before a full adjustment to the previous change has taken place. It is difficult to imagine such circumstances' (Lachmann 1969, p. 156).

Identifying the advantages of economic liberalism with the notion of a tendency toward equilibrium is thus no longer valid. Lachmann is obviously hostile to any interventionism. The market is without doubt superior to any form of socialism when it is a question of managing and transmitting knowledge[24]. In the same way as Mises or Hayek, he believes that State action within the economy disturbs the network of the transmission of present information which is formed by the structure of relative prices. It is here, however, that their ideas diverge and that they go their separate ways. Whereas Hayek considers the rules of just conduct as a powerful factor for the coordination of individual plans, Lachmann establishes the possibility that the evolution of these rules tend, endogenously, to produce a disruption of activity and a failure of plans. If it is a foregone conclusion that State interference with the free functioning of institutions merely serves to reinforce the failure of expectations, then the absence of this interference by no means ensures the success of actors' plans. Lachmann, doctrinally, is not neutral. In the field of the communication of information, Lachmann defends liberalism; but in the field of prediction, he brings its efficacity into question. In order that individual actions should be a success, liberalism may be necessary but in no way sufficient. Therefore, the impact of Hayek's doctrinal message is brought into question[25].

4. Conclusion

Lachmann and Hayek, by distinguishing the implications of information transmission from those of ignorance about the future, have differentiated the theme of price coordination from that of coordinating plans (the market transmits knowledge but does not enable expectations). At the same time they signalled a major break from neo-Austrian tradition post-Mises. Indeed, starting from the same conception of the limits of market, Lachmann and Hayek followed different lines of thought. While Hayek replied to the implications of coordination by defending the notion of the stabilizing nature of institutions, Lachmann took a different stance. With reference to a structural dimension of knowledge governing the action process, he refuses the idea of a regulatory function of the rules of conduct. Institutions identify with gain, by supplying orientation points for individual actions; at the same time they create costs due to their complementarity and to the interdependence of resulting changes. Knowing whether gain is greater than cost is a question to which the economist cannot bring an answer *ex ante*. As such, the compatibility of individual plans is a question which is theoretically undetermined. Its answer belongs to history and in no way (economic liberalism) guarantees future coordinations.

Notes

1 Within the Austrian school uncertainty and ignorance must be distinguished from one another. The former is linked to the phenomenon of knowledge dispersion, a traditional line of thought in Austrian writing. The latter relates to the question of the future being unpredictable.
2 The date of this break is confirmed by Hayek in his posthumous 'autobiography' (*Hayek on Hayek*, 1994): 'What I see only now clearly is the problem of my relation to Mises, which began with my 1937 article on the economics of knowledge, which was an attempt to persuade Mises himself that when he asserted that the market theory as a priori, he was wrong; that what was a priori was only the logic of individual action, but the moment that you passed

from this to the interaction of many people, you entered into the empirical field' (HAYEK, 1994, p. 72).

3 A series of articles is spread over the 1950s and 1960s, of which a good number are published in a writing called *Studies in Philosophy, Politics and Economics,* 1967b. Amongst these, *Degrees of Explanation* (1955), *Rules, Perception and Intelligibility* (1963a), *Notes on the Evolution of Systems of Rules of Conduct* (1963b), *The Theory of Complex Phenomena* (1964), *The Results of Human Action but not of Human Design* (1967a). *Law, Legislation and Liberty* (1973; 1976; 1979) is in fact the most explanatory of Hayek's analyses on the subject. It is however presented in a way that has given rise to a certain number of mis-understandings about the real meaning of Hayek's theory of spontaneous order. Its ambiguity stems from the double meaning of the notion of sponta-neous order. The first, and the most traditional, evokes the undesigned outcome of individual action. It is that of both A. Smith and C. Menger (1883). It is also the one which appeared in *The Use of Knowledge in the Society* (1945). The second dimension is specifically Hayekian, calling, on the contrary, upon the notion of *prediction*. On this question of the double character of spontaneous order theory, see EGE (1992).

4 Indeed, increasing coherence of expectations can only be guaranteed from the moment that existing prices enable future prices to be indicated in one way or another. In *Law, Legislation and Liberty*, Hayek takes up the question to explain the nature and conditions of the process: 'The correspondence of expectations that makes it possible for all parties to achieve what they are striving for is in fact brought about by a process of learning by trial and error which must involve a constant disappointment of some expectations. The process of adaptation operates, as do the adjustments of any self-organizing system, by what cybernetics has taught us to call negative feeeedback: responses to the differences will be reduced. This will produce an increased correspon-dence of expectations of the different persons so long as current prices pro-vided some indications of what futures prices will be, that is, so long as, *in a fairly constant framework of known facts, always only a few of them change*; and so long as the price mechanism operates as a medium of communicating knowledge which brings it about that the facts which become known to some, through the effects of their actions on prices, are made to influence the decision of others' (HAYEK 1976, p. 125).

5 It is important here to remember that this knowledge represented by rules of conduct is expressed by actions and not words. The information necessary for the coherence of life in society is constituted above all by tacit and implicit knowledge, not formalised and thus not transmittable via language, even com-puterised; it is essentially knowledge on the immediate environment, a type of skill which expresses itself through habits, behaviour and traditions in indi-vidual action.

6 There is therefore a *primacy of the abstract* (HAYEK 1969; 1973 . . .): 'Abstract concepts are a means to cope with the complexity of the concrete which our mind is not capable of fully mastering', and constitutes 'the basis of man's capacity to move successfully in a world very imperfectly known to him, an adaptation to his ignorance of most of the particular facts in his surroundings' (HAYEK 1973, pp. 29–30). This element is to be seen in cognitive psychology studies in *The Sensory Order* (1952). Cf. GRAY 1984 and NEMO 1988 on this point.

7 One may also adhere to a more subtle view of this mechanism. The objective data change but more slowly than expectations. This is logical as changes in

these behaviours and their consequences are largely neutralised by the rules of conduct.

8 'Explanation and prediction of course do not refer to an individual event but always to phenomena or a certain kind or class' (HAYEK 1955, p. 9).

9 'Though we are not in a position to specify precisely what to expect, or even to list all the possibilities, each observed pattern has meaning in the sense that it limits the possibilities of what else may occur' (HAYEK 1955, p. 18).

10 These rules 'determine or limit the range of possibilities within which the choice is made consciously. By eliminating certain kinds of action altogether and providing certain routine ways of achieving the object, they merely restrict the alternatives on which a conscious choice is required. The moral rules, for example, which have become part of a man's nature will mean that certain conceivable choices will not appear at all among the possibilities between which he chooses' (HAYEK 1964, p. 56). The rules of conduct thus reduce the scope of subjectivism and the resulting uncertainty. On this point, cf. POLANYI (1962; 1969) whose intuitions are close to those of Hayek.

11 '... the rules governing a spontaneous order must be independent of purpose and be the same, if not necessary for all members, at least for whole classes of members not individually designated par name. They must (...) be rules applicable to an unknown and indeterminable number of persons and instances. They will have to be applied by the individuals in the light of their respective knowledge and purposes' (HAYEK 1973, p. 50).

12 Austrian literature took a belated interest in the work of Lachmann. In the seventies, only Grinder took an interest in Lachmann's theories by assembling a collection of his most important writings with *Capital, Expectations and the Market Process* (1977b). But the first genuine studies date back to the second half of the eighties. See O'DRISCOLL & RIZZO 1985; PRITCHIKO 1986; GARRISON 1987; IOANNIDES 1992; VAUGHN 1994; LAVOIE 1994a; WUBBEN 1995 for the most interesting comments. This revival in interest is probably best illustrated by two collections of studies: *Subjectivism, Intelligibility and Economic Understanding* (1986) edited by Kirzner for Lachmann's eightieth birthday (with special contributions by Ebeling, Fehl, Garrison, Langlois, O'Driscoll & Rizzo ...); and, more recently, a new collection of Lachmann's writings, edited by Lavoie: *Expectations and the Meaning of Institutions* (1994b).

13 On this basis, his thought developed through a series of articles between 1950 and 1991 (see bibliography).

14 'Such interpretation of information is of course an activity. It requires acts of our minds, and each human mind performs it in a different way (...) What needs emphasis is the subjective character of all activity concerned with information and knowledge, as contrasted with the necessarily objective nature of the information market' (LACHMANN 1986, p. 50).

15 The great majority of *The Legacy of Max Weber* (1971) was thus dedicated to the question of the character and the function of institutions.

16 In *The Market and the Economic Process* (1986), LACHMANN insists on the need to distinguish between information and knowledge in order to point out that information only takes on an economic dimension from the moment it is processed and acquires a meaning for individual actors.

17 LACHMANN here remains faithful to the traditional reasoning of Austrian authors, who insist on the structural dimension of economic phenomena. MISES 1912; 1934; 1966 and HAYEK 1931; 1932; 1945 have both demonstrated that a change in price must bring about a transformation within the overall structure

of related prices. In Lachmann's view the rules phenomenon should be considered in exactly the same way.

18 'The ramifications of obsolescence depend on the degree of complementarity between the part of the stock of knowledge affected by obsolescence and other parts. The invalidity of a general rule must have considerably more far-reaching consequences than that of one particular circumstance' (LACHMANN 1986, p. 52).

19 According to Hayek, justice can only evoke an individual desire or action as it is necessarily linked to the notion of responsibility. Illnesses, epidemics and natural disasters cannot therefore be termed 'unjust' as human responsibility is not in question. The idea of social justice means giving society the responsibility for individual situations. Social order is nevertheless the undesigned product of social interaction which no-one controls. It is a game within which talent and merit are in competition and where the notions of chance and luck operate. Because of this, 'the particular results of the social process cannot be just or unjust'. It is the same for the distribution of income: 'if it is not the intented aim or foreseen result of somebody's action that A should have much and B little, this cannot be called just or unjust' (HAYEK 1976, pp. 32; 33).

20 This notion of an ever-increasing State monitoring was already present in *The Road of Serfdom* (1944). Hayek, like Mises, refuses the theme of a third way and the ideal reformer in the manner in which it has been allowed to develop in western economies following World War II. '... there is no third way for the organisation of the economic process that can be rationally chosen to attain any desired goal, in addition to either a functional market within which no-one can determine in what way the situation of the particular groups or individuals or a central management or a group organised for power will determine these situations' (HAYEK 1944, p. 91).

21 HAYEK had already reflected on this point in *The Constitution of Liberty* (1960).

22 HAYEK suggests setting up two chambers, whose respective functions are centred on the distinction between rules of conduct (legislative) and rules of organisation (executive). These two chambers, the Legislative Assembly and the Governmental Assembly are strictly independent from one another. They act within the framework of a Constitution whose spirit is expressed by a 'Fundamental Clause'. Responsible for the Rule of Law, its role is to defend the principles necessary for the exercise of spontaneous orders.

23 'The impossibility of prediction in economics follows from the facts that economic change is linked to change in knowledge, and future knowledge cannot be gained before its time' (LACHMANN, 1959, p. 70). Garrison insisted on the economic implications of this phenomenon: 'The passage of time is necessarily marked by the discovery of new information in the form of fulfilled or disappointed expectations of investors. This is the nature, according to Lachmann, of the market process (...) A new pattern of prices emerges, but the particulars of the new pattern could not have predicted solely from the former pattern or from the sum total of knowledge that underlay it' (GARRISON 1987, p. 79). The process leads to a total impossibility to predict, unlike the clock and a prediction on its movements (contrast between kaleidoscopes and clocks).

24 'A form of economic organization based on voluntary cooperation and the universal exchange of knowledge is necessarily superior to any hierarchical structure' (LACHMANN 1977, p. 308).

25 Garrison makes a good summary of the situation: 'This agnosticism, which permeates much of Lachmann's writings, reinforces his preference for Shackelian

kaleidics over Newtonian mechanics. In a kaleidic world, one pattern of prices gives way to another, but there can be no claim that a given pattern is any closer to a general equilibrium, or represents any higher degree of coordination, than the one that preceded it' (GARRISON 1987, p. 84).

References

BOETTKE, PETER (ed.) (1994), *The Elgar Companion to Austrian Economics*, Aldershot, Brookfield: Edward Elgar.

BUTLER, EAMON (1983), *Hayek: His Contribution to the Political and Economic Thought of our Time*, Worcester: Billing & Sons Ltd.

DOLAN, EDWIN G. (ed.) (1976), *The Foundations of Modern Austrian Economics*, Kansas City: Sheed & Ward.

EBELING, RICHARD (1986), 'Toward a Hermeneutical Economics: Expectations, Prices and the Role of Interpretation in a Theory of the Market Process', in ISRAËL KIRZNER (ed.), *Subjectivism, Intelligibility and Economic Understanding: Essays in Honour of Ludwig M. Lachmann on his Eightieth Birthday*, pp. 39–56.

EGE, RAGIP (1992), 'Evolutionnisme et émergence des normes', in *Cahiers d'Economie Politique*, pp. 1007–1036.

FEHL, ULRICH (1986), 'Spontaneous Order and the Subjectivity of Expectations: A Contribution to the Lachmann-O'Driscoll Problem', in ISRAËL KIRZNER (ed.), *Subjectivism, Intelligibility and Economic Understanding: Essays in Honour of Ludwig M. Lachmann on his Eightieth Birthday*, pp. 72–87.

GARRISON, ROGER W. (1986), 'From Lachmann to Lucas: On Institutions, Expectations and Equilibrating Tendencies', in ISRAËL KIRZNER (ed.), *Subjectivism, Intelligibility and Economic Understanding: Essays in Honour of Ludwig M. Lachmann on his Eightieth Birthday*, pp. 87–110.

—— (1987), 'The Kaleidic World of Ludwig Lachmann', *Critical Review*, été 1987, pp. 77–89.

GRASSL, WOLFGANG & SMITH, BARRY (ed.), *Austrian Economics: Historical and Philosophical Background*, London: Croom Helm, 1986.

GRAY, JOHN (1984), *Hayek on Liberty*, New York: Basil Blackwell.

GRINDER, WALTER E. (1977a), 'In Pursuit of the Subjective Paradigm', in WALTER GRINDER (ed.), *Capital, Expectations and the Market Process*, 1977, pp. 3–24.

—— (ed.) (1977b), *Capital, Expectations and the Market Process: Essays on the Theory of the Market Economy*, Kansas City: Sheed Andrews & MacMeel.

HAYEK, FRIEDRICH A. (1931), *Prix et production*, Paris: Calmann-Lévy, Agora, 1985.

—— (1932), 'L'étalon-or; son évolution', *Revue d'économie politique*, 1966, 6, Novembre-Décembre, Paris: Sirey, pp. 1091–1117.

—— (1935a), 'Nature et historique du problème', in *L'économie dirigée en régime collectiviste*, 1939, pp. 11–48.

—— (1935b), 'Etat actuel de la discussion', in *L'économie dirigée en régime collectiviste*, 1939, pp. 203–243.

—— (1935c), 'The Maintenance of Capital', *Economica*, pp. 241–271.

—— (1937) 'Economics and Knowledge', in *Individualism and Economic Order*, 1948, pp. 35–57.

—— (1939), *Profits, Interest and Investment, and Other Essays on the Theory of Industrial Fluctuations*, London: Routledge & Sons.

—— (1940), 'Socialist Calculation, The Competitive Solution', *Economica* 7, pp. 125–149.

—— (1944), *La route de la servitude*, Paris: Quadrige, Presses universitaires de France, 1985.

—— (1945), 'The Use of Knowledge in Society', in *Individualism and Economic Order*, Chicago: University of Chicago Press, 1948, pp. 77–91.

—— (1948), *Individualism and Economic Order*, Chicago: University of Chicago Press, 1980, pp. 77–91.

—— (1952), *The Sensory Order*, London: Routledge & Kegan Paul.

—— (1955), 'Degrees of explanation', in *Studies in Philosophy, Politics and Economics*, 1967, pp. 3–21.

—— (1960), *The Constitution of the Liberty*, London: Routledge & Kegan Paul.

—— (1963a), 'Rules, Perception and Intelligibility', in *Studies in Philosophy, Politics and Economics*, 1967, pp. 43–66.

—— (1963b), 'Notes on the Evolution of Systems of Rules of Conduct', in *Studies in Philosophy, Politics and Economics*, 1967, pp. 66–82.

—— (1964), 'The Theory of Complex Phenomena', in *Studies in Philosophy, Politics and Economics*, 1967, pp. 22–43.

—— (1967a), 'The Results of Human Action but not of Human Design', in *Studies in Philosophy, Politics and Economics*, 1967, pp. 93–106.

—— (1967b), *Studies in Philosophy, Politics and Economics*, Chicago: The University of Chicago Press, 1967.

—— (1969), 'The Primacy of the Abstract', in *New Studies in Philosophy, Politics, Economics and the History of Ideas*, 1978, pp. 35–50.

—— (1973), *Law, Legislation and Liberty: Rules and Order*, vol. I, London: Routledge, 1993.

—— (1976), *Law, Legislation and Liberty: The Mirage of Social Justice*, vol. II, London: Routledge, 1993.

—— (1978), *New, Studies in Philosophy, Politics, Economy and the History of Ideas*, London: Routledge & Kegan Paul, 1978.

—— (1979), *Law, Legislation and Liberty: The Political Order of a Free Society*, vol. III, London: Routledge, 1993.

—— (1994), *Hayek on Hayek, An Autobiographical Dialogue*, édité par Stephen Kresge et Leif Wenar, Chicago: University of Chicago Press.

IOANNIDES, STAVROS (1992), *The Market, Competition and Democracy: a Critique of Neo-Austrian Economics*, Aldershot: Edward Elgar Publishing.

KIRZNER, ISRAËL (ed.) (1982), *Method, Process, and Austrian Economics: Essays in Honour of Ludwig von Mises*, Lexington: Lexington Books.

—— (1986), *Subjectivism, Intelligibility and Economic Understanding*, New York: New York University Press.

LACHMANN, LUDWIG M. (1943), 'The Role of Expectations in Economics as a Social Science', *Economica*, 10, pp. 12–23.

—— (1950), 'Economics as a Social Science', in WALTER GRINDER (ed.) 1977b, *Capital, Expectations and the Market Process: Essays on the Theory of the Market Economy*, pp. 166–181.

—— (1951), 'The Science of Human Action', in WALTER GRINDER (ed.) 1977b,

Capital, Expectations and the Market Process: Essays on the Theory of the Market Economy, pp. 94–112.

—— (1959), 'Professor Shackle and the Economic Significance of Time', *Metroeconomica*, 11, pp. 64–73.

—— (1966), 'The Significance of the Austrian School of Economics in the History of Ideas', in WALTER GRINDER (ed.) 1977b, *Capital, Expectations and the Market Process: Essays on the Theory of the Market Economy*, pp. 45–65.

—— (1969), 'Methodological Individualism and the Market Process', in WALTER GRINDER (ed.) 1977b, *Capital, Expectations and the Market Process: Essays on the Theory of the Market Economy*, pp. 149–165.

—— (1971a), *The Legacy of Max Weber*, Berkeley: Glendessary Press.

—— (1971b), 'Ludwig von Mises and the Market Process', in WALTER GRINDER (ed.) 1977b, *Capital, Expectations and the Market Process: Essays on the Theory of the Market Economy*, pp. 181–197.

—— (1973), *Methodological Individualism and the Market Economy*, London: Institute of Economics Affairs, 1973.

—— (1975), 'Reflections on Hayekian Capital Theory', in DON LAVOIE (ed.) 1994b, *Expectations and the Meaning of Institutions, Essays in Economics by Ludwig Lachmann*, pp. 198–209.

—— (1976a), 'Austrian Economics in the Present Crisis of Economic Thought', in WALTER GRINDER (ed.) 1977b, *Capital, Expectations and the Market Process: Essays on the Theory of the Market Economy*, pp. 25–45.

—— (1976b), 'From Mises to Shackle: an Essay on Austrian Economics and the Kaleidic Society', *Journal of Economic Literature*, mars 1976, pp. 54–62.

—— (1976c), 'Austrian Economics in the Age of the Neo-Ricardian Counterrevolution', in EDWIN DOLAN (ed.), *The Foundations of Modern Austrian Economics*, pp. 215–227.

—— (1978a), 'An Austrian Stocktaking: Unsettled Questions and Tentative Answers', in LOUIS SPADERO (ed.), *New Directions in Austrian Economics*, pp. 215–227.

—— (1978b), 'Vicissitudes of Subjectivism and the Dilemma of the Theory of Choice', in DON LAVOIE (ed.) 1994b, *Expectations and the Meaning of Institutions*, pp. 218–228.

—— (1982), 'Ludwig von Mises and the Extension of Subjectivism', in ISRAËL KIRZNER (ed.) 1982, *Method, Process, and Austrian Economics: Essays in Honour of Ludwig von Mises*, pp. 31–40.

—— (1986), *The Market as an Economic Process*, Oxford: Blackwell, 1986.

—— (1991), 'Austrian Economics: a Hermeneutic Approach', in DON LAVOIE (ed.) 1991, *Economics and Hermeneutics*, London & New York: Routledge & Kegan Paul, 1991, pp. 218–228.

LANGLOIS, RICHARD N. (1986), 'Coherence and Flexibility: Social Institutions in a World of Radical Uncertainty', in ISRAËL KIRZNER (ed.) 1986, *Subjectivism, Intelligibility and Economic Understanding: Essays in Honour of Ludwig M. Lachmann on his Eightieth Birthday*, pp. 171–191.

LAVOIE, DON (1991) (ed.), *Economics and Hermeneutics*, London & New York, Routledge & Kegan Paul.

—— (1994a), 'The Interpretative Turn', in PETER BOETTKE (ed.) 1994, *The Elgar Companion to Austrian Economics*, pp. 54–63.

—— (1994b) (ed.), *Expectations and the Meaning of Institutions, Essays in Economics by Ludwig Lachmann*, London & New York: Routledge.

MEIJER, GERRIT (ed.) (1995), *New Perspectives on Austrian Economics*, London & New York: Routledge & Kegan Paul.

MENGER, CARL (1883), *Investigations into the Method in Social Sciences, with Special Reference to Economics*, New York and London: New York University Press, 1985.

MISES, LUDWIG VON (1912), *The Theory of Money and Credit*, New Haven: Yale University Press, 1953.

—— (1933), *Epistemological Problems of Economics*, New York & London: New York University Press.

—— (1934), *On the Manipulation of Money and Credit*, New York: Free Market Books, 1978.

—— (1966), *L'action humaine: traité d'économie*, Paris: Libre-Echange, 1985.

NEMO, PHILIPPE (1988), *La société de droit selon F.A. Hayek*, Presses Universitaires de France, Libre-Echange.

O'DRISCOLL, GERALD. P. (ed.) (1977), *Economics as a Coordination Problem: the Contributions of Friedrich A. Hayek*, Kansas City: Sheed Andrews & MacMeel.

O'DRISCOLL, GERALD P. & RIZZO, MARIO (1985), *The Economics of Time and Ignorance*, New York: Basil Blackwell, 1985.

—— (1986), 'Subjectivism, Uncertainty and Rules', in ISRAËL KIRZNER (ed.) 1986, *Subjectivism, Intelligibility and Economic Understanding: Essays in Honour of Ludwig M. Lachmann on his Eightieth Birthday*, pp. 252–267.

POLANYI, MICHAEL (1962), *Personal Knowledge: Towards a Post-Critical Philosophy*, Chicago: University of Chicago Press, 1962.

—— (1969), 'The Determinants of Social Action', in ERICH STREISSLER (ed.) 1969, *Roads to Freedom: Essays in honour of Friedrich A. von Hayek*, pp. 165–179.

POPPER, KARL (1934), *Logik der Forschung*, Wien: Julius Springer Verlag, 1935.

—— (1945), *La société ouverte et ses ennemis*, Seuil, 1979.

PRYCHITKO, DAVID L. (1986), 'Ludwig Lachmann and the Farther Reaches of Austrian Economics', *Critical Review*, summer 1987, pp. 63–76.

SHACKLE, GEORGES L.S. (1949), *Expectation in Economics*, Cambridge: Cambridge University Press.

—— (1955), *Uncertainty in Economics and Other Reflexions*, Cambridge: Cambridge University Press.

—— (1958), *Time in Economics*, Amsterdam: North-Holland.

—— (1961), *Décision, déterminisme et temps*, Paris: Dunod, 1967.

—— (1972), *Epistemics and Economics*, London: Cambridge University Press.

SHAND, ALEX (1980), *Subjectivist Economics, The New Austrian School*, The Pica Press.

SPADERO, LOUIS M. (ed.) (1978), *New Directions in Austrian Economics*, Kansas City: Sheed Andrews & MacMeel.

STEELE, G.R. (1993), *The Economics of Friedrich Hayek*, New York: Saint Martin's Press.

VAUGHN, KAREN I. (1994), *Austrian Economics in America, The Migration of a Tradition*, New York: Cambridge University Press.

WUBBEN, EMIL (1995), 'Austrian Economics and Uncertainty: on a non-deterministic but non-haphazard Future', in *New Perspectives on Austrian Economics*, London & New York, Routledge & Kegan Paul, pp. 106–146.

59

THE SURPRISING PLACE OF
COGNITIVE PSYCHOLOGY IN
THE WORK OF F.A. HAYEK

Jack Birner

Source: *History of Economic Ideas* 7(1–2) (1999): 43–84.

1. Introduction

After a long period of neglect, the work of F.A. Hayek has come back into fashion. Most publications about Hayek address his political and social philosophy, his methodology, his analysis of the division of knowledge and its coordination, and his theory of cultural evolution, and some his monetary theory. However, the fields in which his contributions reached the highest level of analytical sophistication have largely remained unexplored: the theory of intertemporal general economic equilibrium[1], his theories of capital and the business cycle[2] – which is all the stranger since the revival of interest in his ideas dates from his obtaining the Nobel prize for economics in 1974 – and his psychology of perception, about whose existence most Hayek students are ignorant[3]. Yet, Hayek's very first written contribution to science was in psychology, and most of the rest of his work cannot be understood without it. I start by giving a chronological sketch of Hayek's early career.

2. Early career: psychology and economics

When Hayek had returned from his war service in the Austro-Hungarian army, he started to study law. In the winter of 1919–20, "when the University of Vienna was closed because of lack of fuel for heating"[4], he spent "six to eight weeks"[5] in Zürich, where he attended the lectures of someone (who remains as yet unidentified) who discussed the recently published (1918) *Allgemeine Erkenntnislehre* by Moritz Schlick. While in Zürich, Hayek also worked in the laboratory of the brain anatomist von Monakow[6]. About a year later, the result of his Swiss period was laid down in a manuscript with the title *Beiträge zur Theorie der Entwicklung des Bewusstseins* (Contributions to the theory of the development of consciousness)[7], dated September 1920. This manuscript is very remarkable, indeed. When Hayek wrote it, he was only 21 years of age. Yet, it reads like the product of a mature scientist, one, moreover, who moves far beyond the boundaries of received orthodoxy[8].

After Hayek had taken his degree in law, in the Autumn of 1921, he found a job in the Austrian *Abrechnungsamt*, which organized the repayment of debts that had been blocked by the war. In the mean time he studied economics. For that purpose he enrolled for a doctoral degree in political studies, since there was no degree in economics in Vienna at the time. He obtained his doctorate early in 1923. Hayek's dissertation was a study of the link between the value of final products and the value of factors of production (the imputation problem). This problem had been discussed previously by Friedrich von Wieser, with whom Hayek had studied. Immediately after finishing his thesis, Hayek travelled to the United States, where he had been promised a job by Jeremiah Jenks of New York University. Apparently, Hayek had not had enough yet of academic obligations, since he drafted the outline for a thesis which was to have earned him a Ph.D. from New York University. His supervisor was to have been J.D. Magee. The thesis, with the title "Is the function of money consistent with an artificial stabilization of its purchasing power?", was never completed. Its interest lies in the fact that its outline is a sketch of most of Hayek's later work on business cycles and monetary theory[9].

While in New York, Hayek started working on his first publications, all of them in economics (Hayek 1924; 1925 and 1926). They were to be followed by many other articles and several books, about economics and its method. Apparently, he had no more time for his earlier interest in psychology:

> "After I got my law degree in 1921, after three years at the university devoted mostly to psychology and economics, I had to think about earning a living and to confine my extracurricular activities to one of those two subjects. I chose economics, perhaps wrongly; the fascination of physiological psychology never quite left me, though for the next 25 years – struggling to get on as an economist (and rapidly forgetting my law) – I could devote no time to following the development of psychology".
>
> (Hayek 1982, p. 288)

Between 1927 and 1941 Hayek elaborated his theory of the business cycle and the underlying theory of capital. His explanation of cyclical fluctuations in economic activity relies on the distinction between *real* relative intertemporal scarcities, and hence intertemporal relative prices in terms of goods, on the one hand, and the *perception* that individual decision makers have of these relative prices on the other hand. The only prices which individuals perceive in a developed economy are prices in terms of money. The cause of cyclical fluctuations lies in discrepancies between money prices and real relative prices. Disturbances in the money supply due to monetary policy, and also certain changes in the real sector which are amplified by the credit multiplier, may be the causes that money prices no longer reflect real scarcities. Since individuals base their behaviour on the only prices they can observe, viz. money prices, their decisions are not in accordance with the real economic conditions. Therefore, the consumption, saving and investment they undertake, using expectations that are based on money prices, cannot be sustained by the real scarcities that characterize the economy. When in the end the real scarcities assert themselves, the expectations are falsified. In the mean time, however, means of production have been invested in projects whose ex-post profitability does not correspond to their expected, ex-ante profitability. What on the basis of money prices looked like justified saving, investment and consumption decisions, turn out to be mistakes. Since resources are not perfectly mobile, the situation cannot be corrected immediately, and a crisis is the result.

Relative prices that are *locally perceived* by *individual decision makers in their specific circumstances* are crucial to Hayek's theory. One of his earliest criticisms of contemporary explanations of the cycle was that they relied upon the concept of the general price level. Hayek's criticism was that this is a statistical construct which cannot, by its very nature, be perceived by individual decision makers[10].

While he was busy developing his economic theory, Hayek also wrote extensively about the method which he considered to be the correct one for social science. Two principles constitute the most important features of his methodology. The first is that in order to understand and explain social phenomena we have to reconstruct them from the regularities governing the behaviour of individual decision makers. This is the principle of *methodological individualism*:

> "It is to this 'individualistic' method that we owe whatever understanding of economic phenomena we possess . . .".
>
> (*PP*, p. 4)

The second is that since the behaviour of individuals is the result of a decision process that confronts their preferences with the way in which they perceive their environment, the relevant facts of the social sciences are the perceptions and expectations of individuals. This is the principle of *subjectivism*. Hayek is very explicit about the importance of this principle, too:

"It is probably no exaggeration to say that every important advance in economic theory during the last hundred years was a further step in the consistent application of subjectivism".

(*CRS*, p. 31)

Since the explanation of perception is one of the objectives of Hayek's psychology, one might have expected Hayek to have used the results of his psychology in his economics. The surprising thing is that neither his economics nor his methodological writings of the 1930s and '40s contain any explicit reference whatsoever to his psychological theory. This calls for an explanation. However, before going into that, it is useful to discuss Hayek's psychology, his economics, and his methodology in more detail.

3. Psychology of perception

The 41-page long manuscript *Beiträge zur Theorie der Entwicklung des Bewusstseins* of 1920 contains basically the same theory as *The Sensory Order*, which was published in 1952[11]. It was very much ahead of the psychology of its time in that it investigates the problem of consciousness. This had been at the centre of attention of the most prominent German psychologists of the 19th century[12], but the problem had fallen into a long-lasting oblivion afterwards, without having been solved. Hayek did not exaggerate when he wrote in 1952 that "thirty years later, in examining the literature of modern psychology I found that the particular problem with which I had been concerned had remained pretty much in the same state in which it had been when it first occupied me" (Hayek 1952, p. vi). And still in 1982, there was hardly any exaggeration in Hayek's joke that "as far as psychology is concerned, I am really a ghost from the 19th century" (Hayek 1977, p. 287). There was one "fellow-traveller" on the path chosen by Hayek, one whom he discovered only when he had almost finished his book: Donald Hebb, whose *The Organization of Behaviour* was published in 1949. This discovery almost made Hayek give up the project of publishing *SO*.

Hayek's purpose as stated in the ms. is to explain consciousness as it arises out of individual sense impressions, using only the known laws of physiology. Hayek is very explicit that he wants to do so without invoking any non-physiological hypotheses. His purpose will have been reached once all secondary qualities, such as the sensations of colour, heat, and sound, have been explained by means of the laws of physics. In this respect, Hayek's work is consistent with the ideal of a scientific world picture of the Wiener Kreis[13]. This physicalist reductionism distinguishes itself from the atomism and neutral monism of Ernst Mach (and perhaps Moritz Schlick, whose position on the matter in *Allgemeine Erkenntnislehre* is not clear[14]) in that it does not assume a one-to-one correspondence between sense impressions and mental processes. In fact, the discovery that this feature of Mach's theory is not only superfluous[15], but blocks the possibility of making progress in understanding consciousness was Hayek's original incentive to develop his own theory[16].

Hayek assumes that there are two "orders" in which the human mind arranges the objects in the world: the *physical order*, which classifies events as similar or different according to whether they produce similar or different other external events; and the *sensory order*, which classifies events according to their sensory properties. There is no one-to-one correspondence between the elements of the two orders. Events which appear to our senses to be of the same kind may be different in the physical order, and the other way around. How the sensory order of the human mind (or the "microcosm") and the physical order of external events (or "macrocosm"; *SO*, p. 4) are related is the central problem of *SO*.

In contrast to many contemporary psychologists, who pretend to deal with technical problems concerning perception that are of a partial nature, Hayek's theory of perception explicitly addresses the mind-body problem. In that sense, his psychology is much more general than "just" a theory of perception, which is probably why he repeatedly speaks of his book as a contribution to *theoretical* psychology:

> "The relation between the physical and the phenomenal raises two distinct but related problems. The first of these problems presents the task of the physical sciences while the second creates the central problem of theoretical psychology. The task of the physical sciences is to replace the classification of events which our senses perform but which proves inadequate to describe the regularities in these events, by a classification which will put us in a better position to do so".
>
> (*SO*, 1.13)

However, this physicalist reductionism does not make the task of theoretical psychology superfluous. On the contrary. As we make progress in eliminating secondary qualities from physical science, it becomes the task of psychology to explain why these sense impressions appear to us as they do.

> "The task of theoretical psychology is the converse one of explaining why these events, which on the basis of their relations to each other can be arranged in a certain (physical) order, manifest a different order in their effect on our senses".
>
> (*SO*, 1.13)[17]

> "It is because the physical sciences have shown that the objects of the external world do not regularly differ in their effects upon

each other in the same way in which they differ in their effect upon our senses that the question why they appear to us as they do becomes a legitimate problem and indeed the central problem of theoretical psychology".

(*SO*, 1.16)

Repeated physiological impulses or sense impressions stimulate particular neural connections, that are strengthened by this repeated process. The sense impressions are transformed into "values of consciousness"[18] or sensations in that they become incorporated in a system of such connections among neurons. Whenever a particular synaptic chain is activated, other, associated chains are activated as well. This process of physiological association is what would now be called a classifier system: a particular sensation is experienced as being of a particular type, or class, since its occurrence activates the associated set of neural connections. The human mind consists of this complex physiological mechanism which works through a continuous process of classification and reclassification of sense impressions, and the classifications formed from them[19]. This process is located in the "neural order" of the central nervous system, which is part of the physical order. No central guidance is needed for this; the mind is continuously involved in a process of self-organization. It consists of an evolutionary process that leads to an ever more complex set of classifications. The functioning of the mind coincides with its continuous evolution[20].

An evolutionary framework is inherent to Hayek's psychology. The evolution of the human mind is part of the evolutionary process in which organisms (in this case man) struggle to survive:

"Our task is (...) to show in what sense it is possible that within parts of the macrocosm a microcosm may be formed which reproduces certain aspects of the macrocosm and through this will enable the substructure of which it forms part to behave in a manner which will assist its continued existence".

(*SO*, 5.78)[21]

One of the central theses of the book (and one of the great differences with the psychology of Mach) is that

"the sensory (or other mental) qualities are not in some manner originally attached to, or an original attribute of, the individual physiological impulses, but that the whole of these qualities is determined by the system of connexions by which the impulses can be transmitted from neuron to neuron; that it is thus the position of the individual impulses or group of impulses in the whole system of such connexions which gives it its distinct quality; that this system of connexions is acquired in the course of the development of the species and the individual by a kind of 'experience' or 'learning'; and that it reproduces therefore at every stage of its development certain relationships existing in the physical environment between the stimuli evoking the impulses".

(*SO*, 2.49)

Thus, there are no pure sense data or facts, but all facts are embedded in a complex of relations to other facts, which we may call, in the terminology of *SO*, a 'map'. From this map, which serves as a kind of first approximation, more permanent sets of classifications are formed. Hayek calls these "models".

"It is (...) the process of multiple classification which builds the model. What we have before called the 'map', the semi-permanent apparatus of classification, provides the different generic elements from which the models of particular situations are built. The term 'map', which suggests a sort of schematic picture of the environment is thus really somewhat misleading. What the apparatus of classification provides is more a sort of inventory of the kind of things of which the world is built up, a theory of how the world works rather than a picture of it. It would be better described as a construction set from which the models of particular situations are built".

(*SO*, 5.89)

So, these models are not complete representations of the world. That it is possible for the mind to build representations of the physical order from a set of models that is necessarily limited, is due to the accidental fact that the structure of the world is redundant, to use Herbert Simon's term[22]:

"It is (...) no more than a fortunate accident that the different events in the macrocosm are not fully interrelated to any significant degree, but that as a rule it is possible to base predictions of certain kinds of events on a mere selection of a totality of events".

(*SO*, 5.90)

Because Hayek is a physicalist reductionist, one might expect him to hold the idea that it is possible to arrive at a complete description of reality in terms of the laws of physics. But Hayek denies this. The argument relies on the idea that a system A, in order to describe a system B, has to be of an order of complexity higher than B. The mind, or the mental order, is part of the physical order. Therefore, according to Hayek, in order for us humans to give a complete description of reality, we would also have to describe our own minds. That would require our mind to be of an order of complexity greater than itself, which is patently absurd. I will not now criticize Hayek's argument. Let it suffice to observe that here lies the origin of Hayek's notion of explanation of the principle. For he argues that whereas it is impossible to describe the working of the mind in detail, we can explain it in terms of the general regularities governing it. This is one of the "philosophical consequences" of his psychology that form the subject of the final chapter of *SO*.

4. Hayek's research programme in economics

A striking feature of Hayek's economics (and indeed of all his work) is its systematic character. He starts out by stating the problem he wants to solve, and the methodological constraints that a successful solution has to satisfy. Then he gives a historical survey of the solutions that have been attempted, which he then analyzes in the light of his own problem statement and methodological principles. On the basis of this analytical, historical and philosophical analysis, Hayek gives an outline of his own future research[23]. Subsequently, he starts to fill in the outline. This systematic approach justifies discussing Hayek's work as a research programme.

Research programmes are defined by *scientific problems* (or better: problem situations, as problems always arise against a particular scientific background) and *methodological principles*. Two types of problems may be distinguished: global and local problems. Usually, the initial problem situation concerns a global problem. In the case of Hayek, this is the explanation of business cycles. Local problems may be generated by the state of the discipline or by the progress of the specific research programme itself. Thus, in Hayek's case, the global problem of explaining business cycles gives rise to, *inter alia*, analyzing the behaviour of savings, consumption, and investments, since these are theoretical categories that contemporary economics distinguishes. An example of a local problem which was generated by Hayek's own research programme is the question how capital has to be modelled. Initially, Hayek thought he could use Böhm-Bawerk's capital theory, but he soon discovered that Böhm's measure of capital intensity in terms of a unique time-length of the production process was not satisfactory[24].

Philosophers and historians of science have used the elements of problems and methodological principles fruitfully for reconstructing episodes of intellectual history. This approach is also known as the method of rational reconstruction. I follow this method in my presentation of Hayek's economics. A useful instrument is the following scheme of Karl Popper's[25]:

$$P_1 \rightarrow T_1 \rightarrow EE \rightarrow P_{2\rightarrow} T_{2\rightarrow} \text{ etc.}$$

Theories (T_1) are formulated as solutions to problems (P_1). The adequacy of the solutions is put to the test, and possible corrections are applied in a process of error elimination (EE). This usually gives rise to new problems, for whose solutions another theory is formulated, and so on. In presenting Hayek's economics, I will simplify the scheme to a sequence of problems and theories and omit explicit mention of error elimination, as this would involve us more deeply in technical details than the current subject requires.

Hayek's global problem (or original problem situation), which defines the outlines of his research programme, is how to explain fluctuations in the level of production and employment, a dynamic disequilibrium phenomenon, by means of static general equilibrium theory. This indicates two logically possible strategies: either the business cycle is modelled in a way that makes it amenable to analysis in terms of static general equilibrium theory, or general equilibrium theory is dynamized[26]. Hayek chooses the second option[27]. From this global problem setting derive a number of more specific problems of a technical nature, such as the introduction of time, and an appropriate definition of equilibrium.

Hayek states his research programme in economics explicitly on various occasions. Each time he does so, he mentions the methodological requirements it has to fulfil. *Geldtheorie und Konjunkturtheorie* of 1929 (later translated as *Monetary Theory and the Trade Cycle*, 1933) devotes an entire chapter to methodology, and the first chapter of *Prices and Production* (1931) is explicitly methodological in its diagnosis of the stagnation in the development of business cycle theory: economists have adopted the wrong method. Irving Fisher's revival of the mechanistic form of the quantity theory in particular stands accused of having led to "the present isolation of the theory of money from the main body of general economic theory" (*PP*, p. 4), because of the use of "different methods for the explanation of values as they are supposed to exist irrespective of any influence of money, and for the explanation of that influence of money on prices (...)" (*PP*, p. 4). Because that is what economists do when they

> "try to establish *direct* causal connections between the *total* quantity of money, the *general level* of all prices and, perhaps, also the *total* amount of production. For none of these magnitudes *as such* ever exerts an influence on the decision of individuals; yet it is on the assumption of a knowledge of the decisions of individuals that we owe whatever understanding of economic phenomena that we possess; that the modern 'subjective' theory has advanced beyond the classical school in its consistent use is probably its main advantage over their teaching".
>
> (ibid.)

Instead of this aggregate, macro-economic and holistic approach, Hayek firmly puts methodological individualism and subjectivism forward as *the* methods of economic analysis:

"From the very nature of economic theory, averages can never form a link in its reasoning; but to prove this contention would go far beyond the subject of these lectures. I shall here confine myself to an attempt to show in a special field the differences between explanations which do and explanations which do not have recourse to such concepts".

(*PP*, p. 5)

This amounts to a promise of a *methodological* research programme. Hayek is quite explicit that *Prices and Production* is meant as more than a contribution to economic theory. It is also an essay in methodology: "it is the method of approach more than the details of the results which is of importance in what follows" (*PP*, p. 31). By 1931, Hayek's research programme in economics had turned into a methodological programme as well. In the early 1940s Hayek explicitly devoted a series of publications to the methodology underlying his economics. They were collected in *The Counterrevolution of Science*, which will be discussed below.

In the mean time, we can identify the methodological principles that guide the development of Hayek's research programme in economics:

1 Theoretical unification, the principle that all economic phenomena should be explained in terms of a single theory[28]. This is linked with the use of a highly idealized theory which is far removed from empirical reality. In order to re-establish contact with empirical reality the idealized explanations are supplemented with
2 The method of decreasing abstraction[29].
3 Methodological individualism. For Hayek's economics, this principle amounts to the demand that all explanations of the business cycle have to be reduced the theory of rational individual choice, i.e., marginal value theory (Hayek speaks of the pure logic of choice).
4 Subjectivism, the principle that all explanations should involve individual perceptions.

We now have the elements for reconstructing Hayek's research programme. Its theoretical background is static general equilibrium theory. In order for a static theory of equilibrium conditions to explain an inherently dynamic disequilibrium phenomenon such as the business cycle, two problems have to be solved. One is the incorporation of time, the other the introduction of a factor or mechanism that causes the disturbances of equilibrium[30]. Hayek integrates these two problems into the notion of the

333

planning individual, which he introduces in his 1927 and 1928[31]. The concept of a plan implies both a time horizon and a set of perceptions that serve as informational input for rational decisions through time. (Incidentally, this also introduces expectations, which Hayek has been accused of neglecting[32].)

The introduction of the planning individual for dealing with the problems of the incorporation of time and the source of disturbances gives rise to two sub-programmes.

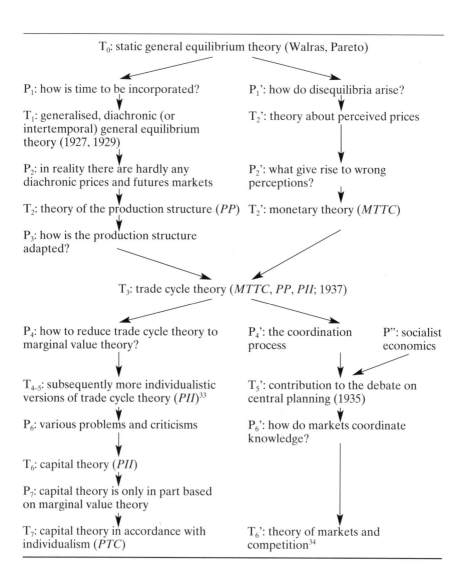

T_0: static general equilibrium theory (Walras, Pareto)

P_1: how is time to be incorporated?

T_1: generalised, diachronic (or intertemporal) general equilibrium theory (1927, 1929)

P_2: in reality there are hardly any diachronic prices and futures markets

T_2: theory of the production structure (*PP*)

P_3: how is the production structure adapted?

P_1': how do disequilibria arise?

T_2': theory about perceived prices

P_2': what give rise to wrong perceptions?

T_2': monetary theory (*MTTC*)

T_3: trade cycle theory (*MTTC, PP, PII*; 1937)

P_4: how to reduce trade cycle theory to marginal value theory?

T_{4-5}: subsequently more individualistic versions of trade cycle theory (*PII*)[33]

P_6: various problems and criticisms

T_6: capital theory (*PII*)

P_7: capital theory is only in part based on marginal value theory

T_7: capital theory in accordance with individualism (*PTC*)

P_4': the coordination process

P'': socialist economics

T_5': contribution to the debate on central planning (1935)

P_6': how do markets coordinate knowledge?

T_6': theory of markets and competition[34]

Hayek links the two main problems, viz. the incorporation of time, and hence the introduction of dynamics, and the source of disturbances of equilibrium, to two distinct methodological principles, which may be considered as defining the two branches or sub-programmes:

(1) The individualist sub-programme. It is defined by the problem how the theory of the business cycle can be reduced to the individualistic theory of marginal value (or the *pure logic of choice* as Hayek called it in "Economics and Knowledge"). The working out of this reductionist programme kept Hayek busy for most of the 1930s. It involved finding solutions to mainly technical problems in capital theory, and the introduction of idealizations. One of these is the description of production processes in terms of single investment processes of which production is supposed to be composed[35].

(2) The subjectivist sub-programme. For Hayek's theory, the perceptions that individuals have of their economic environment (and hence the medium through which individuals perceive their environment) is of crucial importance. He states this very explicitly from his very earliest writings in economics. Hayek is opposed to the use of aggregates in economic theory because they are not the sort of things which individuals perceive. The inspiration for the distinction between perceived as opposed to real magnitudes comes from the works of Wicksell and Mises. And although this distinction is reminiscent of the difference between the sensory and the physical order in Hayek's psychology, there is no evidence whatsoever in Hayek's early work in economics that he was influenced by his own theory of cognitive psychology.

"Economics and Knowledge" of 1937 may be considered as linking the two branches of Hayek's research programme. The article addresses the methodological question what constitutes the empirical content of economic theory. The answer[36] is given by a description of the logical structure of economic theory. Its core is the pure logic of choice, which is tautologous. (Remember that the reduction of the description of all economic behaviour, and particularly investment, to the pure logic of choice is the theme of the first branch of Hayek's research programme.) The empirical content is provided by propositions surrounding this core which describe "how knowledge is acquired and communicated" (Hayek 1937, p. 33). Knowledge of the environment is formed through perceptions. This is the theme of the second branch of the research programme. Knowledge is communicated in an efficient and economical way by the "system of telecommunications" of the price system, as Hayek calls it in his 1937.

Hayek's statement about "how knowledge is acquired and communicated" is another occasion where one would expect him to have applied his own earlier psychological theory. But surprisingly, again he does no such thing. Instead, and even more surprisingly, he confesses that he has made no progress in finding the "concrete hypotheses concerning the conditions under which people are supposed to acquire the relevant knowledge and the process by which they are supposed to acquire it" (Hayek 1937, p. 48). Even though the acquisition of knowledge is now explicitly introduced in the sphere of economics, the acquisition process is not described in cognitive-psychological terms. Rather, the 1937 article is a methodological progress report in which Hayek summarizes in general, methodological terms, the theme of the reductionist branch of his research programme.

In the same article, Hayek does something else. His contributions to the debate on socialism led him to transform or extend the concept of subjectivism. The idea that individual perceptions are the facts of the social sciences is now supplemented by that of the presence of dispersed local information (the division of knowledge). This gives rise to the question how this dispersed knowledge is coordinated. Hayek addresses this problem in a series of publications on markets and competition. So "Economics and Knowledge" sketches the further development of the subjectivist branch of the research programme, which had remained in a rather rudimentary state during the first half of the 1930s[37]. Later, a third transformation of the notion of subjectivism took place. This will be discussed below, in the paragraph on Hayek's methodology.

5. The epistemic turn in Hayek's thought

I propose the following hypothesis for explaining Hayek's neglect of his psychology in his economics.

Hayek was not interested in explaining the misperceptions that cause industrial fluctuations in terms of the working of the minds of individual decision makers. What he wanted to do instead, was to investigate the systematic sources of misperceptions, i.e., the monetary system.

This is the message of "Price Expectations":

"Every explanation of economic crises must include the assumption that entrepreneurs have committed errors. But the mere fact that entrepreneurs do make errors can hardly be regarded as a sufficient explanation of crises. Erroneous dispositions which lead to losses all round will appear probable only if we can show why entrepreneurs should all simultaneously make mistakes in the same direction. The explanation that this is just due to a kind of psychological infection or that for any other reason most entrepreneurs should commit the same avoidable errors does not carry much conviction. It seems, however, more likely that they may all be equally misled by following guides or symptoms which as a rule prove reliable. Or, speaking more concretely, it may be that the prices existing when they made their decisions and on which they had to base their views about the future have created expectations which must necessarily be disappointed".

(Hayek 1933, p. 141)

In terms of the deductive-nomological model of explanation, what Hayek says here is that he takes the *laws* of perception (psychology) for granted, but wants to investigate the consequences of certain changes in *initial conditions*, i.e., price signals.

If this were all there was to the matter, nothing much of a surprise would remain about the absence of an application of Hayek's own psychology to his economics. But matters are more complicated than that. In the same article from which I just quoted, Hayek admits that the formation of expectations and the role of uncertainty and risk have to be developed further (1933, pp. 155–6). He must have been aware that this would have meant going into the details of psychological mechanisms, as has been shown much later by the work of Kahnemann and Tversky and the subsequent literature on problems of framing. Hayek declares himself "in complete agreement with [Myrdal] when he stresses the great importance of this element [expectations] in the further development of the theory of industrial fluctuations", thus leaving a potential role for psychology on the agenda of his research programme. We know that Hayek did not work this out, so some of the surprise concerning his psychology remains. I will turn to that below. First I want to briefly investigate a consequence of my hypothesis.

If Hayek was interested in the systematic sources of disturbance of perceptions, as he was, one would expect him to have devoted a detailed analysis to the functioning of the monetary system. Here we are in for another surprise: apart from some early articles, one chapter of *MTTC*, a brief historical chapter in *PP*, and a series of lectures about the international monetary order which do not directly address problems of the trade cycle (Hayek 1937a), Hayek did not publish anything in that field[38]. What he did do, was to put an elaboration of his monetary theory on the agenda. This was to have become a systematic dynamic theory of the business cycle; for as Hayek indicates in *PTC* (pp. 353–4), the subjects of dynamics and monetary theory are for him the same. He hints that a second volume of *PTC* was to have been devoted to it[39]. That book was never written[40]. And although Hayek refers to war time difficulties which made him curtail his project, this fact seems to corroborate the second hypothesis I propose for explaining the lack of a role of psychology in Hayek's economics:

When Hayek may still have had sufficient interest in developing his ideas about what I have characterized above as the initial conditions of the perception mechanism, i.e., the price system, and hence monetary theory, or about the regularities governing the process in which individual agents form their expectations, he was too busy solving the many technical problems emerging in the elaboration of the individualist branch of his economic research programme. By the time it began to look as if he had reached satisfactory solutions to at least the most important of these, which were in the field of capital theory, his interest had shifted from the role of the individual agent, and from monetary theory, to the social process of coordinating the individual agent's knowledge and actions.

Part of the cause of this shift of interest was internal to Hayek's programme. It reflected what he had learned in the socialism debate, i.e., the importance of local knowledge, its distributed character, and its coordination (the second sense of subjectivism). This internal development was reinforced by an external event. By the time Hayek had dealt with the technical problems of the reductionist programme of methodological individualism in capital theory, Keynes had captured the entire audience of economists. Almost overnight they lost their interest in Hayek's economics, whereupon Hayek diverted his research into a different field so as not to lose all of his audience (as he says; cp. Hayek 1978, 219). He started investigating more general questions dealing with the consequences of the division of knowledge, and with the stability and evolution of society.

"Individualism True and False" of 1945 (*ITF*) marks an important stage in the generalization of Hayek's thought from the domain of economics to that of social theory. The emphasis of "Economics and Knowledge" had been predominantly on methodology, and problems of economic theory were discussed only in a derivative way. In *ITF* it is just the other way around. As is usual in *all* of Hayek's work, methodology does play a role, but the main objective of *ITF* is to work out the consequences of the theory of society of the philosophers of the Scottish Enlightenment. The "individualism [of the Scottish philosophers] ... is primarily a theory of society, an attempt to understand the forces which determine the life of man, and only in the second instance a set of political maxims derived from this view of society" (*ITF*, p. 6). The article bears the traces of Hayek's previous work in other domains. Thus, the observation that "Carl Menger, who was among the first in modern times consciously to revive the methodical individualism of Adam Smith and his school, was probably also the first to point out the connection between the design theory of social institutions and socialism" (*ITF*, p. 4, n. 3), reflects Hayek's contribution to the socialism debate of the 1930s. Hayek's earlier work on

338

general equilibrium theory, planning and particularly the role of expectations underlies passages such as the following, where Hayek observes about the individualism of the Scots that "its basic contention is (...) that there is no other way toward an understanding of social phenomena but through our understanding of individual actions directed toward other people and guided by their expected behavior" (*ITF*, p. 6).

But perhaps the strongest link between *ITF* and Hayek's work in economics is the criticism of aggregates. In *ITF*, this has been generalized into a criticism of holism or collectivism:

> "This argument [of the Scottish philosophers] is directed against the properly collectivist theories of society which pretend to be able directly to comprehend social wholes like society, etc., as entities *sui generis* which exist independently of the individuals which compose them. The next step in the individualistic analysis of society (...) is the contention that, by tracing the combined effects of individual actions, we discover that many of the institutions on which human achievements rest have arisen and are functioning without a designing and directing mind (...) and that the spontaneous collaboration of free men often creates things which are greater than their individual minds can ever fully comprehend".
>
> (*ITF*, pp. 6–7)

This has to be distinguished from the *so-called* individualism of the Cartesian school, which is usually referred to as rationalism. This is why Hayek calls the true individualism of the Scottish Enlightenment *antirationalism*.

> "The antirationalistic approach, which regards man not as a highly rational and intelligent but as a very irrational and fallible being, whose individual errors are corrected only in the course of a social process, and which aims to make the best of a very imperfect material, is probably the most characteristic feature of English individualism".
>
> (*ITF*, pp. 8–9)

Its two main features are that "true individualism is the only theory which can claim to make the formation of spontaneous social products intelligible" (*ITF*, p. 10), and that "true individualism believes ... that, if left free, men will often achieve more than individual human reason could design or foresee" (*ITF*, pp. 10–11).

This has consequences for the political ideas of the Scottish Enlightenment: "the main merit of the individualism which [Smith] and his contemporaries advocated is that it is a system under which bad men can do least harm" (p. 11).

However, true individualism is not just an instance of "negative utilitarianism"[41].

> "The great concern of the great individualist writers was indeed to find a set of institutions by which man could be induced, by his own choice and from the motives which determined his ordinary conduct, to contribute as much as possible to the need of all others (...)".
>
> (*ITF*, pp. 12–13)

Underlying this theory of society is

> "a view which in general rates rather low the place which reason plays in human affairs, which contends that man has achieved what he has in spite of the fact that he is only partly guided by reason, and that his individual reason is very limited and imperfect, and a view which assumes that Reason, with a capital *R*, is always fully and equally available to all humans and that everything which man achieves is the direct result of, and therefore subject to, the control of individual reason. One might even say that the former is the product of an acute consciousness of the limitations of the individual mind which induces an attitude of humility toward the impersonal and anonymous social process by which individuals help to create things greater than they know (...)".
>
> (*ITF*, p. 8)

What we have seen are the following transformations in Hayek's thought:

a   The transformation from subjectivism as the principle that individual perceptions form the facts of the social sciences, to the idea that knowledge in society is distributed[42]. This creates the problem how we explain its coordination, which seems to be an observed fact.

b   The transformation from the distributed nature of knowledge to the idea that individual knowledge is very limited, and that "Rationality" only exists on the level of the social system, i.e., where there are ways of integrating the individual bits and pieces of local knowledge. This creates the problem how to explain that man can, apparently, still cope with his cognitive limitations. The solution that Hayek proposes is that of social institutions as entities which reduce the complexity of social reality, together with the price system as a system of communicating local knowledge in an efficient way.

340

When we think of Hayek's psychology and the influence it had on the development of neural network models[43], the image that begins to suggest itself here is that of (1) social institutions and of society as parallel distributed processes which enable man to cope with his complex environment. In this context, it is not without irony that Minsky uses the reverse metaphor for describing the organization of the mind in terms of a society:

> "I'll call 'Society of Mind' this scheme in which each mind is made of many smaller processes. These we'll call *agents*. Each mental agent by itself can only do some simple thing that needs no mind or thought at all. Yet when we join these agents in societies – in certain very special ways – this leads to true intelligence".
>
> (Minsky 1988, Prologue to ch. 1)

Evidently, relying on Minsky's metaphor in order to get more clarity on the PDP-aspects of Hayek's theory of society would have us running around in circles. But there are more similarities, if not influences, between Hayek's psychology and his theory of society.

(2) The conception of the human mind as a self-organizing system seems ancestral to Hayek's idea that most social institutions are spontaneous orders, which is a prominent feature of his later work[44]. It also justifies the existence of social science:

> "If social phenomena showed no order except insofar as they were consciously designed, there would indeed be no room for theoretical sciences of society and there would be, as is often argued, only problems of psychology. It is only in so far as some sort of order arises as the result of individual action but without being designed by any individual that a problem is raised which demands a theoretical explanation".
>
> (*CRS*, p. 39)

(3) "Rule-guided behaviour" is a theme that emerges in Hayek's social philosophy in the 1960s. It refers to the implicit skills and knowledge which guide most of our behaviour. The notion is directly derived from his earlier description of the functioning of the mind (cp., for instance, Hayek 1962, p. 45). Hayek extends the results of this investigation into an analysis of learning and the transmision of culture in "Notes on the Evolution of Systems of Rules", where he introduces, for instance, the notion of a polycentric order (p. 73), which is taken from his psychology. The same is the case with the idea that individuals derive their meaning to society by the particular place they occupy in the social order (ibid., p. 61). This reads like a direct translation into a social context from the ms. on psychology, where sense impressions are discussed as acquiring

meaning because of their place in the network of neural connections as a whole[45].

(4) In "Arten der Ordnung" (Hayek 1967, p. 36) we find the argument that the genetic and the functional aspects of spontaneous orders cannot be separated. This is strongly reminiscent of the argument of *SO* that the functioning of the mind is identical to the development of its structure.

(5) According to *SO*, all past knowledge is conserved:

> "Sense experience (...) presupposes the existence of a sort of accumulated 'knowledge', of an acquired order of the sensory impulses based on their past co-occurrence; and this knowledge, although based on (pre-sensory) experience, can never be contradicted by sense experiences and will determine the forms of such experiences which are possible".
>
> $(SO, 8.8)$[46]

This reads like a forerunner of Hayek's later argument that spontaneously evolved institutions contain the "wisdom of the ages". The idea that Hayek's conservatism, which is evident in his work after about 1960, has its roots in his psychology is not elaborated here[47].

(6) In his economics and methodology between the 1920s and 1950s, Hayek is a staunch defender of methodological individualism. His later work on institutional and cultural evolution marks a striking turn to a non-individualistic theory. The change seems to have taken place after the publication of *The Constitution of Liberty* in 1960, which is still coherent with individualism. For instance, in "Notes on the Evolution of Systems of Rules of Conduct" Hayek describes the selection process of institutions as taking place at the level of entire institutions and societies, and not, as an individualistic theory would require, on the level of individuals. Individuals are apparently considered to be dependent, as far as the selection process is concerned, on the institutional framework of which they are part. This reminds one of the central thesis of Hayek's theory of mind that individual sense impressions only acquire meaning if they are incorporated in sets of neural connections. The elimination of an individual sense impression will have no consequences for the classification system that makes up the mind, whereas the elimination of a class, or a set of classes, will. This suggests that Hayek's later turn to holism can be explained as a consequence of his applying the ideas of *SO* to his theory of social evolution[48].

This list of similarities (which does not pretend to be exhaustive) strongly suggests that their influence are influences from Hayek's psychology on his theory of society. This impression is supported by Hayek, who says about *SO* that "the work on it has helped me greatly to clear my mind on much that is very relevant to social theory. My conception of evolution, of a spontaneous order and of the methods and limits of our endeavours to explain complex phenomena have been formed largely in the course of the work on that book. As I was using the work I had done in my student days on theoretical psychology in forming my views on the methodology of the social science, so the working out of my earlier ideas on psychology with the help of what I had learnt in the social science helped me greatly in all my later scientific development".

(Hayek 1979, p. 199, n. 26)

There appear to be rather strong links between Hayek's early work in psychology and his theory of society and cultural evolution. This influence is not analytical, in the sense that Hayek's psychology leads deductively to his social philosophy. It is rather of a suggestive nature[49]. In general terms, that much is practically admitted by Hayek, who counts himself amongst the intellectual type of the "foxes" rather than the "hedgehogs"[50]

Before going into the connection between the ms. and Hayek's methodology, I want to address briefly a question that may have arisen from the above discussion. The parallels between *SO* and Hayek's later theory of society seem to suggest that Hayek's answer to the question whether society is mind-like would be affirmative. Surprisingly, it is not. On the contrary, Hayek is rather critical of attempts to apply "brain metaphors" to society.

"Such spontaneous orders as those of societies, although they will often produce results similar to those which could be produced by the brain, are (...) organized on principles different from those which govern the relations between a brain and the organism which it directs. Although the brain may be organized on principles similar to those on which a society is organized, society is not a brain and must not be represented as a sort of super-brain, because in it the acting parts and those between which the relations determining the structure are established are the same, and the ordering task is not deputized to any part in which a model is preformed".

(Hayek 1967, p. 74)

What Hayek rejects in the mind-metaphor for society is a particular way of stating the problem: as the hierarchical relation between mind and body. This is consistent with his idea that except for socialist systems there is no central directing institution which governs society (like the mind governs the body). He has no objections to using the type of mechanism of

343

SO for modelling the evolution and functioning of social institutions. In that sense Hayek does think of society as mind-like.

6. Methodology of social science

In the above, I mentioned that Hayek's research programme in economics is a methodological programme as well. All of his publications of the 1920s and '30s on business cycles and capital theory invariably contain methodological comments, while "Economics and Knowledge" is largely about methodology. *The Pure Theory of Capital* is a systematic exposition of Hayek's economic research programme. *The Counter-Revolution of Science* does the same for his methodology. It collects essays that were written between 1941 and 1951. The theme of the first part is the abuse of reason which consists in the application of what are commonly thought to be the methods of the natural sciences to social phenomena. This has led to holism, the idea that social phenomena are directly given to human perception. In part I of the book Hayek discusses what he considers to be the pernicious consequences of this attitude, the most dangerous of which is the idea that man is capable of shaping society according to his will. Parts II and III are devoted to a historical analysis of holism.

What Hayek does in *CRS* is to reformulate some of the methodological ideas of Adam Smith, Carl Menger, and Ludwig von Mises which he had used in his earlier publications on methodology in terms of his own psychology. In the last chapter of *SO*, called "Philosophical Consequences", Hayek elaborates some of the questions which he had already discussed in the ms. The most important of these is the difference between physics and psychology (in fact, Hayek works out certain ideas of Ernst Mach and Moritz Schlick). In *CRS* this is generalized into an investigation of the differences between the natural and the social sciences, which forms the *Leitmotiv* of *CRS*. Hayek works out the consequences for the social sciences of the fact that even in a reductionist scientific world picture the existence of secondary qualities poses a problem, and hence psychology has a right to exist next to physics. This is the point of departure of his methodology. This background is presented in the second chapter of Part I of *CRS*. It contains a summary of Hayek's psychology, but surprisingly enough *without ever explicitly mentioning his own previous work in that field*.

Before continuing the discussion of Hayek's methodology, I want to formulate some possible explanations for this striking omission. One is that Hayek may have been afraid of losing his credibility (or perhaps, in the light of his own comment about the reason why he withdrew from economics after Keynes' victory, one should say: even more of his credibility) by being seen to have worked as a psychologist. But that would a bit odd, since *The Counter-Revolution of Science* was published after *The Sensory Order*. An alternative hypothesis is that Hayek was too modest to refer to his own work in psychology. In fact, Hayek introduces his paper "Das Wesen des Geistigen" (cp. note 11 above) to what seems to be an audience of psychologists or philosophers rather apologetically by saying that it may seem presumptuous for a mere economist to address the mind-body problem. But I think the real reason for the omission is Hayek's disappointment at the lack of approval for his psychology and theory of the mind-body problem by his friend Karl Popper. This may have made him insecure about his theory of the mind[51].

Let's resume the main argument. In chapter III, Hayek repeats that even in a reductionist scientific world view human consciousness poses a problem that has to be explained, viz. why the world appears to us as it does in terms of sensory qualities. But, he says, that is not what he wants to go into[52]. Instead, he elaborates the consequence of his investigations in psychology for social science:

"the fact that different men do perceive different things in a similar manner which does not correspond to any known relation between these things in the external world, must be regarded as a significant datum of experience which must be the starting point in any discussion of human behavior".

(CRS, p. 22)

Human consciousness provides us with the facts of the social sciences:

"the facts of the social sciences are merely opinions, views held by the people whose actions we study. They differ from the facts of the physical sciences in being beliefs or opinions held by particular people, beliefs which as such are our data, irrespective of whether they are true or false, and which, moreover, we cannot directly observe in the minds of the people but which we can recognize from what they do and say merely because we have ourselves a mind similar to theirs".

(CRS, p. 28; cp. also Hayek 1943)

Social phenomena are never given in the same way as physical phenomena. They are constructs of the human mind. Understanding social phenomena therefore consists in *re*constructing them from the perceptions, opinions and expectations that form the consciousness of individual human beings. This is (1) the *compositive method*, which Hayek takes over from Menger.

Fortunately, the social scientist is capable of this reconstruction, since he has a mind has the same mechanism as the minds of the people he studies. This is the same idea that underlies Smith's *Theory of Moral Sentiments*, which is a psychology of morality. Hayek founds it on his own psychology, which is in fact a rigorous elaboration of the ideas of (British) empiricism[53]. This second element of Hayek's methodology constitutes a further transformation of subjectivism. I will refer to it as (2) the *thesis of the similarity of minds*:

> "the fact that individuals which compose society are guided in their actions by a classification of things or events according to a system of sense qualities and concepts which has a common structure and which we know because we, too, are men (...)
>
> (*CRS*, p. 33. Cp. also the passage on p. 28, quoted above)

The similarity of the minds of social scientists and the individuals whose behaviour they study is the second transformation of what Hayek understands by subjectivism. So now there are three meanings of subjectivism[54]:

i The facts of the social sciences are the opinions of the agents.
ii The agents' knowledge is local, dispersed, and not homogeneous.
iii Both agents and social scientists can understand the actions of other people because they have minds that work according to similar principles.

The fact that agents only have very limited knowledge, together with the fact that they interact with each other, makes that their behaviour will have effects that were not intended by anyone. This, according to *CRS*, is the *raison d'être* of the social sciences. The three subsequent contents with which Hayek fills the concept of subjectivism together constitute the core of the methodology of *CRS*.

From the idea that the facts of the social sciences are the products of human minds, together with the idea that no entity can explain anything that is more complex than itself, which is another of the philosophical consequences of Hayek's psychology, follows the core of Hayek's theory about the limits to human understanding of social phenomena, and hence to the possibility of intervention. This includes his concept of (3) *the explanation of the principle and the related idea of pattern predictions*[55]. Since social phenomena are the consequence of mental phenomena, and since the human mind cannot explain mental phenomena in detail (as this would lead to the absurd consequence that the mind would have to be more complex than it is; cp. the argument in the last section of para. 3 above), the human mind is incapable of reaching an explanation in detail of social institutions and processes.

Another element of Hayek's methodology of social science which I want to discuss briefly is the idea that (4) *social science studies the effects of conscious actions*[56]. This principle of conscious choice is the basis of the methodology of Mises, by which Hayek has been influenced. I have already mentioned Hayek's criticism of Mises' apriorism when discussing

"Economics and Knowledge". Nothing in the content of Hayek's system of thought would have kept him from extending his criticism of Mises to the idea of social science as dealing with conscious choice. Indeed, Hayek's emphasis on implicit or tacit knowledge seems inconsistent with this methodological principle. What comes to mind immediately in this context is sociobiology. The application of the rational choice model (or the model of utility optimization) to the behaviour of animals obviously does not presuppose that conscious choice is involved. But when Hayek criticizes some modern representatives of this discipline, it is not for their applying the theory of rational choice to animals[57]. This indicates that economics as the study of *conscious* choice is not of prime importance for him. But then, why did Hayek not reject this principle of conscious choice? Perhaps here, too, Hayek's own psychological theory can provide us with a new perspective. Subjectivism in the first sense says that the data of the social sciences are the products of human consciousness. Now, in most European languages, the word "conscious" is ambiguous, probably reflecting a particular tradition of thought. For "conscious" means both "mind-like" and "deliberate". I offer as an admittedly very speculative hypothesis that this ambiguity kept Hayek from rejecting this fourth methodological principle.

The compositive method is a reductionist strategy in which social phenomena are reduced to mental phenomena. But we must be careful not to jump to conclusions. Hayek is not a radical reductionist. True, his physicalist reductionism implies that mental phenomena can in principle be reduced to physical laws. But this would not help us in explaining social phenomena:

> "The problem of explaining mental processes by physical ones is entirely distinct from the problems of the social sciences, it is a problem for physiological psychology. But whether it is solved or not, for the social sciences the given mental entities must provide the starting point, whether their formation has been explained or not".
>
> (*CRS*, p. 50)

Here we finally seem to have the answer to the question why Hayek never used his psychology in his economics. Like his brother-in-arms against holism Karl Popper[58], Hayek defends (5) *anti-psychologism*[59]. This is a direct consequence of his rejection of Mach's neutral monism, which was his motivation to write the ms. on psychology in 1920. But again, we must not rush to conclusions. It is very much the question if Hayek had already arrived at this distinction between the tasks of psychology and social science in his early work on economics. There is no evidence of that in his published work. So this is a doubt which will remain, as will the sense of surprise to find Hayek, the arch-integrator and builder of intellectual constructions out of suggestive links (the "fox", or "muddler" in his own terminology[60]), sticking to this sharp demarcation between the mental and the natural orders, between psychology and physics, between social and natural science. So perhaps the real surprise about the place of psychology in Hayek's work lies in this sharp demarcation, from which follow the main tenets of his methodology, subjectivism.

In conclusion, the principal elements of Hayek's methodology of social science all seem to have their source in his earlier work in psychology: subjectivism in its three subsequent versions; individualism (which follows from the first sense of subjectivism); the compositive method (which follows from Hayek's rejection of Mach's neutral monism); the explanation of the principle and pattern predictions (which follow from the self-referential complexity argument); and perhaps even the principle of conscious choice. The principle of theoretical unification, which is one of the four methodological elements of Hayek's research programme in economics, is a direct consequence of the ideal of a unified scientific world picture which is one of the premises of his psychology. Finally, the method of decreasing abstraction which is so prominent in his economics is a natural companion to the principle of unified explanation[61].

7. Conclusion

There have been two recent revolutions in economics, and in social science in general: the cognitive revolution, and the evolutionary revolution. Until even more recently, these two have remained separate. In the work of F.A. Hayek they are intimately connected. The source of his ideas on cognition and evolution is his very earliest scientific contribution, the field of the psychology of perception. However, not only was the manuscript on psychology which he wrote in 1920 left unpublished until 1952, there are no traces of his psychological theory in the long series of publications in economics which he wrote during the 1930s, even though perception plays a central role in it.

From the beginning of his work in economics, Hayek posed himself, and elaborated, a research programme consisting of two branches, a reductionist branch, and a subjectivist branch. As long as he was engaged in the reductionist part, he did not work out the subjectivism beyond the bare essentials necessary for his business cycle theory. For this he did not need cognitive psychology, his own or anyone else's. He could rely on the distinction between economic reality as perceived and subjectively "mapped" by individual agents, and the "fundamentals" of an economy. The explanation of the discrepancy between the two was for Hayek not the subject of psychology, but of monetary theory, a systematic development of which he never undertook. However, a task was left for psychology, in explaining the formation of expectations and the perception of risks. Hayek never even took up this work. By the time when progress in the reductionist branch would have left Hayek with the leisure to elaborate the subjectivist branch of his economic research programme, he had shifted his interest, as a consequence of his study of socialism, from an analysis of the acquisition of knowledge and the formation of expectations by individuals to the coordination of dispersed local knowledge of individuals. From the moment he resumed his work on psychology, the subjectivist part of the programme was generalized into a theory of the coordination of dispersed knowledge, a theory of society, and the methodological principle that the basis of social science is the similarity of the minds of social scientists and the subjects they study. Hayek's psychology shaped his theory of society and its evolution, and it shaped even more strongly his methodology. However, it played no part in his economics.

The influence of *SO* expressed itself in the emergence of the themes of *evolution* and the *spontaneous order*. Evolutionary arguments can already be found in *Constitution of Liberty* of 1960, Hayek's first systematic statement of a liberal social and political philosophy. But they are far less prominent than, for instance, in *Law, Legislation and Liberty*, which was published between 1973 and 1979. In the former book, the evolutionary approach is still consistent with methodological individualism, while in the latter this is emphatically not the case. It looks as if it took a long time for the individualistic theme of Hayek's research programme in economics to lose its momentum, and to be superseded by the evolutionary motive that had become nested in Hayek's subjectivism.

Hayek's rediscovery, or at least elaboration, of what he thought were consequences of his psychology for the methodology of social science opened the door to let in other themes of *SO* in the domain of the study of social institutions and their evolution. If we wanted to characterize the most general common motive in all of these fields, we could single out the idea of knowledge and its limitations. In *CRS*, Hayek finally clarifies his position vis-à-vis the relationship between psychology and social science. It turns out that he is an anti-psychologist, which is a direct consequence of his position vis-à-vis the relationship between physics and psychology.

Although this conclusion benefits from the advantage of hindsight, and need not necessarily constitute the answer to the question why psychology played no role in Hayek's economics, it takes away some of the sense of surprise about the place of psychology in the work of Hayek. But that is not the end of the story. What is perhaps most surprising of all about Hayek's psychology in the wider sense of the word, that is, comprising his solution to the mind-body problem, is that in the end it undermines his entire system of thought, except, perhaps, for his economics, which did not undergo its influence. On further analysis, Hayek's physicalist reductionism turns out to be a straitjacket that leaves no room for any active and creative role of man. One consequence of this is that the existence of science, including that of social science, cannot be explained within Hayek's own system of thought. This is paradoxical because it leaves Hayek's own contributions to social science without a support in his own system. At the same time, this position is coherent with the conservative strain in his thought, which asserts itself with increasing power from about 1960. Hayek's conservatism is a direct consequence of his physicalist reductionism and his identity theory with respect to the mind body problem[62]. These aspects of Hayek's thought have been criticized by his friend Karl Popper, although he never did so publicly. A study of Popper's criticism, and of his alternative approach to the mind body problem and to epistemology throws a revealing light on Hayek's position. But these are topics that have to be left for a more thorough analysis than can be given within the limits of this chapter[63], which, to borrow the words of Alan Musgrave, is as overlong as it is overdue.

Notes

1 Exceptions are MILGATE 1979; DESAI 1994; ROSNER 1994; and BIRNER 1997.
2 Some of the few publications discussing Hayek's theory of the business cycle are STREISSLER 1968; ROSNER 1994; VAN ZIJP & VISSER 1994; and GARRETSEN 1994. For his capital theory, cp., for instance, MEACCI 1994.
3 Some of the few exceptions are BUTOS 1985 and 1997; CUBEDDU 1994; MILLER 1979; and DE VRIES 1984. Cp. also SAMUELSON 1988, p. 324: "You all know the works of Hayek ... few may know that his University of Chicago Press book on psychology is held in awe by such Nobel physiologists as Gerald Edelman of Rockefeller University. (When those two corresponded about the mind-body problem...)".
4 *Hayek on Hayek* (KRESGE & WENAR, eds., 1994), p. 63.
5 *Hayek on Hayek*, pp. 63–4.
6 Ibid.
7 The manuscript can be found in the Hayek archives of the Hoover Institution on War, Revolution and Peace, at Stanford University, box 92/1. It carries a handwritten note by Hayek, saying that the document is a copy which was probably made in the late 1940s of the original typescript. In the sequel, the manuscript or its contents will be referred to as "ms".
8 See below, the paragraph on Hayek's psychology of perception.
9 "The thesis on which I started work while I was registered as a PhD student in New York University (I believe I proposed to call it: 'Is a stabilization of the value of money compatible with its function?'), although neither it nor the German work into which I turned it during the following years in Vienna were ever completed was in many ways the beginning of a continuous development of which most of my publications during the next two years are rather by-products or statements of partial results suggested by a particular occasion. One of the first conclusions at which I remember I had arrived toward the end of 1923 was that stabilization of national price levels and stabilization of foreign exchange were conflicting aims. But before I could anywhere submit for publication the short article I had written on the subject I found that Keynes had just stated the same contention in his *Tract on Monetary Reform*

[1923]. Lest anybody should think that this disappointment in my hope of having made an original discovery is responsible for my later persistent opposition to Keynes I should add that Keynes was then, and remained for a good deal longer, one of my heroes and that I greatly admired this particular work of his" (*Hayek on Hayek*, p. 97).

Hayek's recollection of the title of his thesis is not accurate, and neither is McCormick's, who turns it into: "Is the stabilization of the value of money compatible with the functions of money?" (MCCORMICK 1992, p. 40).

The work in German that Hayek refers to consist apparently of the articles on the history of the English monetary system and its theory that have now been translated and published for the first time in vol. III of the *Collected Works of F.A. Hayek.*

10 Had the concept of the representative individual been around at the time, Hayek would have criticized that as well (except for using it as an idealization to be abandoned later – cp. BIRNER 1997), since it is another aggregate. For a further discussion of these matters, cp. VAN ZIJP & VISSER, eds., 1984.

11 The book is more detailed in that it describes at length the physiological literature. It also contains a chapter, the last, with "philosophical consequences" that Hayek thinks follow from his psychology, which in the ms. are discussed only briefly. For the rest, the crux of the theory is the same, except for a subtle but important difference, which concerns Hayek's position vis-à-vis physicalist reductionism. This is discussed in a paper which I presented to the Wiener Kreis Verein in Vienna in 1998.

The Hayek archives also contain a paper with the title "Das Wesen des Geistigen", which Hayek apparently presented shortly before he published *SO*. (On the first page, he refers to his 30-year long combined interest in economics and physiological psychology. On the other hand, he does not mention *SO*, not even as a project.) It contains the crux of the argument of his psychology and an elaboration on some points.

12 Hayek seems to have made a habit of addressing important and difficult problems rather than easy ones that might have furthered his career. Cp. BIRNER 1994, p. 1.

13 Notice that the Vienna Circle did not exist yet in 1920. Hayek's ideal reflects those of Mach and Schlick. On Schlick's role in the creation of the Vienna Circle, cp. HALLER 1993.

14 Given the fact that Hayek got the inspiration for writing the ms. on psychology from the lectures on Schlick's epistemology and mind-body theory which he attended in Zurich, it is odd that he never refers to this author.

15 *SO*, p. vi.

16 Cp. DE VRIES 1984.

17 Cp. also "Das Wesen des Geistigen".

18 This is a translation of "Bewusstseinswerte" in the ms. There, Hayek also speaks of "Wertungen" (valuations), which are the consequence of the incorporation of physiological impulses into the system of neural connections. These connections constitute the set of "Bedeutungszusammenhänge" (complexes of meaning) of which consciousness is made up.

19 And classifications of classifications, etc. The result is a complex, hierarchical system of classifications.

20 Together with Hebb's book, *SO* was an important source of inspiration for connectionism, or neural network models. Cp. GEORGE 1961, p. 112: "The idea that the human senses worked on a classification principle had *previously* been suggested by Hayek (1952), and Uttley was able to build a simple classification

system in hardware". And: "It was Hayek (1952) who first suggested that the method of human perception was dependent upon a classification system. This suggestion was followed up by Uttley (1954; 1955) ...". (ibid., p. 319). Rosenblatt mentions Hayek's book, together with Donald Hebb's *The Organization of Behaviour* of 1949 as the most suggestive for later work on perceptrons (ROSENBLATT 1958, p. 92).

21 The phrasing of this passage is reminiscent of the title and the theme of an unfinished and unpublished paper by Hayek that is called "Within systems and about systems". It was probably written as a reply to Popper's criticism of *SO*. Cp. BIRNER 1995 and 1999.

22 Cp. SIMON 1968, pp. 109–10.

23 Early statements of the economic research programme are HAYEK 1924, in particular pp. 367, 370, and 378–9; HAYEK 1925, pp. 17, 20 and 25; HAYEK 1927, pp. 68–9, n. 12.

24 Thus anticipating the so-called Cambridge (UK) criticism by some three decades. The idea of a research programme, including the distinction between global and local problems, is applied to the Cambridge debate in BIRNER (forthcoming 2).

25 Cp., for instance, POPPER 1976, ch. 29. The programmatic character of Hayek's economics is analyzed in much more detail in BIRNER (forthcoming 1).

26 Hayek has considered both possibilities. Cp. HAYEK 1933, p. 137: "What we all seek is ... not a jump into something entirely new and different but a development of our fundamental theoretical apparatus which will enable us to explain dynamic phenomena. *Not very long ago I myself still believed that the best way to express this was to say that the trade cycle theory at which we were aiming ought to be organically superimposed upon the existing theory of equilibrium.* I am now more inclined to say that general equilibrium theory itself ought to be developed so as to enable us to use it directly in the explanation of particular industrial fluctuations". The sentence which I have italicized refers to a modelling of the trade cycle in (comparative) static terms. This resolves the interpretation of Hayek's rather puzzling use of "organically superimposed".

For a general description of the adaptation of models to an idealized theory, cp. BUNGE 1973.

27 For the way in which Hayek arrived at the formulation of his intertemporal general equilibrium theory, cp. BIRNER 1997.

28 Cp., for instance, HAYEK 1928; and 1933, p. 137.

29 This approach is followed most systematically in *PTC*. Hayek took over this method from Wieser and Menger. For some consequences on the interpretation of Hayek's contributions to which a neglect of this method leads, cp. BIRNER 1994a.

30 Hayek has a dual notion of equilibrium. One concerns the equilibrium of the individual plan, the other the compatibility of all the individual plans. Cp. BIRNER 1996.

31 Cp. BIRNER 1994a.

32 For instance in LAIDLER 1994.

33 See the next note.

34 The references to publications by Hayek should not be taken as indicating a very strict chronology. As to *PII*: this is a collection of articles written between 1929 and 1939. "Maintenance of capital" (1935), "Investment that raises the demand for capital" (1937), and the article with the same title as the book and written for the occasion are a sequence of attempts to found capital theory on

"microfoundations". I have put T_{4-5} to indicate that there was a sequence, not that there were exactly two attempts.

As to Hayek's "theory" of markets and competition, a whole series of articles may be mentioned, starting with HAYEK 1937, and including HAYEK 1945; 1946; 1947 and 1968. For a discussion of how one may try to integrate the various elements of a Hayekian theory of markets and competition in a coherent framework, cp. BIRNER 1996 and 1999.

35 The recent "time-to-build" models of the business cycle are reminiscent of Hayek's theory. But they lack the rigorously micro-foundational flavour of Hayek's approach.

For the detailed arguments of the reductionist part of Hayek's research programme, cp. BIRNER (forthcoming 1).

36 Which is a reaction against Mises' apriorism. Cp., for instance, *Hayek on Hayek*, p. 72.

37 The problem of the coordination of individual economic plans, together with a dual concept of equilibrium, is stated as early as HAYEK 1928. But it is not worked out there. For this, and the roots of Hayek's intertemporal equilibrium theory in a problem in utility theory, cp. BIRNER 1997.

38 The surprise is compounded by the fact that his monetary theory was one of the reasons for awarding him the Nobel Prize in 1974. The fact that Hayek did not publish much on monetary theory does not mean he had not written about it. Some of these contributions have been published for the first time in the third volume of his collected works.

39 Cp. also *PTC*, p. 3.

40 Cp. also O'DRISCOLL 1977, pp. 133, 136.

41 Which is also the basis of Popper's social philosophy. The expression is due to John Watkins.

42 Hayek distinguishes this second sense of individualism explicitly in HAYEK 1955, pp. 29–30.

43 See note 20.

44 For instance HAYEK 1967a.

45 Cp. note 18 above. Cp. also MILLER 1979, p. 263.

46 The idea dates back to the ms. On p. 29, the principle of conservation is stated in much stronger terms when Hayek says that he finds it encouraging that nothing at all of everything we have experienced is ever lost.

47 It is addressed in BIRNER 1995.

48 BIRNER 1994 argues that Hayek's interest in social evolution itself was kindled by *SO*.

49 Cp. BIRNER 1994.

50 Cp. HAYEK, "Two types of mind", ch. 4 of his 1978. The reference in the text is, of course, to BERLIN 1978. For further discussion, cp. BIRNER 1997a.

51 Popper's criticism and Hayek's reaction are discussed in BIRNER 1995; and 1999.

52 It is here if anywhere that one would have expected Hayek to have explicitly referred to his own work in psychology. Instead, note 16 on p. 22 of *CRS* gives just a summary of the content of his theory.

53 Hayek speaks of "a more consistent and radical application of its basic idea" (*SO* 8.27).

54 Cp. *CRS*, p. 33.

55 Cp. also HAYEK 1955a and 1964.

56 Cp. instance *CRS*, p. 39.

57 See the Epilogue to the third volume of *Law, Legislation and Liberty*. Hayek's

criticism concerns the way in which Pugh and Wilson treat the origins of moral values.

58 Cp. POPPER 1945.
59 RUNDE 1988 has noticed this.
60 Cp. "Two types of mind", in HAYEK 1978.
61 For arguments, cp. BIRNER 1994b, 1996a and forthcoming 2.
62 To give at least a flavour of this connection, I call the reader's attention to the principle of the "conservation of past knowledge" referred to in note 46.
63 The crux of the argument is contained in BIRNER 1995. I elaborated the connection between Hayek and Schlick in a presentation to the Wiener Kreis Verein in Vienna, in 1998. Even though there is not a single reference to Schlick in either the ms. or the published version of *SO*, Hayek was profoundly influenced. He says so explicitly in a letter to H. Mulder (box 61/16 of the Hayek Archives at the Hoover Institution. Part of the analysis of how Hayek's approach to psychology and the mind-body problem influenced the rest of his thought is contained in BIRNER 1999.

References

For some publications by Hayek the following abbreviations are used:
CRS; *The Counter-Revolution of Science* (HAYEK 1955a).
ITF: "Individualism True and False" (HAYEK 1945).
MTTC: *Monetary Theory and the Trade Cycle* (HAYEK 1933).
PII: *Profits, Interest and Investment* (HAYEK 1939).
PP: *Prices and Production* (HAYEK 1931).
PTC: *The Pure Theory of Capital* (HAYEK 1941).
SO: *The Sensory Order* (HAYEK 1952a).
ANDERSON, J.A. & ROSENFELD, E. (1988), *Neurocomputing; Foundations of Research*, MIT Press.
BARTLEY, W.W. III & KRESGE, S. (eds.), *The Collected Works of F.A. Hayek, Vol. III, The Trend of Economic Thinking. Essays on Political Economists and Economic History*.
BERLIN, I. (1978), "The Hedgehog and the Fox", in BERLIN 1978a.
—— (1978a), *Russian Thinkers*, Hogarth.
BIRNER, J. (1994), "Introduction; Hayek's Grand Research Programme", in BIRNER & VAN ZIJP (eds.) 1994.
—— (1994a), "Comment: F.A. Hayek's Research Programme in Economics", in COLONNA, HAGEMANN & HAMOUDA (eds.) 1994.
—— (1994b), "Idealizations and Theory Development in Economics. Some History and Logic of the Logic of Discovery", in HAMMINGA & DE MARCHI (eds.) 1994.
—— (1995), "Connaissance humaine et institutions sociales. L'idée d'évolution chez Popper et Hayek", working paper BETA, University of Strasburg.
—— (1996), "Mind, Market and Society. Network Structures in the Work of F.A. Hayek", working paper 1996/02, Computable and Experimental Economics Laboratory, University of Trento.
—— (1996a), "Cambridge Histories True and False", in MARCUZZO, PASINETTI & RONCAGLIA (eds.) 1996.
—— (1997), "Money, utility, intertemporal general equilibrium, and cyclical fluctu-

ations: on the origins of F.A. Hayek's research programme in economics", working paper 17/97, ICER, Turin, Italy.

—— (1997a), "Between consensus and dissent. The intellectual styles of Keynes and Hayek", working paper 14/97, ICER, Turin, Italy.

—— (1999), "Making Markets", in DOW & EARL (eds.) 1999.

—— (forthcoming 1), *F.A. Hayek's Research Programme in Economics*, Routledge.

—— (forthcoming 2), *Strategies and Programmes in Capital Theory*, Routledge.

BIRNER, J. & VAN ZIJP, R. (eds.) (1994), *Hayek, Co-ordination and Evolution: His legacy in philosophy, politics, economics and the history of ideas*, Routledge.

BUTOS, W. (1985), "Hayek and general equilibrium analysis", *Southern Economic Journal*.

—— (1997), "Hayek and Rational Expectations", in KEIZER, TIEBEN & VAN ZIJP (eds.) 1997.

COLONNA, M., HAGEMANN, H. & HAMOUDA, O. (eds.) (1994), *Capitalism, Socialism and Knowledge*, Edward Elgar.

COLONNA, M. & HAGEMANN, H. (eds.) (1994), *Money and Business Cycles. The Economics of F.A. Hayek*, Edward Elgar.

CUBEDDU, R. (1994), "From the Sensory Order to the political order", *PP* 12, University of Vienna.

CUNNINGHAM, R.L. (1979), *Liberty and the Rule of Law*, Texas A & M University Press.

DESAI, M. (1994), "Equilibrium, Expectations and Knowledge", in BIRNER & VAN ZIJP (eds.) 1994.

DOW, S.C. & EARL, P.E. (eds.) (1999), *Economic Organisation and Economic Knowledge. Essays in Honour of Brian Loasby*, Edward Elgar.

EARL, P.E. (ed.) (1988), *Psychological Economics. Trends, Tensions, Prospects*, Kluwer Academic Publishers.

GARRETSEN, H. (1994), "The Relevance of Hayek for Mainstream Economics", in BIRNER & VAN ZIJP (eds.) 1994.

GEORGE, F.H. (1961), *The Brain as a Computer*, Pergamon Press.

HALLER, R. (1993), *Neopositivismus. Eine Einführung in die Philosophie des Wiener Kreises*, Wissenschaftliche Buchgesellschaft.

HAMMINGA, B. & DE MARCHI, N. (eds.) (1994), *Problems of Idealisation in Economics, Poznan Studies*.

HAYEK, F.A. (1924), "Das Stabilisierungsproblem in Goldwährungslandern", *Zeitschrift für Volkswirtschaft und Sozialpolitik*.

—— (1925), "Die Währungspolitik der Vereinigten Staaten seit der Überwindung der Krise von 1920", I & II, *Zeitschrift für Volkswirtschaft und Sozialpolitik*.

—— (1926), "Bemerkungen zum Zurechnungsproblem", *Jahrbücher für Nationalökonomie und Statistik*.

—— (1927), "Zur Problemstellung der Zinstheorie", *Archiv für Sozialwissenschaft und Sozialpolitik*.

—— (1933), "Price Expectations, Monetary Disturbances and Malinvestments", in HAYEK 1939.

—— (ed.) (1935), *Collectivist Economic Planning*, Kelley 1975.

—— (1937), "Economics and Knowledge", in HAYEK 1949.

—— (1939), *Profits, Interest and Investment, and Other Essays on the theory of Industrial Fluctuations*, Routledge & Kegan Paul.

—— (1940), "Socialist Calculation III: The Competitive 'Solution'", in HAYEK 1949.

—— (1941), *The Pure Theory of Capital*, Routledge & Kegan Paul.

—— (1943), "The Facts of the Social Sciences", in HAYEK 1949.

—— (1944), *The Road to Serfdom*, Routledge & Kegan Paul.

—— (1945), "Individualism True and False", in HAYEK 1949.

—— (1945a), "The Use of Knowledge in Society", in HAYEK 1949.

—— (1946), "The Meaning of Competition", in HAYEK 1949.

—— (1947), " 'Free Enterprise' and Competitive Order", in HAYEK 1949.

—— (1949), *Individualism and Economic Order*, Routledge & Kegan Paul.

—— (1952), *The Sensory Order*, Chicago University Press.

—— (1955), *The Counterrevolution of Science*, The Free Press.

—— (1955a), "Degrees of Explanation", in HAYEK 1967.

—— (1963), "Rules, Perception and Intelligibility", in HAYEK 1967.

—— (1963a), "Arten der Ordnung", in HAYEK 1969a.

—— (1964), "The Theory of Complex Phenomena", in HAYEK 1967.

—— (1965), "Kinds of Rationalism", in HAYEK 1967.

—— (1967), *Studies in Philosophy, Politics and Economics*, University of Chicago Press.

—— (1967a), "Notes on the Evolution of Systems of Rules of Conduct", in HAYEK 1967.

—— (1968), "Competition as a Discovery Procedure", in HAYEK 1978.

—— (1969), "The Primacy of the Abstract", in HAYEK 1978.

—— (1969a), *Freiburger Studien*, Tübingen: Mohr.

—— (1977), "The Sensory After 25 Years", in WEIMER & PALERMO (eds.) 1982.

—— (1978), *New Studies in Philosophy, Politics, Economics and the History of Ideas*, Routledge & Kegan Paul.

HEBB, D.O. (1949), *The Organization of Behaviour*, Wiley.

KEIZER, W., TIEBEN, B. & VAN ZIJP, R. (eds.) (1997), *Austrian Economics in Debate*, Routledge.

KRESGE, R. & WENAR, L. (eds.) (1994), *Hayek on Hayek. An Autobiographical Dialogue*, Routledge.

LAIDLER, D. 1994, "Hayek on Neutral Money and the Cycle", in COLONNA & HAGEMANN (eds.) 1994.

MARCUZZO, C., PASINETTI, L. & RONCAGLIA, A. (eds.) (1996), *The Economics of Joan Robinson*, Routledge.

MCCLOUGHRY, R. (ed.) (1984), *Money, Capital & Fluctuations; Early Essays [by] F.A. Hayek*, Routledge & Kegan Paul.

MCCORMICK, B. (1992), *Hayek and the Keynesian Avalanche*, Harvester/Wheatsheaf.

MEACCI, F. (1994), "Hayek and the Deepening of Capital", in COLONNA et al. (eds.) 1994.

MILGATE, M. (1979), "On the Origin of the Notion of 'Intertemporal Equilibrium'", *Economica*.

MILLER, D. (ed.) (1983), *A Pocket Popper*, Fontana.

MILLER, E.F. (1979), "The Cognitive Basis of Hayek's Political Thought", in CUNNINGHAM 1979.

MINSKY, M. (1987), *The Society of Mind*, Simon & Schuster.

O'DRISCOLL, G.P. (1977), *Economics as a Coordination Problem*, Sheed Andrews & McMeel.

POPPER, K. (1945), "The Autonomy of Sociology", in MILLER (ed.) 1983.

ROSENBLATT, F. (1958), "The perceptron: a probabilistic model for information storage and organization in the brain", ANDERSON & ROSENFELD 1988.

ROSNER, P. (1994), "Is Hayek's Theory of Business Cycles an Austrian Theory?", in BIRNER & VAN ZIJP (eds.) 1994.

RUNDE, J. (1988), "Subjectivism, Psychology, and the Modern Austrians", in EARL (ed.) 1988.

SAMUELSON, P.A. (1988), "The Passing of the Guard in Economics", *Eastern Economic Journal*.

SIMON, H.S. (1968), *The Sciences of the Artificial*, MIT Press, 1975.

STEEDMAN, I. (1994), "On *The Pure Theory of Capital* by F.A. Hayek", in COLONNA & HAGEMANN (eds.) 1994.

STREISSLER, E. (1968), "Hayek on Growth: A Reconsideration of his Early Theoretical Work", in STREISSLER (ed.) 1968a.

—— (ed.) (1968a), *Roads to Freedom, essays in honour of Friedrich A. von Hayek*, Routledge & Kegan Paul.

DE VRIES, R. (1994), "The Place of Hayek's Theory of Mind and Perception in the History of Philosophy and Psychology", in BIRNER & VAN ZIJP (eds.) 1994.

WEIMER, W.B. & PALERMO, D.S. (eds.) (1982), *Cognition and the Symbolic Process*, Erlbaum, Hillsdale, N.J.

VAN ZIJP, R. & VISSER, H. (1984), "Mathematical Formalization and the Domain of Economics: the Case of Hayek and New Classical Economics", in BIRNER & VAN ZIJP (eds.) 1984.

60

THE HAYEK/KEYNES CONTROVERSY IN THE LIGHT OF MODERN BUSINESS CYCLE THEORY

Richard Arena

Source: *History of Economic Ideas* 7(1–2) (1999): 227–253.

The drastic changes which have been affecting our modern economies since the mid-seventies implied a revival of business cycle theory. This revival was substantial and durable, and, therefore, it convinced some economists to come back to the inter-war period to draw some lessons from the debates of this epoch. Obviously, this analysis 'in retrospect' could not be independent of contemporary preoccupations and, especially to the attention paid by economists to the role played by information and knowledge within the context of microeconomic decisions. It suggested however that modern controversies in macroeconomics are directly connected to the inter-war period debates and, especially, to the famous Hayek/Keynes controversy.

Macroeconomics has indeed become today the battle-field of two currents of thought, the so-called 'new classical' and 'new Keynesian economics'. Thus, focusing business cycle theory, Scheide (1986, p. 556) wrote:

> 'The discussions of both approaches showed that it would not be appropriate to claim that Austrians have developed the only theory of business cycles which refers to individual behaviour and choice. New classicals have rediscovered this approach and used many of the tenets for their explanation. This is not to say that new classical theory completely follows Austrian traditions. But many of the differences appear to be small or are only semantic in character'.
>
> (See also Laidler 1982, p. IX; and Hoover 1988, p. 237)

358

On the other hand, Greenwald & Stiglitz (1987, p. 127) observed that:

'The new Keynesian economics provide a general theory of the economy, derived from micro-economics principles (...). It succeeds both in filling the lacunae in traditional Keynesian theory (...) and resolving the paradoxes and inconsistencies of more traditional Keynesian theory. It provides an explanation both for an equilibrium level of unemployment (...) and for business fluctuations'.

(See also Mankiw, Romer 1991, vol. 1, pp. 1–3)

In other words, it is often argued that new classical and new Keynesian approaches do provide modernized versions of the Hayekian and the Keynesian theoretical constructions. If this assertion is accurate, it means that the re-reading of the Hayek/Keynes discussion might cast new light on the present state of the macroeconomic debate between New Classical and New Keynesian economists. We however know the danger of a purely retrospective view of the history of economic thought – but, in our particular case, the danger is strongly decreased by the temporal closeness of both debates and our proximity with them.

It seems therefore reasonable to wonder abethes some of the main themes of the discussion between Hayek and Keynes in the thirties did revived in the late eighties and the early nineties through new classical and new Keynesian economics.

The question is obviously complex. On the one hand, various interpretations of the Hayek/Keynes controversy are available and it is clear that the number of issues raised by the debate was pretty large. It would be, therefore, impossible to consider them systematically here. On the other hand, the modern debates on business cycle theory also exhibit an extensive range of possible approaches and the purpose of the present paper is not to discuss them. We shall preferably point out three main thematical areas which emerged from the Hayek/Keynes debate and were revived by modern business cycle theory.

1. Information and coordination

As Hayek noticed, both Keynes and himself regarded basically the business cycle as a disequilibrium phenomenon, i.e., as 'a general disproportionality between supply and demand'.

In other words, both Hayek and Keynes belong to what Leijonhufvud (1981, p. 132) called 'the saving-investment approach to income fluctuations'. Hayek was perfectly aware of this common theoretical origin and stressed it in his survey of the *Treatise on Money*:

'That the new approach, which Mr. Keynes has adopted, which makes the rate of interest and its relation to saving and investing the central problem of monetary theory, is an enormous advance on this earlier position, and that it directs attention to what is really essential, seems to me to be beyond doubt'.

(Hayek 1931, in Hayek 1995, vol. IX, p. 120)

Now this saving-investment approach is well-known. Its use for the analysis of

'income fluctuations is predicated on the hypothesis that the inter-est rate mechanism fails to co-ordinate saving and investment decisions appropriately. This is where all the Wicksell connection theories differ from monetarism. In monetarist variants of the Quantity Theory, saving and investment have to do aggregate income or the price level. This is true because Monetarist theory assumes that the interest rate mechanism can be relied upon to co-ordinate the intertemporal decisions of households and of firms (...).

The original idea is simple. In allocation theory, we learn that household saving decisions and entrepreneurial investment decisions are to be co-ordinated by the interest rate mechanism. In money and banking, we learn that "the" interest rate is gov-erned by the supply and demand of securities (or of "credit")'.

(Leijonhufvud 1981, pp. 132–133)

However, the common Wicksellian origin of Hayek's and Keynes's the-ories of business cycle must not conceal the drastic differences which appear when we consider the concepts of equilibrium privileged by both authors and the explanations of the 'general disproportionality between supply and demand' they provide.

1.1 Keynes

Keynes's equilibrium in the *Treatise* corresponds to the equality between the natural and money rates of interest, i.e., between saving and invest-ment. The same definition might be proposed to characterise Hayek's equilibrium in *Prices and Production*. However, as we know, the words 'saving' and 'investment' do not have the same meaning for both authors. In Keynes, if equilibrium prevails, aggregate windfall profits are zero. Now, if the natural rate is suddenly driven to a position where it is above the market rate, firms will be pushed to define new investment projects and, therefore, investment spending will exceed saving and positive wind-fall profits will appear. Hayek did not accept Keynes's use of windfall profits. He however agreed that a lowering of the market rate of interest below the natural rate would induce entrepreneurs to increase their investment spending, creating investment-excess in relation to saving. However, this investment-excess would not result in capital and consumption goods inflation but in a change of their relative prices according to the place assigned to them by the capital structure.

Furthermore, the origin of the discrepancy between investment and saving in Keynes is not a preliminary increase of the quantity of credit or money, as Hayek wrongly argued:

> 'What Hayek has missed, according to Keynes, was the claim that savings and investment could "get out of gear" within the framework of the *Treatise* for any of a number of reasons that were independent of changes in the amount of credit in the system. Keynes suggested that Hayek's misreading was due to his being trapped within an old framework, one in which only changes in credit could cause savings to differ from investment'.
>
> (Caldwell 1995, p. 29)

The true origin of the discrepancy between saving and investment in Keynes was different. Global production includes the production amounts of consumers and investment goods. Now the income amount earned by productive factors in both sectors is either consumed, or saved, or hoarded. As Keynes stressed it clearly,

> '(...) The division of the output between investment and goods for consumption is not necessarily the same as the division of the income between savings and expenditure on consumption. For workers are paid just as much when they are producing for consumption; but having earned their wages, it is they who please themselves whether they spend or refrain from spending them on consumption. Meanwhile, the entrepreneurs have been deciding quite independently in what proportions they shall produce the two categories of output'.
>
> (Keynes 1931, in *Collected Writings*, 1971, vol. V, p. 123)

In other words, Keynes attributes the very origin of the inequality between saving and investment to what he will call in the *General Theory* the problem of *effective demand*. Leijonhufvud (1981, pp. 152–153) explained that the Wicksellian conception of economics lead to the characterisation of a notion of 'circular flow' in which three social groups of agents (firms, banks and households) enter into contact and participate in the process of transformation of saving into investment. Now, this conception is also present in Keynes's *Treatise on Money* and expresses, in its way, a specific characteristic of market economies, namely the systemic division between entrepreneurs and households. Entrepreneurs borrow money from banks to implement their productive decisions at a moment when they do not know what the demand will be. Therefore, this *systemic uncertainty* – inherent in the organisation of market economies – induce firms to make *expectations* on future consumption without being sure whether these expectations will prove to be accurate. Hayek very uneasily understood this conception of the co-ordination problem. Significantly, he contested the very notion of circular flow, when he noticed that

> 'profits cannot be explained as the difference between expenditure in one period and receipts in the same period or a period of equal length because *the result of the expenditure in one period will very often have to be sold in a period which is either larger or shorter than the first period*'.
>
> (Hayek 1931, in Hayek 1995, p. 127)

Keynesian disequilibria are not transitory but cumulative. We know that the disequilibrium process begins with an increase of the natural rate of interest. This increase is passed on to the increase of the price of capital goods. Therefore, the firms belonging to this sector will raise their profits and be induced to revise their production plans. The volume of industrial circulation then expands, either through a decrease of the volume of the financial circulation or through an increase of the money supply.

Furthermore, the increase of investment goods production implies a rise of employment, income and spending. This new purchasing power will permit to demand and, therefore, to produce more consumers' goods. The increase of production is then general and the needs of new markets create a rise of wages. The volume of industrial circulation has therefore to be risen again and this pressure on the supply of credit and money will sooner or later result in a growth of the market rate of interest.

However, meanwhile, the generalisation of expansion to all types of goods has implied new rises of the natural rate of interest, so that the growth of the market rate proves to be now insufficient to stop the disequilibrium process. Counter-tendencies then occur; monetary constraints become more and more stringent; long-term profit expectations begin to be less optimistic and this growing pessimism is reinforced by the rise of the market rate of interest. These counter-tendencies accumulate and finally imply a progressive decrease in the natural rate of interest which, combined with the increase of the market rate, favours a new phase of depression. Now, because of the successive emergence of optimistic and pessimistic long-term expectations and of the permanence of the structural independence of production and spending decisions, there is no reason why business cycles would naturally stop and be replaced by a tendency to equilibrium (see Arena & Raybaut 1998).

1.2 Hayek

The most popular opinion concerning Hayek's conception of co-ordination and equilibrium within business cycle theory is that he adopted a Walrasian approach. According to this view, Hayek would have been a strict Walrasian economist before he saw the light at the end of the thirties, becoming thereafter a new man, Hayek II. Such an opinion is, for instance, defended by a very authoritative Austrian economist, Ludwig Lachmann, who wrote:

'For Hayek Paretian general equilibrium was the pivot of economic theory, the centre of gravity towards which all major forces tended. For him, the task of trade cycle theory was to show how it came about that these major forces were temporarily impeded and their effects delayed, and since the cycle was supposed to start with a boom and end with a depression, he saw in the depression the ultimate triumph of the equilibrating forces'.

(Lachmann 1986, p. 227)

Hayek himself seemed to welcome this opinion when, referring to his crossing from economic analysis to economic methodology, he wrote:

'I was somehow in thinking through anew these problems [related to the theory of welfare economics-RA] which had much occupied us in Vienna ten or fifteen years earlier that I had suddenly the one enlightening idea which made me see the whole character of economic theory in what to me was an entirely new light and which I tried to convey in my presidential address to the London Economic Club on *Economics and Knowledge*'.

(Hayek 1963 in Hayek 1995, p. 62)

However, Hayek's remarks are not unambiguous, and we have some doubts about the validity of the thesis of a rupture between Hayek I and Hayek II.

We indeed think that Hayek chose to refer to a standard concept of equilibrium in his business cycle theory because he wanted to discard any psychological approach to the cycle. Marina Colonna noticed that

'Hayek's confidence in the working of the price mechanism appeared first in his criticism of those non-monetary theories of the trade cycle which explained cyclical fluctuations by introducing the assumption of a "general misconception" as regards the economic situation due to the entrepreneur's miscalculations, ignorance, or psychological errors of pessimism and optimism and so on. All those factors justified some sort of break in the working of the price mechanism and hence the development of a trade cycle. But, according to Hayek, the authors of such theories failed to explain why, in the absence of money, those factors should ever exist: why, for example, expectations should generally prove incorrect, or entrepreneurs should suddenly become pessimistic or optimistic. According to Hayek the fundamental error in all those theories arose from their misconception of the significance of the price mechanism for, he says: «so long, at least, as disturbing monetary influences are not operating, we have to assume that the price which entrepreneurs expect to result from a change in demand or from a change in the conditions of production will *more or less* (emphasised by me – RA) coincide with the equilibrium price (1933, p. 69)»'.

(Colonna 1993, p. 33)

In other words, Hayek considers that it would be too easy to explain a disorder implying a business cycle by behavioural errors or mistakes. Hayek's position is sharp and clear. The economist must assume that agents are rational and, therefore, that they do not commit systematic errors. This view does not however imply that prices are the only accurate signals agents have to take into account. He notices that

'no one would deny, of course, that errors can arise as regards the future movements of particular prices. But it is not permissible to assume without further proof that the equilibrating mechanism of the economic system will begin its work only when the excessively increased product due to these mistaken forecasts actually comes on the market, the disproportional development continuing undisturbed up to that time. At one point or another, all theories which start to explain cyclical fluctuations by miscalculations or ignorance as regards the economic situation fall into the same error as those naive explanations which base themselves on the "planlessness" of the economic system. They overlook the fact that, in the exchange economy, production is governed by prices, independently of any knowledge of the whole process on the part of individual producers, so that it is only when the pricing process is itself disturbed that a misdirection of production can occur. The "wrong" prices on the other hand, which lead to "wrong" dispositions, cannot in turn be explained by a mistake'.

(Hayek 1966, pp. 84–85)

This conception of agents' behaviour is obviously supported by Hayek's belief in the existence of a natural tendency of the economy towards equilibrium. The reason why agents cannot make the same mistakes over and over again is that they *learn* from market experiments. Hayekian agents are indeed learning more than rational ones: 'they *cannot* know more than a tiny part of the whole of society, 'and ... therefore all that can enter into [their] motives are the immediate effects which [their] actions will have in the spheres [they] know' (Hayek 1946, p. 14).

Thus, interindividual market relations provide the opportunity for the diffusion of private knowledge which forms 'the unlimited variety of human gifts and skills' (Hayek 1946, p. 15) and which is a priori unequally distributed among agents. From this point of view, the main problem of agents is the *discovery* of new information through the economic signals revealed by the market process. Prices are some of these signals but, as Hayek expressed it,

'price expectations and even the knowledge of current prices are only a very small section of the problem of knowledge as I see it. The wider aspect of the problem of knowledge with which I am concerned is the knowledge of the basic fact of how the different commodities can be obtained and used, and under what conditions they are actually obtained and used, that is, the general question of why the subjective data to the different persons correspond to the objective facts'.

(Hayek 1937, p. 51)

On the one hand, Hayek's conception is neither axiomatic nor universal. He notes that

'apparently subsidiary hypotheses or assumptions that people do learn from experience, and about how they acquire knowledge ... constitute the empirical content of our propositions about what happens in the real world'.

(Hayek 1937, p. 46)

Therefore, agents' behaviour essentially concerns the creation of knowledge through experience and not the use of given natural endowments.

On the other hand, however, Hayek himself wrote that we 'have to make use of the logic of equilibrium theory', adding in a footnote

'By "equilibrium theory" we here primarily understand the modern theory of the general interdependence of all economic quantities, which has been most perfectly expressed by the Lausanne School of theoretical economics'.

(Hayek 1966, p. 42)

In spite of this reference to Walras or to the Lausanne School, the view according to which Hayek would have been a follower of Walras, appears to be superficial.

We might first note that the footnote in *Monetary Theory and the Trade Cycle*, often quoted, is incomplete. Hayek adds a final sentence: 'The significant basic concept of this theory was contained in James Mill's and J.B. Say's *Théories des Débouchés*. Cf. L. Miksch *Gibt es eine allgemeine Überproduktion?*, Iena, 1929'.

This sentence clearly means that, in Hayek's mind, equilibrium theory includes James Mill as well as Say and Walras. Now, those three authors have developed drastically different theories of prices. The reference to equilibrium is therefore more general than a kind of intellectual oath of allegiance to Walras. It visibly refers again to Hayek's belief that there is a natural tendency in the economic system to clear markets. This, however, is not the whole of the subject.

Our view is immediately confirmed, since Hayek adds after his footnote:

> 'Yet this logic, properly followed through, can do no more than demonstrate that such disturbances of equilibrium can come only from outside – i.e. that they represent a change in the economic data – and that the economic system always reacts to such changes by its well-known methods of adaptation, i.e., by the formation of a new equilibrium'.
>
> (Hayek 1966, pp. 42–43)

In other words, after having referred to 'the logic of equilibrium', Hayek notes its inability to take economic fluctuations into account. The same critique is developed when Hayek explains why the Walrasian-Paretian approach cannot cope with business cycles. Let us indeed recall that for Walras and Pareto, as well as for their follower in the 1930s, Henry Moore, dynamics was described as a succession of 'moving' or temporary equilibria disturbed by recurrent changes of the data. No evidence is given *a priori* which confirms that this succession will take the shape of a cycle.

Evidently, Hayek did not agree with this conception. This is already clear when we compare the Walrasian and the Hayekian processes of reaching equilibrium. There is little common room between Walras is *tâtonnement* and Hayek's market discovery. But Hayek does not even accept the notion of stationary state with which Schumpeter and others interpreted Walras (Donzelli 1986; Arena 1992) during the 1920s and 1930s:

> 'since equilibrium is a relationship between actions, and since the actions of one person must necessarily take place successively in

turn, it is obvious that the passage of time is essential to give the concept of equilibrium any meaning'.

(Hayek 1937, pp. 36–37)

Having characterised Hayek's equilibrium according to its temporal dimension, it is now necessary to examine the notion in more detail. We have already introduced the notion of 'market discovery'. Beyond this, Donzelli (1986, p. 192) has shown that the Hayekian notion of equilibrium is better understood if we associate it with the notion of 'economic order' (Hayek 1976). The idea is that Hayek's equilibrium offers a direction for the natural tendency of the economy. On this path intertemporal disequilibria can appear but, if they are not 'too large', they can be included in an 'order' which corresponds to the normal working of the economic system. Obviously, such an 'order' is vaguer than Walrasian equilibrium and cannot be formalised through a *tâtonnement* process.

The equilibrium is therefore a norm in regard to which disequilibria might be estimated:

'if we want to predict at all, it must be on the basis of the plans which entrepreneurs are likely to make in the light of their present knowledge, and of an analysis of the factors which in the course of time will determine whether they will be able to carry out these plans or whether they will have to alter them. It seems natural to being by constructing, as an intellectual tool, a fictitious state under which these plans are in complete correspondence without, however, asking whether this state will ever, or can ever, come about'.

(Hayek 1976, pp. 22–23)

The path of the economy towards equilibrium cannot be investigated analytically, as is the case in a *tâtonnement* process:

'Its justification is not that it allows us to explain why real conditions should ever in any degree approximate towards a state of equilibrium, but that observation shows that they do to some extent so approximate, and that the functioning of the existing economic system will depend on the degree to which it approaches such a condition'.

(Hayek 1976, pp. 27–28)

It is easy to understand this view if we have in mind the distinction introduced by Hayek between 'logical (or axiomatic) and empirical (or causal) analysis' (Klausinger, 1990, p. 66). Now, the proposition according to which there exists a 'natural tendency towards equilibrium' is clearly of the second type, in sharp contrast with the Walrasian view:

367

'Whatever may occasionally have been said by over-pure economists, there seems to be no possible doubt that the only justification [to admit the fictitious state of equilibrium] is the supposed existence of a tendency towards equilibrium. It is only with this assertion that economics ceases to be an exercise in pure logic and becomes an empirical science ... The assertion of the existence of a tendency towards equilibrium is clearly an empirical proposition, that is, an assertion about what happens in the real world which ought, at least in principle, to be capable of verification'.

(Hayek 1937, p. 45)

The Hayekian conception of economic equilibrium, therefore differs from the Walrasian one. The differences, however, do not only concern the *nature* of equilibrium but also the *characteristics* of the *convergence process* towards it. Hayek explicitly refuses to consider the Walrasian *tâtonnement* process as an argument in favour of a logical demonstration of economic stability. By the way, this view is confirmed by Hayek's 1937 article. Far from being a sign of Hayek's allegiance to Walras, this contribution shows that the conditions required by the theory of intertemporal equilibrium are too strong to be accepted by the economist. In other words, the article appears to be a negative proof against a Walrasian type of co-ordination: it is only casually that an intertemporal general equilibrium can be achieved in a decentralised economy (Hayek 1937, pp. 41–45).

As we saw, a drastic difference is already clear between Hayek's and Keynes's conceptions of equilibrium and co-ordination. No room is afforded in Hayek's approach for mass psychology, 'bearishness', 'propensity to hoard' or 'animal spirits'. But Hayek's conception also differs from Keynes's about the origin of disequilibrium and its permanence or, even, its cumulative character. As we saw, for Keynes, disequilibrium and, therefore price changes are not necessarily related to a change in the volume of money but to a divergence between spending and production decisions. Hayek took the opposite view. The origin of the investment excess is indeed located in the growth of money supply. To put it in different words, macroeconomic disequilibria come from the fact that, far from limiting their part to their 'natural' role of *intermediary* agents, banks act as *creators* of money and, therefore, are responsible for the excess of investment. According to Hayek, equilibrium between saving and investment is indeed reached when the natural and the market rates of interest coincide, that is, when banks are pure intermediaries and do not create any money *ex nihilo*. However, in the Hayekian perspective, monetary authorities are unable to control the supply of credit with sufficient care, in order to equalise both rates. Therefore, in a monetary economy, business cycles are unfortunate but unavoidable phenomena. Therefore, when banks choose a market rate superior to the natural rate, the credit demand of firms is above the given reserves supply. In this framework banks can no longer act as pure intermediaries on the credit market, transmitting savings to entrepreneurs in order to finance their investments. They create a net quantity of money, which is precisely the cause of investment excess. Starting from a full employment equilibrium, the economy will then decrease its consumers' goods production, increase their price and induce a given volume of forced saving. We are then in an expansion phase: prices, profits and the credit quantity increase. However, little by little, the effective reserve rate of banks is decreasing and they become more and more illiquid, so that they finally decide to raise their monetary rate of interest. The expansion phase comes therefore to an end and, through a recessive phase, the economy tends again towards an equilibrium position.

Here also, the contrast with Keynes's view is eloquent: the disequilibrium process is not cumulative and the function of money creation by credit is regarded as pathological and not as natural.

1.3 'New' business cycle theory

What is remaining today of those Hayek/Keynes differences concerning the concepts of equilibrium and co-ordination?

Real business cycle theory clearly avoids any problem of co-ordination. Shocks to the economy that cause the interest rate to rise or the wage to be temporarily high, induce people to work and, therefore, to produce more. Agents instantaneously and rationally adapt to the impulses, noticeably through intertemporal substitution decisions. Real business cycle theory indeed assumes that wages and prices always adjust perfectly to clear markets.

Lucas's equilibrium theory of business cycle was more interesting from our viewpoint since it assumed that information was imperfect. Therefore, shifts in labour or goods supply were supposed to be induced by a misperception about intertemporal opportunities of exchanging leisure and consumption. However, according to Lucas, as well as for the real business cycle theory, output and employment fluctuations are conceived as the equilibrium consequences of shifting labour demand or labour supply curves, not as disequilibrium movements along those curves.

The new Keynesian literature on co-ordination failures is one of the few echoes of the debates of the thirties. The problem to be faced is not, however, that of 'disequilibrium co-ordination', to use Howitt's expression (Howitt 1990). Here, an implicit auctioneer is supposed and the problem is related to the existence of external economies. We indeed know that, only in the absence of any form of external economy, private and social net benefits of individual decisions coincide. In this case, the equilibrium prices announced by the auctioneer on the basis of individual excess demand functions provide the sufficient and accurate signals to solve the co-ordination problem according to the general economic equilibrium approach. Whenever external economies are present, the usual standard solution is no more appropriate. It is based on excess demand functions, i.e., on individual behaviours but it cannot take into account the full global impact of individual decisions. The problem to solve is then Howitt's equilibrium co-ordination problem: how consistent individual plans can generate a socially preferable outcome?

The external economies considered might be of various types: spillovers, strategic complementarily, complementarities in price adjustment, competitive imperfections, etc.... Their common feature is the existence of any influence (as slight as it may be) of an agent's decision on the utility of all other agents. This presence of co-ordination failures can then entail macroeconomic underproduction or underemployment and, in some cases, a multiplicity of macro-equilibria. Obviously, this type of co-ordination problem is very different from those Hayek and Keynes had in mind. The essential contrast lies in the attention paid today by *new-Keynesian* economists to the theme of micro-foundations. The problem of information failures is therefore coped with in Keynes as well as in New Keynesian economics but the analytical tools differ. Keynes favours radical uncertainty, while new Keynesians prefer asymmetric information.

The new Keynesian literature permits to connect macroeconomic co-ordination failures with microeconomic specific phenomena and, from this point of view, it could offer some progress if we compare it with the intuitive macroeconomics of the thirties. However, the price to pay in order to take this increase of rigour into account is very high: we must go back to the general equilibrium framework which both Hayek and Keynes, each of them in his own way, tried to quoid, especially when they thought about micro-foundations.

2. Money and credit

Hayek's and Keynes's theories of business cycles tried to build a framework in which real and monetary phenomena were mixed in order to explain economic dynamics and, especially, business cycles. Here again, our authors proposed two very different solutions.

2.1 Keynes

As we know, the traditional view on banks was defined by Irvin Fisher who assimilated them to price intermediaries. This assimilation was considered as the very condition of equilibrium between investment and saving. E. Cannan illustrated it according to the famous 'cloak-room' image. Then, Marshall took into account the possible existence of a rigid deposit multiplier. Keynes defended, in his *Treatise*, a different line of thought. He referred to Wicksell's and Robertson's distinction between a metallic money system and a credit money system. Now, within a credit money system – i.e., a modern monetary economy – bank money predominates, so that it can be assimilated with 'current money' (Keynes 1931 in Keynes 1971, *Collected Writings*, vol. V, pp. 27–28).

> 'It will, therefore, simplify the argument, without seriously detracting from its generality, if we assume not only that all the central bank money is held by the member banks, but also that all the current money in the hands of the public is member bank money, i.e., bank deposits'.

Bank money presupposes the generalisation of the 'overdraft' banking technique, which plays a main role in the process of money creation. Therefore, for Keynes banks are not intermediaries between savers and investors. They finance the *totality* of production, as in Wicksell's pure credit economies. Thus, saving is no longer a pre-condition of investment. On the contrary, investment through the use of finance produces its own corresponding saving. Therefore, Keynes is right when he does not attribute the responsibility of over investment to the quantity of credit. Credit is a necessary condition of investment excess but not a sufficient one, as it is in Hayek's theory. The increase of money supply is, very often, a consequence more than a cause of disequilibrium.

2.2 Hayek

Hayek seemed to welcome Keynes's conceptions of money and credit in his survey of the *Treatise*. He wrote:

> 'Book I gives a description and classification of the different kinds of money which in many respects is excellent. Where it gives rise to doubts or objections, the points of difference are not of sufficient consequence to make it necessary to give them space which will be much more urgently needed later on'.
>
> (Hayek 1931 in Hayek 1995, p. 123)

We already saw that Hayek gave credit a place which sensibly differed from the one Keynes attributed to it. As we know, Hayek was indeed convinced that there were two types of credit.

The first type is the one which corresponds to an equivalent amount of saving deposited in the banking system. Each monetary credit unit may be defined as a token which circulates but represents an equivalent amount of saving. If banks do not accept to give more than this type of credit to firms, both the natural and the market rates of interest coincide, saving is equal to investment and no disequilibrium can occur.

A second type of credit appears when it is created by banks *ex nihilo*, without any equivalent in the bank system deposits. This second type of credit creates a discrepancy between saving and investment since it permits to the banks to create money without any counter-part in saving. It allows banks to become money creators and not only monetary intermediaries.

We understand now why, in Hayek, money takes an important part in the origin and persistence of economic fluctuations.

We have already noted that, in a Hayekian barter economy, there is a natural tendency towards the equilibrium between supply and demand:

'so long, at least, as disturbing monetary influences are not operating, we have to assume that the price which entrepreneurs expect to result from a change in demand or from a change in the conditions of production will more or less coincide with the equilibrium price'.

(Hayek 1966, p. 69)

The introduction of money changes the working of economic activity:

'in a barter economy, interest forms a sufficient regulator for the proportional development of the production of capital goods and consumption goods, respectively. It is admitted that, in the absence of money, interest would effectively prevent any excessive extension of the production of production goods, by keeping it within the limits of the available supply of savings, and that an extension of the stock of capital goods which is based on a voluntary postponement of consumers' demand into the future can never lead to disproportionate extensions, then it must also necessarily be admitted that disproportional developments in the production of capital goods can arise only through the independence of the supply of free money capital from the accumulation of savings; which in turn arises from elasticity of the volume of money'.

(Hayek 1966, pp. 91–92)

We know that referring to the Wicksellian tradition, Hayek locates the origin of the cycle in an increase in the equilibrium rate of interest (the Wicksellian 'natural' rate) associated either with a decrease in the ratio of voluntary saving of individuals or with an increase in the investment demand of firms.

The first case corresponds to an intertemporal substitution of present for future consumptions. The second derives from the implementation of technical changes within the firms of the economy.

Still in compliance with Wicksell's theory, if we are in a monetary economy, the market rate of interest ceases to move according to the self-regulatory principles which rule the working of a barter economy. The equilibrium rate of interest increases while the market rate remains fixed.

What is happening then is a change in the volume of money, as an answer to the preceding variations of saving or investment. Now, 'a change in the volume of money ... represents as it were a one-sided change in demand, which is not counterbalanced by an equivalent change in supply' (Hayek 1966, p. 93).

We can therefore see that the causes of the cycle can be real as well as monetary. Money, in any case, is a necessary condition of the cycle because it prevents the self-regulating working of the economy.

But the original of the working of the money market is not sufficient to ensure the permanence of fluctuations. As Hayek noted 'the successive changes in the real structure of production [...] constitute those fluctuations' (Hayek 1966, p. 17). The effect of the variation of the volume of money is not indeed a change in the general level of prices but a change in the relative prices of goods, according to their places in the structure of production. For instance, if the voluntary saving of agents increases, the prices of production goods will increase in proportion to the prices of consumers' goods.

This interpretation is confirmed by Hayek's *Profits, Interest and Investment* – a book which, however, is often interpreted as the locus of a drastic change in Hayek's approach to business cycles. Commentators frequently stressed Hayek's description of the natural rate of interest as rate of profit (Hayek 1939, pp. 3–4) and his insistence on real more than monetary causes of fluctuations:

> 'We have seen that if the rate of interest fails to keep investment within the bounds determined by people's willingness to save, a rise in the rate of profit in the industries near consumption will in the end act in a way very similar to that in which the rate of interest is supposed to act, because a rise in the rate of profit beyond a certain point will bring about a decrease in investment just as an increase in the rate of interest might do'.
>
> (1939, p. 64)

However, the necessary and logical condition for the existence of business cycles is the short-term rigidity of the monetary rate of interest:

> 'If the rate of interest were allowed to rise as profits rise (i.e. if the supply of credit were not elastic), the industries that could not

earn profits at this higher rate would have to curtail or stop production, and incomes and the demand for consumers' goods and
profits in the consumers' goods industries would cease to rise'.

(1939, p. 32)

We might interpret this assumption of a rigid short-term rate of interest
as a concession to the Keynesian context of the epoch. But this is not the
important point. More relevant is the fact that in a monetary economy the
profit and interest rates do not move simultaneously and, therefore, imply
the possible occurrence of business cycles. The explanation of the sticki-
ness of the monetary rate of interest might be Wicksellian (banks' behaviour), or Keynesian (distinction between short and long periods) but, in
both cases, the monetary characteristic of the rate of interest remains and
allows the birth of cycles.

2.3 'New' business cycle theory

Here again, real business cycle has little to tell us concerning the legacy of
the Hayek/Keynes controversy. Lucas's approach is more monetary oriented but its relation to Keynes or Hayek perspectives is very weak. Thus,
exogenous shocks in Lucas's approach are not related to a variation of the
equilibrium rate of interest but to a set of stochastic injections of money
units. Their global volume and the general level of prices are taken into
account as such, in contradiction with Hayek's views. Then, intertemporal
substitution effects do not enter into the realm of production, as they do in
Hayek's model, when he defines the structure of different stages of productive activity.

The most interesting modern approach to business cycles is here again
the new Keynesian one and, more specifically, the approach which relates
credit rationing and macroeconomic fluctuations. Obviously, this approach
sensibly differs from Hayek's as well as Keynes's theories. It does not
define the credit market as both authors did. However, two important features might be stressed which do not contradict the flavour of the thirties.

On the one hand, Keynes and Hayek did not accept the Fisher-Cannan
predominant approach to the credit market according to which banks were
pure intermediaries and the modes of financing did not interfere with the
types of investment decisions.

In a similar way, new Keynesian economists do not accept the modern
usual approach of Modigliani and Miller which stresses the complete
neutrality of financing choices. Therefore, Hayek, Keynes and the new
Keynesians share the same conception according to which *credit matters*
and exerts its influence or real activity.

On the other hand, Hayek, Keynes and the New Keynesians also share
the same interest in saving and investment co-ordination failures. Hayek

and Keynes even thought it was the key to the permanence of business cycles. The New Keynesians prefer to stress the problems of credit and equity rationing, which means that they are more preoccupied by under-investment phenomena, due to the behaviours of banks confronted to imperfect information. Moreover, Hayek, Keynes and the New Keynesians welcome the specificity of credit and consider it cannot be treated as a pure commodity. Its market is particular and the usual supply and demand alloca-tive mechanisms do not work fully in this case. It is therefore important to check if, as Keynes, Hayek or Stiglitz often pretended, there exists an eco-nomic logic of banking which does not coincide with the logic of the market.

The preceding reflections however imply a more careful consideration of the causes of credit rationing in New Keynesian economics.

Now, we can easily identify these causes with the existence of informa-tional asymmetries and appropriate individual behaviours. The problem is then to evaluate New Keynesian originality from this perspective. It is easy to show that the main results reached by New Keynesian economists derive from a mixture of standard microeconomic behaviours combined with a specific theory of information. That is why, reflecting on Greenwald and Stiglitz's aggregate supply modes, Hall wondered about its Keynesian label and the predominant role attributed to rigidities. He pointed out that Greenwald and Stiglitz wrote

> 'as if there were a huge gulf between their own model and the real business cycle model, a gulf as great as the one between Keynes and the Classics. They could equally well have portrayed them-selves as members of the real business cycle school. They con-tribute to new theories within the general framework that applies standard tools of equilibrium analysis to macroeconomic ques-tions. A model with financial rather than technological shocks as the source of movements in the demand for labour would be taken seriously by real business-cycle theories ... A much more significant watershed in macroeconomics ... is between the real school ... and the nominal schools'.

(Hall 1988, p. 26)

3. Microfoundations of macroeconomics?

The pre-eminent role given by Hayek to the tendency towards equilibrium and his defence of methodological individualism combine to explain his refutation of macroeconomics, seen as an autonomous or an aggregate level of analysis:

> '[Lorsque nous essayons d'établir des relations causales directes entre la quantité totale de monnaie, le niveau général de l'ensemble

des prix et éventuellement la production totale], aucune de ces grandeurs en tant que telle n'exerce jamais d'influence sur les décisions des individus; pourtant, les principales propositions de la théorie économique non monétaire sont fondées sur l'hypothèse d'une connaissance des décisions individuelles. Nous devons notre compréhension, quelles qu'en soient ses limites, des phénomènes économiques à cette méthode "individualiste" '.

(Hayek 1975, p. 63)

3.1 Hayek and Keynes

Considering what was argued above, according to Hayek, the heterogeneity and the interdependence of agents have to be taken explicitly into account, in order to build what we could call a microeconomic theory of business cycles. This attempt implied some important consequences.

Hayek first gave up using the notions of volume of money and general level of prices. This renunciation, which was necessary for 'further progress' (Hayek 1975, p. 62), meant discarding the quantity theory:

'Si la théorie monétaire essaie encore d'établir des relations causales entre agrégats ou moyennes générales, c'est à cause de son retard sur le développement de la science économique en général. En fait, ni les agrégats ni les moyennes n'interagissent, et il ne sera jamais possible d'établir entre eux des relations systématiques de cause à effet, comme on peut le faire pour des phénomènes individuels, des prix individuels, etc'.

(Hayek 1975, p. 63)

But this rejection of aggregate analysis also appeared in the theory of capital. Hayek indeed expressed his doubts with regard to the treatment of capital goods as a single homogeneous quantity. He wrote:

'the problems that are raised by any attempt to analyse the dynamics of production are mainly problems connected with the interrelationships between the different parts of the elaborate structure of productive equipment which man has built to serve his needs. But all the essential differences between these parts were obscured by the general endeavour to subsume them under one comprehensive definition of the stock of capital'.

(Hayek 1976, p. 6)

This conception of aggregation obviously led Hayek to consider the *Treatise* rather critically. According to Hayek, the book did not provide any rigorous macroeconomic foundation to the macroeconomic edifice.

This absence or these imprecisions contributed to explain why profits and investment were inaccurately defined according to Hayek. More precisely, according to Hayek, Keynes had to build or accept a specific theory of capital:

> 'As I shall repeatedly have occasion to point out, [Keynes] treats the process of the current output of consumption goods as an integral whole in which only the paces paid at the beginning for the factors of production have any bearing on its profitableness. He seems to think that sufficient account of any change in the relative supply (and therefore in the value) of intermediate products in the successive stages of that process is provided for by his concept of (positive or negative) investment, i.e., the net addition to (or diminution from) the capital of the community. But this is by no means sufficient if only the total or net increment (or decrement) of investment goods in all stages is considered and treated as a whole, and the possibility of fluctuations between these stages is reflected; yet this is just what Mr. Keynes does'.
>
> (Hayek 1931, in Hayek 1995, p. 125)

Keynes, as we know, accepted Hayek's critique but he also expressed his doubts on the possibility of building a satisfactory theory of capital. That is why he wrote:

> 'Dr. Hayek complains that I do not myself profound any satisfactory theory of capital and interest and that I do not build or any existing theory (...) This is quite true; and I agree with Dr. Hayek that a development of this theory would be highly relevant to my treatment of monetary matters and likely to throw light into dark convers [...] But there is no such theory at present'.
>
> (Keynes 1931, in *Collected Writings*, 1971, vol. V, p. 154)

3.2 'New' business cycles theory

The echo of Hayek's insistence on the necessity of providing microfoundations to the business cycle theory is present in the various modern approaches.

Real business cycle theory defined its research program as the very extension of the general economic equilibrium approach to the realm of business cycle theory. This search for Walrasian microfoundations is significant in itself but it has no connection with the Hayek/Keynes debate.

Lucas's approach is less uninteresting for us. According to Lucas, the key problem with macro theory is indeed that the sound and rigorous ground of general equilibrium theory has been progressively abandoned –

the whole process beginning with Keynes. Too many Keynesian macroeconomic propositions reflect *ad hoc* assumptions on individual behaviour and are inconsistent with the rationality postulate. Therefore, these propositions must be discarded and macrodynamics should be studied within the framework of general equilibrium, using the principle of utility maximization and referring to a specific approach of imperfect information. This view is not completely different from Hayek's.

Finally, New Keynesian macroeconomics surely provide the largest variety of possible microfoundations to macroeconomic theory. It will be useless to discuss them here. Two conclusive remarks might, however, be made.

On the one hand, those microfoundations offer a significant example of what a part of the profession would call *ad hoc* constructions. However, those constructions share with Hayek's or Keynes's approaches a fundamental interest for what happens in the 'real world': we would be more skeptical with a theory like the real business cycle theory which, even today, explains unemployment as the voluntary result of an intertemporal consumption substitution effect. From this point of view, New Keynesian economics offers new routes which are worth exploring.

On the other hand, the conception of microfoundations which is present in New Keynesian economics is sensibly different from the Keynesian one. A vertical approach to production has indeed little in common with a microeconomic theory of imperfect competition. However, for us, the multiplication of different angles and *ad hoc* attempts in New Keynesian economics is a proof more of its vitality and originality than of its lack of rigour.

The precedent development shows the opposition between New Classical and Keynesian approaches is far from a simple re-play of the Hayek/Keynes controversy. On the one hand, real business cycle has nothing in common with the Austrian or the Hayekian tradition and its only *raison d'être* is the paradoxical extension to macrodynamics of a Walrasian framework which is now confined into the field of microeconomics. On the other hand, New Keynesian economics have absorbed many of the analytical preoccupations of the thirties, even they express them in a standard language and in a usual formalization. If these impressions are right, they prove that history of economic analysis is not an *éternel retour* but that, sometimes and in a somewhat strange way, it can exhibit scientific progress. In this case, no doubt is possible: to answer to Hicks's question, both 'Hayek and Keynes were right'.

Note

The author would like to thank all the participants in those conferences and School and, especially, Harald Hagemann, Heinz Kurz, David Laidler and Axel Leijonhufvud for their comments, critiques and suggestions. Usual disclaimers apply.

References

ARENA, R. (1992), 'Schumpeter after Walras: "economie pure" or "stylized facts"?' in T. Lowry, *Perspectives in the History of Economic Thought*, vol. VIII, Aldershot: Edward Elgar.

ARENA, R. & RAYBAUT (1998), 'Credit and financial markets in Keynes's conception of endogeneous business cycles', in G. Abraham-Frois (ed.), *Non-linear Dynamics and Endogeneous Cycles*, New York: Springer Verlag.

CALDWELL, B. (1995), 'Editorial foreword' in B. Caldwell (ed.), *The Collected Works of F.A. Hayek*, vol. IX: *Contra Keynes and Cambridge*, London: Routledge.

COLONNA, M. (1993), 'Hayek's trade cycle theory and its contemporary critics' in M. Colonna & H. Hagemann (eds.), *Money and Business Cycles*, vol. I: *The Economics of F.A. Hayek*, London: Edward Elgar.

DONZELLI, F. (1986), *Il concetto di equilibrio nello teoria neoclassica*, Rome: NIS, Economica.

GREENWALD, B. & STIGLITZ, J. (1987), 'Keynesian, new Keynesian and new classical economics', *Oxford Economic Papers*, no. 39 (1).

HALL, R. (1988), 'Examining alternative economic theories: comment', *Brookings Papers on Economic Activity*, no. 0 (1).

HAYEK, F.A. (1931), 'Reflections on the pure theory of money of Mr J. M. Keynes', *Economica*, vol. XI, no. 33 reprinted in F. Hayek (1995), *The Collected Works of F.A. Hayek*, vol. IX, *Contra Keynes and Cambridge*, London: Routledge.

—— (1937), 'Economics and knowledge' reprinted in F.A. Hayek *Individualism and Economic Order*, London: Routledge & Kegan Paul, 1949.

—— (1939), *Profits, Interest and Investment*, London: Routledge & Kegan Paul.

—— (1946), 'Individualism, true and false' reprinted in F.A. Hayek *Individualism and Economic Order*, op. cit.

—— (1966), *Monetary Theory and the Trade Cycle*, New York: Augustus M. Kelley, First English Edition 1933.

—— (1975), 'Foreword' to the first French edition of *Prix et Production*, Paris: Callman-Levy.

—— (1976), *Choice in Currency: A Way to Stop Inflation*, London: IEA.

—— (1963), 'The economics of the 1930s as seen from London' in B. Caldwell (ed.) *The Collected Works of F.A. Hayek*, vol. IX, *Contra Keynes and Cambridge*, London: Routledge, 1995.

HOOVER, K. (1988), *The New Classical Macroeconomics*, Oxford: Blackwell.

HOWITT, P. (1990), *The Keynesian recovery*, Ann Harbor: University of Michigan Press.

KEYNES, J.M. (1931), *Treatise on Money* (vols. I and II) *Collected Writings*, vols. V–VI, Cambridge: Cambridge University Press, 1971.

KLAUSINGER, K. (1990), 'Equilibrium methodology as seen from a Hayekian perspective', *Journal of the History of Economic Thought*, vol. 12 (1), Spring.

LACHMANN, L. (1986), 'Austrian economics under the fire: the Hayek-Sraffa duel in retrospect', in W. Grassl and B. Smith (eds.), *Austrian Economics: History and Philosophical Background*, London: Croom Helm.

LAIDLER, D. (1994), 'Hayek on neutral money and the cycle' in M. Colonna and H.

Hagemann (eds.), *Money and Business Cycles. The Economics of F.A. Hayek*, London: Edward Elgar.

LEIJONHUFVUD, A. (1981), *Information and Coordination*, Oxford: Oxford University Press.

MANKIW, G. and ROMER, P. (eds.) (1991), *New Keynesian Economics*, vol. I, Cambridge: MIT Press.

SCHEIDE, J. (1986), 'New classical and Austrian business cycle theory: is there a difference?' in *Weltwirtschaftliches Archiv*, no. 122 (3).